DUFF: A LIFE IN THE LAW

# DUFF
## A Life in the Law

DAVID RICARDO WILLIAMS

UNIVERSITY OF BRITISH COLUMBIA PRESS
IN ASSOCIATION WITH THE OSGOODE SOCIETY
Vancouver
1984

# DUFF: A LIFE IN THE LAW

©The University of British Columbia Press 1984
All Rights Reserved

This book has been published with the help of a grant
from the Canada Council

**Canadian Cataloguing in Publication Data**

Williams, David R., 1923–
  Duff

Includes index.
Bibliography: p. 279
ISBN 0-7748-0203-0

1. Duff, Lyman Poore, Sir, 1865–1955.  2. Judges — Canada —
Biography.   3. Canada. Supreme Court — Biography.   I. Title
KE8248.D83W54 1984          347.71'03534          C84-091253-6

ISBN 0-7748-0203-0

*Printed in Canada by T.H. Best Printing Co. Ltd.*

To Laura

# Contents

# Illustrations

following p. 98

The Duff Brothers, about 1873.
Isabella and Emma Duff, about 1874.
The Reverend Charles Duff, about 1890.
The Speedside (Eramosa) church.
The University of Toronto class of 1885.
Lyman Duff, in 1895.
Duff in the B.C. Court of Appeal, 1895.
The Vancouver Courthouse.
Duff's home in Victoria, about 1904.
The Alaska boundary tribunal in London, 1903.
The Ottawa Supreme Court building in the 1880's.
Duff in the Supreme Court of Canada.
The Privy Council in session, 1920.
Lizzie Duff, about 1920.
Duff's home in Ottawa, in 1911.

following p. 194

The Privy Councillor
Haldane as Lord Chancellor, 1924.
Cartoon of Thornton, Beatty, and Duff.
Cartoon of the Transportation Commission.
Cartoon of Duff at the Canadian Bar Association.
Duff and Annie on board the *Duchess of Athlone.*
Duff at the University of Pennsylvania, 1940.
Duff the Administrator.
The unveiling of Duff's bust, 1947.
Duff's wartime passport.
Duff in old age.
Douglas Alexander.

*"Every lawyer knows that no system of law worthy of the name, whether it be cast in the form of a code or not, can be a mere collection of mechanical rules. By the law, a lawyer means the law in operation, the law in action; the law as it is commonly said is a living organism, possessing like every living organism, within limits, of course, the power to adapt itself to changing circumstances."*

Lyman Duff, 1915

# Preface

This is the first biography of Sir Lyman Poore Duff, a judge of the Supreme Court of British Columbia from 1904 to 1906, and from the latter year until 1944, of the Supreme Court of Canada. For nearly forty years he held high judicial office, and during the last eleven of these years he stood at the pinnacle of the Canadian judiciary as chief justice of Canada. Not only because of his long service on the Supreme Court of Canada — no one has equalled his time there — but also because of his massive intellect, his reputation as Canada's most distinguished jurist remains unchallenged.

The role and function of judges, and the extent to which their influence is felt in the lives of ordinary people, are not well understood or appreciated. Certainly, the most visible judges in Canada are those appointed by provincial governments to preside over the lower courts. But there are higher courts, to which judges are appointed by the federal government: in ascending order of seniority, these are the county or district courts, the superior trial courts — bearing different names in the various provinces — the courts of appeal, and, at the peak of this system, the Supreme Court of Canada. All courts work on the principle that the higher the court, the more important the decision. Judges make law, and decisions handed down by the high courts often touch those who may be unaware of the process or its effects. Canadians need an understanding of how the court system operates in this country and how judges do their work. With that understanding, they can recognize the system's strengths and weaknesses, but above all, they will have seen that the law is close to the heart of any orderly society.

This is the theme of my book as it was the theme of Duff's life. I have worked substantially from primary source materials: letters, private papers, diaries, memoirs, and recollections of relatives, friends, and close associates. Duff himself left a mass of correspondence and other documents, now in the Public Archives of Canada, most of them of a formal rather than personal nature. He left no diary or memoirs, so that to reach the inner man, one has to read between the lines. There are enough revealing personal letters, however, some of them from boyhood, to let me draw what I think is a reasonably accurate picture of the man and his views.

Over a long judicial career, Duff wrote, or participated in, decisions in nearly two thousand lawsuits. I have examined all of these. Some are of no interest or importance; some have trivial value; the truly important ones I have read with the care of a practising lawyer and historian/biographer.

In my task, I have received a great deal of encouragement and help from various people. The late Chief Justice Bora Laskin of the Supreme Court and his colleagues, Mr. Justices Martland, Dickson, Estey, and McIntyre, have smoothed my path. The registrar of the Supreme Court, Bernard Hofley, and his staff obligingly located material for me when asked. Numbers of people sent me information and anecdotes about Duff in response to a request which appeared in newspapers across Canada, and to them I am especially grateful. Some of these contributions appear directly in the text, but all have guided me. My correspondents from Nova Scotia, particularly Dr. S.B. Bird of Liverpool, have been helpful and enthusiastic; Nova Scotians have a special feel for history. I have asked many lawyers and judges, serving and retired, for comment and advice, and most have obliged. Marianne McLean of Ottawa has been an indefatigable and highly intelligent researcher who made it unnecessary for me to spend inconveniently long periods of time in the Public Archives at Ottawa, where much of the material related to this book is to be found.

In England, Eric Mills, the registrar of the Privy Council, D.H.O. Owen, the chief clerk, and their staff were extremely helpful. Without their assistance I would not have grasped the full extent of Duff's work on the Judicial Committee of the Privy Council. And to Lord Denning, Viscount Simon, Lord Edmund-Davies, Sir Brian McKenna, and the late William Forbes of the Law Commission, I am indebted for insights into Duff's work on the Privy Council as well as that of his English colleagues. Lady Rosalind Hayes gave me most charming recollections of Duff's lighter side. Mrs. William Machin of Worksop helped me trace Duff's family in Nottinghamshire and led me to his grandmother's grave. In this country, Mrs. Sheila Waugh of Ottawa, a cousin of Duff's, helped me greatly in tracing the Canadian family.

I must acknowledge my indebtedness to the Association for Canadian Studies, the Faculty of Law at the University of Victoria, and to Richard F. Gosse. In 1979, the association announced a competition for three Canadian biography awards. I had contemplated a biography of Duff, and the announcement prodded me into making up my mind. I received one of the awards which, quite apart from its monetary aspect, was valuable because it imposed on me a deadline for the completion of the work.

The then dean of the law faculty of the University of Victoria, F.M. Fraser, on learning of my proposed work, invited me to join that faculty as writer in residence. It has been a happy and fruitful experience for me. Indeed, as I write, the experience continues, since the present dean, Lyman Robinson, has extended my appointment until 1986. Diana Priestly, librarian of the faculty, and her staff have been unfailingly helpful. I should add that the views I express on constitutional law, or any other field of law, are entirely my own, and I bear full responsibility for any frailties in them. I should also mention that the British North America Act which formed so large a part of Duff's professional life has been renamed the Constitution Act as part of the arrangements of 1981. I have throughout the text used the name by which it was known to Duff.

My friend Richard Gosse, now deputy attorney-general of Saskatchewan, had for years intended writing a biography of Duff, but events conspired against him. Learning that I intended to do one and that I could bring it to completion, he turned over all his research notes and material, a magnanimous gesture that shortened my task significantly. I am deeply grateful to him.

I must record my special gratitude to W. Kenneth Campbell, formerly Duff's private secretary, and, after Duff's retirement, his close friend and confidant. Kenneth Campbell spent days with me recalling as much as he knew — and it was a great deal — of Duff, his career, opinions, and attitudes, and has obligingly helped me in numerous other ways.

When I was well into the drafting stage, the Osgoode Society of Toronto expressed interest in taking the work on as one of its publications. I am grateful to the members of the publications committee of the society and to Professor Peter Oliver, the editor, for their encouragement in bringing the work to term and their support for its publication in conjunction with the University of British Columbia Press.

My partners in my law firm have accepted my frequent and prolonged absences with good grace, as have my family. My former secretary, Margaret Filion, has given valuable assistance in typing and offering advice. My secretary of many years, Carole Daem, has been unfailingly helpful and typed for me the whole of the final draft. Maureen Campbell, my secretary at the law faculty, typed most of my research notes and much of the earlier draft. Professor W.R. Lederman, Q.C., of the faculty of law at Queen's University, offered to read the manuscript when he was a visiting professor at Victoria, and gave me much encouragement. Professor DeLloyd J. Guth, also when a visiting professor, read the work and offered much useful advice. And to those many other persons who helped me in differing ways, I express my indebtedness.

David Ricardo Williams
Duncan, B.C.
April 1984

# 1

## "I am all bully"

LYMAN DUFF was one of the many outstanding Canadians to have sprung from Scottish forebears. His lineage, however, is unknown and perhaps unknowable. Not only was he indifferent to his family tree, but he was dispassionate about relatives of his own generation, and never during the many trips he made to Britain did he visit Scotland, or for that matter, those parts of England where his paternal grandparents had lived.

His grandfather Charles was the only member of that generation of whom Duff knew anything at all. He was a Perthshire man, born on 6 June 1796 in the fine city that straddles the river Tay as it winds through a verdant plain on its course to the North Sea, and looks north and west to the Grampians which, like sentinels, guard the passes to the western highlands. Even though in Charles's time Perth was a sizeable place with fifteen thousand inhabitants, it was evidently not busy enough to keep him working at his stonecutter's trade. There were better opportunities in England, and Charles left Scotland never to return.

He went to Nottinghamshire to look for work, arriving some time after 1817 and settling in the district around Hucknall Torkard, now a grubby mill town near the city of Nottingham. The county has been made famous by the exploits of Robin Hood, and it is almost as well known for its associations with the Byron family, particularly the poetical sixth Lord Byron who in 1817 sold the ancestral home, Newstead Abbey, nine miles north of Nottingham, to stave off bankruptcy. The purchaser, Colonel Thomas Wildman, embarked on an extensive programme of restoration which took ten years to complete. Charles found a steady job at the abbey, working as a carver rather than a mere cutter of stone, a less skilled craft.

Some of the restoration work was done by a family whose name was spelled variously as Lindley or Linley. Through them, Charles met their relative Ann

Linley, who lived at Linby, a small, attractive village nestling beneath the handsome tower of the twelfth-century parish church of St. Michael. In this church they were married on 16 May 1830. They lived in the village of Papplewick, even smaller but just as pleasant, and an easy walk from Linby across grassy fields bordered by oaks. There Ann became the village shopkeeper, helped perhaps by Charles, whose trade as a stonecarver began to falter from lack of work. Within eight years of their marriage the couple had four children, all born at Papplewick; John, Charles, George, and Sarah. By 1848 the elder Charles, no longer able to find steady work, had decided on a drastic course: the family should emigrate to Canada. Ann would have none of it. The anxious discussions, if not arguments, may be imagined; in the upshot Charles, accompanied by two of his sons, young Charles and George, left for Canada West, or Ontario. Ann had insisted that her eighteen-year-old son John remain with her, and it made obvious sense for Sarah, aged ten, to stay at home too. Husband and wife were never again to meet; young Charles and George did not see their mother again, nor John and Sarah their father.

The younger Charles, destined to be Lyman Duff's father, was sixteen at the time of the voyage across the Atlantic, a journey frequently uncomfortable and sometimes dangerous. The Duffs' accommodations would have been below decks in cramped and smelly quarters; in addition to human passengers, the sailing ships of the day carried livestock and poultry to supply fresh milk and meat. There was the ever-present danger of shipboard fire from the flames of cook-stoves and the candles which a crew member had the task of extinguishing in early evening. Still, the crossing does not seem to have been an unpleasant one. Once when the vessel lay becalmed, the adventurous young Charles leapt overboard for a swim in the ocean, much to the consternation of the ship's captain.

Charles and his two boys took up a parcel of farmland near Balmoral in Walpole Township, Haldimand County, Canada West. George, barely twelve, could not have been much use to his father, but young Charles pitched in manfully to do his share. They had hardly broken the ground on the homestead when the father died in August 1850. Less than a year later, saddened by the separation of her family and grieved by her husband's death, Ann Duff died at Papplewick. John and Sarah left for Canada soon afterwards to join their brothers. As the eldest son, John inherited the farm, and took his younger siblings under his wing. Thirty years after the mother's burial at Annesley Hall churchyard near Papplewick, he had a tombstone erected over her grave and inscribed with a typical Victorian eulogy, the first four lines of which were adapted from the one on his father's stone at Balmoral.

| | |
|---|---|
| A faithfull mother lieth here | When nearly 30 years had passed |
| Beloved by all her children dear | Her eldest son returned at last |
| Great is the loss that they sustain | And gratefully this tribute gave |
| But hope in Heaven to meet again. | In honour of his mother's grave. |

Ann's tombstone still stands mouldering in the now deconsecrated and abandoned churchyard.

John stayed on the farm for some years after his father's death, but in 1867 moved to Hamilton to start the grocery business which he and his descendants ran for eighty years. That side of the family was a prolific one, but Lyman saw little of them after his early years and never displayed more than a perfunctory interest in his many collateral relations.

Young Charles, as well as being venturesome, was studious. He had done well in his schooling at Hucknall Torkard, where he was a pupil-teacher by age sixteen; his son Lyman would follow much the same path, teaching to put himself through university. Like his brother, Charles was on the farm for some time after the father died, until he enrolled in 1855 as a charity student of the humanities at Union College in Schenectady, New York. He left after two years without taking his degree, probably because the charitable funds had run out or were inadequate to support him.

He decided to become a minister of the Congregational church, an outgrowth of seventeenth-century English Puritan dissent that had flowered in the New England colonies and been transplanted to Nova Scotia in the mid-eighteenth century; the denomination spread to the Canadas, now Quebec and Ontario, in the early nineteenth. Congregationalists were evangelicals: they looked to the Bible for guidance in all aspects of life and religion. They also insisted on "full recognition of the distinctive principles of Congregational churches, namely, the Scriptural right of every separate church to maintain perfect independence in its government and in its administration."[1] These self-governing Congregational parishes formed "unions" to represent their collective interests in various regions of the country. The unions also organized the training of clergy in such colleges as the Congregational Theological Institute of Toronto from which Charles graduated in 1862.

In its obituary on Charles, the Toronto *Globe* suggested the reasons for his adherence to the Congregational church: "As a lad in England he had been a disciple of Bright and Cobden and as a non-conformist, when dissent was neither so powerful nor popular as it has become, he saw the crushing injustice of class and religion privileges."[2] Disapproval of the authority vested in official church and state no doubt weighed with him, but he must also have been attracted by the fundamentalist cast of his denomination; it did not attract Lyman, who in adulthood became an Anglican.

As a theology student Charles frequently did missionary work in Meaford, Ontario, where, immediately after his ordination in 1862, he remained to minister to the small parish. Meaford is still a pleasant, quiet town on the south shore of Georgian Bay, shaded in the summer by leafy trees but gripped in winter by hard frosts and buffeted by winds coming off the lake. With a population of about five hundred in those days, it was an out-of-the-way place, not easily reached from the communities to the east and west. To journey southward to the larger town of Fergus, the traveller took the trail up the gently rising slope of Beaver Valley to find himself on a broad plain of splendid farmland dotted with large stone houses.

Soon after he was ordained, Charles married Isabella, the daughter of James Johnson of Bolton, Ontario, whom he had met while she was visiting Meaford relatives. An Irishman trained to the law, Johnson had emigrated to Iowa, where Isabella had been born. Afterwards the family moved up to Bolton where Johnson became a local worthy. Isabella had been raised in the Roman Catholic faith, but on marrying Charles she became a Protestant, an unusual conversion showing an independence of mind which carried over into the upbringing and education of her four children. Charles was an evangelical, Isabella an intellectual. To her, books and classical literature were on a plane with formal religion. At the end of his life, Duff spoke not of his father but of his mother, who died in 1902. True to the temper of the times, his father had been a strict parent, and it was the memory of his mother's gentleness that lingered in him.

Charles laboured mightily in the vineyards of the Lord, but church membership rose only slightly. He and Isabella had great joy, however, in the birth of two children at Meaford. Their first, Rolph, arrived in 1863, the year construction started on Charles's first church, a small building rather like a schoolhouse near the family's brick home on the north side of Parker Street. There, on 7 January 1865, a Saturday, Lyman was born. At Sunday service the next morning, Charles offered prayers of thanksgiving for his wife's safe delivery. In naming the baby, Charles recalled his ordination, at which two clergymen present had been the Reverend Mr. Lyman and the Reverend Mr. Poore. Lyman's Aunt Sarah later described the baptism for John Duff and his wife.

> Mr. Poore, a missionary from New Zealand and Australia, came to visit this mission field and he baptized the baby. They called him Lyman Poore though that is not a very suitable name for he is very fat. He is a sweet little fellow, always laughing and crowing...[3]

In October 1865, discouraged by the slow increase in church members, Charles made the first of many moves from one pastorate to another, accepting a call from the congregation at Speedside, a hamlet a few miles east of Fergus in the township of Eramosa. He took up his new work early in 1866 to remain there barely a year, though even in that brief time he and Isabella endeared themselves to the congregation, for they were invited back nine years later for a much longer stay. When Charles accepted a call to Liverpool, Nova Scotia, the Speedside faithful presented Isabella at a farewell ceremony with "one of Raymond's sewing machines and a beautiful box in which to keep it, and several hundred dollars besides." Charles was given a pocket Bible "filled with worked mottos of an appropriate character," as well as a "purse containing upwards of $60."[4] Thus did the Duffs depart for what was probably, from what Charles hinted later, a somewhat more prosperous congregation.

The family left Toronto by train on 16 January 1867 to travel to Portland, Maine, where they took a steamship for St. John, New Brunswick. Isabella, pregnant with her daughter Emma, had an uncomfortable time of it. The voyage to St. John was not unpleasant, but from there they had to travel in a small sailing packet across the Bay of Fundy to Digby, Nova Scotia, then to Annapolis, and on to Liverpool over the snow "in an open one-horse sled," as Charles later recalled.[5]

On the last day of the week-long journey, just as they were arriving in Liverpool, Lyman became seriously ill with a fever which lasted seven weeks. His parents despaired for his life, and according to a family story told by his sister Annie, at one stage he was even allowed to be treated by an old sea-dog with a cup of rum. In later life Lyman used to say that he could still taste the rum.

Charles arrived expecting to take charge, not only of the Liverpool parish, but also of those at Brooklyn and Beach Meadows, the latter being the smallest. All three communities stood on the sweep of Liverpool Bay. The first settlers of the area, who had come from New England in the 1750s, were augmented later by Loyalists fleeing the revolutionary United States. Their descendants, pious, earnest men, made fishing their livelihood, although a few still worked at boat-building or lumbering. Not infrequently, Charles's income would be supplemented by payment in fish and game: pollock — a white fish — haddock, scallops, lobster, and venison. The family lived at first in a house close to Brooklyn on the sea-front, but within a few months they had moved a short distance to their permanent residence, a handsome two-storey parsonage just a few steps from the water. In it they were to spend the next seven years, a period indelibly impressed on young Lyman's mind.

By the time Charles arrived in Nova Scotia, Congregationalism had lost many of its adherents, principally to the Baptists. It was a mark of his successful ministry that he reversed this trend in his Nova Scotia parishes: he recorded the reception of many people into the church and exalted in the "most wonderful and extensive revivals that it has ever been my privilege to have dealt with."[6] Though successful, his ministry was marred at the outset by parish politics. A group of Liverpool parishioners had protested their congregation's dismissal of Charles's predecessor, and for a period he did not minister there, confining himself to the parishioners at Brooklyn and Beach Meadows, who had removed themselves from the Liverpool congregation. This disagreement and others related to it festered for several years, with Charles moving back and forth between the Brooklyn and Liverpool parishes almost as the wind blew, but by the time he left the area in 1875, he had won the hearts of all his congregations. Perhaps because of the parochial unpleasantness, or possibly because he needed the money, he became school inspector for the county of Queen's, a post he held for four years and which led some time later to an honorary master of arts degree conferred on him by Acadia University. He had well understood the character of his parishioners: "The people here are so heterogeneous that religious and political influences sweep localities as fires sometime do in forests."[7] Though a transplanted "Canadian," that is one from central or "Upper" Canada, he quickly absorbed the Maritime attitude and espoused Joseph Howe's views: "Canada has [all] along misunderstood N.S. You may depend upon it, there is no play about the repeal movement."[8]

Young Lyman's first experience of education was on rough wooden benches in the one-room school at Brooklyn. His brother Rolph, two years older, attended the same school; they were probably joined later by Emma, born a few months after their arrival in Liverpool. No record exists of Lyman's school attendance in Brooklyn, and he left no written recollection of it himself. We can be sure, however, that the curriculum was based solidly on the "Three R's."[9]

Like any young lad compelled to go to church at least twice on Sunday, he was sometimes obstreperous. Once he fought with his brother in church, obliging his father to build a special pew for the two boys beneath the pulpit, where he could control them. He earned a little pocket money selling lobsters which he carried around in a wheelbarrow. His sister Annie has said that this merchandising experience prompted him to talk of becoming a shopkeeper. Lyman found life pleasant, even though children thereabouts pretty much had to make their own entertainment. He went swimming and played sand-lot baseball, and he had a new little sister, Annie, born in 1873. There was no road to Halifax; travel was only by ship, and journeys elsewhere were difficult. The seafaring tradition of the area — the boats, the fishing, the sailors — all fascinated Duff, who acquired a lifelong love of the sea.

It must have been a disappointment to the ten-year-old boy when his father decided that his three children of school age, all of whom showed promise as students, would get a better education in Ontario. While he was in Montreal for a meeting of the Congregational Union, Charles put out feelers for a return to Speedside, a smaller parish than any of the three to which he had ministered in Nova Scotia. Receiving his invitation late in 1875, he was installed for the second time as pastor and moved with his family into the red brick manse which still stands next to the present church building.

The district around Speedside, or Eramosa, as the parish is more correctly called, epitomizes the farm country of southern Ontario. Speedside is set on a level, fertile plain which stretches for miles in all directions. At age thirteen, Duff gave a whimsical description of it in a letter to his friend Douglas Alexander, who had asked what the place was like and whether there were any lawyers.

As to lawyers, there number is 0. There names "None." At the westerly extremity of Speedside runs the Brook Speed spanned by a bridge tottering with old age, and ready to "give up the ghost" at any moment. As you pass the hill east the "bridge" you come to Speedside. Population of it is something like 20 — the number of horses 6, including a Post Office & grocery store (4 ft. x 10 ft.) There are also a Blacksmith + Carpenter's shop.[10]

The tiny village was still the hub of a region, though a very minor one, because of its church, and this is the case even now. Charles came back in 1875 to the same church building where he had preached ten years earlier, but under his stewardship a new building was erected in 1880 which stands virtually unaltered today, except for a parish hall joined to it. It is a rare Canadian example of an octagonal church, with peaked tower and Gothic windows. The interior is equally attractive, with the pews placed on the fine planked floor at exactly the proper angles to the pulpit in line with the eight sides of the building, so that the minister can take in the congregation at a glance. It is not known what part Charles Duff had in the design of this lovely church.

Ten-year-old Lyman easily made the transition from the Atlantic seaboard to the heartland of rural Ontario. He was enrolled at once in the grey stone schoolhouse at Speedside, where for a year, he spent six hours a day at his books. Built in 1861, it was the sort that found its way into a government report on school accommodation which deplored the dangers to health of overcrowding and poor ventilation, particularly in winter:

> The air — especially near the close of the day, when it sometimes becomes almost pestilential — indicates a sad lack of Ventilation and much uncleanliness of person and clothing. The dietetic habits of the children will inevitably attract attention. They eat before School, at recess, after School, sometimes during School hours — eat pies, doughnuts, fried meat and other heavy indigestible food, sure to ruin the health early, or late.[11]

To reach this school, Duff walked only a short distance down the road from the manse and across the bridge over the river Speed; he spent many an idle hour in the shallow waters of the languid stream, fishing or paddling under a canopy of arched trees. He was a bright pupil. By age ten, under his mother's influence, he read Hansard regularly as well as novels by Dickens, books of English history, the plays of Shakespeare, and accounts of famous battles and soldiers; he never lost his fascination with military history. His sister Annie has said that Lyman would as soon sit with a book as play with his fellows.

Instructions to elementary schools of the day set out the virtues of a general education:

> Every youth, whether in Town or Country should be able so to read that reading will be a pleasure and not a labour, otherwise his little knowledge of the reading will be seldom, if ever, used to acquire information; he should be able to write readily and well; he should know Arithmetic so as to perform readily and properly any financial business transactions, and be able to keep Accounts; he should be able to speak and write with correctness the language of the Country. The subjects are the first essentials of education for every youth, and in which he should be primarily and thoroughly taught.[12]

In addition, Duff learned geography; he was required to "point out on a Map of the World each Continent and ocean and know which part of the Map is north, south, east or west."[13] He studied "linear drawing," using a slate. He was taught some science and physics, and as well, "the first principles of Christian Morals." Because he lived in the country, he was also given *First Lessons in Agriculture*, written by the famous Dr. Egerton Ryerson. After school, he would be expected to do homework for two hours.[14]

In late December 1876 he travelled to Elora, a pretty town on the Grand River not far from Fergus, to sit for the high-school entrance examinations. Of the twenty-seven students who spent two consecutive days writing, he was the youngest. Excelling in mathematics, he achieved a mark of 100 per cent even though he had needed only one of the allotted two hours to complete his paper.

As if in celebration of his success, a merry party took place at the manse. A lively account of these festivities appeared in a church newspaper.

> New Year's eve falling on Sunday, Saturday evening was chosen by the young people of Speedside congregation and church to make a raid upon the parsonage. Accordingly at about 7 o'clock, half-a-dozen sleighs containing about forty of them landed at the gates, and just when the inmates were thinking and preparing for an early retirement to the rest needful for the morrow, that number of laughing, sportive youths and maidens, were suddenly and unexpectedly launched into the quietude of the Speedside country-parsonage. Well, if change is best, that visit was beneficial in its influence on the next day's sermon as a much earlier retirement.

Gifts were presented to the Duff family, and "entertainment and enjoyment" followed. One of the visitors read a "flattering address" to Charles "in the most breathless stillness, which we doubt not was felt by them all." Everybody then enjoyed a "pleasant repast which they themselves had taken great care to provide and bring with them." Following prayers, the visitors rode off into the night in their sleighs in time to get home before the arrival of the Sabbath morning.[15]

Like his father who moved so often from parish to parish, Lyman moved from school to school during the years leading up to university. In 1877, Charles enrolled him for six months in the Hamilton Collegiate Institute. In Hamilton, he stayed reluctantly with his Uncle John, whom he disliked; one of John's children, almost exactly Lyman's age, also attended the collegiate.

For some undisclosed reason, perhaps because he did not get on well with his uncle, Duff spent the next eighteen months at the Fergus high school. Going to classes there while living at Speedside meant a journey of seven or eight miles, depending on the route or short-cut taken. Lyman drove to school by horse and buggy, sometimes accompanied by his brother Rolph, who was going to school in Elora and boarding there. The two of them once landed in a ditch while trying to drive over a cow lying in the narrow road, an event which must have caused the tongues to wag. The school inspector's reports for the period of Lyman's stay at Fergus speak favourably of the "new stone building" and the quality of education: "This school is highly efficient."[16] Along with some sixty or seventy schoolmates, Lyman now studied algebra and geometry in addition to the other basic subjects, and he did well in all of them.

His progress at Fergus was interrupted, however: Charles decided that the boy, now thirteen, should return to Hamilton, and back he went for a continuous stay of two years, boarding again with the uncle's family. Duff looked back with affection on his time at the collegiate there, no doubt because he became fast friends with a few of his schoolmates, notably Charles Fields, later professor of mathematics at University College in Toronto, and Douglas Alexander, whose close friendship with Duff would span some seventy-two years. After studying law at Osgoode Hall, Alexander ended up in the United States, where he had a long and distinguished career as president of the Singer Manufacturing Company that included guiding it through strategic production in two world conflicts. As boys, he and Duff were avid correspondents, and many years later on one of his regular visits to Canada, he brought his old friend the letters Duff had written more than a half-century before. Luckily for a biographer, Duff kept them. They are invaluable because they cover the period of his shaping, the years from age twelve to seventeen; in them Duff writes boyishly, cleverly, frankly, and above all, affectionately. Very seldom in later life did he write anything of such a private character. Perhaps the most remarkable feature of the letters is that over the six-year period, Duff charted a course for himself in life, stage by stage, which he followed in every important particular.

The intermediate examinations that preceded the matriculation process were an important hurdle for serious-minded students like Duff and Alexander. Duff told his friend, in a letter written just after his twelfth birthday, that he planned to write them soon expecting to fail. His prediction was correct, since he did not pass until he was thirteen, helped by copies of the examination papers which Alexander, being a year older, had already written. But at twelve, Duff was not downhearted: "I am all bully, and suppose you are something of the same stamp..." He ended his letter with mock seriousness:

> I have the honour to be
>
> Sir
>
> Your obedient servant
>
> L.P. Duff[17]

Alexander started work in a law office, apparently copying documents. Already thinking of a career in law himself, Duff wrote, "Do you only have the writing to do in your office; and do you have the use of the law books! I am thinking something of trying to get a situation in one next winter."[18] Alexander wangled an offer of a job in a law office for him, but Duff declined for the reasons he gave in a letter of December 1878.

> I rather intended going to school next winter and trying to push ahead and matriculate in arts in a couple of years if possible. By so doing I might obtain a certificate as assistant teacher in a High School even before 18 years of age. I am not exactly sure whether I will take a course in Arts or in Law, there are a good many arguments in favour of both, but I think I would prefer the Law. So, if I could teach for a while, so as to obtain some *footing* I think that with a little help I might be able to get through. However, I am sure that I will go to school likely at Hamilton after Christmas and I am very glad that you are going too.[19]

Duff did in fact get a position as a teacher, in Barrie; he did get some "footing," as he called it, and he did prefer the law.

For the moment, there was Hamilton. The collegiate there was a large one for the day, with an enrolment of over four hundred and a teaching staff of sixteen. There were attendance fees: for non-residents, sixteen dollars a year, and for residents, twenty cents a month for each subject taken. The inspector's reports for the school in the two years Duff attended, 1879 and 1880, speak highly of the building, classroom equipment, and, most important of all, the excellent instruction given by a well-qualified staff. It seems to have been a good setting for Duff's natural ability as a student.

Though he spent the lazy summer days at Speedside, Duff did not give up his studies; at least, he was expected to continue them. In the summer of 1879, he wrote Alexander blithely,

> Yours to hand several days ago. Glad to hear that John Brown, Hon. Ass and premier of Essayists, are doing well....You wanted to know how I have been studying since I came home. The answer is short, I have been doing little or nothing in that line. I would just feel tip-top then, if it wasn't so Orful, Orful, HOT...P.S. When you see Hon. Geo. Rev. Bell, again, give him my compliments, with success to his oratorical powers and tell him he's a full-blown ass.[20]

He embellished his letter with multiple flourishes and underlinings of words.

By the following summer, when he was fifteen, Duff had made up his mind about his future. Writing to Alexander, he referred first to his brother Rolph's academic plans.

> You wanted to know how long it would be before R.J. was going to law....Well — July, August, ad infin:...He has given up the idea of becoming a Pettifogger of Law M.A., Ll.D., and his occupation will be commencing some time...which requires the arranging of skulls across legs — grave robbing, etc. — and others better imagined than described.

As it happened, Rolph did study law, not medicine, at the University of Toronto, but he did not go into the profession. Alexander was aiming at law like Duff, who said in the same letter, "I suppose you will soon be initiated into the mysteries of *Our Profession*. I hope you'll like it — in your last you said you had mailed a catalogue of Law Books — it didn't come." The conduct of a common acquaintance in debating circles had evidently annoyed both of them. "I wrote to him a long while ago — but I guess I so disgusted him with assishness that he thought it was better not to write back for fear I should treat him to another dose."[21]

Lyman left Hamilton at the end of 1880. Early the following year he went to St. Catharines to attend the collegiate institute there, probably boarding with church acquaintances of his father or uncle. The school, though a little smaller than Hamilton's, was also a good one. Duff was remembered by schoolmates for his prowess in debate, a natural talent that apparently flowered in St. Catharines. Fifty years later, one of them recalled Duff as "a small red-headed boy" who, in the words of another from that time, made "shreds of the opponent's arguments." After one forum on the virtues of a monarchical as opposed to a republican form of government, the local newspaper had high praise for the "splendid and determined opposition of Messrs. Mustard and Duff."[22] Duff lost for republicanism. In true debating tradition he had argued a cause he did not personally support; his belief in the value of the monarchy was one he held all his life.

A month or so later, after a debate on whether a limited franchise was preferable to universal suffrage, his efforts again attracted favourable notice from the press. And using another of his talents, "Mr. Duff recited 'The Lady of Provence' in a manner creditable to himself and interesting to the [Literary] Society."[23] He also sang with the Glee Club, an activity he did not pursue in later life.

Duff thought he received a first-class education at the school and spoke in the most glowing terms of the quality of his teachers. He was thoroughly enjoying life in general and ready for experience, as revealed in a letter to Alexander soon after his sixteenth birthday.

> This hour I suppose, it being 9 p.m. the 3rd day of April is a happy one with you — trudging along with "my dear Susan Jane" hanging on your arm and listening with rapture to the sweet accents which fall from your beloved lips, telling of things you know better than I do. Well, I suppose you'll think I'm about as barbarous a critter as one is likely to meet in these days of general enlightenment — and you will be about right too.

His eyes still on the law, Duff finished by saying, "You see I am on a fair way to becoming a lawyer (in the matter of writing). You will have to look up. I am beating you all to pieces."[24]

By the summer of 1881 he had passed an important milestone: at age sixteen, he successfully wrote the examinations for junior matriculation, the threshold of the University of Toronto. He had only passing grades in such subjects as Latin and Greek, French, and natural philosophy, but in mathematics he won the second-highest mark among the 153 students across the province writing the examination. His brother Rolph sat for the same examinations, getting a first in English. A boy at Brantford whom Duff had yet to meet, Gordon Hunter, took a first class in both classics and mathematics, and respectable seconds in the other subjects. Their later friendship would be important for both of them.

# 2

# Undergraduate

AT SOME STAGE, Duff attended Jarvis Collegiate Institute in Toronto; the puzzle is to know precisely when. Since he did not complete his intermediate examinations until the end of 1878, and for the two following years and the first half of 1881 he was in Hamilton and then St. Catharines, he could only have gone to the Toronto school before entering university towards the end of the latter year. He could have had two reasons for doing so. He may have wanted a senior matriculation, which reduced by a year the time required for a bachelor of arts degree; and knowing that he would have to help pay his way through university by teaching his best subject — mathematics — he may have gone for extra courses to an institution with an unexcelled reputation in the discipline.[1]

In October 1882 his father tendered a resignation which the Speedside parish refused to accept. He agreed to stay on, but he and his parishioners must then have realized how unsatisfactory an arrangement this was, for he left Speedside permanently at the end of the year. Apparently in an unsettled frame of mind, he went to Winnipeg, intending to do missionary work on the Prairies. While there, in the spring of 1883, he received an invitation to take charge of a Toronto parish and declined. Yet a few months later, in August, he accepted a call to form a new parish in the west-end Toronto district of Parkdale, with its church to be built on the corner of Brock and Maple Grove avenues, and thus combine his pastoral work with his duties as chairman of the Congregational Union of Ontario and Quebec. He had experience at this sort of thing, having twice served as chairman of the union in the Maritimes. The advantage for Lyman, of course, was that from 1883 on the family lived in Toronto, and he could stay inexpensively with his parents while studying at the university. His two sisters, Emma and Annie, were also at home, both of them attending school.

From 1883 until his death in 1905, all Charles's time was spent in the Toronto area except for three years beginning in 1897 when he was at his old parish of Brooklyn. He left without his wife; Isabella's decision not to accompany him is reminiscent of Ann Duff's refusal to emigrate to Canada with the elder Charles. Her reasons are not known; perhaps she felt that she should stay with her two daughters, by then teaching school in Toronto but living at home, or perhaps she had simply had enough of Nova Scotia. In 1894 Charles had taken on the editorship of the *Congregationalist*, the journal of the Congregational churches, and this seems to have been the last job he did for the denomination as a whole.

Though Lyman, in what correspondence has survived or in the recollection of friends and acquaintances, never acknowledged his father's influence, it must have been considerable. Without question, Charles Duff was an upright man, inclined to sternness but remembered warmly and thought of highly by those to whom he brought the Gospel. He was capable but not particularly well read — Lyman acquired his voracious reading habits from his mother. Yet it was Charles who first encouraged his son to study the law, clearly perceiving some talent in him. Directly or indirectly, Charles also influenced his son's political beliefs. The Toronto *Globe* said of him in its obituary that

> in his political sympathies Mr. Duff was a Liberal among Liberals. It was in no mere party sense that Mr. Duff was a Liberal and allied himself with the Reform movement in Canada, but because he knew democracy with all its perils is safer than Toryism. Mr. Duff contributed frequently to these columns and never without saying something worthwhile, without bitterness or malice.[2]

By the time Lyman presented himself at the university, his political views were exactly in accord with those of his father; they would remain unchanged throughout his life, form an important element in the development of his character, and motivate many of his actions as both lawyer and judge.

More by indirection than direction, Charles influenced his son in another important respect. He was an unbending teetotaller, utterly opposed to the use of the "demon liquor." As early as 1862 he presided at public temperance meetings in central Canada, and later did the same in Nova Scotia. His convictions and those of others like him were expressed in a popular verse of the day:

> Water is best for the trees of the forest,
> Water is best for the flowers of the field,
> Water is best for the rich and the mighty,
> Water is best for the humble that toil.[3]

Charles could not persuade his own son Lyman to temperance, however. The young man rebelled openly against his father's views, and must have caused him some small distress by the way he carried on with his convivial companions, particularly Gordon Hunter, later chief justice of British Columbia. In fact Lyman's drinking habits, actual or reputed, were to dog his career until he became chief justice of Canada in 1933, and not even then were his excesses forgotten.

The record of his progress through the University of Toronto and Osgoode Hall is muddled, partly because of the interruption in his studies during the four years he taught school and also because of changes in university structure and curriculum. The founding of a new Osgoode law school in 1889 and his unexplained stay there for five years when he should have finished in three, as well as gaps in the records at both the university and Osgoode, contribute to the difficulty of retracing his career. We do know that he entered University College in the autumn of 1881. Until 1889, the relations of the constituent and associated colleges with the University of Toronto, established as the provincial university in 1867, were complicated ones. Essentially, the university was the examining and degree-granting body and the work of instruction was entrusted to University College, which had been in existence since 1853. When Duff entered the college, it was *the* visible university. Enrolment barely exceeded three hundred, all male; women did not gain admission until 1884.

Lyman plunged into university life energetically and enthusiastically, with the zest of one who had been looking forward to it for four years. He had not been on campus a month before he kicked over the traces by becoming involved in a freshman hazing incident that won notoriety at the time, and, soon afterward, in a billiard-room brawl. The first incident, occurring in November 1881, also involved Gordon Hunter, by then Duff's friend, and Stuart Henderson, a brilliant student who moved to British Columbia eventually as did both of the other culprits, emerging as possibly the cleverest criminal lawyer ever to practise in that province. The matter was really nothing more than a typical example of freshman initiation, but it did reflect the division between those favoured students who resided in the college and the less favoured ones who, like Duff himself, lived off campus. The former tended to view themselves as superior mortals, reluctant to associate with the hoi polloi. The *Globe* branded it piously as "probably the most disgraceful outrage that has ever yet occurred in college circles in the city."[4]

After trading insults with a group of freshmen, about fifteen upperclassmen grabbed Duff and his friends along with a fourth man, bound them hand and foot, and locked them in upper rooms at University College. Hunter managed to free himself, and escaped by tying bedsheets together and lowering himself to the ground, where he raised a hue and cry. Duff and the two others were then dragged away to the edge of a creek into which the upperclassmen threatened to fling them, and made to ridicule themselves and other freshmen by singing a disparaging song. Perhaps because the *Globe* reported that some forty bottles of whisky had been drunk by college seniors in the course of the evening's events, the president of the university promised to launch a full inquiry. Nothing came of it.

Not surprisingly, the university newspaper, the *Varsity*, took the relaxed approach that it was "the custom in all colleges for the freshmen to treat the seniors with respect and to enforce this by *mild remonstrances* or more stringent measures when refused."[5] Identifying Duff and his friends as the "leading insurrectionists," the paper said that they had sought legal advice from one of the largest law firms in Toronto only to be "told that they deserved their fate." The *Varsity* printed a letter from "Leveller" advocating the rights of freshmen; one wonders if it might have been written by Duff or his friends. The anonymous writer argued that

> too much importance is attached to differences of academic standing in the social system of University College. It seems to me to be high time that the old party lines of "resident" and "outsider," where there are no principles to contend for which are worthy of the exertions put forth at election times, should be forgotten, and a new party formed whose leading plank might be equal rights for all undergraduates. The ungenerous manner in which First Year men are wont to be treated at College and the wearing of caps and gowns, might then be ranged side by side as relics of barbarism; and some effort might be made for the abolition of both grievances.[6]

The excitement had hardly begun to die down when the second incident took place. A number of freshmen, Duff among them, had jammed into a billiard room on Yonge Street, then as now Toronto's main thoroughfare. There was so much tumult that the proprietor called the police, who waded into the crowded room swinging their night sticks and arrested half a dozen students. Duff and others escaped into the street pursued by policemen, one of whom struck Duff from the rear. When Duff retired as chief justice in 1944, a student who had been in the brawl read a newspaper account of his career that made reference to his "unfailing courtesy" and wrote him to recall the affair. When he was hit by the policeman, it seems, Duff thought mistakenly that he had bumped into an innocent bystander, whereupòn "you ... straightened up quickly and said humbly, 'I beg your pardon.' "[7] Duff himself, describing the affray to his friend Douglas Alexander at the time, said that it occurred in the wake of a big meeting called to form a students' union: "we had quite an episode with the police about which I suppose you have already heard considerable. They followed us to Yorkville and then turned around and walked back — quite amusing I suppose for them."[8] Apparently he worked off all his steam in these episodes; his fighting was confined thereafter to the debating forum and the floor of the mock parliament he founded at University College, with any surplus energy used up in association football.

Though in later life Duff attended church only for marriages or funerals, in his university days he had not shaken off the habit drummed into him by his parents. He wrote Alexander urging him to come to Toronto solely to hear a Dr. Wild whose sermons often contained "a good deal of solid worth," and ended on a note of gaiety that would become less evident as he grew older:

> I hope that, like a good little boy who always does as his conscience tells him, you are working hard. Of course — don't hurt yourself, take care of yourself, strain neither mind nor body — still you *must* get that scholarship. Finally, be good — don't swear, don't smoke anymore, and above all, keep clear of women.[9]

As the tone of his letters grew gradually more serious, his nickname of "L.P." gave way to "Lyman" and sometimes — a liberty allowed to a few — "Lyme." The same seriousness came to bear on his studies, and for the rest of his time at university Duff kept his nose to the grindstone. He would go to hear cases, telling Alexander,

> I usually spend an hour or two daily down at the courthouse and police courts. There is often a great deal of fun. Often, too, there is a great deal that is as dry as chips. I suppose if I understood a little law, it would not appear so. I wish you were here, the chancery court is sitting a great deal of the time in Osgoode Hall and Blake and McCarthy are doing a great deal of work there now. You would have a splendid chance of hearing good pleading if you were in an office here instead of in Hamilton.[10]

Edward Blake and D'Alton McCarthy, both members of dynastic Toronto law firms, were giants of the profession and considerable public men.

Duff kept his eye on law as a career, but the university in his time did not possess a law faculty as such; its LL.B. did not confer the right to practise, which could be granted only by the Law Society of Upper Canada at Osgoode Hall on the basis of requirements that changed from time to time. Duff chose to enrol in arts as a preliminary to the bachelor of laws degree. The two were linked in a practical sense, since a degree in arts would reduce by a year the time needed for the one in law. If, as in Duff's case, it was intended to study law at the university, courses in the arts faculty were chosen with that in mind. He also opted for the lustre of the honours programme that meant focussing on subjects in one of five departments, among them mathematics and mental and moral science along with civil polity, in addition to such pass-course material as Greek and Latin, English, history, and, if one was not a candidate for honours in mathematics, that subject also for two years.[11] As might have been expected, Duff first elected the mathematics programme, but he soon switched to philosophy in the belief that it would better prepare him for law. Accordingly, under the tutelage of the renowned Dr. George Paxton Young, he studied the works of Locke, Hume, and Bishop Berkeley, and such commentators on classical thought as T.H. Green.

He vied with his brother Rolph on the one hand and Gordon Hunter on the other. All three were clever students, though Hunter achieved greater academic distinction than either Lyman or his brother did. In fact Duff seems to have spent as much time debating as he did at his books; he was a keen member of the college Literary and Scientific Society, which in the variety of its activities was more like a contemporary alma mater society. The many accounts of him in formal debate and the arena of the mock parliament all use such terms as "forcible," "direct," "lucid," and "eloquent" to describe his performances. One was even attended by the famous Edward Blake, which must have given an added fillip to his argument. His efforts at recitation or "readings," however, were less successful; in its report of a rendering Duff had given from the poetry of the now scarcely read Mrs. Hemans, the *Varsity* complained of "a certain ungracefulness of gesture," something the same paper, reviewing Duff on another occasion, characterized as "exaggerated emphasis."

By the end of 1884, his third year at University College, it must have been evident to him that he would be financially incapable of completing his fourth for the bachelor of arts degree. Presumably the father supported his sons as far as he was able; he may have decided that Rolph as the elder of the two, though not quite so good a student as Lyman, deserved what limited money he could afford. There may have been another reason: Rolph, like his father, was a teetotaller, and this may have weighed with Charles when it came down to whether one or the other, not both, would continue at the university. In the end, only Rolph returned to graduate with the class of '85, though Lyman, who did not graduate until two years later, always considered himself none the less a member of that class.

He now found it necessary to earn money before resuming university, and, as he had foreseen, became a schoolteacher. In January 1885 he was appointed to teach mathematics in Barrie Collegiate Institute at a salary of six hundred dollars per annum, rising later to seven. His sister Annie has said that he chose Barrie because he had a friend on the staff then leaving whose place Duff could take: "This seemed to attract Lyman, who was always ready for an adventure. It did not attract his father."[12] With an enrolment of just over a hundred, the school was not a large one, but the inspectors' reports for the four years Duff was there speak highly of the place. He turned out to be an excellent teacher, not only of mathematics but of other subjects he sometimes gave, usually French. A pupil in his mathematics class recalled how he "insisted on his students doing their work in ink and not in pencil, believing that this led to greater accuracy: a mistake in pencil could be rubbed out and corrected without leaving a trace of the mistake, but a correction in ink would remain apparent."[13] When Duff left at the end of 1888, the inspector commented regretfully that the standard of mathematics instruction became "weaker" with his departure.

At Barrie, Duff remained keen on football, playing halfback on the school team; the fullback on the team recalled that he "sure knew how to give and take knocks — football was no parlour game to him."[14] He also kept up his interest in public speaking, joining not one but two literary debating societies the tastes of which seemed to run more to evening readings than cut and thrust. Duff's role as critic of readings from the works of Oliver Goldsmith given by another member drew favourable comment from a Barrie newspaper;[15] another time, again as critic, he urged the virtue of concentrating on one main point in an argument when time was limited, and deprecated the "too free use of notes" in speechmaking.[16]

This obvious talent as a public speaker when he was a young man stands in sharp contrast to his performance in later years. His reputation as counsel or courtroom lawyer rested on learning and careful preparation, not on quickness of speech or eloquence. After becoming a judge at age thirty-nine he made many speeches, but invariably wrote them beforehand, labouring over them so that, when read, they lacked fire and spontaneity. Even on occasions when only a few words were required, or when he was in front of old friends or colleagues, Duff was virtually incapable of speaking extemporaneously. He found it difficult to talk easily and gracefully to an audience, however intimate.

The year 1885 was a comparatively easy one for Duff, but the ensuing three must have taxed his physical and mental energies to the limit. In 1886, while still teaching, he resumed his studies in the university's arts faculty, taking fourth-year courses and beginning second-year law as well, and doing all the work extramurally. The LL.B. course curriculum had been changed in 1885, but he appears to have studied, among other subjects, the law of contracts and real property. In 1887, during his third year of law, his arts degree was "granted Aegrotat with Honours in Mental and Moral Philosophy."[17] He did not, in other words, write the final examinations, presumably because these conflicted with his school duties, but earned the degree based on his term work. The pace became a little less hectic in 1888, when he had only to teach, which he did until year end, and study fourth-year law, reading such dry subjects as Roman law and, once again, the law of real property.

The money he saved from teaching, combined with a scholarship he had won, enabled him to return to the university on a full-time basis early in 1889. His connection with Barrie did not end, however. He had met the family of Henry Bird, a respected citizen of the town who had been a shoe merchant and later town clerk, and taught two of Bird's children, one of whom, Edward, was barely two years younger than himself. Duff's relationship with Edward Bird persisted over many years with unfortunate financial consequences. Edward's sister Elizabeth, or "Lizzie" as she was called by her family, was herself a schoolteacher in Barrie, though not at the collegiate institute. How well Duff knew her in Barrie is not known, but the friendship continued over the years to culminate in their marriage in 1898.

By 1889, significant changes had occurred in the teaching of law at both the university and Osgoode Hall. As the result of the Federation Act passed in 1887 and proclaimed in 1889, which amalgamated the university and certain related colleges, the university revived a full-fledged law faculty which it had abolished nearly forty years earlier. It was hoped that this faculty, besides academic law, would also teach the practical side of law to prepare students for entry into the legal profession. In February 1888, the university met with representatives of the Law Society of Upper Canada to consider empowering the new faculty to represent the legal profession as well as the academic community and thus offer students complete training in a single institution.[18] The society rejected these overtures, however, and in late 1888 decided instead to reorganize its own law school, which had existed since 1881 and for intermittent periods prior to that date. Attendance by those planning to practise law was made obligatory, a decision which determined for sixty years the shape of legal education in Ontario.[19]

Duff did not complete his fourth-year studies for the LL.B. until mid-1889, when he received his degree with respectable first-class standing, though not the highest mark. He had become a student-at-law of the Law Society of Upper Canada at Osgoode Hall on 8 December 1888, but he had to complete his degree and wait for the reorganization of the law school in October 1889, under the principalship of W.A. Reeve, before beginning formal study.

As well as attending the prescribed lectures on a whole range of legal subjects for two days a week from October to June for three years, each student in those days spent the rest of the week in a law office, either under articles — the lawyers' version of apprenticeship — or if he was a university graduate, doing bona fide work for a barrister. We do not know whether Duff entered into formal articles or simply, as a university man, met the second requirement. According to his sister Annie, he worked for one year in the law office of Gordon Hunter's brother William in Toronto; the other two were spent with N.M. Monro, a lawyer in Fergus. As a working student in either capacity, he would perform such tedious chores as the hand-copying of documents; with experience, he would begin interviewing witnesses and clients and assist the lawyer in court, perhaps appearing by himself on a client's behalf. It seems that when he was with Monro, Duff took a considerable share of responsibility for the work in the office.[20]

Yet his progress through Osgoode Hall was slow, delayed by two unexplained interruptions. He was almost a year late writing the examination for his first year's studies, though in the end he did well, receiving the highest marks in his class and the top scholarship of one hundred dollars. In that same year, 1890, along with several others who had evidently fallen behind schedule, he tried to persuade the law society to abbreviate their period of qualification by allowing them to be called to the Bar on the strength of successfully writing the third-year examinations. The society turned them down. Duff and his fellow students were probably hard-pressed for money, and no doubt they pleaded this in asking for special consideration. A society rule that prohibited students from sullying their hands with work outside a law office caused great difficulty for the poorer ones, as articling was unpaid at the time; often, indeed, a student or his parents had to pay the office simply to get him into it. According to his sister Annie, Duff solved his problem by ignoring the ban on outside employment and quietly taking a job in the assessment office at Toronto's city hall.[21] Somehow, he did manage to write the second-year paper in the spring of 1891, though he gained no honours; then, oddly, he disappears from the law society's records not to emerge again until his call to the Bar on 20 November 1893. There is no trace at Osgoode Hall of his having written the final examination; certainly, he won none of the gold, silver, and bronze medals for achievement.

When he did emerge, Duff the newly qualified lawyer was not quite twenty-nine years of age. His studies and training had been protracted, and he had fallen behind those friends who had joined him in 1881 as young freshmen at the University of Toronto; Gordon Hunter, for example, had gone straight through to open a Toronto law office in 1888, immediately after his call to the Bar. On the whole, Duff's academic career had been good though not outstanding. Had he been able to study continuously without the distraction of outside work, it might have been better. However, as so often happens, academic supremacy is no guarantee of professional supremacy; Duff achieved the latter, if not the former. He seldom spoke of his time at Osgoode Hall, but he had affectionate memories of his university days, often receiving letters from former classmates to whom he replied warmly, though never easily or freely. No doubt his fondness for the institution induced him to serve later, and for many years, as a member of its board of governors.

# 3

# Junior counsel

HAD DUFF ACHIEVED better standing in his final Osgoode year, he might have been offered a position with one of the prestigious law firms in Toronto. And his fervent membership in the Toronto Young Liberal Club[1] might have interested a firm sympathetic to the cause. If he had such an offer, however, he did not accept it. Duff chose instead to practise amid scenes of his childhood in Fergus, the market town for a region which included the old home at Speedside and stretched as far north as his birthplace in Meaford. Settled by Scots, the town on the banks of the Grand River is still graced by handsome stone buildings, many of them grey like their counterparts in so many such towns in Scotland itself. There were only two other lawyers in Fergus. A rural practice which called him into such disputes as the ownership of pigs and other livestock can hardly have aroused his unbounded enthusiasm. Yet he settled in to work with N.M. Monro, the man who had taken him on as a student, and, like Duff, a strong Liberal; both were active in constituency business.

The only lawsuit of any significance that Duff handled in Fergus began disagreeably. A bitter family dispute arose when a wealthy local farmer died without a will. A son sued the administrators of the estate, for whom Monro and Duff acted, alleging that his father had owed him a substantial sum in unpaid wages. While the case was in its early stages, the son met Duff on the street, began talking heatedly, and finished by knocking him to the ground. Duff, who suffered cuts and bruises as well as a broken tooth, laid a charge of assault against the man, who was convicted and duly fined; a few months later, he lost the suit as well.

Two circumstances combined to make his stay in Fergus a short one. Belle Armstrong, whose parents had been Charles's parishioners, fell deeply in love with him, and while he clearly encouraged her feelings, he did not return them. Matters were complicated by his continuing interest in Lizzie Bird, whose regard for Duff, as with Belle's, was a good deal warmer than his for her. Lizzie, whom he had known for nearly ten years, lived some distance away in Barrie, but Belle, whom he may have known since childhood and almost certainly since coming to Fergus as a law student in the early 1890s, lived right in the town. Apparently unable or unwilling to summon the courage to break off with one or both of them, Duff gladly accepted what he later described as an "urgent invitation" from Gordon Hunter to join him in partnership in Victoria, British Columbia, where he had moved from Toronto a year or two earlier.

Duff left Fergus at the end of April 1894 with the Guelph *Daily Mercury* predicting "a bright future....He is a young man of exceptionally good natural talents which have been improved by a University education and thoughtful reading."[2] Besides the two girls, however, he also left behind some indebtedness, the forerunner of a host of similar problems in the future. He and a grocer named James Philp had borrowed money for a purpose not now known; Duff sent his share of the monthly payments from Victoria, but Philp, who was hard up, kept them and spent the money on himself. The debt was ultimately paid, but the episode, trifling in itself, is an early indication of Duff's bad judgement in the selection of business associates as well as his chronic carelessness in matters of money.

In the early summer of 1894, Duff boarded a C.P.R. train at Toronto to head west on the first of his many transcontinental journeys. He lived when one still travelled in the ease and comfort of a Pullman coach, instead of being hurled through the skies in an aluminum envelope. It was the finest time of year for travel. The train, after crossing the farmland of central Ontario, reached the rock and scrub of the Laurentian Shield and the shores of Lake Superior. In turn, the harshness of the northern Ontario landscape gave way to the magnificent expanse of the Prairies. Two days later the Rockies loomed into view, still wearing their winter snowcaps. The train snaked through them, creeping down the narrow valleys and winding round the sharp crags of the Selkirk and Purcell ranges of British Columbia. Soon Duff reached the semi-desert of the British Columbia interior, from which the railway made its painstaking descent down the narrow canyon of the Fraser, where the whistle of an engine echoing from the steep rock walls remains one of the most evocative sounds a Canadian can hear. Gradually, the river valley widened to reveal the lush green of the Pacific shore.

No doubt Duff's constitutional views were shaped by his cross-country journeyings. By the time he went to the Supreme Court of Canada in 1906 he had gone back and forth from the Pacific to Ottawa many times. He saw, understood, and was sympathetic to regional differences; for him, the provinces were political expressions of geographic realities neither inferior nor subordinate to the federal power. Many commentators on his role as an interpreter of the Canadian constitution have suggested that he tended to favour them, and unquestionably, though he disavowed any conscious intention of affirming provincial jurisdiction at Ottawa's expense, he saw Canada as a federal state and not a legislative union, an alliance among equals rather than a unitary state controlled from the centre.

He reached Victoria in July 1894. The rules of the Law Society of British Columbia required six months' residence before he could practise. He earned some income reporting the courts for the Victoria *Daily Colonist*, and continued to do so for a brief period after his call to the Bar on 28 February 1895. In mid-March he launched his career as a courtroom lawyer, working exclusively as counsel, arguing and pleading cases in court. There were not many lawyers in the entire province at that time, just over thirty in Victoria and another seventy-five or so elsewhere; those few who practised in the courts saw themselves as a select group, and were inclined, rather in the tradition of English barristers, to view solicitors, or lawyers who did not go to court, as an inferior breed. Duff himself said many years later that he had joined a "band of brothers," and with the sentiment of old age, wrote to a friend:

> In the British Columbia Bar, as I knew it there was in our relations with one another as professional men, a thoroughgoing disregard of differences which embitter people so much in other parts of the world — differences, for example, of creed and politics. That was not only a happy state of affairs for the Bar itself, it was a good thing, an ineffably good thing, for the general body politic; and I do most sincerely hope that the members of the British Columbia Bar will never forsake this kind of attitude toward these potential causes of internal antagonism.[3]

Besides his close friend and partner Gordon Hunter, there were other Toronto graduates: Peter Secord Lampman, later a county court judge in Victoria, G.H. Barnard, afterwards a senator, and E.P. Davis, destined to be the leader of the British Columbia Bar for many years and a formidable lawyer of whom Duff observed late in life: "I can say, without the slightest affectation, that I have never known either in a Court of First Instance or in a Court of Appeal, advocacy more powerful than his."[4]

The residents of Victoria, numbering about twenty-five thousand in 1895, believed that they lived in a favoured land; the opinion is still held by its present-day citizens. Across the strait, Vancouver was an upstart community, a stigma which, in the eyes of many Victorians, it has never lost. Duff experienced for the first time the delight of a west-coast summer, moving into bachelor quarters on a street not far from the site of the Parliament Buildings then under construction.

He had not been in Victoria long before poor Belle Armstrong began a fruitless pursuit of him through the mails. Only three of her letters to Duff have survived with their tale of unrequited love, but it is clear that she sent many more to which she received only occasional and then cold, off-hand replies. At Christmas she wrote to tell him that her present was on its way, only a small gift, all she could afford, but explaining, "I am sorry I could not send you something nicer but you know it is not the gift itself — and you know better than I can say what I could and do wish it to express."[5] A letter he had written crossed with hers of Christmas, and its contents distressed her: "You say you do not write to reproach me, but you have done worse. You have been thinking unkindly of me all these weeks." And she suffered still greater distress on learning that Lyman seemed fonder of Lizzie Bird than of herself. Visiting Belle's parents, Annie Duff had talked of the pair; Belle bit her tongue and appeared unconcerned. Later the same day, Annie proclaimed that "Lyme has no business engaging himself to anyone." Belle told Lyman: "I didn't like it — I remembered you and didn't pay attention to them."[6] She extracted from Annie a promise not to discuss her views on a suitable match with Charles and Isabella. Feeling that in some way she had done wrong, she then wrote abjectly,

> Surely you know I would rather do anything on earth than willingly displease you. I wish I could see you, it would be so much more satisfactory and I am almost sure you would not blame me....Perhaps I have tired you by writing so much. I wish you knew how it all was.[7]

In July 1895, evidently realizing that she had lost the game, she addressed a mournful last letter to Lyman.

> I have intended writing you...but have put it off thinking that you might possibly write me....Certainly I must think you care little or nothing for me. When you didn't in any way acknowledge the Christmas gift I sent you, I thought it was lost or mislaid in some way and that you didn't get it — but when you didn't have time to answer my letters after you were ill I began to think there was something more...

She then speaks more sternly:

> Lyman, I ask this of you, in the name of all you hold dear, I know I am not asking too much, only what is just and surely it is due me. I have trusted and still trust you and I ask you to tell me the truth. Do not put me off.

Please remember I do not mean to insinuate that you haven't always been truthful with me, but I know you will understand me — I want to thank you for all your kindnesses to me and if I did not always seem to appreciate them it was because I could not show it even when I would like to have done so, and so often it was that way....If I could only see you for just one half hour or even five minutes, but I cannot so write me as if you were with me — I ask you to burn this letter please. You will do that much for me, surely.

She did not end this with her customary farewell of "lovingly," but, "always your friend — Belle," and then, as if to drive home her independence of spirit, added in a firm hand underneath, "Belle Armstrong."[8]

Lyman never received the letter. Not having heard from him, and uncertain of his address after his call to the Bar, Belle mailed it to Gordon Hunter. Perhaps he suspected what its contents might be; at all events he placed it in a desk drawer in his office where it was found unburned and unopened seventy years later, ten years after Duff's death. By contrast, Lizzie's correspondence of the same period, which was opened, is pedestrian. After all, she held the inside track. She wrote mainly about family gossip and the comings and goings of relatives. Lyman was little more diligent in replying to her than he was to Belle.[9]

Whatever inner turmoil all this may have caused Duff, it had no visible effect on his career as he rapidly eclipsed most lawyers who had come to the province before him. Within three years of his call to the Bar in British Columbia, and only five years after his call in Ontario, he had achieved a formidable reputation and a handsome income.

Gordon Hunter had practised originally with Theodore Davie who, early in March 1895, succeeded Sir Matthew Baillie Begbie as the province's chief justice. Duff, newly qualified, then joined his friend to form the firm of Hunter & Duff; it was a move that gave much pleasure to Lyman's family, who often had Hunter's relatives to tea in Toronto. The pair set up practice on Bastion Street, just up from Victoria's Inner Harbour and across the road from the turreted courthouse (now the Maritime Museum) that had opened in 1889. They lived virtually cheek by jowl on Belleville Street, Hunter in a mansion that is now a tourist trap and Duff in a boarding house a door or two away. And they enjoyed life. Their talents, nourished by education, flowered in the gentle climate of Victoria. They were brilliant, Hunter probably more so than Duff, though the sparks that flew from him were ephemeral.

Duff was also lucky enough — perhaps a portent for the future — to win his first case. The legal problems were not complex, but the case involved the considerable sum for the era of over seven thousand dollars, adding a little keenness to the newcomer's gratification. For the next two years, Duff and

Hunter were exceedingly busy, winning success for their clients and professional acclaim for themselves. Duff also staked a reputation, maintained throughout his professional life, as an expert in the law of mining. Indeed, his understanding of the intricacies of that industry might well be placed next to his universally acknowledged accomplishments in constitutional law. He knew the technology of the trade as well as its statutes, and late in life, looked back with pride on his skill in the field.

In the first two or three years of his career, Duff also acted for accused criminals, though with little success. The successful practice of criminal law requires persuasiveness if not actual eloquence before juries; it also calls for a certain identification with clients who are often disreputable. In Duff's day, certainly, long before the advent of legal-aid schemes, it demanded the commitment of considerable time for an uncertain financial reward. Moreover, his talents and temperament were not suited for the hurly-burly of the criminal courts — his strength as counsel was intellect, not badinage.

Oddly, the only two important cases in criminal law that he dealt with as a defence lawyer involved exactly the same situation. The well-known rule of law that makes second-hand or "hearsay" evidence inadmissible is varied in murder cases, where a witness can give statements by a dying victim in evidence if the victim was convinced that death was inevitable. The rationale for this comes from the Christian belief in the hereafter: no one about to meet his Maker would tell an untruth. In the first case, the dying victim could not speak; when asked to point out the person who had shot him, the man had pointed to Duff's client. A police officer testified to that and a jury convicted the accused, who was hanged. In the other case a Native woman, mortally wounded, could speak no English. She had told an interpreter in Chinook, the Native lingua franca of the last century, "I think I be dying," and through the same interpreter identified the accused as her killer. Duff argued that the intervention of the interpreter made the statement doubly hearsay and hence inadmissible. That client was hanged too.

Hunter and Duff were partners for only two years. Though close friends, they found that they could not practise comfortably together and separated without recrimination or hard feelings. Perhaps there was not enough work to go round: each man spent all his professional time in court or else preparing for court, and as the senior, Hunter may have aroused Duff's resentment by taking the more important and interesting cases. Their drinking habits were certainly a factor in the breakup, though not the immediate cause. Hunter cut quite a swathe; Annie reported to Lyman that a Vancouver visitor had described him as the "biggest drinker and gambler in Victoria," but hastened to reassure her brother that as far as his own conduct was concerned, "we have contradicted all these reports, especially when the person said that you had refused to have anything to do with him on account of his dissipation."[10] Annie's loyal optimism has not been borne out, however, by two men who knew both Hunter and Duff very well, James Lawson of Victoria and Senator J.W. deB. Farris of Vancouver. Senator Farris has recalled that the two partners were "great drinking buddies when Duff first came out."[11] On an occasion when Duff and Hunter were drinking in a hotel room, one of them put a chamber-pot over his head, where it became stuck and had to be broken to be removed. This may have been Duff's doing, for according to James Lawson, Duff was a "boisterous drinker" and Hunter a "quiet" one.[12]

Duff's career did not suffer from the break with Hunter, for he joined E.V. Bodwell, another giant of the early British Columbia Bar, and Paulus Aemilius Irving, who soon afterwards went to the bench. Almost at once, he found himself arguing cases with Hunter as his opponent. Duff came out the immediate winner in the first three of these encounters, and in one, he argued a point of constitutional law for the first time.[13] The litigation grew out of familiar facts: animals wandering on to an unfenced rail line had been killed by a train. Under provincial legislation, rail operators were obliged to fence rights-of-way, but the railway came within federal jurisdiction because it had been declared a work for "the general advantage of Canada."[14] Since federal law did not require a fence, Duff argued successfully that the provincial law was inapplicable and hence the unfortunate owner of the cattle could not recover damages from the company. Hunter appealed the ruling and lost. The case, though of little lasting interest in itself, was the harbinger of a long series of notable constitutional cases in which Duff figured.

Duff's meteoric rise to prominence as a courtroom lawyer coincided with the beginning of an active role in the affairs of the Liberal Party in British Columbia. He arrived at a time when provincial governments were formed by alliances of individuals; premiers, though perhaps of Liberal or Conservative persuasion, did not build their administrations along party lines. Towards the end of the century, however, there was a ferment of change. Duff, who favoured party government, emerged in public support of the Liberal interest a year or so after coming to the province, and from then until his elevation to the bench in 1904 he was in the thick of political activity.

In November 1896, Israël Tarte, public works minister in the newly formed Laurier government at Ottawa, visited Victoria. The Liberal establishment turned out in full force for a dinner chaired by Duff's future partner E.V. Bodwell and ornamented by visiting dignitaries who included the premier of Prince Edward Island, F.L. Béique, the leader of the Quebec Bar, and the rising nationalist Henri Bourassa. Duff gave one of the toasts; no dinner of that era was complete without interminable toasts to all manner of institutions and individuals. Also present was William Templeman, publisher of the

Victoria *Times* and a man who would play a critical role in the advancement of Duff's career. His later choice of Duff as a protegé may have been the result of a letter the younger man wrote to Laurier the following May:

> I am given to understand that Mr. Templeman of this city would, if offered the appointment to the office of Lieutenant-Governor of this Province, accept it. I hope you will pardon my intrusion upon your attention with the object of assuring you that such appointment would meet with the approval not only of the Liberals but of the people generally of this community.
>
> I sincerely hope that you and your government will find it possible and expedient to recognize Mr. Templeman's services to the Liberal Party and his admirable personal qualities by conferring upon him this distinction.[15]

Gordon Hunter, Duff's equal as a party stalwart, wrote to Laurier a few days after this to urge the appointment of another man. Laurier chose to ignore both recommendations and appoint Senator T.R. McInnes to the post, but he did reward Templeman by naming him to the Senate.[16]

In October 1897, Duff attended a Liberal Convention held at New Westminster as a first-time Victoria delegate. Others present included Bodwell, Templeman, Gordon Hunter, and a brilliant, brash, and rather dandyish young lawyer called Archer Martin. The following February, Duff became president of the Young Liberal Association of Victoria, with Templeman elected honorary president.[17] That June, after a provincial election had been called, Templeman, Duff, and others strongly advocated that Liberals abandon the old notion of personalities and vote the straight party line. Liberals were not unanimous on this; Gordon Hunter wrote a long letter to the *Daily Colonist*, attacking Templeman and others for their views and airing his credentials as a long-time party supporter and charter member of the Toronto Young Liberal Club founded in 1881. Duff, of course, had been a charter member too.

Before election day, however, Duff went east. The time had come to marry Lizzie Bird, with whom he had an "understanding." He was thirty-three, she thirty-eight, but Lizzie, and apparently her family also, successfully concealed her real age from him.[18] Charles Duff married the couple with the assistance of Rolph, who, abandoning the law, had become like his father an ordained minister of the Congregational church; yet even in the midst of this family affair, Lizzie declared her age as thirty-five on the marriage-licence application. When Duff registered the particulars of her death in 1926, he gave her age as sixty though in fact she had been sixty-six: the deception apparently lasted. There were other odd aspects. Duff, giving particulars for the marriage certificate, disclaimed church membership. And opposition from his own family may explain why, immediately after the quiet ceremony at Barrie that was attended only by relatives, Lyman and Lizzie left by train for the Pacific coast, travelling on this occasion by an American railway.[19]

Lizzie Duff was a woman of pleasant appearance, though of rather full figure. She had never been known to be interested in any man but Lyman, and held herself available until he decided to marry. She had worked for thirteen years as a dutiful and possibly subservient teacher. When a school inspector decreed that students be taught to write with vertical strokes of the pen, he requested that teachers follow suit in their private correspondence; thereafter, Lizzie wrote to Lyman in the new style. She was not clever; close friends of Duff's have agreed that the gulf between their intellects led to frequent embarrassment throughout their married life. A nephew of Lizzie's described his aunt as a "mouse" who "didn't grow with Duff," going so far as to say that Duff was "intellectually contemptuous of her."[20] She was inclined to be a nervous, "twittery" person who found it difficult to encounter people with ease. Though she entertained widely, she did so out of a sense of duty rather than for enjoyment.

It has been suggested by John Stevenson, Duff's intimate friend and for many years Ottawa correspondent of the London *Times*, that Duff would have preferred to marry Lizzie's sister Bertha, who had been his student in Barrie.[21] In fact, Stevenson said there was a rumour that he had proposed to Bertha by mail, but Lizzie had intercepted the letter. Whatever the truth, Duff did remain "very fond" of Bertha, who eventually married and moved to Vancouver.[22]

Lizzie proved nonetheless to be a steadying influence on Duff. His own relatives have described him as someone "never organized" for whom Lizzie always had to do the "arranging."[23] Admitting his inability to deal with the practical details of a household in which there was frequent entertaining, he "used her as a sheet anchor."[24] She grew ambitious for him; when Mackenzie King made Anglin chief justice in 1924 instead of Duff, Lizzie snubbed the Anglins. She learned French to converse with guests from Quebec; she entertained the right people, and she did it very well.

Though there were no outward signs of serious difference between them, they probably did not enjoy a warm, compatible home life. For one thing, Duff remained difficult to live with; his favourite niece, who often visited the Duffs, said that he gave Lizzie "a very rough time."[25] Senator Farris, in London for the sessions of the Privy Council, once asked him to dinner; Duff declined, saying he felt he should remain at his hotel with his wife because "it's the least I can do — I've given her a pretty hard time."[26]

The fact that the couple had no children may have caused sadness to both, but there was a medical reason. Professor Henry Angus of the University of

British Columbia, a member of the Rowell-Sirois Commission and later chairman of the British Columbia Public Utilities Commission, had known Duff in Victoria and met him one time towards the end of his life when he was somewhat in his cups. Angus recalled his saying of his marriage that "they were disappointed that they couldn't have children....If she had brought proceedings for nullity she would have succeeded," and that his impotence explained his drinking.[27] If Duff really meant physical incapacity for the sexual act rather than infertility, this might indeed explain both his drinking and the "tough time" he gave his wife. It may also account for the fact that he made no attempt to remarry after Lizzie's death.

# 4

## Learned in the law

MR. AND MRS. LYMAN DUFF returned to Victoria on polling day, 9 July 1898. The results stirred up political turmoil that lasted for months. Lieutenant-Governor McInnes declined to call on the outgoing premier, J.H. Turner, to form a new government, on the grounds that the public had lost confidence in him by refusing him and his supporters a clear majority. He called on Robert Beaven, a defeated candidate, to head a government; Beaven gave up for want of support. The next call went out to Charles Semlin, who did manage to form one. These extraordinary events, which created enormous excitement in British Columbia and Victoria, were symptomatic of the difficult transition from personal government to party politics, a process that reached a new stage in 1903 when Richard McBride led an avowedly Conservative regime.

Not only did the 1898 election provide political excitement for Duff, but it generated lucrative legal business as well. Thirty election petitions were issued by defeated candidates trying to overthrow declared winners. Duff acted in a number of these, the two most important of which had to do with the elections in Lillooet and Esquimalt.

A J.D. Prentice had won the upper Fraser seat of Lillooet for the Liberals. One Stoddart, a defeated candidate represented by Hunter, sought to invalidate the election on the grounds of impropriety. Duff applied to strike the petition out by raising preliminary objections to its contents in a proceeding heard in November 1898 by Archer Martin, who had been appointed to the provincial supreme court that same fall. In some articles printed after the court proceedings but before the decision, the *Daily Colonist* criticized Martin for hearing the case at all on the ground that he was disqualified by "partisan" activity in the recent elections which constituted at the very least a "judicial anomaly." Duff applied for a citation of contempt of court against the manager and editor of the newspaper, which, here again, Hunter represented. At the hearing that took place before Mr. Justice Drake, Hunter's principal submission was startling and possibly unprecedented in Canada: he pointed out that British Columbia's Supreme Court Act required a judge to have practised as a barrister in the province for at least ten years,[1] and since Martin had not arrived until 1894, there could be no legal contempt of a judge not legally appointed. Hunter's argument, an ingenious one, may not have been sound; there was always a lurking constitutional doubt as to whether provincial legislatures could place residential conditions on judges who, like Martin, were named by the federal authorities. That Drake presided over the hearing was unusual in itself, since applications for contempt of a judge are normally heard by the one concerned. He said that he would take a day or two to think about his decision.[2] The next day, Martin ruled against Duff by holding that the election petition had been properly launched; the day following, Drake disposed of the contempt application by ruling that there had been a technical contempt, but not of such seriousness as to warrant imprisonment.[3]

Heady with this result, the *Colonist* permitted itself a caustic attack on Duff's conduct of the affair. The paper pointed out that while he was preparing the case he had sent a messenger boy to its offices to get the names of the manager and editor, later using this information in an affidavit along with a statement the boy had vouchsafed about the paper's "political attitude." The *Colonist*, which had been in existence since 1858, observed with the primness of a Victorian matron that it "had a political record before that boy, or Mr. Duff either, was out of swaddling clothes," going on to describe Duff as a "busybody of a solicitor" interested only in a "bill of costs" who "came before the court without offering...the slightest reason to justify him in so doing."[4] The paper reprinted an editorial from the Ottawa *Journal* that summed the whole episode up very neatly under the head, "Judge Martin's Cropper."

> One of the funniest legal developments on record is on deck in British Columbia. It concerns the contempt of court idea, that relic in large part of barbarism. In British Columbia a judge is being hoisted with his own petard....Here was a man [Martin] who wasn't legally a judge proposing to punish without trial by his peers a critic who said that he was not the right kind of judge.[5]

The British Columbia government moved to scotch Hunter's argument in 1899 by enacting a law to repeal the earlier law, and to make doubly sure, declaring the latter "never to have had any force or effect."[6] Archer Martin never forgave Hunter: when the latter became the province's chief justice in 1902, the animosity between the two men blossomed into active hostility which did not end until Hunter's death in 1929, and was at the root of a public controversy almost fatal to Hunter's career that Duff, by then in Ottawa, was asked by Laurier to mediate.

While the Prentice case was moving through the courts, Duff and Hunter found themselves on opposite sides of the Esquimalt election case in which all participants were well-known Victoria personalities. W.F. Bullen had been declared the winner on election night by a narrow margin over Frank Higgins, a prominent Liberal lawyer. A fellow Liberal for whom Duff acted challenged this result on the grounds, first, that some ballots rejected by the returning officer ought to have been counted, and secondly, that Bullen and his supporters had bought votes with "whisky and money and cigars."[7] The trial judge in the first hearing overruled the returning officer by ordering a count of the rejected ballots which gave Higgins the seat by a single vote. Duff had the bit in his teeth, however, for he pressed on with the charges of corrupt practices. He elicited the fact, for example, that bottles of whisky had been hidden behind shrubbery near polling stations where voters could help themselves. One witness was asked, "You went down and got some?" — and to the great amusement of those in the courtroom at once replied, "Certainly."

Duff and Hunter reached an accommodation by which the bribery allegations were withdrawn in return for Bullen's admission of the disputed ballots' validity. The two lawyers also agreed on Prentice, whose election was confirmed. The settlement of these two noteworthy election disputes evidently defused other pending cases, for these were not pursued and the furore subsided. Duff came out well, but his newfound reputation as an expert in election cases did not produce a flood of further business in that line. Disputed elections involving bribery and corruption formed a link between law and politics which even in Duff's time had become less common and has all but vanished today. In British Columbia, certainly, the 1898 election was the high-water mark for this class of litigation.

Some other lucrative legal work, however, arose out of that election. In January 1899 Chief Justice McColl, acting as royal commissioner, reported on alleged overpayments to the contractors for the recently finished Parliament Buildings. Construction of the handsome complex designed by F.M. Rattenbury had started in 1893 and finished late. in 1897. The general contractor hired at the outset had died part-way through the work, and his successor who completed it put in a claim for over thirty thousand dollars more than the contract sum in so-called "extra" work. A sub-contractor lodged a similar though smaller claim. The government led by J.H. Turner had authorized payment of these claims not long before the July 1898 election. Suspecting skulduggery by the defeated Turner regime, the new government was no sooner in office than it appointed the commission, and Turner retained Duff to represent him. It was an indication of Duff's stature as counsel that after only three years in the province he was called on to act in such weighty matters.

Civil servants testified that the claims were not reflected in work done, and one went so far as to describe them as "scandalous." Rattenbury stated unequivocally that payment was made against his advice; the contractors had given him no statement of the extra work they claimed to have done. Turner differed from him, and, under Duff's guidance, described "stormy sessions" between Rattenbury and the contractors which had ended in hard feelings and no agreement. Eventually, Turner said, the government decided that despite what Rattenbury thought, the contractors "had a good deal of right on their side,"[8] and paid virtually the full amount. They did so partly because "the government was not overconfident of the architect's figures."[9] Later that same day, however, Turner hastened to correct a wrong impression he thought he might have given by questioning Rattenbury's figures: the errors were "clerical," and the government "had the greatest confidence in him." Corrections were very much in order. Unfortunately or perhaps deliberately, the former premier, who had then also been finance minister, put a special warrant through the legislature to authorize the payments without showing them as separate items. They were buried in a lump sum that encompassed other expenditures related to the buildings' construction. The suspicion that greeted this discovery was not altogether surprising. However, the royal commission absolved Turner and his colleagues of actual wrongdoing.

Duff attracted his share of trivia, and from time to time, like most lawyers, argued cases which he believed to be devoid of merit. He once argued unsuccessfully that a man who had lost a sealskin jacket and wolf robes on a Yukon railway could not be compensated since these items were not "wearing apparel." The trial judge informed Duff tartly that what is worn in the Yukon differs from what is usual in Honolulu.[10] He even triumphed in a case only to find himself pressing exactly the opposite view a few months later — an incident made even more remarkable by the fact that the judge, Mr. Justice Walkem, had already made a ruling on the question and then, rather like Duff, taken the opposite view and reversed himself.[11]

Some prominent clients who could afford to pay large legal bills might have had dubious cases, but they were attracted to Duff, not by flamboyance, but by a capacity for meticulous hard work. It was not uncommon for courtroom lawyers of his day, particularly when they were in front of juries, to use any histrionic device to attract attention. Duff relied on careful preparation, knowledge of the facts, their effective presentation, and mastery of the law.

He was an excellent trial lawyer, though his skills were more suited to the appellate courts which concern themselves chiefly with arguments over points of law. Some barristers never appear at a trial or see a witness, spending their entire careers in the appellate courts; Duff appeared at all levels. Slight and relatively short with close-cropped red hair and a beard, he did not have a commanding physical appearance, and yet there was something about his demeanour and visage that caught the attention of witnesses, particularly those whom he cross-examined. He did not intimidate them, but unquestionably he dominated them. Volumes have been written about cross-examination, which is an art and not a science, of all the skills of an experienced advocate probably the most demanding. Painstaking preparation of a case is the key to success in the courtroom, but effective cross-examination requires an extra dimension that sets the really skilled cross-examiner apart from his fellows; the art is compounded of knowledge of human nature, theatrics, intuition, a good memory, patience, stamina, and judgement. With Duff, the theatrical element was relatively minor, but his phenomenal memory and his ability to size up a witness were paramount. Equally, his judgement and intuition told him when to stop asking questions: a danger of the art is that one question too many may undo the value of everything that was drawn out beforehand.

His first "big" case involved a lawsuit brought by Dennis Harris, a relative of Sir James Douglas, against Joan Dunsmuir, a member of the prominent Victoria family and owner of the Wellington Coal Mines near Nanaimo on Vancouver Island. She had commissioned Harris in writing to sell the mines for what was at that time the astronomical sum of $2.6 million. The legal question had to do with her liability to pay Harris despite his failure, after much effort, to find a purchaser. The case had an unusual history, with three trials and as many appeals. Duff and his partner Bodwell acted throughout for Harris, but after the second trial Mrs. Dunsmuir fired her lawyer and engaged another. She had been present at the first two trials, which had both been by jury, but missed the third through illness; her lawyer at the third trial had not been present, of course, at the first.

When the third trial began, Duff and his colleague chose as one of the jurors a man they knew to have been a member of the first jury, which had given a verdict in Harris's favour. Neither he nor Bodwell breathed a word of this to the opposition. Not until after the last jury had pronounced for Harris did Mrs. Dunsmuir's advisors learn of the twice-sworn juryman. She appealed the verdict to the Supreme Court of Canada. The judges of that court decided that the lawyers at the third trial could have checked the names of the jurors of the earlier trials, and since they had not done so there was no legal ground for complaint. The ruling may have been correct, but the ethical question lingers.

As the century drew to a close, Duff became involved in a cause célèbre. He felt himself that it was one of the most important cases on which he had worked; undoubtedly it was one of the most lucrative. At the western extreme of Vancouver harbour, close to Stanley Park, is the low-lying Deadman's

Island, named for its old use as a Native burial ground. Surveying this insignificant piece of real estate, now the site of a naval reserve establishment, one marvels that it could have given rise to so much expensive litigation; in 1899, however, it became a bone of vital contention involving the city of Vancouver, the federal authorities, and the government of British Columbia.

Vancouver, just beginning to feel its economic muscle, wanted control of Deadman's Island to remain in local hands; a sawmill operator by the name of Ludgate proposed to build a mill there that would employ many people and thus feed the city's prosperity. Ottawa, which claimed the island, wanted it to form part of a military reserve, but was prepared to lease it to Ludgate for the time being. Victoria, which also claimed it, strenuously opposed the island's being controlled from outside the province. But the real bitterness of the Deadman's Island affair stemmed chiefly from personal animosity between two members of the provincial cabinet — Francis Carter-Cotton, a Conservative, and Joseph Martin or "Fighting Joe" as he was called, a Liberal.[12]

Martin, a colourful, abrasive, clever lawyer and attorney-general of British Columbia to boot, was not prevented by the law of the day from acting for private clients while holding cabinet office. He represented Ludgate, who, with the city's blessing, managed to lease the island from the federal government. When the entrepreneur started to fell trees to clear a site for his sawmill, however, the Victoria authorities, spearheaded by Cotton, obtained an injunction to stop development on what they alleged to be the province's land. Incredibly, at one stage in the proceedings, Martin appeared as attorney-general in opposition to his own client:[13] when asked by a reporter how he could represent the province and Ludgate at the same time, he responded with profanities.[14] Ludgate kept cutting trees in violation of the court order, only to be arrested and jailed. Cotton, who represented Vancouver in the legislature, might have been expected to take a stand favourable to the city, but his intense dislike of Martin outweighed any parochial interest. The dispute heated up to white-hot pitch, with Conservatives supporting Cotton and the province, and Liberals supporting Martin, the Laurier government in Ottawa, and, by association, the city of Vancouver. Martin himself eventually resigned from the cabinet and took no part in the subsequent litigation.

Duff's role in the case was a curious one. On the initial application by the provincial government to secure an injunction to prevent Ludgate from clearing trees, he appeared as one of the lawyers retained by the federal government. He took no part in the argument, but held a "watching brief" and sat in the courtroom each day as an observer.[15] When the preliminaries ended and the main litigation began, however, he acted for the province. In fact, he had been hired to conduct the provincial case in June 1899 at Cotton's own instance. This was no doubt a factor in Martin's exit; Duff was said by a Vancouver paper to owe his appointment entirely to the "loss of confidence in Martin by his cabinet colleagues."[16]

The actual litigation was far less interesting than the events leading up to it. The case dragged through the courts for years. At the trial, Duff and Bodwell secured judgement in their client's favour. The federal government launched a successful appeal, and in turn the province appealed unsuccessfully to the Privy Council, which affirmed federal jurisdiction over the islet on the principle that it had been designated on maps as a military reserve during the colonial or pre-Confederation period. Since in the earlier period jurisdiction over military matters had rested with the Imperial government, the Dominion government had as it were inherited Deadman's Island. Duff, moving on to the bench, did not see the case through to its weary end.

The bitter dispute between Martin and Cotton and their respective adherents contributed to the fall of the Semlin government in 1900. In March of that year the Lieutenant-Governor made the controversial move of calling on Joseph Martin to form a government even though he had no supporters in the assembly; McInnes actually read the speech proroguing the legislature to a house that was empty except for Martin himself. His administration was virtually still-born, lasting just over one hundred days. He had the moral support of some Liberals in Vancouver, but Duff and the Victoria wing of the party opposed him, perhaps because they saw him as a threat to Templeman's ascendancy; Bodwell, for example, described Martin as a "menace" to the province.[17] As for Lieutenant-Governor McInnes, his role in these remarkable events led to his dismissal and replacement by Sir Henri Joly de Lotbinière. James Dunsmuir succeeded Martin as premier.

With the excitement in provincial politics dying down by mid-1900, Duff and his fellow Liberals prepared for the coming federal election. Talk of Duff seeking the nomination for one of the two Victoria seats drew the somewhat patronizing comment from the *Daily Colonist* that "Mr. Duff...is comparatively well known, fairly popular and considered to possess a fair amount of ability." The newspaper gave him no chance of winning a seat against the two Conservative incumbents it supported.[18] Duff did not seek nomination, but he did campaign vigorously for the party. At one meeting, his carrot for voters was the possible siting of the Royal Mint in Victoria, an event that could occur only if the provincial capital returned to the Liberal fold.[19] Of this and other campaign orations Duff made, the *Colonist* observed, "He is a picturesque speaker and must not always be taken too seriously." The Victoria *Times* sniped at its rival for branding Duff as "picturesque," but the tory paper had the last word, doubting if Duff objected to an epithet that "was intended to be, and was, complimentary."[20] The *Colonist* went on to excel itself in a colourful report of a speech in which Duff

> started out by declaring that he was not in favour of parochial politics...in his strictly non-parochial way he asked the people present to believe that a vote for Messrs. Prior and Earl [the Conservative members] is against the

most vital and immediate interests of Victoria. To other people than Mr. Duff this would seem very much like ultra-parochial politics. Speaking also non-parochially, we assume, he then told the audience that we have many favours to ask from the Dominion Government and therefore should elect Liberals. By the same logic, if there is any sort of chance that the Conservatives may come in, it is the duty of the people to elect Conservatives. Mr. Duff elaborated this point at considerable length, and appears to have evoked laughter and applause, which is not a matter of surprise, because, as we have said, he is a picturesque speaker; but it was dreadfully parochial, and this is something which Mr. Duff abhors. How he must have hated himself when he got through with it.[21]

All Duff's efforts were in vain; both Conservatives retained their seats, though by narrow margins. No Royal Mint has materialized in Victoria, and in 1900 Duff seemed to have exhausted his political energies; he remained out of public politics for the next two years.

In the middle of the campaign, Duff went into court on a case unique in British Columbia, at least in this century, that of an eight-year-old boy charged with murder. Before the days of the first Juvenile Delinquent Act passed in 1908, the common-law rule prevailed: any person over age seven could be held capable of crime, murder included. The young accused, Ernest Chenoweth, lived in Rossland, British Columbia, with his mother, who had employed a Chinese cook. It was the time of the Boxer Rebellion in China, an event which inflamed the always considerable anti-Chinese feeling in the province, and prompted inflammatory articles in the local newspapers about the supposedly murderous nature of that people. Young Chenoweth became infected by the racist poison, and, loading a rifle which belonged to an older brother, went into the kitchen, where he found the cook preparing beans for the evening meal. Aiming the weapon at the unfortunate man, he said, "Here you go, John" — "John" was a more or less opprobrious generic title used by whites for Chinese — and shot him in the head. The boy told the police coolly that he "smiled when I pointed the gun at him, but the smile left his face mighty quick when I shot him," and, a little while afterwards, said to a friend he "had never seen a man die so quick."

Ernest Chenoweth's preliminary hearing took place before a magistrate who ordered him to stand trial. Duff entered the case when the defence lawyer in Nelson, where the trial was to take place, asked him to make application for bail to the Supreme Court in Victoria. In that era, courts seldom granted bail for accused murderers; Duff argued, however, that it should be granted in Chenoweth's case, first because of his age, and secondly because the prosecution's case against the boy rested on a confession of doubtful legality. The court fixed bail at five thousand dollars to be posted by four bondsmen. Duff took no part in the trial, which the deputy attorney-general prosecuted himself; the trial judge ruled the boy's confession inadmissible and the jury acquitted him to cheers from the assembled spectators.[22]

Duff's professional and social standing suggested appropriate quarters. By 1900, he and Lizzie were living on Rockland Avenue, close to Government House, in a splendid establishment designed by F.M. Rattenbury; it is still standing, though with an altered exterior.[23] According to students of Rattenbury's work, the house is not typical of his domestic architecture. It seems possible that someone else had a hand in its design — perhaps even Duff himself, since the place was built for him, possibly in 1898.[24] At least, construction may have started in that year. Both this date and that of the Duffs' occupation are uncertain, since Duff did not become the legal owner until 31 January 1901.[25] He paid two thousand dollars cash and assumed a five-thousand-dollar first mortgage.[26]

Since the building-permit records of the city of Victoria for this period have disappeared, one can only speculate why, if Duff and his wife lived in the house before 1900, they took so long to take title to the dwelling. It may well be that Duff, with characteristic inattention to business, did not bother to arrange the transfer even after he had moved in; perhaps too, the builders did not finish the place until late in 1900. It has been suggested that Duff brought Lizzie to the new house as his bride, which would certainly make 1898 the completion date, but we know that Duff lived on Belleville Street in the James Bay area of Victoria until some time the following year.[27]

It is more interesting to speculate how Duff could afford such magnificence after only three years or possibly five in Victoria. He had been in debt when he went there and he was plagued by debt all his life. There may have been some arrangement with Rattenbury; the two men had known each other for some time and even lived for a period in the same house in the James Bay area.[28] As the architect of the Parliament Buildings, Rattenbury had won celebrity status; Duff was hardly in that category yet, and he had little if any money set aside. Rattenbury may have agreed to do the house at a reduced rate in return for services rendered. It will be recalled that at the Parliament Buildings inquiry, Turner, when testifying in the morning, gave the impression that Rattenbury's accounts were not all they might have been; in the same afternoon and for no apparent reason, he went out of his way to defuse any suggestion of impropriety and declare complete confidence in Rattenbury. Did Duff suggest to Turner that he dispel any imputation against the architect? There may be some significance in the fact that Duff, though representing Turner, did not actually appear before the commission until his client was to testify. It is a very odd circumstance indeed that he did not show up earlier. In acting for Turner, it was Duff's job to mitigate by cross-examination any evidence unfavourable to his client, particularly that given by Rattenbury, whose evidence went unchallenged. Whatever the truth may be, Duff obviously impressed Rattenbury by his skill as counsel: when, in 1904, the architect was facing truly serious allegations of fraud, he called on Duff to help him and came out unscathed.

Duff and Lizzie lived in their Rockland Avenue mansion until his appointment to the Supreme Court of Canada in 1906. They were happy there. Though it was far larger than would be needed by a childless couple, Lyman had ample space for his many books and Lizzie had spacious rooms in which to entertain. As with every other asset Duff owned, however, this investment turned to ashes through either bad luck or bad judgement. In 1905 he placed a second mortgage on the property, though he did manage not long afterwards to pay off the first. In 1907, a year after his appointment to the Ottawa court, he sold the house and two-acre property for twelve thousand dollars. Four years later, the purchaser resold the property at very nearly double what he had paid Duff for it. Duff made no money whatever from the house; in fact, he probably lost.

By 1900 he had reached a peak in his profession; he had numerous clients, he was an insider in the British Columbia Liberal Party, and he had a gracious home in which he and his wife lived agreeably. Besides being the seat of government, Victoria was the Pacific coast station for the Royal Navy, and Duff attended many rounds of entertainment at Government House and the nearby military establishments as well as in the private houses of his prosperous friends. Prominent barristers like Duff were high on the social scale, and if he and his wife were not at the pinnacle of turn-of-the-century Victoria society, they were certainly not far from it. He lacked but one distinction.

The dignity of Queen's Counsel is conferred in British Columbia on the recommendation of the attorney-general. In 1900, the governing legislation limited appointments to no more than two persons annually, though they could be and generally were accumulated to be made every few years. In England, where the distinction originated, barristers applied to the Lord Chancellor to become Queen's Counsel by "taking silk" — fine court robes to distinguish them from junior counsel who wore only cotton. In Duff's day, as now, politics often directed the award to particular persons, but the accolade then, however politically motivated, went only to courtroom lawyers of demonstrated skill. On 31 December 1900, by a notice in the *Provincial Gazette*, Duff received this honour. His former client J.D. Prentice, then provincial secretary, made the appointment under his hand and seal. Also named were Gordon Hunter, W.J. Bowser, later premier of the province, and Aulay Morrison, a future chief justice of the Supreme Court of British Columbia. Thus did Duff join twenty-two other lawyers in the province as, in the ancient, pleasing language of the appointment, "one of Her Majesty's Counsel learned in the Law." He was thirty-five years old, well liked by his colleagues, acknowledged by them to be gifted, and destined to surpass them all.

# 5

## Senior counsel

THERE WAS a practical advantage in being Queen's Counsel: one could charge larger fees. In the three years between this appointment and his elevation to the British Columbia Supreme Court, Duff experienced a time of prosperity such as he never knew again. True, he spent all his income, but clients persisted in asking for his services, and rather than turn them away he asked for more money.

There is a well-known story about the eminent English barrister Sir Edward Carson who, when a solicitor complained of his fees, led him to a window, and, pointing out dozens of other law offices near by, told him that any of the lawyers in them would be pleased of the business. The solicitor retained Carson. So it was with Duff; he acted for wealthy clients who never niggled about his fees — a happy situation for a lawyer. In those years, he argued four cases in the Supreme Court of Canada, winning two and losing two. He could not be said to have enjoyed a notable career as counsel in that court.

Early in 1902, Duff as the new president of the B.C. Liberal Association caught the public spotlight in spectacular fashion. The *Daily Colonist* reported a February meeting of the association under the page-one headline, "Resort to Their Fists. Prominent Liberals Appeal to Arms to Settle Their Differences."

After last night's session of the Liberal Association, an unfortunate occurrence took place at the Hotel Vancouver. Mr. Joseph Martin was endeavouring to explain to Senator Templeman his position in the political fight and the view he took of the situation, when he was challenged in his statements by a jocular remark of Mr. Duff of Victoria. Mr. Martin took the remark in earnest and resented it, calling Mr. Duff a liar, so the story goes. Mr. Duff resented this by striking Mr. Martin. Mr. Martin struck back at Mr. Duff and the combatants were immediately quieted down by friends. The incident was the result of hasty tempers on both sides. Both regretted the incident and parted without harbouring resentment.[1]

In this Vancouver incident, as in the university brawls, Duff showed a certain pugnacity; the same quality may have incited that unfortunate litigant who knocked him down in Fergus. The fight with Martin had brief repercussions. At a meeting of the Victoria Liberals in May, the *Daily Colonist* reported poor attendance because of a "slight rift...between the various sections of the party."[2] All the same, Duff was returned as president, and Senator Templeman, the *éminence grise* of the party in Victoria, became honorary president.

That same year, after a good deal of political jockeying among aspirants, Laurier appointed Gordon Hunter chief justice of British Columbia. Then as now, prime ministers decided personally who the provincial chief justices were to be. The appointment had ramifications that affected, not only Hunter's career, but also those of Duff and Archer Martin, Hunter's bête noire. Martin found himself junior in rank to the man who had questioned — perhaps correctly — his very right to be a judge at all. For his part, Hunter found himself at the head of a court to which Martin had in his view been improperly named.

With the spring of 1903 Duff gave up the presidency of the Liberal Association, though not his interest in its activities. Ever since the 1898 election provincial politics had been volatile, with cabinet membership endlessly shifting and changing. In June 1903 the Lieutenant-Governor dismissed the premier, Colonel E.G. Prior, and called on Richard McBride, a charismatic lawyer from New Westminster, to form a government. Though a Conservative, he had some support elsewhere, and he proceeded to consult with Liberals both in and out of the legislature — among them Duff, Bodwell, and A.E. MacPhillips, later a judge of the appeal court. However, McBride's Conservative supporters persuaded him to select his cabinet from that party's ranks alone. He did so, and the first government in British Columbia constituted along purely party lines came into being. Non-tories like Duff who supported him were "consigned," as the *Daily Colonist* put it, "to the tender mercies of the Liberal Party."[3] Though not one of the midwives at the birth of party government in British Columbia, he had at least donned a mask for the delivery room.

Duff took several important cases in the last year of his practice, between 1903 and 1904, but one of them, putting him at the top of his profession in British Columbia, undoubtedly led to his appointment to the supreme court of that province and ultimately the Supreme Court of Canada. In the summer of 1903, he was made one of the team of Canadian lawyers joining their British counterparts before a tribunal in London that had been set up by the United Kingdom and the United States to settle the boundary between Canada and Alaska.

The dispute involved the demarcation of the Alaska Panhandle, a narrow tongue of land five hundred miles long which runs southeasterly from the main bulk of Alaska to a point on latitude 54°40′. Alaska had formed part of the Russian Empire until 1867, when the Russians sold it to the United States for $7.2 million. Earlier, in the 1820s, the boundary between Russian and British North America had formed the subject of negotiations between those two powers that led to a treaty of 1825, the terms of which (or rather, the interpretation of which) gave rise to heated argument at the London hearings. Purchasing Alaska, the United States acquired whatever rights the Russians had enjoyed, and Canada, becoming a Dominion in the same year as the Alaska purchase, inherited the rights of the British.

The central issue was the location of the eastern boundary of the Panhandle. Did it, as the Russians and later the Americans contended, lie well east of the heads of all inlets in the region, effectively excluding the British and thus the Canadians from access to tidewater? The British and Canadians held that because the general configuration of the coastline was so far removed from the heads of the major inlets, with the Lynn Canal chief among these, Canada should have access to salt-water ports in at least some of them. The 1825 treaty defined the Panhandle with reference to a line to be drawn northward from 54°40′ to various survey points:

> Whenever the summit of the mountains which extend in a direction parallel to the coast...shall prove to be the distance of more than ten marine leagues from the ocean, the limit between the British possessions and the strip of coast which is to belong to Russia...shall be formed by a line parallel to the sinuosities of the coast, and which shall never exceed the distance of ten marine leagues therefrom.[4]

The negotiators had no certain information about the location of the mountains. The entire region was mountainous, a "sea of mountains" in fact, and no pattern of ranges could be discerned.[5] In fixing the ten-league line with reference to ranges whose existence was not real but imagined, what mountains does one select for use as boundary markers? Official British maps published before 1867 and Canadian maps after that date showed a land barrier between the heads of all inlets and the mountains, a circumstance that denied Canada all access to tidewater. It was evidence of this type which prompted Theodore Roosevelt, who became the architect of the eventual award, to point out with relish that in the very cabinet room of the British Government stood a globe, prepared by the Admiralty, which showed the Panhandle exactly as the Russians and Americans interpreted it.[6]

With the Americans in Alaska and development reaching the region, some disposition of the matter became urgent. In the closing years of the nineteenth century, the gold rush in Canada's Yukon, with massive influxes of fortune-seekers across disputed territory, put a certain strain on relations between the two powers of the Pacific northwest. After protracted meetings and correspondence, principally between the embassies in Washington and London, the Hay-Herbert Treaty was signed on 24 January 1903 entrusting the solution to "six impartial jurists of repute." Lacking a formal or legal seal, John Hay, the American Secretary of State, pressed into the soft wax by his signature a ring once owned by Lord Byron. Considering that Byron lost all his possessions and was "sold up," there was a certain grim irony in the circumstance.

A year and a half before the signing of this treaty, an assassin cut down U.S. President McKinley. Theodore Roosevelt, the vice-president, succeeded to the presidency, and his entrance on the stage of the Alaska negotiations had a decisive effect. For all practical purposes, he took charge of them, though he retained Hay as secretary. Roosevelt vehemently upheld the American position, scorning the British, who "didn't have a leg to stand on." His truculence caused Hay, an acknowledged anglophile, some embarrassment. During the two years after McKinley's death, Roosevelt quite openly and cynically moulded the course of events, guided by two principles: to arrange the composition of the tribunal so that the United States could not lose; and afterwards, make sure that the United States won.[7] To get the treaty through the Senate, or so he claimed, Roosevelt let it be known that in selecting the "impartial jurists of repute" he would look for men whose views on the weakness of the Canadian case coincided with his own. He made perfunctory attempts to enlist justices of the United States Supreme Court, but in the end chose Senators George Turner and Henry Cabot Lodge, and Elihu Root. It was made clear to each of them that if, through some miscalculation, the award went against the United States, he would reject it and send in troops to bolster the Americans already in occupation, leaving the British to do their worst.[8]

The Hay-Herbert Treaty confronted Canada with the delicate problem of choosing its representatives on the tribunal, who did not necessarily have to be Canadian, as well as lawyers to argue its case. Weighing these appointments, the Laurier government bore in mind the goal of peace in the political household and, as consistent with that as possible, the desirability of making appointments that would placate British Columbia, whose interests were clearly affected. The government resisted the temptation to call on representatives as blatantly partisan as the Roosevelt nominees. Lord Alverstone, the

Lord Chief Justice of England, accepted appointment, as well as two Canadians, Sir Louis Jetté and Allen B. Aylesworth. The former, the Lieutenant-Governor of Quebec, had been a judge in that province, and the latter was a distinguished Toronto lawyer.

Senator Templeman wrote from Victoria to Clifford Sifton, the agent for Canada and Great Britain, urging Duff's appointment as one of the lawyers.[9] Unfortunately, Templeman jumped the gun by leading Duff, in March 1903, to believe that the matter had been settled. Duff assumed, naively perhaps, that Templeman's word carried enough weight in Ottawa to guarantee the assignment. As late as the end of July, however, Sifton had still not made up his mind.[10]

In the meantime Duff, like any busy courtroom lawyer, had to schedule his trials for the coming months, a task made difficult by the uncertainty of his appointment to London. From Sifton's correspondence with Templeman, it seemed that either he or Aimé Geoffrion of Montreal would be chosen.[11] However under further pressure from Templeman, who pointed out that there should be someone from British Columbia, Sifton decided to call on both men. On 29 July he wrote a letter, rather offhand in its tone, as if he had not really convinced himself that Duff's presence was either necessary or desirable, inviting him to be one of the junior counsel. He emphasized that he would have no opportunity to address the tribunal; his function would be limited to advising senior counsel. Not surprisingly, Duff, who had for five months believed his appointment secure, wrote a testy reply. Sifton had used language to suggest that he was a mere place-seeker, an allegation which cut Duff to the quick. He replied,

> apparently it is thought that in this matter so materially affecting the interests of this province I have expected to be provided with an occupation....I do not see how if my diagnosis of your views be correct I can justify myself in acting on your letter.[12]

In the end Duff swallowed his pride, and ten days later, accompanied by Lizzie, sailed with Sifton from New York on the German liner *Kaiser Wilhelm*. He joined Geoffrion, who had sailed earlier, F.C. Wade of Vancouver, S.A.T. Rowlatt of England, and John Simon, later Lord Chancellor, as junior counsel. Appointed to lead the argument for Canada and Britain were Sir Robert Finlay, the English attorney-general, Christopher Robinson of Toronto, a leading barrister, and the old Liberal stalwart Edward Blake, who had moved from Toronto to England and a lucrative law practice. Unfortunately, after slaving over the Canadian argument for six months, Blake suffered a nervous breakdown in July and was replaced by Sir Edward Carson, then English solicitor-general. The Canadian lawyers were beset with illness; Robinson, far from well, would have preferred not to participate in the argument at all, but his colleagues persuaded him otherwise.

Duff arrived in England days before the tribunal sat. As part of the Canadian strategy to persuade it to concentrate on the strict wording of the 1825 treaty, he developed an argument to get around the awkward fact that the Hay-Herbert Treaty empowered the tribunal to take into account not only the phrasing of the 1825 accord but also the subsequent actions of the various countries. In 1892, the Americans and Canadians had signed a convention establishing a commission "with a view to the ascertainment of the facts and data necessary to the permanent delimitation" of the boundary line, and providing that once these data had been gathered, the governments would proceed to consider a permanent boundary.[13] In 1895, the commissioners' reports sparked renewed interest by the governments in a definitive settlement, which came ultimately by way of the Hay-Herbert Treaty. Duff contended that by signing the 1892 convention the Americans had waived all claim to the Panhandle based on their occupation of the country and the boundary line shown on various maps. Equally, he argued, they had agreed to restrict themselves to a determination of the boundary line based solely on the language of the treaty of 1825. Looking at the language of the 1892 convention, one is hard-pressed to see the interpretation Duff placed on it, but there were so few weapons in the Canadian arsenal that he can hardly be blamed for trying.

The tribunal assembled on 3 September 1903 in the imposing Foreign Office reception room in Whitehall.[14] After choosing Alverstone as its president, it decided on the order in which the various lawyers would present their arguments and other procedural matters before adjourning to the 15th for the commencement of argument. At the conclusion of hearings on 8 October several of the main participants voiced appropriate pleasantries. General John W. Foster, the American agent, expressed his gratification that "no harsh word had been uttered on either side — no manifestation had been given of disturbed or irritated feeling. He prayed that this might be an indication of the character of the decision which would be rendered."[15] In the light of Canadian reaction to the decision, these were hollow words indeed. But the courtly behaviour and fine words were really part of the overall pretence that the tribunal would act judicially, that is reach a decision after carefully weighing evidence and arguments as would a true court of law. The reality, of course, was very different. The main actor was far away in Washington.

Ten days or so after the hearings started, Lodge reported to Roosevelt that Alverstone had accepted the main point of the U.S. contention, that the boundary line be drawn beyond the heads of the inlets, but that he believed the Panhandle should be narrower than the Americans were proposing. Roosevelt agreed as a slight concession that the Americans could relinquish their claim to the several islands at the entrance of the Portland Canal so long as they got the main point, emphasizing to Lodge that "we must not weaken on the points that are of serious importance."[16] Meanwhile Aylesworth and Jetté, sensing that Alverstone had decided to concede the unbroken Panhandle, confided their fears to Sifton. He wired Laurier the day before the hearings ended, provoking the vigorous but futile reply that "our commissioners must not withdraw. If they cannot get our full rights, let them put up a bitter fight for our contention on Portland Canal, which is beyond doubt...shame Chief Justice and carry that point."[17]

Duff and his colleagues were unaware of all these undercurrents, although Finlay, who as attorney-general held cabinet rank, might have had some inkling of the true state of affairs. As hard-working lawyers, Duff, Geoffrion, and Simon spent hours together at the end of each day of argument, reviewing the day's events and devising rebuttals to the important points made by the American lawyers. They continued to think that their labours might actually contribute to a reasonable decision, and with luck, one favourable to Canada. But there were diversions. Simon took Duff up to Oxford to tour his old college. The Duffs spent a number of weekends in the country, in tune with the habit of all upper-class Englishmen of the period who could be found in London on a Saturday or Sunday only in an emergency. Duff and Geoffrion saw a good deal of each other. Geoffrion, a superb lawyer with his gallic wit, quick mind, and great personal charm, was completely bilingual, and as much at home in English-speaking Canada as he was in Quebec. Duff said many years later that he had "spent two months arguing with him — or perhaps conducting reciprocal slang matches with him would be a better description."[18] They became firm lifelong friends.

After adjournment of the public hearings, Alverstone and his colleagues held daily conferences to discuss the award. As the only one of the six who made any real attempt to act impartially, the Lord Chief Justice found himself more and more in the role of an unwilling intermediary between proponents of two irreconcilable views. He had decided fairly early in the proceedings, as he told Lodge, that "on the law and the facts" the American argument that "the line goes around the heads of the inlets" was unanswerable.[19] On 12 October he prepared a draft opinion accepting the American position on the heads of the inlets but conceding to Canada four disputed islands lying at the entrance to the Portland Canal; he showed this to the Americans. Lodge took him aside, and as he had done before, reminded him of Roosevelt's view that the tribunal represented Canada's "only chance." If it failed to reach a decision conformable to the American stand, Canada "would get nothing."[20]

That evening, the Lord Mayor of London, Sir Marcus Samuel, invited a company of about one hundred guests to a gala dinner at the Mansion House — all the members of the tribunal, all the lawyers, Canadian and American, the aldermen of the City of London, various judges and eminent English lawyers, and a number of English academics. Nothing could better illustrate the contrast between the appearance and reality of the tribunal's work than this banquet and the speeches made at it. The guests dined in the Egyptian Room, the grand banqueting hall of the Mansion House. The lofty chamber is barrel-vaulted and spacious; fluted pillars on either side support a gallery above which stained-glass clerestory windows admit a subdued light. Duff sat across a table from Senator Lodge and Lord Alverstone. Such delicacies as *côtelettes de homard* and *bécassines en caisse* were served with appropriate wines. While they feasted, the band of His Majesty's Royal Life Guards — the Blues — played, with a nice eye to the occasion, a selection of European and American band music. At the conclusion of the repast, the speeches began.

Sir Marcus looked about him when the dessert wines had been poured. He had no notion of the political pressures on the Canadian and American members of the tribunal. In accordance with convention, but in total ignorance of Roosevelt's real role, he proposed a toast to the one who embodied "in his own person...all that the president of the United States should be." It is recorded that this toast was "drunk with enthusiasm."[21] Sir Marcus then gave toasts to the members of the tribunal who, unknown to him, had for days been arguing bitterly among themselves. He eulogized them and all those connected with the hearings. Stating that the submission of such a dispute to such a tribunal "was an example which should become historic, and would undoubtedly influence the course of events throughout the world" — a remark which brought loud cheers from the audience — he expressed his confidence that "the gentlemen who had undertaken the duties of the tribunal would carefully and impartially follow the dictates of their consciences, and be guided entirely by the evidence submitted to them in arriving at a decision." The entire assembly applauded and cheered.

Lord Alverstone followed. The words he used convey some sense of his uneasiness, but few of those present would have been aware of it.

> He wished some of those people who did not understand and appreciate the difficulties of the task they had to perform would abstain from imputing motives to members of the tribunal, and from suggesting that they were going to be governed by anything but a desire to do what they thought right on the evidence before them.[22]

Jetté spoke in a similar vein, although he too well knew the true basis on which the decision would be reached, and Lodge followed to more cheers with a poker-faced "tribute to the President for his uniform kindness, courtesy, patience, and consideration." Only Elihu Root, of all the members of the tribunal and those connected with it who spoke that evening, took any pains to avoid dissimulation, confining himself to platitudes about the "reasonable-ness of the Anglo-Saxon race."

On 17 October the decision was announced. The Americans got a panhandle that was slightly narrower than they had hoped for; the line was drawn at 54°40′, and they were awarded two of the four islands at the entrance to the Portland Canal. In short, they gained virtually all they wanted.

The ownership of the four islands had not been a major issue in the hearings, yet after the hearings ended and during discussion among the six commissioners, they became a bargaining stratagem. Knowing that Alverstone was theirs on the main issue and intent on coming away with as much as possible, the American commissioners told him that the Panhandle should be widened. Believing it to be wide enough already, he suggested as a compromise that the United States should have the smallest two of the four islands. The American commissioners knew, of course, that such a proposal would be acceptable to Roosevelt, and so they agreed. Thus the award was settled, Lord Alverstone joining the three American commissioners to form the majority. The two islands awarded to Canada were by far the most important of the four; Laurier himself had told Sir Joseph Pope that "he wd be satisfied to get Wales and Pearse Islands, but if they [the American commissioners] went against us in that, he wd feel we were badly sold. He evidently does not expect a favourable decision on inlets."[23] And so, seventy-eight years after the 1825 treaty, and with a great deal of diplomatic manoeuvring, the Alaska Panhandle was located almost exactly as the Russians had drawn it in a map of 1827.

Duff and Geoffrion had worked very hard, giving their client good value in a lost cause. Although Duff believed to the end of his days that Alverstone had made a wrong decision, he evaluated the Lord Chief Justice's actions by standards applied to judges sitting in courts; Alverstone presided not over a court but over a tribunal, the American members of which would never have ruled against their own country.

In the aftermath of the ruling, emotion ran high in Canada. Laurier, who knew that the Canadian case had little merit, professed resentment. In view of what he had told Pope, we must conclude that he engaged in theatrics. The aggrieved Canadians lashing out at the turncoat Alverstone and the bully in the White House might have done better to look at the conduct of their own prime minister. For Laurier never resolutely took up the cudgels on behalf of his country. By admitting the weakness of the Canadian case in 1902 to the American representative in London, he cut the ground out from under his own commissioners; worse, he literally encouraged Roosevelt to continue his pressure. Moreover Laurier never once reminded the public of the real possibility of an adverse decision, nor did he try to check the tide of a belief that the Panhandle was Canada's by right. But then, Laurier was playing politics, an art that was foreign to those on the spot, like Duff, making his "frantic endeavours to save Alaska for Canada."[24]

Duff stayed in London for a few days after the award. When a reporter interviewed him on his return to Victoria, he echoed the lofty tones of the Lord Mayor's banquet, concluding that "the whole affair proceeded on that high plane that might be expected in the case of men who were accustomed to move in wide circles in dealing with large affairs."[25] He had hardly unpacked his bags before he was acting in another lucrative case. He and Bodwell represented the well-known American actress Edna Wallace Hopper, step-daughter of Alexander Dunsmuir, a scion of the wealthy Victoria family. Not long before his death from alcoholism Dunsmuir had married her mother, but instead of leaving his very large estate to his wife, he had left it to his brother James. Mrs. Hopper brought the court action to set aside the will on the grounds that Dunsmuir, being drunk at the time he had executed it, could not have understood what he was doing. After his death, Alexander's widow had signed away all legal rights to the estate in return for a substantial annual payment from the Dunsmuir family; the action sought also to invalidate that arrangement. The case proved a bonanza for the lawyers involved. Not only did all the clients have a great deal of money, but the affair also went on for a long time; after extensive and expensive preliminary skirmishing, the trial itself took a month to complete. In a decision announced in February 1904, the court ruled against Duff's client. A subsequent appeal also failed, though Duff, by then on the bench, played no part in it.

That case out of the way, Duff turned his attention to the problems of the architect F.M. Rattenbury, who faced a potential scandal. What proved to be Duff's last case as a lawyer arose out of the contract for the reconstruction of Government House in Victoria following a disastrous fire in 1899. Architects regarded the commission to design the new official residence as valuable both financially and professionally, and a flurry of manoeuvring went on. The government announced that it would choose from competitive designs. Rattenbury, who had won a competition to design the Parliament Buildings, disdained to enter this one, feeling perhaps that it was now beneath his dignity; privately, however, he hankered for the work, and privately, he went after it.

After two Vancouver architects won the competition, he planted doubts that their design could be built within the budget, and persuaded the government to appoint the accomplished Victoria architect Samuel Maclure instead. He then worked out a back-door arrangement with Maclure that made him the effective supervisor, and when, not long afterwards, Maclure fell ill, Rattenbury took full charge. As it transpired, his activities went far beyond those associated with architectural design: he ordered materials in his own name, receiving, it was later alleged, discounts from suppliers who would normally have dealt with contractors. And as in the case of the Parliament Buildings, Rattenbury's own accounts were in a state of disarray. In particular, he took a casual attitude towards "extras," frequently omitting or not bothering to get authorization for them — a practice for which he had condemned the contractors of the legislative building.

It eventually came to the attention of Richard McBride, who had become premier in June of 1903, that Government House would cost more than half as much again as the original contract price. He appointed an arbitration board to examine the contractor's accounts. Two of the three members were architects in whom Rattenbury's habitual arrogance had aroused dislike, and his undoubted talent, envy. They awarded the contractor an additional sum and laid much of the blame on the architect. Worse, they alleged that marble destined for and billed to the Government House project had found its way into the kitchen of Rattenbury's handsome house, now the Glenlyon School, on Beach Drive in Oak Bay, and that an expensive grate in Rattenbury's dining room had been charged to Government House. If substantiated, these accusations could have led to criminal charges. Rattenbury called on Duff to extricate him.

As a direct consequence of the arbitrators' report, the government appointed a legislative committee to inquire into the allegations against Rattenbury in February 1904. In contrast to his conduct at the Turner inquiry five years earlier, Duff attended every session. Because the affair had been brewing since at least June of the previous year, it seems that Rattenbury asked Duff to represent him at that time. In agreeing to act, Duff must have felt a strong obligation, for he deferred acceptance of a judgeship until the conclusion of the inquiry.

The most damning evidence at the committee hearing came from Thomas Hooper, a Victoria architect who had been one of the arbitrators, but severe cross-examination by Duff deprived his testimony of much of its effect. Hooper still managed to get in a few good thrusts. When Duff said to him sarcastically, "We quite understand, Mr. Hooper, that you have a strong leaning towards commissions that are paying twenty-five dollars a day" — an allusion to the discounts offered to contractors but not architects by material suppliers — Hooper retorted that "he didn't know about that, but that [Mr. Duff] would not be there if Mr. Rattenbury were not paying him that much and more."[26] Hooper, like many self-righteous men, had very conspicuous feet of clay; he too had purchased materials and taken discounts. When Duff pointed out that Hooper had given sub-contracting work to his own brother, all he could find to say was that it had been done with the contractor's knowledge.

Such cross-examination could not, however, explain away the Government House marble in Rattenbury's kitchen. Only Rattenbury could do that. His answers were plausible but unconvincing. Having so much work and so many commissions to fulfil, it was often difficult for him, he said, to keep proper accounts of the delivery of materials, particularly when he had been building his own house at the same time; suppliers might easily confuse an order for him personally with one intended for Government House. But why was the Government House grate in his dining room? Quite understandable, he replied; the room at Government House for which the grate was intended required a larger one, which he had ordered, but regrettably the supplier had billed the government for both. Duff must have stage-managed the hearings very cleverly, for at the end of Rattenbury's evidence the committee concluded that it could take no more time, and adjourned. Thus, Rattenbury did not have to endure cross-examination by the lawyers representing Hooper and the contractor. Reporting to the legislature a few days later, the committee exonerated Rattenbury, whose conduct they described as "honourable and satisfactory," but they did express a nagging doubt by saying that with more time they might have reached a different conclusion.[27] The committee did not reconvene or conduct further inquiries. Duff had won his first case in British Columbia; now he had also won his last.

# 6

# Junior judge

ALTHOUGH DUFF was by now collecting very healthy sums in fees, the advantages of a fixed income independent of the vagaries of clients had always appealed to him. Even before his marriage, he had told a friend that a judgeship in the county court represented the height of his ambition so that he could receive a guaranteed sum each month.[1] Duff also believed that a lawyer, if offered a judgeship, should accept it out of a sense of duty. Then, there was always the prestige.

On 16 October 1903, the *Daily Colonist* announced that Duff had been named to the Supreme Court of British Columbia. It described him as a man of "sterling integrity, of brilliant parts, endowed with great energy and untiring industry."[2] Word of this story reached him in London. He had agreed to accept an appointment if one were offered, but the report was embarrassingly premature. More than one prospective judge has lost out by such untimely disclosure, and so on his way home, Duff stopped in Ottawa, undoubtedly to assure the justice minister or his deputy that the item had appeared without any knowledge or complicity on his part. In fact, several other men were in the running for the vacancy that would occur with the expected retirement of Mr. Justice Walkem, among them F.C. Wade, Duff's colleague in London, and F.B. Gregory, both active Liberals. Another was Aulay Morrison, the Liberal M.P. for New Westminster, who had various political supporters write to Ottawa urging his case.

Templeman, the dispenser of Liberal patronage in British Columbia, favoured Duff personally but wished not to be too obvious. He pointed out to Laurier that Morrison's appointment would require a by-election in New Westminster at a time when there was thought of calling a general election; Morrison should be "patient until the announcement of an election is made."[3]

Laurier took Templeman's advice on this point but delayed on Duff. Templeman wrote to him more openly early in February 1904:

> Personally, I have always inclined to Duff. In every respect he is the ablest, best man for the position. There are, of course, many applicants and our friends the members have their own views in regard to each....If you are averse to a bye-election in New Westminster and Morrison can be placated for the present, it would seem to me that the best thing to do is to fill the position at once by appointing Duff.[4]

Laurier telegraphed Templeman on 9 February agreeing to Duff; the M.P. could be "tabled for early appointment," that is have the next vacancy.[5] When Morrison, who happened to be in Ottawa at the time of this correspondence, called on the prime minister two days later, he expressed displeasure. Laurier placated him by suggesting that "we might...reserve to him the succession of Mr. Justice Drake, who, I understand, is willing at an early date to take his pension."[6]

Duff's appointment won approval from all the papers. He was referred to as one of "the keenest legal minds in British Columbia."[7] No Conservative lawyer such as Sir Charles Hibbert Tupper in Vancouver had been considered, of course; the selection of judges in those days was frankly political. Duff travelled to Vancouver for a private swearing-in on 16 March 1904 at the courthouse then located on what is now Victory Square, at Hastings and Cambie streets. His old friend Gordon Hunter administered the oath of office in the presence of only one other person, the registrar, to the Honourable Mr. Justice Lyman P. Duff, a Puisne Judge of the Supreme Court of British Columbia. By a curious anachronism, he had to pay twenty dollars for his formal document of appointment. He was expected to reside in Vancouver but though he may have commuted between Vancouver and Victoria for several months he kept his home in Victoria.

Drake obliged Laurier by retiring that September; the prime minister kept his word and appointed Morrison who, though appeased, now found himself junior to Duff. He became the resident judge on the mainland; not for many years did the judicial pendulum swing away from Victoria. F.C. Wade meanwhile, bitterly disappointed at being twice passed over, wrote Clifford Sifton and Laurier to vent his anger. Word of these recriminations became public, and the *Daily Province* reacted.

> The question which reflecting men in Canada today are asking themselves is how far the suspicion, which is undoubtedly prevalent among the people and which is harboured by all classes of the community, that judicial positions are becoming the spoils of party strife and the rewards of

partisan fidelity, is justified, and if justified what consequences it involves, where it will end and in what it will result?"

The newspaper went on to say that the issue "strikes at the very root of our social organization."[8] This drew fire and brimstone from Templeman, who told Sifton that the editorial

was no doubt written by Wade; he threatened something of that kind in the press or on the platform. Note the argument of the hypocrite — judges should be appointed solely because of character, probity, ability. His only plea to me was that he had fought for the party in Manitoba, and had spent $20,000 on its behalf!

Templeman went on to depict himself as an even-handed man, immune to the crassness of Liberals like Wade:

Patronage of such a general character as the appointment of judges of the Supreme Court and a Senator is all that I have any considerable say in; if I cannot handle that I can do nothing. I must be the judge of what is best and right in all matters of the kind, and I don't think my recommendations of the past have been very far wrong. Certainly they have all been in the interest of the public and the Liberal party.[9]

Laurier eventually rewarded Wade by making him commissioner of the Yukon Territory.

Duff would now have an assured income, but by no means a bigger one. There is no record of his earnings at the Bar, since his fee books and office records are lost. We can, however, arrive at a reasoned estimate. The 1890 Rules of the Supreme Court of British Columbia, which governed the legal profession during all the years of Duff's practice, incorporated a scale of fees barristers could recover. They were entitled to charge a minimum twenty-five dollars for each day in court, but in important cases they could get fifty. This scale applied only when a client disputed an account; wealthy and grateful clients no doubt paid more. There were no trials in July or August, though there would have been other court business, hearings before judges or court registrars in preliminary stages of litigation. At the height of his career in the years 1902–04, Duff probably worked two hundred and fifty days of the year, and if he averaged forty dollars a day his annual income would have been ten thousand dollars, a tidy sum for the time.

Since judges of the Supreme Court were paid only four thousand annually, accepting the judgeship involved a substantial loss of income — as is often the case even today, when many capable lawyers refuse appointments for economic reasons. There was, however, a cogent motive for successful lawyers to accept judicial appointments at financial sacrifice: prestige, a factor not lost on Duff, who, from humble beginnings, had made his way in the world entirely by his own exertions. Supreme court judges in Duff's time had more status in the community than is the case today. And his sister Annie has said that he viewed judgeship as a means of professional advancement. Perhaps he thought to emulate Oliver Mowat, who left the bench to become premier of Ontario; such opportunities were in fact later available to him. If he did not have an eventual political career in mind, he must have believed that the British Columbia court would serve as a stepping-stone to a wider judicial sphere.

The status of a newly appointed judge necessarily alters his relations with former colleagues at the Bar. He avoids mingling too closely in public with those lawyers, however good friends they have been, who might appear before him the next morning to argue a case. A judge may hobnob with architects or pharmacists without compunction, but he must withdraw himself from close public association with other lawyers. Late in life, Duff described the gap as the "river of Lethe," the mythological stream whose waters induced forgetfulness. He meant by the metaphor that judges must remain to some extent aloof, forgetting previous associations to administer the law impartially to the best of their ability. Yet Duff said that the river had been narrow in his case, one he could easily cross to visit his former brethren. It is, of course, impossible for a judge to divorce himself from his education, professional experience, political activity, if any, and habits of mind; Duff's own career on the bench is abundant proof of this.

Duff's colleagues on the Supreme Court when he joined it, besides Hunter as chief justice, consisted of Drake (soon to be replaced by Morrison), Martin, and Irving. They sat mainly in Victoria, but individual judges travelled about the province "on assize" to conduct criminal trials as well as civil litigation. There was no separately constituted court of appeal until 1909. Appeals from judges sitting at trial were heard by the Full Court consisting of three of the Supreme Court judges. Thus, all members of the court found themselves sitting in rotation as a de facto appeal court to rule on judgements rendered by their brethren.

The judges wore wigs until the year after Duff's appointment when, mainly at the instigation of his old college friend Stuart Henderson, who had strong egalitarian feelings, the legislature abolished them. Many lawyers and certainly all the judges regretted the change, but Archer Martin, by a quirk, could circumvent the edict in some cases. He had been appointed as a judge in Admiralty to adjudicate shipping cases which came under federal jurisdiction. Contending that the provincial government had no power to regulate dress in a federal court, he insisted to the end of his days that every lawyer appearing before him in an Admiralty case wear a wig.

Of Duff's colleagues, only Hunter and Martin have left any mark on the jurisprudence of British Columbia. Morrison eventually became chief justice, but his decisions, in the lawyer's phrase, "lack authority." Irving's judgements are unspectacular. Martin's, notwithstanding his erratic and volatile personality, are still treated with respect by lawyers and judges. And Hunter, who was chief justice for twenty-seven years until his death in 1929, is one of the most underrated Canadian judges of this century. If one takes as the criteria for a sound judge learning, the ability to express legal principles correctly in plain language, the absence of pedantry, and perhaps a sense of humour, Hunter satisfied all of them. In 1938 Duff spoke affectionately of his old friend's "brilliant intellectual gifts...his power of attracting the good will of everybody who came within his influence...his robust common sense...the humor which ever and anon lit up the dullest subject."[10]

Once on the bench, Duff had to adapt himself to an entirely different way of life: instead of making arguments, he settled them; instead of talking, he had to listen; instead of taking sides, he had to be impartial; instead of being scornful of the claim of an opponent, he had to adjudicate, possibly in favour of a disagreeable litigant represented by an equally disagreeable lawyer. Instead of exhibiting the theatrical impatience favoured by courtroom lawyers of his era, he had to remain patient; instead of arguing passionately, he had to speak soberly and reasonably. Judges, particularly those newly appointed, are very conscious of changes in their working conditions. They understand that, by their decision in a given case, they are, though perhaps only within a narrow compass, breaking new ground, making new law. They know that the more significant the case, the more carefully their judgement will be studied. Under the English system of common law which, except for civil lawsuits in Quebec, Canada has inherited, a decision of a judge with reference to a given set of facts may be considered as a guide by a future tribunal seeking to solve a legal problem that arises from similar facts or circumstances. This is the application of the rule of precedent, or *stare decisis*. If it can be found that an answer to a question has been given by a court of equivalent or higher standing than the one in which the question is asked, then the latter is obliged to follow suit.

At the conclusion of the evidence in a case, and after the lawyers have presented arguments on behalf of their clients, the judge retires to his office to formulate a ruling. In recent years, judges have tended, at least in the higher courts of Canada, to write their judgements after giving themselves time for reflection rather than delivering them orally at the ends of cases. Oral judgements were more common in Duff's day than they are now, but even so the great majority of decisions were "reserved" or deferred.

Duff, like all other judges in the Anglo-Saxon legal tradition, found himself obliged daily to make a choice between opposing viewpoints. The more effective presentation of one point of view than another sometimes makes it difficult to choose between them, for one poorly presented might on analysis have greater merit than one skilfully advanced. A good judge must seek out the merits of a case without yielding to the superficial blandishments of lawyers. Judges are on the bench to solve unpleasant disputes between individual litigants. But a great judge will look beyond the confines of a private dispute to a wider horizon; he will not merely enunciate correctly the principles by which the dispute should be resolved but will proclaim those principles in a large and ample fashion. Every judge is conscious of the need to speak not only for the present, but for the future, a dichotomy which is the subject of endless discussion.

For a new judge, the writing of his first judgement can be a daunting experience. If they do not make law, at least judges deliver a plausible interpretation of existing law and in the process create a literary work, however imperfect it may be. To blend learning with literary style so that style will drive home the legal truth is a great judicial art. In examining Duff's written judgements from the point of view of style and literary expression over a period of nearly forty years, one is struck by a remarkable fact: his technique of judicial writing is constant throughout. He settled early on an approach that was his for all his days on the bench. One of his judgements written in 1943, the year before his retirement, might just as well have been written in 1904. Using an antiseptic style and elaborate syntax, he brought to bear on the most trivial case the same degree of concentration that he applied to the most important one. This should not be surprising if one recalls his skilled, dedicated, but humourless advocacy.

Duff did not serve long enough on the Supreme Court of British Columbia to make any real impact. Undistinguished though his career there was, and although few of his judgements are referred to by present-day lawyers, a pattern began to emerge. In his first published judgement, he enunciated a rule for the interpretation of legislation which he applied on many occasions thereafter:

> Parliament, not usually parsimonious of language, has...employed a precise phrase; I must look to the words themselves for the policy of the Legislature, not elsewhere. In no case...can I press the words of the Legislature beyond their fair and natural sense.[11]

In an important case of 1918 in which he held valid an order-in-council revoking exemptions from conscription, he stated this principle at somewhat greater length:

> It is the function of a Court of Law to give effect to the enactments of the Legislature according to the force of the language which the legislature

has finally chosen for the purpose of expressing its intention. Speculation as to what may have been passing in the minds of members of the legislature is out of place, for the simple reason that it is only the corporate intention so expressed with which the court is concerned. Besides that road — the road of speculation — leads into a labyrinth where there is no guide.[12]

In so ruling, Duff adopted the traditional role of statutory interpretation in the belief that Canadian courts could not do otherwise. He contrasted the approach of courts in Canada with the one in United States courts by remarking that "eminent American judges, in the application of legislative enactments, do permit themselves a latitude of interpretation which a Canadian court would not feel itself free to exercise."[13] In his interpretation of the British North America Act, the two points of view are most sharply contrasted. At the same time, Duff, although he declined to follow the more imaginative American practice in interpreting statutes, showed an early willingness to look to decisions of American courts for assistance in solving Canadian problems. Judges tend nowadays to view problems in a broader setting, but it was not at all fashionable then to pay attention to rulings made in the United States. Duff acquired a wide knowledge of leading cases decided by the higher courts of that country and referred to them constantly. He often quoted decisions of a century before by a giant of the U.S. Supreme Court, Chief Justice Marshall, whom he greatly admired.

He believed firmly that lawyers conducting cases in court should play strictly by the rules; having taken one position on a client's behalf, a lawyer should not be allowed to shift ground on appeal in a higher court by arguing propositions differing from those advanced previously. Such conduct drew anger from Duff throughout his career. In one of the first cases in which he gave a judgement in the Full Court of British Columbia, he spoke of "the rule long established, which holds the litigant to a position deliberately assumed by his Counsel at the trial....The rule is...that litigants shall not play fast and loose with the course of litigation."[14] In a well-known case heard late in his career, he reiterated this view. At a murder trial, the prosecuting lawyer, summing up the case for the prosecution, had told the jury that the accused should either be convicted of murder or acquitted. The jury acquitted him, and the Crown appealed on the ground that the trial judge should have told the jury it could have taken a middle way by finding a verdict of manslaughter. Refusing the Crown appeal, Duff described such tactics by the prosecution as "a dangerous practice."[15] The common-law system is an adversary system, not a process of arbitration; contending clients represented by contending lawyers confront each other, and a judge resolves the argument. Duff always maintained that the system, imperfect as it may be, would be even more imperfect if one allowed clients and lawyers to be elusive and changeable as quicksilver.

In one important area of the criminal law, the admissibility of statements made by an accused person, Duff's early views were to remain unaltered. The law allows a prosecutor, by satisfying certain conditions, to ask a police witness to testify to what an accused person said. One of the conditions is that the statement be "voluntary," that is not obtained by force or coercion. To dispel any future suggestion that a statement was not made voluntarily, police officers usually deliver a caution or warning, telling the person that it is not necessary to say anything, but what is said can be used in evidence; in the United States, this is done by reading an accused person his "rights." Duff ruled in 1904 that a statement was inadmissible unless the accused had first been warned, a ruling which favoured the accused rather than the prosecution.[16] In 1943, the Supreme Court of Canada made a similar ruling; although Duff did not write the judgement, he participated without dissent in the views expressed by Mr. Justice Taschereau. Six years later, when Duff had retired, the Ottawa court modified its earlier decision, holding that the presence or absence of a warning merely formed one element to be considered with respect to the admissibility of a statement. It is doubtful if Duff would have agreed.[17]

He had some disagreeable moments on the bench in British Columbia. After sentencing a man to prison at Nelson, Duff walked from the courtroom to be confronted by a friend of the prisoner who hit him on the head with a baseball bat; he suffered a broken nose, the scars of which he carried for the rest of his life. Pronouncing sentence of death on a young murderer caused him such great distress that he became physically ill, and he remained sick at heart for a year. Despite this experience, Duff believed throughout his judicial career in capital punishment for premeditated murder or murder done during the commission of a serious crime. At his first trial of a murder charge, the accused, a Chinese, was convicted. When he had uttered the ritual words ordering that the man be taken to the place of execution where he would hang by the neck until dead, and these words had been translated into Chinese, the prisoner spoke. Duff asked the interpreter, "What does he say?" The interpreter replied, "All right, judge."[18]

During the two years Duff spent on the British Columbia court, he found himself in the crossfire of the battle between Hunter and Martin which had been raging since 1902. The increasing virulence of relations between the two men embarrassed their colleagues and everyone else who had contact with the court — lawyers, registrars, and courthouse staff alike. Within a year of Duff's appointment, the situation had become so poisoned that Martin would not speak to the chief justice, communicating only through such intermediaries as the court usher, librarian, or registrar. As Hunter's closest friend, Duff must have been particularly uncomfortable, all the more since he respected Martin's obvious ability. He must have been relieved to escape the conflict by going to Ottawa.

On the bench, Duff had new and continuing financial woes. Perhaps he reflected that he ought to have delayed accepting a judgeship until he had a reasonable nest egg. Not only did he suffer a reduction in earnings, but he managed badly what money he did have. In 1918, Duff wrote to congratulate a man who had recently been named deputy attorney-general of British Columbia. The occasion jogged his memory to recall that he had not requested reimbursement for travelling expenses incurred on his last circuit through that province in 1906. Duff had no record of expenses, but he asked to be paid a sum based on a reasonable estimate of costs for travel to the various cities where he had held court. The response is not known; one can hardly believe that the attorney-general's department would have paid after so long a time. [19]

# 7

# First Ottawa years

SECTION 101 of the British North America Act gave the Parliament of Canada the authority "from Time to Time to provide for the Constitution...of a general Court of Appeal for Canada." Not until 1875, however, did the lawgivers exercise their power and establish a "Court of Common Law and Equity in and for the Dominion of Canada which shall be called 'The Supreme Court of Canada'." Sir William Buell Richards, chief justice of the Ontario Court of Common Pleas, became the first chief justice of the court, followed by four others before Duff's time, of whom one, Sir Charles Fitzpatrick, appointed in June 1906, served as chief justice longer than anyone else. In most instances the right to appeal in a civil case then depended only on the amount of money involved in the litigation, whereas the present-day litigant must apply for permission to appeal, granted only in significant cases. In criminal matters, appeals were and are still governed by different rules from those applying to civil cases; belief in the importance of the liberty of the subject has meant, generally speaking, that cases of serious crime can be appealed more readily.

Fitzpatrick had had a distinguished career as a criminal lawyer, his most notable client being Louis Riel. After serving in the Quebec Legislative Assembly, he was elected to the House of Commons in 1896, and served as a minister under Laurier. At the time of his appointment to the Supreme Court, that body had five other members. Mr. Justice Girouard, like Fitzpatrick, came from Quebec. Louis Davies, a former premier of Prince Edward Island, had been elected in 1882 to the House of Commons where he served until his appointment to the court in 1901. John Idington and James Maclennan both came from Ontario; Robert Sedgewick was a Nova Scotian on whose death in August 1906 Laurier decided to find his replacement in western Canada.

Duff had been mooted as early as 1903 as a possible appointment to the court. His partner Bodwell telegraphed Laurier in that year emphasizing the need for British Columbia to be represented and urging that consideration be given to Duff.[1] Templeman felt that Duff had not yet achieved the necessary stature for appointment to Ottawa, but did not exclude the possibility.[2] In 1906, Laurier's idea of a westerner ran into some initial opposition from his chief justice. Fitzpatrick, who as the former justice minister had in effect appointed himself, wrote to the prime minister soon after Sedgewick's death: "Please do not forget Judge Cannon from Quebec as personal favour."[3] This was blatant nepotism: Cannon's son, who did later become a Supreme Court judge, had married Fitzpatrick's daughter. To his credit, Laurier did not indulge the chief justice. He offered the appointment first to E.P. Davis of Vancouver, who declined because his wife loathed Ottawa and refused to move there.[4] In then asking Duff to join the court, Laurier may have been influenced by A.B. Aylesworth, who had become justice minister, and perhaps too by Aimé Geoffrion; both had been associated with Duff at the London tribunal of 1903. Duff accepted without hesitation. No longer would he be obliged to sentence men to death.

At age forty-one, he became the youngest person thus far appointed to the court, and he would serve longer than anyone else. His salary went from four thousand dollars in British Columbia to six thousand in Ottawa. Immediately after his swearing-in he took part in his first case; it involved the validity of an election, a subject in which he had considerable experience. A newspaper described Duff's first appearance in the court:

> Physically, he [is] rather over-shadowed by the burly form of Mr. Justice Idington...but his features...suggest intellect, sensibility and good humour, and the keen eyes appear to take in everything. The new judge with his ruddy hair and his closely cropped pointed beard of the same hue, looks quite youthful alongside some of his learned brethren.[5]

The Supreme Court until 1946 occupied a handsome building, at the corner of Bank and Wellington streets in Ottawa, which had been built in the 1860s as a workshop and used later as a carriage shed. The courtroom itself resembled a chapel: peaked beams formed the ceiling; the rich wood panelling of the walls, graced by carved scrolls with a floral motif, glowed with the patina of age. The judges from their dais peered at the counsel, who were seated according to rank, the K.C.s — King's Counsel now that the old Queen was gone — enjoying pride of place. Behind the lawyers were low-backed pews ranged on both sides of a central aisle.[6] The hot-water radiators sometimes distracted attention in the courtroom. On one occasion, a radiator began to shake and rattle; two ushers rushed up to it, clutching the ends of the monster like grooms trying to subdue an unruly horse. As they tried desperately to quell the rattle Duff, seemingly oblivious, continued to question the lawyer presenting his case.[7] With all its defects, the room had atmosphere. No one could doubt that he was in the hall of justice.

On their arrival in Ottawa, the Duffs plunged into a whirl of lunches, teas, and dinners. They met the same people or, at all events, the same types of persons at the same sorts of functions: senior civil servants, eminent lawyers, fellow judges, diplomatic staff, and high-ranking politicians. One wonders how much of this was pleasure and how much duty, and yet they kept up an extremely active social life until the outbreak of war. In 1910 they built a large, handsome house on Golbourne Avenue. During its construction, Lizzie had let it be known that she could not "receive" that "season," but in November of that year she had two large "at homes" to christen her new mansion, and thereafter frequently entertained in it.

Duff, however, did not plunge into the work of the court as he did into Ottawa society. There was in him a certain diffidence about taking an active part in the deliberations of his fellow judges, an understandable reaction from a relatively young westerner suddenly finding himself a member of the highest court in the land. He did not, as Anglin did after his appointment in 1909, start writing judgements in important cases at once, choosing rather to side with one or another of his colleagues. Not until he had been on the court for two months did he write a judgement, and even then it was an uncharacteristically short one.[8] And not until he had been four months on the court did he write his first judgement to express the views of the court as a whole.[9] In fact, Duff used this whole prewar period to develop his judicial talents. By 1914, he had done so to the high level which distinguished his work until retirement.

His effectiveness as a judge depended on a number of factors; the same can be said of other judges, but Duff added an extra dimension of achievement to the jurist's basic skills. He read widely on legal subjects in both French and English; he kept abreast of decisions from the higher courts in Canada and the United Kingdom, as well as those of Australia and New Zealand. With his reading he combined a prodigious memory, perhaps a better qualification than any other for success in the law. Duff's photographic memory allowed him as rapid information retrieval as was possible in the pre-computer age. He constantly astonished colleagues and impressed observers. The Ontario attorney-general's department once inquired about his knowledge of a memorandum written by Oliver Mowat in 1875, when he headed the department, on the obscure legal doctrine of escheats. Duff wrote back at once giving the name of the book in which the memorandum could be found and apologizing for not remembering the page. Then, after thinking for a minute or two, he remembered it and put it in a postscript.[10]

He got straight to the heart of any legal problem, often leaving the lawyers behind. One who had thoroughly worked his case up and looked at it from every point of view had nothing to fear from Duff, even if the outcome was unfavourable, but Duff could not abide slovenly preparation; woe betide the lawyer who had not done his homework. By the time arguments had ended his mind was made up. He usually knew more law than the lawyers and was confident that he knew more. This was not arrogance but competence. Very rarely did he change his mind. If he did so, he admitted it. As he said in a 1931 judgement,

> I ought, I think, to add this, that at the conclusion of the first argument, and indeed for some time after the second argument, I thought my brother Smith was right, and more than once expressed myself in that sense. But I have changed my opinion and to that opinion I must now give effect.[11]

After the argument ended, he would turn to write his judgement with Roget's Thesaurus at his elbow. He worked on several cases at once, keeping in his chambers piles of books relating to each. Unlike many of his colleagues, he made copious notes during the argument of a case. While dictating judgements, he strode up and down his chambers jingling the change in his pocket. He dictated with great precision; his judgements seldom required much reworking. He launched right into the legal issues of a case, unlike many judges who were in the habit of prefacing their legalities with a recital of the relevant facts.

Duff regarded every problem brought before him as a serious one to be solved in a serious fashion. Not once in his judgements over nearly forty years did he permit himself a literary allusion or reference to contemporary events. He believed that appellate judgements should be written for lawyers and possibly for posterity, but certainly not for litigants. Never did he use humour, even where it would have been excusable and even helpful. In an unusual case, a claim for slander of title, the court considered the legal effect of a newspaper item describing an alleged haunted house that told of the antics of various ghosts in the dwelling. The owner, who had contracted to sell the house, lost the sale because the purchaser refused to buy after reading this story, and won a suit against the paper for damages. The claim might have had to do with dryrot or vermin for all the reaction these ghosts drew from the judges, Duff included. In another case turning on whether or not the comic strip "Buster Brown and Tige" could be registered as a trademark, no judge smiled. Seldom did Duff write a vigorous judgement; he controlled his feelings to give well-reasoned but dispassionate decisions. The tricks of fraudulent businessmen and cheats seemed to be the only subjects which provoked him to discernible judicial wrath.

Duff's judicial style can be compared with that of his colleague John Idington, who came to the court in 1905. Considered by most lawyers to be a judicial lightweight, Idington has often been referred to as the "Great Dissenter," out of step with his colleagues. His intellectual ability may not have equalled that of some of them, but he made up for this in common sense and humanity. Beyond question, judgements reveal men; Duff's show him as a serious student devoted to intellectual solutions for problems, and Idington's show him to have been a bluff, hearty, forthright, no-nonsense person. He invariably spoke his mind. He and Duff obviously respected each other's abilities, as, particularly during Duff's first years, they were so often on the same side of a legal question. They dissented regularly from colleagues' opinions, and such harmony speaks well for both men. When Idington died in 1928 — he had retired in 1927 at the age of 87 — Duff spoke feelingly of him in court the next morning:

> I personally sat with him for nearly twenty years. I must say that I owe him much. I feel that not only a notable influence has passed out of my life but that I have lost a very dear and valued friend. As you all know, he was a man of great strength, mental and physical; conspicuous for marked individuality. As in the case of many men of great force of character, those who knew him were aware of a very wide and deep reserve of kindness and tenderness. He had, and did not hesitate to shew, the loftiest disdain for anything mean, or shabby, or anything resembling chicanery or intrigue, or, to use a well-worn phrase, "the little arts of little men."

Duff concluded that "a more valiant judge never lived."[12]

He soon mastered the French language and the Civil Code, with the help of his colleague Girouard. He eventually became bilingual and could easily discuss cases in French with lawyers from Quebec, although in his day the formal arguments presented to the court were printed in English. The underlying evidence in Quebec cases was often in French, however, and Duff commonly questioned the accuracy of translations from one language to the other. Moreover the challenge for lawyers of English mother tongue, trained in the common-law tradition, trying to understand the Quebec Civil Code, was more than linguistic. The Code came into effect in 1866, adapted to Quebec needs from the great French *Code Napoléon*, and is concerned mainly with what lawyers call "private law," dealing with such subjects as marriage, family relationships, property, and wills; lawyers practising in it pay much more attention to writers of legal texts — doctrine as distinct from jurisprudence — than those working in the English tradition do. Although in the event of conflict jurisprudence would be given greater weight than doctrine, the Civil Code in Duff's time did not explicitly recognize the rule of precedent which lies at the heart of the common-law system. His skill in both the language and the law of Quebec was rewarded by honorary doctorates of law from Laval, McGill, and Montreal universities.

Duff had a high regard for the role of lawyers paid to persuade a judge to their client's point of view, and nothing pleased him more than engaging in parry and thrust with skilled advocates. He looked on them as an integral part of the judicial process; they should not aim darts at the judge on the bench, but in tandem solve a legal problem by a rational, intellectual process. Duff described these qualities of advocacy with eloquence on the occasion of the unveiling of a bust of Eugene Lafleur, who had died in 1930:

> You cannot, of course, lay bare with the scalpel of analysis the springs of individual power in any great practical art, least of all in the arts of the forum. The power to captivate, to fix, to hold the attention of the tribunal; the power to predispose the tribunal to a favourable view of the cause of your client; the power, in a word, to persuade — you recognize it, but you cannot explain it or decompose it into its elements.

He went on to talk about the great virtues of "excellence" and objectivity that successful advocates must possess:

> Matthew Arnold says somewhere, in commenting upon the writings of a famous French critic, that the intellectual gift of lucidity is not without some significant relationship to character. And of this I am sure, that lucidity bears a very close affinity to a mental quality which, in its perfection is extremely rare; a quality that, for want of a better term, may be designated by a phrase we sometimes hear — "intellectual honesty." It is a quality which involves a great deal more than mere honesty in intention and purpose. It presupposes a faculty of seeing things as they are, unmoved by bias or passion or excitement. I think this detachment is, perhaps, characteristic of the really great lawyer and it is a characteristic which competent observers always recognize when they encounter it. In Lafleur's case it was conspicuous. [13]

Although the decision of a lower court is governed by that of a higher, judges who want a particular result sometimes confront an adverse decision by a higher court. Various devices are available to them for isolating the awkward ruling: they can conclude that the facts were substantially different, for example, or that the apparent rationale was based on an incomplete examination of the law. Not long after Duff went to Ottawa, the court ruled in favour of Ontario in a dispute arising from a treaty between the Ojibways of that province and the federal government. When a boundary survey revealed that a large portion of the land the Ojibways occupied was in Ontario rather than Manitoba as had formerly been believed, the federal government claimed compensation from Ontario for money spent among Natives residing on that province's land. Since the eminent English judge Lord Watson had expressed the opinion in a Privy Council ruling that Canadian provinces had jurisdiction over Crown lands, counsel for the federal government argued that Ontario should therefore be required to pay for the support of Natives living on such lands.[14] Duff expressed due regard for Lord Watson's views, but declined to follow suit as they were gratuitous in the sense that he had not heard full legal argument before expressing them.[15] What makes Duff's finding curious is that hardly a year later he was citing Watson's language with approval.[16] He was not often guilty of such lapses.

Early in his career on the Supreme Court, Duff made interesting decisions in two areas of law that are now very much in the public eye — women's rights and the rights of racial minorities. He confirmed a tendency first observable in British Columbia towards a relaxed attitude to the claims of common-law wives against the estates or property of the men with whom they lived.[17] He also had a certain sympathy for illegitimate children in this respect. In a Quebec case, a mother brought a claim for damages after the death of such a child in an automobile accident. Duff stated that Quebec law recognized claims only for legitimate children, but helped her by absolving her of responsibility as the unsuccessful party for the payment of court costs. In the course of his judgement, he said,

> One additional observation I feel obliged to make. We have before us a dry question of law, and I do not think it incumbent upon me to express either approval or condemnation of the well-known and traditional attitude of the common law, of England as well as of France, towards illegitimacy.[18]

A 1914 case concerned a Saskatchewan law prohibiting "white female" employment in "places of business and amusement kept, owned or managed by Chinamen." On a challenge to the constitutionality of the legislation, Duff and all the other judges but one upheld the validity of the law on the grounds that such legislation fell within the powers of the province, to which the British North America Act gave jurisdiction over "civil rights." Duff again declined to follow language used by Lord Watson, this time from a celebrated 1899 Privy Council appeal that threw out a British Columbia law forbidding the employment of Chinese in underground coal mines. Only Idington, in his characteristic blunt manner, came down on the side of the Chinese, holding that "this legislation is but a piece of the product of the mode of thought that begot and maintained slavery."[19] Evidently, the plight of Orientals in Canada aroused no revulsion in Duff against legislation aimed at them, but the same could be said of virtually all his contemporaries on the bench. Only a few, Sir Matthew Baillie Begbie, who died in 1894, and Idington among them, saw such legislation as an invasion of basic human rights.

Duff's early mastery of mining law saw regular use in Ottawa; in virtually every mining case coming to the Supreme Court of Canada in his time the leading judgement was written by him. Occasionally too, he turned to his experience of political controversy. Disagreeing with his fellow judges, he once ruled that a newspaper allegation according to which a Liberal nominee had withdrawn from a political race because he was offered a "price" to do so did not amount to a charge of corruption. Many people, Duff said, used such words in political battles without intending any accusation of corruption.[20]

Before 1914, the important criminal cases coming to the court were few as compared with the numbers being heard towards the end of Duff's career. One reason was Canada's still relatively small, mainly rural population; statistically, the growth of cities fostered crime. Another was the state of the law itself; the principle that a person is presumed innocent until the prosecution can prove guilt beyond a reasonable doubt remained unsettled until 1935.[21] Sir Charles Fitzpatrick declared in 1912, with Duff in agreement:

> I have always understood the rule that the Crown, in a criminal case, is not required to do more than produce evidence which, if unanswered and believed, is sufficient to raise a prima facie case upon which the jury might be justified in finding a verdict.[22]

Two significant criminal cases from Duff's early years may be mentioned. The decision in one, an appeal from a conviction for murder, is still referred to by lawyers. The victim fled from an armed pursuer who, although he dropped his gun, continued the chase until the victim reached a group of men, shouting at them as he ran, "Hold on, hold on, he shot me and he will shoot me again. Hold on, boys, hold on!" Could evidence of these statements by the deceased be given by the witnesses to whom he spoke? The situation is analogous to that of a dying person's declarations. The Supreme Court ruled that the statements were admissible since they formed an integral part of the very event in question, the shooting which gave rise to the murder charge.[23] In the other case, Duff dissented from the decision of his fellows to uphold a conviction in a police murder during the serious miners' strike at Frank, Alberta in 1908. The convicted man had set out at night with a companion intending to commit theft, assuming that he would not be caught because of the turmoil caused by the strike. When he returned home, he told a friend that he had killed a person whom he believed to have been a secret police constable. The accused said that the dead man had pointed a pistol at him and had told him to "go to hell," whereupon he had shot him. A majority of the judges of the Supreme Court of Canada agreed that the trial judge had been correct in telling the jury that they had only two options, to acquit the accused or convict him of murder. Duff did not agree. He believed that the description of the event by the accused gave the jury a basis for finding a reduced verdict of manslaughter on the ground of provocation or perhaps self-defence. Unavailingly, he urged a new trial.[24]

His dissent in this case is another early example of a tendency observable during his years on the bench. In a case evenly balanced between the accused and the prosecution, he took the side of the accused. Just why this should be so is not easy to explain. It may have had unconscious origins in his sympathetic involvement with the case of the eight-year-old Chenoweth boy. Or perhaps, again unconsciously, he was trying to compensate in some way for his own lack of success in defending criminals. It could be that his decisions were a reflection of his classic liberalism — the belief in the essential goodness of men buffeted by forces of repression in a hostile world. Whatever the reason, the admirable tendency is clear.

In 1911 the court heard an appeal in an unusual dispute. The well-known Toronto firm of Morang, publishers of the "Makers of Canada" series, had commissioned W.D. LeSueur, an author of repute, to write a biography of William Lyon Mackenzie, the rebel grandfather of William Lyon Mackenzie King. After paying LeSueur the agreed sum for the delivered work, Morang declined to publish it as being unsuitable for its series but refused to return the manuscript. LeSueur, evidently on the advice of his lawyer, sent the publisher's money back and demanded his work. Still the publisher would not give it to him. LeSueur started court action. He won his case at the trial and before the Ontario Court of Appeal. Morang than launched an appeal to the Supreme Court, and not long before it was due to be heard a direct attempt to influence the decision of the court was made by then labour minister Mackenzie King. LeSueur had used material given him by Mackenzie's descendants, who objected strongly to his portrayal, feeling that it did not do justice to their ancestor. King wrote the judges of the court urging that the publisher be allowed to retain the work since the author had made unfair use of the material made available to him.

This was, of course, a highly improper attempt to influence, if not subvert, the course of justice. A majority of the court, including the chief justice and Duff, resisted the pressure, ordering Morang to give the manuscript back. Duff recognized the special character of a literary work by ruling that failure to publish it implied an obligation to return it. Possibly because of King's intervention, Duff declared in a rare fit of judicial anger that

> a suppression of this manuscript would so manifestly defeat the intention of both parties — is indeed so monstrous a fraud upon the agreement

upon which the appellant Morang obtained possession of it that the Court will, if possible...overcome all technical difficulties to make that impossible.[25]

Mackenzie's heirs later obtained a court injunction to block publication of the manuscript, and it was not issued until 1979.

Recalling the incident fifteen years later, Duff wrote that King's "offence was passed over without comment, unfortunately, as I thought at the time."[26] He made that comment a year after King had chosen Anglin over himself for the chief justiceship in 1924, and undoubtedly had a jaundiced opinion of the then prime minister. At the time of the Morang case, however, the two were on excellent terms.[27] They had first met when King was studying at the University of Toronto and Duff at Osgoode Hall. In 1940 the Liberal leader referred to their "friendship of some 50 years."[28] Duff admired King. In 1910, he wrote to congratulate him on his role in settling a strike by employees of the Grand Trunk Railway:

My dear King,

Just a line to congratulate you upon the success of yr. efforts in settling the strike. I quite appreciate the position of the co. from *their point of view* in declining to accede to the principle of a definitive *arbitration* although the methods of Mr. Hayes were certainly rather suggestive of those of the proverbial "pettifogging attorney." On the other hand it would have been a disastrous blow to the cause of industrial conciliation had the moral force of the community as represented by you failed to bring about an adjustment. This as representing the moral socially progressive force of the community as affecting the relation of capital and labour — I am quite convinced — that you are...to be congratulated. The personal triumph is nonetheless gratifying to your friends.

Duff's letter was an odd one from a judge who had supposedly drunk of the river Lethe. King responded with regret that he had not been able to convey his thanks personally.[29] The association between the two men was not always so cordial, but it proved to be perhaps the most important single influence on Duff's career.

Soon after the Morang case, Duff and his colleagues considered the validity of "mixed marriages" in Quebec between Protestants and Roman Catholics. This case, which aroused more controversy than any with which Duff had hitherto been involved, inflamed religious passions throughout Canada. It stemmed from the decree *Ne Temere*, proclaimed by the Pope in 1907 and made effective in the province of Quebec the following year, according to which mixed marriages were unlawful in the church's eyes unless performed by priests acting under special dispensation. The effect of the decree was bolstered by a provision in the Quebec Civil Code which gave priests the right to refuse to perform marriages that did not conform to the dictates of the church.

Protestant zealots, particularly those in the fundamentalist churches and the Orange order, made fiery speeches when the decree began to be applied in a glare of publicity. They contended that a duly ordained clergyman of any denomination should be able to perform a legally binding marriage, and that it was "grossly insulting" to prevent Protestant clergymen from doing so. Resolutions denouncing the decree were passed by numerous parishes across the country with increasing frequency and mounting anger. The uproar contributed to the 1911 defeat of the Laurier government, which had supported the validity of the Quebec marriage laws; Ontarians in particular translated their loathing for the decree into anti-Laurier votes.

The Protestant outcry prompted E.A. Lancaster, an Ontario backbencher in the newly elected Borden government, to bring forward a private member's bill in 1912 that managed to get as far as second reading. It provided that

> every ceremony or form of marriage heretofore or hereafter performed by any person authorized to perform any ceremony of marriage by the laws of the place where it is performed, and duly performed according to such laws, shall everywhere within Canada be deemed to be a valid marriage, notwithstanding any differences in the religious faith of the persons so married and without regard to the religion of the person performing the ceremony.
>
> ...the rights and duties as married people of the respective persons married as aforesaid, and of the children of such marriage, shall be absolute and complete, and no law or canonical decree or custom of or in any province of Canada shall have any force or effect to invalidate or qualify any such marriage or any of the rights of the said persons or their children in any manner whatsoever.

The validity of this proposed legislation depended upon two provisions in the British North America Act. One gave provinces the jurisdiction to enact laws for "the solemnization of marriage," and the other gave the federal government jurisdiction to pass laws relating to "marriage and divorce." Into which of these categories did the draft law fall?

In the debate on Lancaster's bill, Borden pointed out that the former justice minister and the deputy minister of justice both believed legislation of the type proposed to be invalid because it had to do with solemnization of marriage. Borden, in a move which drew vitriolic accusations of cowardice from newspapers outside Quebec, adjourned debate so that he could ask the

Supreme Court of Canada for an opinion on the bill's legality. The Act creating the court gave the federal government the right to do this, and such requests, known as "references," have often been resorted to by governments. Early in 1912, the Duke of Connaught, the Governor-General, approved an order-in-council referring the bill to the court. In the hope of alienating as few voters as possible, Borden decided not to take a firm position in the court; E.L. Newcombe, the deputy justice minister, was instructed simply to make a courtesy appearance and place the issue before the judges.

The case was so highly charged that not even the judges could preserve their aloofness. Sir Charles Fitzpatrick, an Irish Roman Catholic, found himself in a particularly difficult position because he had some sympathy for the Protestant point of view. Not long before the reference came to the court, he wrote a confidential letter to Borden pointing out that though the Treaty of Paris in 1763 had guaranteed Quebec Catholics their special privileges, Protestants in Quebec under *Ne Temere* were not to be afforded the same degree of religious tolerance.[30] After this understandable protest, however, Fitzpatrick joined with Duff and two other judges to declare the bill invalid because it fell within provincial jurisdiction. Religious passions gradually subsided, but it was not until the Lesage era in Quebec half a century later that the decree's last vestiges disappeared.[31]

Within a few months of Duff's arrival in Ottawa, he heard his first appeal involving the constitutional law of Canada, *Canadian Pacific Railway Co. v. The Ottawa Fire Insurance Co.*[32] His greatest judicial contribution to his country would be made in that somewhat nebulous but vital area, and the case provides a good clue to the drift many of his decisions would take in the thirty-five years to come.

Canada's constitution derives from various sources that include statutes and long-observed usages, but the single most important source in Duff's lifetime was the British North America Act, the law passed in 1867 by the Parliament of the United Kingdom to bring about the Confederation of Canada. Many of the British North America Act's provisions provoked litigation which ended up before the Supreme Court of Canada or the Judicial Committee of the Privy Council in London, but the two that stimulated the most significant legal questions were sections 91 and 92. The former empowers the federal government to pass legislation in various areas, criminal law, trade and commerce, and banking being chief among them. In addition, the section gives Parliament the general power, sometimes referred to as the "emergency" power, to "make Laws for the Peace, Order and good Government of Canada" in areas outside provincial jurisdiction. Section 92 assigns provincial legislatures a number of other subjects, including property and civil rights, direct taxation, the "incorporation of companies with provincial objects," and "generally all works of a merely local or private nature." The determination of the validity of provincial or federal legislation tested in the light of these sections has given rise to decisions that have had profound influence on the conduct of business, politics, and personal lives in Canada.

During all the time Duff sat on the Supreme Court, the Judicial Committee of the Privy Council in London was the court of last resort for Canada in civil cases. The economic and constitutional rights of Canadian citizens were determined offshore. Because judges on a "committee" sitting in London, however "judicial" it might be, settled important questions in Canada, Canadians did not regard their own supreme court as the principal actor in the main stream of the country's legal activity. Americans have always been far more conscious of their supreme court since it was enshrined in their constitution as the tribunal of last resort. Ottawa had passed legislation in 1887 abolishing appeals to the Privy Council in criminal cases,[33] but the statute and its subsequent re-enactments remained legally ineffective until passage of the Statute of Westminster in 1931.[34] Strictly speaking, then, the Privy Council had jurisdiction to hear criminal appeals from Canada up to that time, but in fact it heard none after Louis Riel's in 1885, though at least one unsuccessful attempt to appeal was made.[35] When it came to the constitution, however, things were otherwise. A few such cases ended with a ruling by the Supreme Court, but almost every important one went to London, with the result that authoritative interpretation of sections 91 and 92 of the B.N.A. Act rested with the Privy Council. By a series of decisions in the last two decades of the nineteenth century, that body laid down a scheme for interpreting those sections that has persisted to this day, even though Privy Council appeals were abolished in 1949. Despite the presence on the Judicial Committee of an outstanding judge like Duff, many Canadians saw the role of the Privy Council as evidence of servitude or colonialism; the shortcomings or perceived shortcomings of our constitutional arrangements could be laid at the door of an institution not of this country. Since 1950, when the Supreme Court of Canada assumed the mantle of judicial infallibility, it has nominally had a determining influence on those arrangements, but the court has not yet renounced its fealty to the rulings of the Privy Council.

Duff's importance as a constitutional lawyer springs, not from innovation or originality, but from his entrenchment of earlier London rulings. His decisions gave them respectability. In those rulings, the Privy Council had declared that the British North America Act must be interpreted like any other statute: by looking at the plain meaning of the words, without regard to the supposed political intentions of their sponsors.

This traditional approach led the Privy Council by two of its judges in the Victorian era, Sir Montague Smith and Lord Watson, to make rulings according to which Canada was in effect a federation of provinces and not a legislative union. The distinction was crucial. The provinces in their jurisdictions were as powerful as the federal government was in its field, and the Privy Council rejected any interpretation of the British North America Act which would have permitted the federal government to invade provincial fields, for example by exercising federal powers of legislation with respect to trade and commerce or criminal law. Moreover, the Privy Council whittled down — some would say emasculated — the general federal power to make laws for the peace, order, and good government of Canada. It ruled that to allow Ottawa full rein to legislate by virtue of what appeared to be a clause giving it residuary power would deny provinces the exercise of specific powers under section 92 of the Act. There have been many critics of the Privy Council in this, though some commentators have supported them. For his part Duff endorsed the Privy Council's interpretation. And in fact even had he not been convinced of its correctness, he would still have been obliged to support it; the decisions were binding on the Supreme Court by the rule of precedent, and Duff was a firm believer in the utility of that rule. He never considered taking a fresh look at the B.N.A. Act.

The point at issue in the *Ottawa Fire Insurance* case was

> whether or not a company incorporated under the authority of a provincial legislature to carry on the business of fire insurance is inherently incapacitated from entering into, outside the boundaries of its province of origin, a valid contract of insurance relating to property also outside those limits.

A majority of the court — Idington, Maclennan and Duff — held that a company was not incapacitated and could enter into those contracts. In this they skirted language used in a Privy Council decision of some years before, in which Sir Montague Smith, drawing his expressions from yet another Privy Council case, seemed to state clearly that only a company incorporated under Dominion legislation could carry on business throughout the Dominion: "the Parliament of Canada could alone constitute a corporation with those powers."[36]

In his judgement, Duff said that this language must be viewed in the context of the facts in the case; the precise point now raised had not been argued before the Privy Council. His own language is a good example of the method by which judges circumvent inconvenient decisions.

> We are not to seize upon the statement that only companies incorporated by the Parliament of Canada have the capacity to carry on their business throughout the Dominion, detach it from its context, from the subject under discussion, and imputing to it the broadest signification which it will bear, give effect to it in that sense as expounding a binding rule of law.

He pointed out that if provincially incorporated companies could not enter valid contractual obligations outside the province, their whole business would be futile. If that capacity were denied,

> no provincial life insurance company could insure against a death, no accident company against an accident occurring outside the province [with the result that] in effect no provincial company could engage in the business of life, accident or marine insurance except upon conditions which would in practice make it impossible or almost impossible for it to obtain any business to do.

Thus, in his first constitutional case, Duff took a point of view favourable to the provinces. He saw Canada as a federal state with equal members whose legislative powers, as an English judge later put it, were like "watertight compartments." That view of Canada's constitution led him ultimately to the firm belief that the federal government could not act unilaterally in any way that affected the legislative powers of the provinces.

The *Ottawa Fire Insurance* case was the precursor of a flurry of constitutional cases that came before the court before and just after the outbreak of war involving the extent to which companies incorporated in one part of Canada, or under federal law, could do business in other provinces and territories. In one of these, *John Deere Plow v. Agnew*,[37] Duff ruled that a company incorporated under Dominion legislation could ship goods to British Columbia, and bring a lawsuit in B.C. courts to recover the cost of the goods, without being said to be carrying on business in the province, which would have required registration under the provincial Companies Act.

In 1910, the federal government formulated a bill requiring all insurance companies doing business in Canada to get a licence from Ottawa. On a reference, the Supreme Court declared it invalid. Duff's opinions in the case make a good example of his interpretive approach. He held that the insurance business could not be categorized as "trade and commerce" and hence amenable to federal regulation; it fell into the category of "property and civil rights," and was thus subject only to provincial regulation. Moreover, the federal government could not use its general power to oust provincial jurisdiction over a "local" matter merely because a particular activity, in this case insurance, was an important element of the country's business. The federal government appealed unsuccessfully to the Privy Council whose judgement, given by Lord Haldane, agreed with Duff: the federal power to regulate trade and commerce could not be invoked to regulate "a particular trade in which Canadians would otherwise be free to engage in in the provinces."[38]

In another reference, the court answered several questions about the legal capacity of provincially or federally incorporated companies to carry on their business and the territorial limitations of such companies; the various judges gave various opinions, the accumulation of which was not helpful in defining what a federally or provincially incorporated company had power to do, or where it could operate. A year later, however, on a direct appeal from British Columbia which bypassed the Supreme Court, the Privy Council at last began to shed some light on this vexed question. It invalidated British Columbia legislation which required licensing by companies incorporated under federal law as a condition for doing business in the province, on the grounds that a province could not inhibit the capacity of such federally incorporated companies.[40] This was a corollary to Duff's earlier ruling in the *Agnew* case on the powers of federally incorporated companies. And in the *Bonanza* case of 1916, the Privy Council authoritatively relaxed the territorial limitations placed upon the two classes of companies by holding that despite such limitation, a company "with provincial objects" acquired the capacity to do business in another province, or another country for that matter, if it chose.[41] In this ruling, the Privy Council reversed a Supreme Court decision by Duff and his colleagues. In fact, it is hard to reconcile the views Duff expressed in the *Bonanza* case with those of *Ottawa Fire Insurance*; in the one, he and two other judges took a limited view of companies' extraterritorial capacity, while in the other he had taken a broad view.

The appeals to the Privy Council in the *Bonanza* case and the reference on the insurance question were heard at the same session, and concluded before it heard the appeal on the companies reference. By the time the latter arrived, the Judicial Committee felt it had had enough appeals from Canada on the powers of companies; Haldane expressed exasperation at the government's practice of seeking references on abstract questions.[42] His concern, which was shared by all the judges, was that since references were by nature abstract, involving opinion only, such opinions lacked the binding character of decisions in actual lawsuits.

These early Ottawa years during which Duff established the basis of his reputation were on the whole satisfying professionally as well as pleasurable socially. However, one matter which had caused him distress in British Columbia continued to cause concern. The festering dispute between Hunter and Martin exploded into notoriety and became a public scandal which Laurier and Duff tried to quell. The contumacious but clever Martin was simply not suited to sit on the bench with Hunter, also clever but an urbane bon vivant. Jealous of Hunter's appointment as chief justice, Martin refused to accept judicial duties that did not suit his convenience. In retaliation, Hunter had persuaded the attorney-general to enact a Rule of Court specifying the chief justice's power to assign judges to particular cases. Martin took this as a personal affront and refused to carry out any assignment that was not made in writing and in meticulous detail.

The war was waged largely in private until 1907. Early in that year, however, there was open friction in an appeal to the Full Court heard by Hunter, Martin, and another colleague. Hunter and the third judge decided to make an immediate ruling but Martin wished to "reserve" his to allow himself time to think it over. When Hunter remonstrated with him, Martin left the bench remarking that it seemed his services were being dispensed with. The chief justice responded by saying sarcastically "that his services could be dispensed with all right."[43] Provoked by this and other incidents with Martin, Hunter, who shared Duff's weakness for liquor, began to drink heavily during the day, at the Union Club if he was in Victoria or at the Vancouver Club on the mainland, afterwards falling asleep on the bench. Early in 1908, when Hunter's misconduct could be ignored no longer, Laurier asked Duff's assistance in bringing his old friend to his senses.

Duff was not optimistic — "I have not much hope of doing anything with Hunter"[44] — but he did make a journey to British Columbia that turned out to be futile. He saw Hunter again early in 1909, and this time his visit may have borne fruit, though it was too late to stop the whole unseemly business from being aired in the Senate, where Senator Hewitt Bostock moved successfully for a public inquiry.[45] Based on what Duff told him, however, the justice minister felt that Hunter would reform himself, and he recommended to Laurier that no further action be taken. Laurier reluctantly followed this advice, but when Hunter sent a grateful note, he wrote to castigate him.

> I am in receipt of your letter and I hasten to reply to it. You owe me no thanks whatever, for I must tell you frankly that if I had been in charge of the matter, the petition brought against you would have been dealt with differently, but the Minister of Justice thought otherwise and I felt bound to defer my judgment to his own.
>
> You may deem my language harsh; I do not think so, nor do I believe that you can have that impression yourself. If you will remember the circumstances under which you were appointed, I had your word conveyed to me by a mutual friend that you would never touch a drop of liquor. I leave it to you to answer if you have kept that promise. When I say I leave it to you to answer, I do not mean that you should give me your answer but that you should answer to yourself.

Hunter had said he had learned to be particularly careful of his behaviour in a "small community," and this angered the prime minister.

> I must tell you frankly that I do not like this sentence. Whether it be in a small or large community, I expect a man to keep his word.
>
> If you will keep the resolve which you conveyed to me in which, I

believe, you were quite sincere, but which unfortunately you forgot, and if once more you take the resolve to be true to it, I have no doubt you will be an honour to the Bench because everyone acknowledges, and I am the first in that respect, the great ability with which you have been endowed and which ought to bring you in the very front ranks of the eminent judges of the land.[46]

Laurier wisely removed Martin from Hunter's court that same year, naming him to the newly established court of appeal of which he eventually became chief justice. Hunter continued in his post until he died in 1929.

There was some parallel between Hunter's problems and those of his friend. Duff may have been denied the chief justiceship of Canada in 1924 because of his drinking, and when R.B. Bennett finally gave him the promotion in 1933, he did so only after expressing serious reservations and extracting a pledge of good behaviour.

Financial woes, reaching all the way from British Columbia, also continued to plague Duff. He had no sense of business management; money came to hand and was as soon spent. With luck, some was left over for investments that might have proved profitable if Duff had taken independent financial advice and not relied for counsel on his well-meaning but incurably optimistic brother-in-law J. Edward Bird, who had moved from Barrie to Vancouver to practise law. When Lizzie and Duff left Victoria for Ottawa in 1906, Duff placed such small amounts of money as he had in Bird's hands. Lizzie possessed a bit of family money of her own, and her brother looked after this as well.

There is an old truism that one should avoid business dealings with relatives; they frequently lead to trouble or embarrassment. In Bird's correspondence with Duff over many years, the same theme recurs constantly: the investments are always sound, but there is always a shortage of cash to make payments on the borrowings which provided the money to make the investments in the first place. On such occasions Duff, whose personal spending habits left him perennially broke, had to raise money. In 1913 he borrowed a thousand dollars from a bank as a contribution towards some investment property in Vancouver; he was not able to repay the loan until four years later.[47] Somehow, his personal relations with Bird remained cordial none the less.

In June 1914 he and Lizzie sailed for Europe intending to spend four months in England and on the Continent, but the outbreak of hostilities abruptly forced their return to Ottawa. The Great War interrupted the even flow of their lives, but it also turned Duff into a national figure.

# 8

# Public figure

BY 1914, of the judges serving at the time of Duff's appointment, Maclennan and Girouard had gone, to be replaced by F.A. Anglin and L.P. Brodeur. Sir Charles Fitzpatrick presided over a court of five justices, in order of seniority after himself, Davies, Idington, Duff, Anglin, and Brodeur, with Duff still the only westerner. Although cut from the same political cloth as Fitzpatrick, Duff remained wary of him; a man of powerful intellect and many talents, the chief justice was inclined to deviousness. Davies, a decent man, has left no imprint on the jurisprudence of this country; Brodeur was an undistinguished judge. Idington, an attractive figure, stood out as the most outspoken man ever to sit on the Supreme Court of Canada. Anglin, the same age as Duff, had been appointed in 1909 after five years as a judge of the Ontario High Court.

Until fairly recently, and certainly until the 1930s, appointment to high judicial office depended as much on politics and religion as it did on talent. If in Britain the Church of England is the Conservative party at prayers, in Canada, from 1900 until Duff's retirement in 1944, the Supreme Court of Canada was the Liberal party in court. Common political backgrounds did not ensure harmony among the judges, however; Duff himself had no real intimate in the prewar court, and no truly close friendship with any colleague until the appointment of Mr. Justice Davis in 1935.

By the outbreak of war, Duff had established his reputation as a hardworking judge whose legal opinions commanded respect among fellow judges and lawyers; early in 1916, a scandal concerning munitions supply made a reputation for him with the general public. The political storm brought down on the Borden government swirled chiefly around one of the two central figures, the colourful minister of Militia and Defence, Sir Sam Hughes. His relationship with Col. J.W. Allison, the other central figure, and their joint relations with the Shell Committee, the British War Office's purchasing agency in Canada for munitions, led to the appointment of a royal commission with Duff and Sir William Meredith, chief justice of Ontario, as its members.

Soon after war began, the British government had asked Canadian officials about the availability of shells and fuses in Canada, whether manufactured there or in the United States. Hughes had persuaded them to set up the Shell Committee, an unincorporated body with no legal status in itself, to act as procurement agent. The two senior army officers running the committee's affairs in Canada and authorized to contract for munitions purchases were answerable only to the British government and spent only British money. The Canadian government had no financial responsibility for its operations, but did, of course, have an understandable interest in the committee as one means of successfully prosecuting the war, particularly since Hughes had always worked in close co-operation with it.

Allison, a Canadian, was a munitions dealer, a broker who represented the Vickers company in the United States and spent most of his time in that country, where he was well known to American munitions manufacturers and other middlemen who also made handsome sums from the sale of arms. He lived in a mansion near Brockville, Ontario, and moved in the shadowy world of weapons suppliers where intrigue in financial arrangements was general and political connections always useful. His close links with the Liberal Party were remarked on in the ensuing publicity.

In February 1915, Allison and an American arms broker with the unlikely name of Yoakum signed a secret agreement by which they would split equally any commission either of them received for arranging or procuring government munitions contracts. In the spring and summer of that year, the Shell Committee endeavoured on War Office instructions to procure a substantial quantity of high-explosive shells and fuses; discovering that no Canadian manufacturer could supply these within a short period of time, however, the committee turned to U.S. sources. Hughes advised its directors to see Allison, who had American contacts. Allison introduced them to Yoakum, who in turn arranged a contract with an American company, which also agreed to pay him a large commission. Allison's share, though never precisely determined, would exceed $220,000.

Hughes had no inkling of the arrangement between Allison and Yoakum; Allison had beguiled him into believing he was entirely disinterested and had brought Yoakum into the negotiations only out of friendship for Hughes. Early in 1916, however, rumours circulated that corrupt profits had been made on the previous year's fuse contract and Allison and Hughes were involved. The Liberal opposition in Parliament, or some members of it, hired a New York private detective to ferret out the details of the two men's involvement. The fact that this detective turned out to have pro-German sympathies later attracted harsh comment from Conservative newspapers, which accused the Liberals of giving away sensitive information about the Canadian war effort.

Parliament debated the alleged improprieties by Hughes and Allison throughout March 1916, but not until the end of the month did the Liberals have enough data to make specific accusations. On 28 March George Kyte, a Nova Scotia Liberal member, charged in the House that Allison and Yoakum had divided a commission of $475,000 from the fuse contracts and were to receive still further commissions for other contracts from the Shell Committee. (As it turned out, no other commission was paid.) Kyte, by innuendo, implicated Hughes in all this, since he had given written approval for the fuse contract.

With sardonic humour, Borden recorded in his diary that Kyte had "finally exploded his bomb."[1] And realizing the serious political implications of the charges against Hughes, the prime minister acted quickly. On the 29th, he informed the Governor-General of his intention to issue a royal commission even though no Canadian funds were involved in the alleged scandal, and on the same day he sent a long telegram to High Commissioner Sir George Perley in London, giving the substance of Kyte's charges and asking him to notify the British of the government's plan to hold an inquiry.[2] Borden also cabled this information to Hughes, who was in the United Kingdom; Hughes replied at once, asserting his innocence and announcing his return by the first available ship to defend himself and the government.[3] On the following day, the 30th, Borden met with his cabinet to discuss the commission's appointment; all ministers agreed on its necessity, and discussion was limited to its composition. In view of the nature of the charges against Hughes, Borden decided at the outset to avoid anything that could be seen as a tory cover-up. He recommended a commission of two judges, one Conservative by background and the other a Liberal. Duff and the Ontario chief justice, a former Conservative, were his choices. After the cabinet meeting Borden telephoned the two men, both of whom readily agreed to serve, and later that day he disclosed the plan to an excited House of Commons. His alacrity had taken the wind out of the opposition's sails; he noted with pleasure how "Laurier was evidently non-plussed & showed his disappointment & irritation in a very petulant manner."[4]

Newspapers throughout Canada applauded both Borden's decision and the choice of members, with many remarking on the political balance. Borden's even-handedness went still farther. He agreed that the government would pay for a lawyer selected by Kyte to represent him at the hearings, as well as one chosen by Laurier to represent the official opposition. Meredith and Duff, following Borden's example, acted with almost equal speed. After a few private meetings, they convened their first session on 19 April in the dignified atmosphere of the committee room of the Board of Railway Commissioners. At the first session, an array of outstanding counsel appeared before them: Eugene Lafleur and the great Canadian nationalist J.S. Ewart represented Hughes, who had chosen from the best; Wallace Nesbitt and J.C. Laflamme appeared for the Shell Committee, and I.F. Hellmuth represented the government. E.F.G. Johnston acted for the Liberal opposition, and F.B. Carvell was there for Kyte. Allison had instructed G.F. Henderson to represent him.

Judges acting as commissioners do not sit as judges. Courtroom decorum is not always observed, and the technical rules of evidence do not invariably apply. Even so, politeness and civility are expected. Given the number of lawyers appearing on behalf of opposite points of view in the midst of a widely publicized political scandal, it is no wonder that verbal dogfights were frequent. The hearings were often acrimonious, and at times Meredith and Duff were hard-pressed to keep the squabbling lawyers in order. There were accusations of leaked documents, and worse, of a break-in at Hughes's office to get hold of confidential papers. The bitterest exchange occurred after Nesbitt insinuated that Carvell had stolen documents. The latter complained to the commissioners, "I don't want any nasty insinuations from Mr. Nesbitt ....That's the second time he has done that sort of thing and I don't intend to take it." "You will take anything I please to give you either here or elsewhere," Nesbitt fired back. Meredith protested, "This will have to stop." But Carvell persisted: "I don't think I should have to stand for this. It is not for him to cast contemptible slurs across the table at a man trying to conduct an examination in an honourable way." Duff then intervened. "Just a moment, please," he said: "Mr. Nesbitt's observation should not have been made and if that sort of thing is to continue I cannot sit here any longer." As a former judge of the Supreme Court of Canada, Nesbitt ought to have known better; he had overstepped the bounds of professional decorum.

Yoakum testified, freely admitting that he had received the commission; he saw the agreement between himself and Allison as a perfectly normal business transaction. Allison testified to the same effect. His bland denial of impropriety failed to impress Duff, who "declared with emphasis," as the Ottawa *Evening Journal* put it, "Here is the situation...Allison, as the confidential adviser of the Minister of the Militia and the Shell Committee put his hand into the till to the extent of $220,000." This drew the comment from Allison's lawyer G.F. Henderson, "That is a strong expression," to which Duff replied, "Of course it is a strong expression...I intended it to be a strong expression."

The star witness was undoubtedly Sam Hughes. Pugnacious, argumentative, unrepentant, he dominated the hearings from the witness stand and overpowered the lawyers who dared to cross-examine him. He had alienated his cabinet colleagues, however, and caused the Borden government acute embarrassment by his persistent and intemperate defence of Allison long after it must have been obvious that Allison had played him for a fool. Even as late as 13 May, well after the hearings had started, Hughes defended Allison in the House as one "who has the honour of being Vickers' representative of the British government as agent in the United States of America in respect of very large matters of international concern." And he vilified one senior official who questioned the transactions, claiming that Allison had "more honour in his little finger than the Auditor-General has in his whole carcass."[5] Under the headline, "Some Hughes High-Explosives," the Ottawa *Evening Journal* offered a selection of his thrusts at opposition lawyers: "I am not here to gratify any lawyer who is paid ten dollars an hour to cross-examine me;" "I am not the keeper of Allison's conscience," and, "I am not directing the war; if I were things would go differently."[6] These sallies drew loud laughter from an appreciative gallery.

Six weeks after the hearings, Meredith and Duff brought down their report. They exonerated Hughes from all charges of corruption; Allison's conduct could not be "justified or excused." Newspaper reaction was generally favourable, although a few journals thought that corruption might have been uncovered by an investigation with wider terms of reference. No criminal charges were laid against Allison, but his regiment, at the request of a reluctant Hughes, stripped him of his colonelcy, perhaps the unkindest cut of all.

Feeling that he had done a conscientious job, Duff was hurt to receive no word of thanks from Borden or any member of his government. This rankled: late in December 1916 he spoke of it to an official who reported the conversation to the prime minister:

> At your request and because of his high regard and admiration for you, [Duff] accepted what was to him a rather distasteful task as a member of the commission to investigate the charges against General Sir Sam Hughes. He thought he had carried out his part of it to the satisfaction of the Government, yet you had not said one word about it to him since.[7]

Borden repaired the omission by sending Duff a New Year's message of gratitude for his services.[8] But there was an additional reason for Duff's rancour. The government had offered him and Meredith honoraria of five thousand dollars apiece. Meredith accepted, but Duff refused: the Supreme Court Act prohibited any judge from "holding any other office or emolument," and another federal statute forbade any federally appointed judge (and this would have included Meredith) to engage directly or indirectly "in any occupation or business other than his judicial duties."[9] What is more, the province of Ontario already paid its judges an added thousand dollars a year for extra services they might be called upon to perform "under any Act of the legislature."[10] Meredith felt able to steer through the reefs of the law because the payment was described as an honorarium. Duff, to whom it would have been a godsend amounting to two thirds of his annual salary, refused on principle, believing that acceptance would violate the intent of the legislation. He was outraged when he found out that Meredith had taken the money. Duff remained consistent in his view; he accepted only his out-of-pocket expenses, and even then reluctantly, for work on later commissions and public inquiries.

As the war ground on into the summer of 1917, the Borden regime faced a leadership crisis, and Duff was among those seen as possible strongmen in a reconstructed government. Added to the debilitating strain of the all-out war effort was that of a crisis then shaking the whole country: the crisis over conscription. Forced enlistment for military service was an explosive issue, especially in Quebec, but such were the pressures and such the need that the government felt it had to be done. Cabinet had at its disposal the War Measures Act of 1914 that gave it unlimited authority to make emergency regulations for such purposes as censorship and the arrest and detention of citizens; although the Act did not expressly refer to it, conscription would certainly have come within its ambit. However, in mid-1917 the Borden government brought in specific legislation, the Military Service Act, to meet the increasing demand for men to serve in the trenches of Europe. Borden, who favoured conscription, had members within his government opposed to it; Laurier, who opposed it, had caucus members in favour of it. Western Canada mainly supported the measure; French Canada was dead set against it.

With division both in the country and in its two major political parties, Borden considered as early as May 1917 forming a coalition or union government, to include pro-conscriptionist members of both parties, so that the measure could be passed with the minimum of damage to the unity of the country. He invited Laurier to join, but the Liberal leader, deeply worried about his position in Quebec, did not wish to be a member of a government committed to compulsory military service. When even pro-conscriptionist Liberals who were possible candidates expressed doubts about serving under Borden as prime minister, he cast about for a likely successor.

On 9 June Dr. J.D. Reid, the customs minister and one of Borden's confidants, told him that "Justice Duff is willing to join" as a representative of the west; if this was confirmed, Reid "would take him and run him in Victoria, B.C."[11] This proposal did not involve government leadership, simply membership: Borden mulled it over along with proposals for such other new men as T.A. Crerar and N.W. Rowell, the Liberal leader in

Ontario. In considering Duff's suitability, he noted that Fitzpatrick "distrusts Duff and thinks he is intriguing against the government."[12] Fitzpatrick, like Duff, never completely shed his political colours.

On 5 July both Borden and Arthur Meighen met with Clifford Sifton, who suggested Duff for leader of a new government; Sifton called him the "leader the Liberals had in mind."[13] Although Borden recorded in his diary that he and Meighen resolved to speak to Duff, apparently he did not do so until the following month, when, after talks with him on the 10th and 11th, he told Meighen and Reid of "my idea of advising gov.gen. to call on Duff to form Union government."[14] His two listeners were appalled at the plan which, if carried out, would in their opinion destroy the Conservative Party.[15]

In spite of this strong opposition from his two closest colleagues, Borden did not discard the idea. After receiving a telegram from a group of Liberal stalwarts in western Canada urging a "change of leadership" by the choice of Sir George Foster or Duff or Sir Adam Beck or Sir William Mulock, he decided he would speak to Duff again when he had met his caucus. On 29 August, caucus gave him so tumultuous a vote of confidence as leader that he was moved to tearful silence. From then on he abandoned any idea of resigning. It has been suggested that Borden extracted the vote by a calculated threat to go,[16] but no hint of any such motive appears in his memoirs or diaries.

The day before caucus, the Ottawa *Citizen* and Toronto *Daily News* had carried stories about the proposal that either Duff or one of the three other men assume the leadership of a new government. Duff wrote Borden on the same day to disclaim any intention of seeking the leadership,[17] and the prime minister replied before going to the meeting:

> I should be glad to find some honourable path to relief from my present duties and responsibilities which are severe beyond the conception of anyone who has not been brought closely in touch with them. If I should lay them down, they could be taken up by no hands more capable than your own.[18]

From 29 August on, however, his talks with Duff were about coming into the cabinet. They next met on 31 August, when Duff said he would join on condition that W.N. Tilley of Toronto be invited also. Borden recorded that the judge "spoke in highest terms of Tilley's character and ability. Told him I would consider."[19] The following day, Borden "played golf with Duff and beat him badly."[20] No doubt the two of them discussed affairs of state between strokes. The prime minister made a determined effort to persuade Tilley to join the cabinet and thus get Duff in. Both Borden and Reid saw Tilley, Borden telling him that "it was his duty to enlist in public life for the rest of the war and that his actions would create a profound expression."[21] It was all to no avail; Tilley remained adamant, so did Duff, and neither entered the government. Borden was disappointed, not to say exasperated: "Duff and Tilley evidently have not idea of entering the government. They lack the spirit which prompted our young men to cross the seas and go over the parapet."[22] Borden formed his union government in October by taking a number of Liberals into the cabinet, among them N.W. Rowell and Hugh Guthrie, each of whom became Duff's close friend. At the general election in December, Borden won a substantial mandate.

Duff's insistence that Tilley join the government may possibly be explained by a wish to have a close confidant by him if he risked exchanging high judicial office for an uncertain political career. Whatever his reasons, he had lost his last chance at political office. The astonishing thing about the whole affair is that a junior judge of the Supreme Court of Canada should even have been thought of as a potential cabinet minister and conceivably prime minister. It was certainly not because of broad popularity or countrywide acclaim. The answer lay in the machinations of politics. Clifford Sifton, who suggested him as a prime-ministerial candidate in 1917, had in 1908, unknown to Duff, advised Laurier to take him into the cabinet.[23] When one recalls Sifton's lack of enthusiasm in appointing Duff as one of the Canadian counsel to the 1903 tribunal, it does seem odd that only a few years later he should give Laurier that advice, and odder still that in 1917 he should be telling Borden to consider Duff as the head of a union government.

What is clear is that Duff, though he might have accepted a cabinet portfolio, would not have given in to a draft to make him prime minister. By 1917 he had discarded any thoughts of political greatness he might have had. In a 1943 interview, he told the Winnipeg journalist Grant Dexter that he was quite unfitted to hold the highest political office in the land, and that when he heard his name being bandied about, he at once disclaimed any intention of seeking it. One is left with the impression that in 1917 Duff lost either his nerve or his desire for any career in politics. Perhaps it is not irrelevant that Fitzpatrick had become restless in office by 1917; he left the next year to become Lieutenant-Governor of Quebec. It is likely that Duff saw in his eventual departure a possibility of advancement to the chief justiceship, in his eyes a greater opportunity for self-achievement than mere cabinet rank. However, the Borden government that Duff had declined to join made Davies chief justice instead. Duff went back to biding his time; he could not have anticipated having to do so for another fifteen years.

Debate in Parliament on the cause of the 1917 turmoil, the Military Service Act, ended with its enactment in late August; Duff, in his capacity as Administrator, gave the royal assent. Hardly a week after he had refused a cabinet post, he found himself chosen by Borden as the central appeal judge under the Act, charged with the "fundamentally difficult [task] in co-ordinating the Military and Civil needs of the Dominion, in a country already stripped of its finest personnel."[24] The Military Service Act conscripted men into six groups according to age and marital status, with younger bachelors liable for service in the Canadian Expeditionary Force, either in Canada or overseas, before older married men. Unlike the American selective draft of more recent years, it imposed the duty to serve on every male below age forty-five. All those potentially liable to be called up were required to register, but they could apply for exemption to a "local tribunal" of laymen; if they were unsuccessful there, they could go before an "appeal tribunal," a single judge of a high court; and if still unsuccessful a claimant could, with permission, appeal to Duff who presided in Ottawa as the central appeal judge for the whole country. By a similar process, a "public representative," as he was called, could appeal a decision granting exemption on behalf of the military.

Although Duff did hear appeals involving individual exemptions, he did so only in instances viewed as test cases or where matters of principle were involved. The Military Service Act allowed exemption from military service only if this was consistent with the "national interest." Such people as farmers, skilled and irreplaceable tradesmen, and vital workers on the railways, would generally be exempted. What Duff tried to do was define a rule applicable to future cases that would "balance judicially and impartially the necessities of the individual against those of the State, and the civil against the Military requirement of the nation."[25] He looked at groups of cases so that a single decision could dispose of a number of individual appeals. For example, he made a ruling in a case involving several thousand clerks employed by all the chartered banks of Canada. The process was intentionally impersonal: men appealing to local or appeal tribunals were discouraged from appearing personally, and the law prevented them from engaging lawyers to represent them; all appeals to Duff were in writing, and he ruled without seeing or hearing the persons affected. Sometimes the justice minister referred a difficult question of eligibility for Duff's opinion, much in the style of a "reference" to the Supreme Court of Canada by the Governor-General in Council.

With the Act's proclamation on 30 August 1917, the justice department embarked on a crash implementation programme that finished early in December, although no men were actually called up for service until a month after this. The laborious task of hearing appeals for exemption began in mid-November and, with the exceptions of Quebec and Saskatchewan, was substantially completed by the end of that month. By the end of January, most appeals to the appeal tribunals from local decisions had been disposed of, and Duff's work began in earnest. For the next five months, he and his staff toiled to assemble individual appeals into groups for collective rulings. Group appeals carried the risk that the merits of an individual's case might be overlooked; this was an ever-present danger and one of continuing concern to Duff and his colleagues. During those five months, he disposed of over forty-two thousand cases; even though the bulk of these were accounted for in groups, the task placed a severe strain on his health, particularly since he attempted to keep up with his court duties, and by August he was in a state of nervous collapse. Among the group appeals decided were ones involving law students and university professors. None persuaded Duff that the national interest required them to remain in civilian life.

Quebec opposition to the Military Service Act posed special problems. Many citizens in other provinces felt, with the Act's director, that in Quebec there was "no universal recognition of the obligations of citizenship."[26] Many French Canadians opposed conscription on the grounds that it forced men to fight for England; English Canadians, seeing France as the great ally, puzzled endlessly that their centuries-settled francophone compatriots did not feel the same solidarity with that country that they themselves felt with the British Isles. Duff blamed the church:

> The Church in Quebec was against us in the war — that is to say, it was Catholic in the hierarchical ultra montaine sense — sympathetic with Austria and with the Spanish hierarchy. The Bishops did everything in their power to prevent people enlisting. The populace in itself was indifferent at the beginning....Generally, Quebec was sullen with the Church antagonistic. Then, in 1917, conscription threw the whole population of the Province into the hostile camp.[27]

In conscription's early stages the Quebec local tribunals granted exemptions, as Borden said in the House, "almost wholesale," impelling the government

> to see to it that by appeals we brought these cases up to the Central Appeal Judge so that in the end there would be a fair, a just, a uniform and an impartial administration of that Act for all the provinces and all the people of Canada.[28]

The prime minister blamed this state of affairs on Henri Bourassa and Armand Lavergne, the editors of *Le Devoir*, who had been preaching "agitation and sedition."[29]

Late in March 1918, serious riots broke out in Quebec City; crowds rampaged through the streets destroying military property, files, and documents. Though the riots got beyond police control, the civil authorities took no steps to quell them. The officer commanding the military district called out the troops to restore order on his own initiative. Despite continued bitterness in French Canada, no further disturbance occurred, and in fact, partly because the public representative speeded a host of appeals on to Duff, Quebec, according to the director, eventually did "reasonably well in furnishing men under the compulsory draft."[30]

Laurier attempted to use his influence with Duff for personal favours; though he was not the only person to do so he was certainly the most notable. He first requested exemption for his secretary. Duff wrote a circumspect reply, telling him in a "personal" letter that the man's case would likely be reviewed at some future time. Weeks later, Laurier tried to intercede again, this time on behalf of his valet. On this occasion Duff, not quite so circumspect, told Laurier that he would consider the application on receipt of a medical report. A month later, Laurier took up the cudgels once again on behalf of a widow, asking Duff's help in having her son discharged from service.[31] It is not known what reply was made to this request.

By April 1918 manpower was running so short on the Western Front that Ottawa felt obliged to enlarge the categories subject to conscription. Wanting to proceed with all possible haste, the cabinet decided to make the change by order-in-council rather than the more time-consuming process of amending the Military Service Act itself. The decision gave rise to notable litigation. Section 13 provided that nothing should "limit...the powers of the Governor-in-Council under the War Measures Act, 1914." The latter Act, as will be recalled, conferred wide powers for securing the country's defence. The first of two orders-in-council passed in April directed all men aged nineteen to register, though in the end none was called up for service, and the second called up all men between the ages of twenty and twenty-two. This effectively cancelled every exemption previously allowed to men of those ages. An exempted man named Gray applied to the Supreme Court of Canada for a writ of habeas corpus, arguing that an exemption granted under the Military Service Act after due process could not be nullified by a mere order-in-council. A majority of the Supreme Court, including Fitzpatrick and Duff, decided otherwise.[32]

The decision, an important one, is still valid and will be for as long as the War Measures Act remains in force in its present form. In 1970, Prime Minister Trudeau invoked the very provision the Borden government relied on in 1918, the right of the Governor-in-Council to pass emergency orders in a case of "war, invasion or insurrection, real or apprehended." The Supreme Court of Canada decided in the *Gray* case that the War Measures Act overrode a specific statute dealing with one aspect of the emergency.[33] The case virtually marked the end of Duff's work, although his duties did not terminate formally for another year. It had been a massive operation: by the war's end, local tribunals had heard over three hundred thousand appeals, granting exemption in approximately fifty-six thousand of them; appeal tribunals heard roughly one hundred and twenty thousand cases, granting exemption in eighty-six thousand. Of approximately forty-two thousand persons involved in appeals before Duff, roughly half were ordered to service.

There could be endless argument about the actual value of the Military Service Act in providing reinforcements. By the date of its passage, more than four hundred and thirty thousand Canadians had gone overseas as volunteers; its operation coincided with the last year of the war, during which just over a hundred and thirteen thousand were conscripted as "fighting fit." As to whether it had all been worthwhile, Duff himself had reservations. In 1940, he wrote optimistically to an English friend:

> We are exceedingly fortunate in the fact that Quebec recognizes the duty of Canadians to put forth all their strength. As you know, the attempt to enforce conscription in Quebec in the last war had effects which produced a certain kind of isolationism in that province that a good many people thought constituted a menace to the real political unity of the Confederation. The King and Queen, however, on their visit here made an extraordinary appeal to the natural chivalry of the French-Canadian people, and the attitude of the French-Canadians today is most gratifying to everybody.[34]

A year later, he had modified his views. In December 1941 Grant Dexter, a journalist who had Duff's ear, spoke to him about conscription and the proposed government referendum on the issue, keeping a record of this talk. Though disclaiming any wish "to take part in any political discussion: which might "injure the position of the court," Duff freely offered his views. "Conscription," he told Dexter, was "like prohibition — unenforceable except by the assent of the people." He had made inquiries and was informed that "the situation in Quebec was much more favourable than in the last war. To take a club to the province would be a tragedy." With gathering enthusiasm, he went on. "Nobody," he thought,

> except himself was aware of the fact that practically no French-Canadians were rounded up. The Quebec tribunals, although headed by superior court judges, gave exemptions automatically to French-Canadians and it was meaningless for the National Appeal Court to reverse their decisions. But they applied conscription against the English-speaking minority in Quebec with a rigor unparalleled. They gave no exemptions on any grounds and they thus created the deepest division, hatreds and so on.

Duff told Dexter that "to go for overseas conscription direct would be a disaster," and that he "took occasion to tell this to King when Hump Mitchell, Minister of Labour, was sworn in. King was very worried."

He finished by claiming with pardonable exaggeration that "the only two men who really knew what went on and who were still alive were Biggar and himself." The reference was to Oliver Mowat Biggar, who had left his Edmonton law practice for Ottawa to join the Military Service Council, the supervisory body that administered the Military Service Act in its early stages. The advice Duff gave King at the time of the second war is telling in two respects. Duff obviously believed that it would be unwise to use conscription again, and the fact that he, as chief justice, said so at all is significant. If King's Delphic phrase, "Not necessarily conscription, but conscription if necessary," did not originate with Duff, King must at the very least have been reinforced in his belief in the correctness of his approach by Duff's opinion. The episode is further confirmation that politics always coursed through the judge's veins.

Though he closed his office in June 1919, Duff retained all the records, moving them to the Supreme Court building for storage. A few years later, after the end of the war, he burned them with a secretary's help in what must have been a time-consuming task. Duff gave Dexter his reason for this extraordinary auto-da-fé:

> After the last war he could not bear the thought of having the conscription records placed anywhere where the public could reach them. The papers of the local tribunals and appeal bodies in Quebec were full of hatred and bitterness and would have been a living menace to national unity.

He told Dexter it was "after an illness" that he decided they had to be incinerated, and "he was glad to say that no real records of conscription existed."[35] Whether by design or coincidence, E.L. Newcombe, then deputy justice minister and later Duff's colleague on the court, also burned records he had amassed as chairman of the Military Service Council. Both men, both honourable men, believed they had acted in the national interest by denying future researchers the opportunity of ascertaining the truth.

# 9

## Privy councillor

BY AND LARGE, except for the constitutional cases, wartime litigation produced no important decisions. There were a few of interest. For example, the Supreme Court concluded by a majority in 1915 that fire insurance on a dwelling intended to be used as a "sporting house," a euphemism for "brothel," could not be enforced, since the insurance facilitated the carrying out of an immoral purpose. Duff disagreed, not because he approved of brothels but because he thought that since the same company insured brothels in other parts of the city of Calgary, areas apparently sanctioned unofficially by the police, or "licensed" as they were said to be in the case, the illegal purpose was irrelevant to the insurance risk. He had nothing but "impatience" with

> the posture of this company whose interest in the public morals finds adequate expression in a distinction between bawdy houses protected by the police, according to clearly understood convention, and bawdy houses whose toleration is more "irregular and precarious."

This elaborate passage of restrained contempt is a rare display of judicial emotion.[1]

Among the others Duff heard in wartime was his first case of labour law, in which, again dissenting from his colleagues, he ruled that union officials were justified in expelling two members for breaking union rules, even though they had lost their jobs as a result.[2] Two other decisions of that period illustrate Duff's mastery of the Quebec Civil Code. In the first of these he wrote a dissenting judgement filled with references to texts and opinions on doctrine and jurisprudence in the interpretation of the code[3] that he felt were applicable to the provisions featured in the litigation. In the second case the Supreme Court ruled, Duff again dissenting, that the French version of the code prevailed over the English. He pointed out that the enactment in English was intended to modify the provision as found in the French of the *Code Napoléon*, and thus decisions by French courts and writers were of no value in interpreting plain English language.[4] The earlier case went on to the Privy Council, which held that if the wording of the Civil Code is clear then it is wrong to rely on the opinions of French jurists as aids to interpretation. Ironically, Duff's view in the first case received implied criticism from the Privy Council whose opinions coincided with those expressed by him in the second. The apparent contradiction in Duff's thinking is but another illustration of the legal cliché that circumstances alter cases.

In 1918 came the first of several major shifts in the court's composition during Duff's time on it. When Sir Charles Fitzpatrick resigned on 21 October, Borden persuaded his cabinet colleagues to stifle their objections to Louis Davies's Liberal background and concur in naming him chief justice. Both Lafleur and Tilley were suggested for the vacancy created by this promotion, but it was P.B. Mignault, a former Conservative from Montreal, who joined the court.

Though he was junior to Davies, Duff felt he had a claim on the chief justiceship. His work in wartime had recently brought recognition for his extraordinary abilities in the broadly political as well as the judicial sphere. When word of his disappointment reached Borden, the prime minister saw him late in the month for an "interesting interview," at the end of which he told Duff that he would recommend him for creation as an Imperial privy councillor.[5] Since 1897, each chief justice of Canada, though no puisne or junior judge, had been sworn as a privy councillor: Strong, Taschereau, and Fitzpatrick had all been reasonably active as members.

The King's Privy Council had existed since the Middle Ages, but the Council's Judicial Committee did not come into existence until 1833, by an Act of the British Parliament. Though called not a "court" but a "board," the committee served in fact as the final court of appeal for the Empire (or Commonwealth) — not, however, for the United Kingdom itself, where the final appeal court has always been the House of Lords. Before 1833, appeals had been taken to the Privy Council, or, really, to the foot of the throne in accordance with historical tradition, but not until that year were they heard before only judges, a changing company whose numbers later included men from such overseas countries as India, Canada, Australia, and various British colonies.

Duff was immensely gratified by Borden's recommendation, and his emotion was in no way diminished by the simultaneous but inevitable recommendation of Davies. Both appointments were made on 1 January

The Duff brothers, Rolph (at left) and Lyman, about 1873. *W. Chase/Public Archives of Canada*

Isabella Duff and Emma on the beach at Liverpool, Nova Scotia, about 1874. *Public Archives of Canada*

The University of Toronto class of '85, with Lyman Duff seventh from the left in the second row up. Rolph is in the top row, fourth from the right, and Stuart Henderson at the far right in the bottom row; Gordon Hunter is fifth from the right in the fourth row. In the cameo, President Wilson; Paxton Young is second from the right in the row of professors. *University College Archives, University of Toronto*

The Reverend Charles Duff about 1890

The Speedside (Eramosa) church that was Charles Duff's first charge. *Photo by Rev. Robert Hyde*

Duff as he appeared when he was called to the British Columbia Bar in 1895

Duff (second from the left) on his first appearance in the British Columbia Court of Appeal. Others present include Aulay Morrison at the left and, second to fourth from the right, E.V. Bodwell, E.P. Davis, and L.G. McPhillips. *City Archives, Vancouver*

The Vancouver courthouse as it was during Duff's years in British Columbia.
*City Archives, Vancouver*

Duff's Victoria home at 1745 Rockland about 1904. *Public Archives of Canada*

The Alaska boundary tribunal outside the Foreign Office in Whitehall,
London 1903. Duff, bearded, is on
the right at the back. Aimé Geoffrion
stands in the same position on the
left, with F.C. Wade next to him at
the end of the back row. The tribunal
members are at the front: from the
left, Root, Jetté, Turner, Alverstone,
Lodge, and Aylesworth. *Public Archives
of Canada*

The Ottawa Supreme Court building
of Duff's time, shown here in the
1880s with the West Block of Parliament in the background. *Public
Archives of Canada*

Duff as he appeared soon after his
swearing-in for the Supreme Court of
Canada in 1906. *Public Archives of Canada*

The Privy Council in session, July 1920. From left to right: lords Atkinson, Cave,
Haldane, and Dunedin, and Duff. *Public Archives of Canada*

Lizzie Duff about 1920

The Duff residence on Golbourne Street, Ottawa, in 1911. *Public Archives of Canada*

1919. After Duff wound up his work as central appeal judge, he sailed for England with his wife late that June. On the morning of 1 July, wearing "plain dress (with frock coat)" as he had been instructed to do by the clerk of the council, he drove to Buckingham Palace to wait on King George and his councillors, among them the Archbishop of Canterbury and Lord Curzon. Duff and his fellow councillors-to-be stood in line before His Majesty. As their names were read by Curzon, Lord President of the Council, they knelt to take the oath of allegiance collectively. Then, individually, each moved forward to kneel and kiss the King's hand. They returned to their standing position to hear the clerk of the council read the oath of office, each councillor holding a New Testament in his lifted hand and repeating to himself the words,

> I do swear by Almighty God to be a true and faithful Servant under the King's Majesty as one of His Majesty's Privy Council....I will in all things to be moved, treated, and debated in Council, faithfully and truly declare my Mind and Opinion according to my Heart and Conscience; and will keep secret all Matters committed and revealed to me, or that shall be treated of secretly in Council....I will to my uttermost bear Faith and Allegiance to the King's Majesty.[6]

After shaking hands with his fellow councillors, the Right Honourable Lyman Poore Duff, for such was now his designation, left the royal audience to take his seat on the board that same day with the Earl of Birkenhead presiding. As F.E. Smith, Birkenhead had had a brilliant career as a barrister; he had just been created Lord Chancellor and, like Duff, sat for the first time on the Privy Council. Lord Haldane, politician, statesman, scientist, philosopher, and former Lord Chancellor, sat next to Birkenhead. The two other members of the board, lords Buckmaster and Parmoor, were distinguished English jurists.

Since 1833, the Judicial Committee's hearings have been held in a splendidly proportioned, lofty room in the Privy Council office on Downing Street immediately next door to what is now the residence of the prime minister. Antique oak chairs upholstered in red leather stand against finely panelled walls; graceful windows admit an ample light. The conduct of appeals here differs markedly from court proceedings in Canada. The judges enter the courtroom first to take their seats; only then do the lawyers go in. Lawyers wear robes and wigs; the judges do not. The lawyers sit like schoolboys at worn, sloping desks with inkwells. They address arguments to the judges sitting only a few feet away at a handsome semi-circular table. The result is that appeals are conducted in an intimate atmosphere, gentlemen chatting with gentlemen. In reaching a decision, the judges render "advice," since, though judicial officers, they are members of the Privy Council whose ancient role has always been to advise the Monarch. The advice of the Judicial

Committee is invariably taken, and forms a binding judgement. In Duff's time, only one judge gave advice, in a single opinion. Dissenting opinions were not recorded or disclosed, but they certainly existed. Duff occasionally dissented; in such instances the registrar sent a draft majority judgement to the dissenters, who were invited to comment, though as a rule they said nothing. In a famous Canadian case on which Duff did not sit, a dissenting judge wrote angrily in the margin of the formal record: "Lord Blanesburgh strongly dissented from this judgement which is generally considered to be wrong."[7] And there is a well-known Canadian constitutional case in which Lord Haldane, who wrote the judgement, had a very difficult time persuading two of the other four judges to come round to his point of view.[8]

Generally, judgements were rendered more speedily than they would be in Canada. By the time a case reached London, its bones had been well picked over by a series of lower courts, and their decisions had narrowed the issues. Because the overseas judges liked to dispose of cases before they sailed for home, judgements tended to be shorter and written in a compressed style. The style of judgement writing in the Privy Council differed unmistakably from that used by the same judges when sitting in other courts. It tended to produce brief statements of general principle rather than elaborate dissertations larded with quotations from other cases. The change of style is graphically illustrated by Duff himself. One would hardly deduce from reading the dozen or so judgements he wrote in the Privy Council that they were drafted by the same man who prepared a thousand or more, many of them tendentious, in Canada.

Trips to the Privy Council were prized by Canadian lawyers, for they became great social occasions. Starting with a train journey, they sailed as cabin-class passengers to England and stayed in the best hotels. Duff usually stayed in an apartment-hotel, though sometimes at the Hyde Park; he would visit lawyers if they were not actually engaged in a case before him, and they visited him. There was a chumminess among them.

A remarkable instance of this camaraderie occurred in 1927. The Supreme Court of Canada had ruled against the province of British Columbia in its attempt to levy a tax on the first purchaser of fuel oil, holding that the tax was indirect and hence beyond the province's jurisdiction, for the cost would be passed on to the ultimate consumer. Duff joined the majority, for whom Anglin wrote the judgement. The province appealed to the Privy Council, where Senator Farris appeared on its behalf before a board headed by Haldane. Duff did not sit on the appeal since he had made it a rule not to sit on any appeal from the Supreme Court, even in cases in which he had not participated; many of the Canadian cases, however, came directly from provincial courts of appeal, the *per saltum* appeals that bypassed Ottawa. The hearing started on a Friday; at the end of the day, Farris met Duff and lamented that he seemed to be losing. Duff, commiserating with his friend, invited Farris to join him at his hotel room the next morning to discuss the case. Fortified by gin fizzes, the two of them spent most of the day trying to devise arguments that would reverse Anglin's — and Duff's — judgement. Both lawyer and judge were unsuccessful. The case resumed the following Monday; the board heard Farris out, then told opposing counsel that they need not say anything as the appeal would be dismissed.[9]

On another occasion, Farris found his case shoved down the list, and this jeopardized his return voyage to Canada. Haldane, who was presiding, refused to accommodate him by readjusting the schedule. Duff leaned over to speak privately with Haldane, who then announced grudgingly that the appeal would be heard as originally scheduled. Later in the day, Duff remarked to Farris, "We mustn't let those beggars push us around, you know."[10]

Duff remained in London during July 1919 hearing fourteen cases, all from Canada, and delivering judgements in two of them. His colleagues all found the "heavy mass" of Canadian appeals, as Haldane described them, onerous work. That hard taskmaster, who replaced Birkenhead as president of the board, drove "through the Canadian Appeals, and the Indian Petitions ruthlessly...tolerating no delay." Buckmaster's health broke down under the strain, but still Haldane lamented, "My difficulty is to keep my colleagues at work."[11]

The remark was not directed at Duff, with whom he had quickly developed a close rapport that may have stemmed from a common interest in Liberal politics, but at Birkenhead. Haldane tended to regard Birkenhead, for all his brilliance, as a judicial butterfly, incapable of "real work,"[12] and quite willing to take credit for the labours of others:

> The Lord Chancellor is energetic in getting people to blow his trumpet. But...those interested know well that the law of Real Property [a massive and notable piece of legislation] is not a subject with which he is familiar, and that he did not fashion the Great Bill.

Haldane himself had had a considerable hand in the preparation of this important legislation, but there is no doubt that Birkenhead got the credit, since it is still referred to as one of his great achievements in office. He at least had the decency to give Haldane some recognition in the House of Lords, as the latter observed wryly: "The L. Chancellor made me sit by him in front of his Throne in a cocked hat & robes — to give the Royal Assent to the great Law of Property Bill. Well, I smiled, but did not refuse."[13]

A cryptic Haldane remark from the 1923 sessions seems to have been made with reference to Duff. "Yesterday," he wrote, "we made very substantial progress…and the end is coming in sight. I have to keep firm command of the Judge."[14] In the case in question, his colleagues were Birkenhead, Lord Sumner, Sir Henry Duke, and Duff. Duff was the only colleague to whom he could have referred in that vein; he would certainly not have spoken of Birkenhead as "the judge." Duff got on extremely well with Birkenhead despite the differences in their politics and personalities; they shared many intellectual pursuits and a common weakness, alcohol. Haldane's remark implied that the two of them had succumbed to temptation.

Duff's close friendship with Haldane, a mutually expressed "affection,"[15] became important. The law lord's influence on the Canadian constitution in the twentieth century was as pervasive as Watson's had been in the nineteenth. And his view of the nature of Confederation and the distribution of powers among its governments confirmed Duff's own opinion. Haldane knew his own strength:

> I have to write practically all the judgements in the Constitutional cases, for the good reason that since Lord Watson's time there has been no other who knew this branch of learning. The Canadians now call me the "father of the Privy Council" and want my portrait hung up there.

A month later, writing about a dinner party Duff and his wife had attended at his house, he made the comment that "he & I are the repositories — so the Prime Minister of Canada says — of learning about the Canadian Constitution" — the prime minister presumably being Meighen, then in office.[16] Haldane noted with pride the day on which his judgements equalled in number those written by Lord Watson.

Although Duff may have taken comfort from Haldane's views, he himself had been responsible for their formulation in at least one and perhaps two important respects. In the *Insurance Reference* case, Duff rejected the notion that the federal government's use of its general "peace, order, and good government" power to regulate a particular business could be justified simply on the grounds of size: "I do not think that the fact that the business of insurance has grown to great proportions affects the question in the least."[17] In the Privy Council appeal, Haldane picked up this theme, remarking, "No doubt the business of insurance is a very important one, which has attained great dimensions in Canada," but ruled that the federal government's claim to regulate it merely because of its dimensions still amounted to an intrusion on provincial authority.[18] He may also have been swayed by Duff's powerful argument in the *Companies* reference that to allow the federal government to exercise its general power because a matter was "truly of national interest or importance" would leave the provinces "very little of that local autonomy which the parties to the Confederation Compact believed they had reserved to them."[19] Duff went on to point out that "those who were responsible for the scheme of Confederation deliberately rejected the American system of constitutional limitations," by which he meant that provinces were paramount in their spheres, free from intrusion by Ottawa, a view with which Haldane heartily agreed.

The *Board of Commerce* case decided by the Supreme Court of Canada in 1920 involved the validity of combines legislation which prohibited unfair profits on the sale of the necessities of life. Three judges saw nothing wrong with the legislation, but Duff and two others declared it invalid. Duff rejected the argument that the law could be supported as a legitimate exercise of the general power, holding that this power could be exercised only if the "matter dealt with shall be one of unquestioned Canadian interest and importance," and then only if the law invaded none of the specific fields of legislation reserved to provinces.[20] On appeal, Haldane agreed, but taking the proposition slightly farther, he enunciated for the first time what has become known as the "emergency test" of the extent of the general power:

> Circumstances are conceivable, such as those of war or famine, when the peace, order and good government of the Dominion might be imperilled under conditions so exceptional that they require legislation of a character in reality beyond anything provided for by the enumerated heads in either Section 92 or Section 91 itself.[21]

In the *Fort Frances* case Haldane used the word "emergency" for the first time in this context:

> The general control of property and civil rights for normal purposes remains with the Provincial Legislature. But questions may arise by reason of the special circumstances of [a] national emergency which concern nothing short of the peace, order and good government of Canada as a whole.[22]

Thus, Duff seems to have inspired the "emergency" doctrine of the general power which has given rise to so much discussion and litigation,[23] the anti-inflation law of recent years being a notable example. In the *Board of Commerce* case, Duff reiterated the traditional approach to the interpretation of Sections 91 and 92 of the British North America Act, one he shared with Haldane:

> The ultimate social, economic or political aims of the legislator cannot, I think, determine the category into which the matters dealt with fall in order to determine the question whether the jurisdiction to enact it is given by Section 91 or Section 92. The immediate operation and effect of

the legislation, or the effect that the legislation is calculated immediately to produce must alone, I think, be considered.[24]

Of the judgements Duff delivered in the Privy Council, only one, the *Reciprocal Insurers* decision of 1923,[25] has become a leading case. The federal government sought to regulate insurance companies by making it an offence under the Criminal Code for them to carry on business without a licence from Ottawa. Duff and his colleagues lords Haldane, Buckmaster, Shaw, and Sumner, heard the arguments in July but Duff took an unusually long time to prepare the judgement, undoubtedly because it was his first in an important case. Late in November the Privy Council registrar wrote discreetly to inquire when Duff would complete his task, and Duff's reply is illuminating:

> I found myself thoroughly dissatisfied with the judgement as I had written it, and I shall still keep it a few days longer. The judgement is a most important one; more important, from our point of view in this country, than any which the Privy Council has delivered for a long time. The practical effect of it will be that, in the revision of the Dominion Statutes, a great amount of Dominion legislation will have to be discarded as *ultra vires*. Many of the statutes to be discarded are statutes dealing with practical matters of business which are constantly in practical operation, and the disappearance of Dominion legislation will necessarily lead to the enactment of similar legislation by the provincial legislature. In course of this, the judgement will be subjected to critical examination by journalists and politicians as well as by lawyers, and will be the subject of much general discussion, not only in the Dominion Parliament but in the Legislatures of various provinces. It is therefore important that it present as few vulnerable points as possible. I do not think there is any real urgency, although insurance people are no doubt vitally interested.[26]

A month later he finished it, sending it off to Haldane:

> I am enclosing the judgment of the insurance case...I must apologize for the unconscionable time it has taken to hatch, but...the decision will in fact necessarily attract a great deal of attention, and I have given it the best attention I could....I thought it better...to bring out the fact that there is nothing new in the doctrine on which the decision rests by referring to some of the earlier cases. The Alberta decision in 1916, taken together with the Board of Commerce decision in 1922, is of course conclusive, but I think it is on the whole better that there should be some elaboration. I am afraid that I elaborated too much; I hope you will be ruthless in applying the pruning knife wherever it occurs to you to do so.[27]

Neither Haldane nor the other judges applied any "pruning knife"; they accepted without textual change what Duff had written. In his judgement which struck down the federal regulation, he referred to a decision of the United States Supreme Court dealing with "colourable" legislation, that is the enactment of illegal legislation under the guise of legality. He commented to Haldane that

> the discussion of the judgment of the Supreme Court of the United States is, I suppose, a little out of the ordinary course, but it seemed to me rather useful as shewing that the doctrine of colourable legislation is a natural and necessary development in view of the character of the Constitution.[28]

Duff's first visit to the Privy Council exhilarated him. He had met some of the outstanding lawyers and great judges of Britain, and he had sat with all of them as their equal. The experience had been so successful and so rewarding personally that he gladly accepted an invitation to return, and spent one month of each of the five succeeding years at its sessions.

That five-year period, which ended with Davies's death in 1924, saw the number of appeals to the Supreme Court in criminal cases increase noticeably. In one of these, Duff laid down the rule that an accused person pleading insanity as a defence is not required, as is the prosecution, to prove the issue beyond a reasonable doubt but only by a preponderance of evidence, the onus applicable in civil cases. He reiterated these same views late in his career, again displaying his general tendency to take a position favourable to the accused.[29]

Soon after his return in 1919, the court heard its first products liabilities case, involving the sale of surplus wartime Ross rifles which could be fired with the bolt unlocked though it might appear not to be. Because the weapon carried no warning of the condition, Duff and his colleagues concluded that the manufacturer had negligently created a "trap."[30] At about the same time, the court settled an unseemly dispute as to which of two judges could correctly by styled the "Chief Justice of Alberta." In extraordinary confusion, the federal government had appointed two men to the position, and was forced in embarrassment to ask the Supreme Court to decide which of them actually held it. Duff's old university and political friend Horace Harvey, represented in court by Eugene Lafleur, contended with D.L. Scott, who was not represented at the hearing, presumably because he found the controversy distasteful. Harvey won out, but not unanimously: Duff and three of the five other judges ruled in his favour.[31]

A few days before that case, Duff and his colleagues sat on an appeal in which the Canada Law Book Company, a well-known legal publisher, sued another publishing firm. The case is of no interest but for the fact that Duff sat on it at all, since the head of Canada Law Book, R.R. Cromarty, who figured personally in the litigation, knew him very well. The Supreme Court gave unanimous judgement for his company, with Duff writing one of the principal judgements. This same Cromarty had been consistently taking advantage of the friendship by pestering Duff with allegations that his firm's *Dominion Law Reports* were being discriminated against by the other judges of the court, who preferred a series brought out by a rival publisher; that the court registrar was treating him unfairly by reducing the purchase of his books, and so on. Duff listened to the whole litany of complaints and must have responded to some. Cromarty even spoke frankly of "the many favours that you have done this Company..." The unquestionable (and unexplained) hold he had makes it all the more remarkable that Duff should have sat on the appeal.[32]

In one case, amusing to read though the judges treated it with the utmost seriousness, the Supreme Court concluded that a railway locomotive pushing a tender did not constitute a train. When a train had no engine in front, the law required that a man be stationed at level crossings to warn traffic. As a result of this judgement, however, there had been no train, and the father of two young boys killed by a locomotive and tender at an unguarded level crossing could thus recover no damages for their deaths. The father managed to finance an appeal to the Privy Council, where lawyers for the railway company said that a tender formed an integral part of an engine, and notwithstanding that in the case in question the tender went first rather than last, only an engine and not a train went down the track. This ingenious piece of special pleading failed to impress Lord Shaw, who remarked that a tender was a tender and an engine an engine, and when one had an engine and a tender, in whatever order, one had a train. Only Idington in the Supreme Court had displayed the same common sense.[33]

Two connected cases from British Columbia raised the problems of legislation restricting the employment of Orientals. Such problems were not new to the court; as noted earlier, a majority decision had upheld the right of Saskatchewan to forbid the employment of white females by Chinese. Both these new disputes had their origins in 1902, when the British Columbia government, issuing permits by order-in-council for logging Crown lands, attached a condition that the permit holder not employ Chinese or Japanese. This resembled legislation passed by the same province in the 1890s to forbid the employment of Chinese in underground coal mines, which the Privy Council, in a liberal-minded decision, declared unconstitutional as an invasion by the province of the exclusive power of the federal government to legislate for "aliens."[34]

When, in 1921, the British Columbia legislature validated the earlier orders-in-council, the Japanese protested to Ottawa that this was in conflict with the treaty negotiated between Japan and Canada in 1911 by which

Japanese in Canada were placed on the same legal footing as British subjects. They argued that the legislation derogated from the rights conferred by the treaty and that the federal government should observe its treaty obligations by taking steps to invalidate it. At the same time, a logging company in British Columbia with a permit containing the race restriction applied to have it declared illegal. The two cases, the one brought privately by the logging company and the other brought by the federal government on a reference to the Supreme Court of Canada, came out quite differently. In the first, both the Supreme Court, and on appeal, the Privy Council agreed that the provincial government had the authority to impose the condition; the logging permits were issued for Crown lands over which the province had exclusive jurisdiction under section 92(5) of the British North America Act. Duff gave tortuous reasons for arriving at his decision. The main fact was that the company had agreed to the condition; if such a condition was unconstitutional, then the licence became invalid and the company could do nothing about it; if the condition was valid, the company could not complain either. Even Idington, who had rebelled against his colleagues' views in the *Saskatchewan* case, thought this legislation could be supported as relating to the province's unquestioned power to regulate the use of provincial Crown lands.[35]

In the other case, however, the courts took a different approach. Both the Supreme Court and the Privy Council considered the problem in the abstract; there was no logging firm to be concerned about here. The judges of the Supreme Court held the legislation invalid, but for differing reasons. Duff reiterated his view expressed in the logging-company case that the province could do virtually what it pleased with Crown lands, but he concluded that the federal government, using its exclusive treaty-making power under section 132 of the British North America Act, had entered into a treaty with Japan that overrode powers the province could otherwise exercise. The Privy Council agreed with Duff, but unlike him it perceived the absurdity of deciding on the one hand that the logging company would lose its logging permits if it employed Orientals, and on the other that the restriction was unconstitutional. Lord Haldane, trying to steer between Scylla and Charybdis, held,

> This conclusion does not in any way affect what they [the Privy Council] decided on the previous appeal [the logging-company case] as to the title to a renewal of the special licenses relative to particular properties. It is concerned with the principle of the statute of 1921 and not with that of merely individual instances in which particular kinds of property are being administered.[36]

No judge saw the legislation as discriminating against racial minorities. Sir

Matthew Baillie Begbie, whose views on such questions were reflected accurately, though posthumously, in the Privy Council decision in the *Union Colliery* case, would have inveighed against the approach Duff and his colleagues took both in Ottawa and in London. But Duff stuck to his opinion of the federal treaty-making power, most notably in the *Labour Conventions* case of 1936.[37] Such a view is surprising. Lord Watson, Haldane, and Duff himself built strong walls to repel federal attacks on the provincial domain. Now Duff would have given Ottawa a ladder for scaling them. The Privy Council held firm, however, eventually overruling him.

Duff's views in the *Aliens* and logging-company cases would not draw praise from today's civil libertarians; nor would the opinions he expressed in the *Bedard* case at about the same time. As part of an anti-prostitution campaign in the early 1920s, Quebec passed legislation authorizing the forcible closing of a dwelling if an occupant had been convicted under the Criminal Code of operating a bawdy house. The legislation was challenged on the ground that it amounted to criminal law and hence lay beyond the jurisdiction of a provincial government. Duff disagreed, saying somewhat laboriously that the

> legislation impugned seems to be aimed at the suppressing of conditions calculated to favour the development of crime rather than at the punishment of crime. This is an aspect of the subject in respect of which the Provinces seem to be free to legislate.[38]

After Duff's retirement from the bench, the Supreme Court heard several appeals stemming from attempts by the Quebec government to prohibit Jehovah's Witnesses from preaching and enforce the so-called Padlock Law designed to combat the spread of communism. Duff applauded the majority decisions of the Supreme Court which frustrated the attempts; he particularly admired the opinions given by Mr. Justice Rand. It must have caused Duff some chagrin, however, to find that his *Bedard* decision had been relied on heavily by the lawyers for Quebec in arguing the validity of the repressive legislation. What is more, the dissenting judges in two of the cases relied on it as well. The majority judges in the Padlock Law case did not refer to his opinion specifically, being perhaps embarrassed by it, but they did say that the *Bedard* case had to do with a use of private property amounting to a common nuisance in the legal sense of this phrase, whereas the Padlock Law restricted freedom of speech and discussion.[39]

In the early postwar years, honours and distinctions began to accumulate. In 1922 his old university conferred on him an honorary doctorate of laws, the first of nine such degrees he eventually received. His connection with the University of Toronto continued when, three years later, the premier of Ontario appointed him to its board of governors. He accepted a request to serve on the committee to select Rhodes scholars from Ontario, a job he discharged conscientiously, chairing the committee for three years.

In 1923, he accepted an invitation from Harvard University to become a member of the "Committee to Visit The Law School." The famous Dean Roscoe Pound, wrote to congratulate him: "We have had many students here from Canada in recent years, and I think nothing could be more timely than to have so eminent a representative of the profession in Canada upon the committee."[40] Duff joined a group composed of such illustrious legal figures as Benjamin Cardozo and Augustus Hand. Their functions were largely honorary, but they were expected to preside over mock trials in the annual Ames competition. Duff did so in 1924. He wrote Pound to commend the system,[41] but he obviously felt that the standards achieved were low, for he wrote on the same day to one of the professors that he was "grievously disappointed" with the result.[42] Duff kept up his Harvard connection for ten years, relinquishing it only on becoming chief justice in 1933. He approved of the methods of legal education there, reference to actual cases as illustrating a legal principle rather than teaching legal principles in generalities. He told Pound that

> you have succeeded in an extraordinary degree in providing for the pursuit of the study of modern law as modern law in an environment which, while it encourages workmanlike efficiency, reminds the students how much the law of today is a heritage.[43]

The admiration each man had for the other ended only with his death. And Duff also met Felix Frankfurter at Harvard, on the faculty then but later a justice of the United States Supreme Court. Frankfurter held liberal views, though he became more conservative on the bench, and he and Duff liked one another at once. They continued to meet occasionally, both there and in Ottawa. Frankfurter regarded Duff as "one of the most significant judges during his service in any country among English speaking judiciaries," but even more, as "an authentically great man."[44] For his part, Duff saw in Frankfurter an enormous legal talent: "How you succeed in producing so much work of the highest class is always a puzzle to me."[45] He valued their friendship, of which he was "very proud."

Grand social events had reared above the general level of mundane luncheons and dinner parties. The Duffs entertained the outgoing viceregal couple, the Duke and Duchess of Devonshire, on the eve of their return to England in 1921. Later that year in London, Duff was a guest at a large dinner presided over by the Duke of Connaught for Lord Byng, about to leave for Canada as Devonshire's successor. Sir Arthur Currie gave one of the toasts, coupling

Duff's name with others who had achieved eminence by "perseverance and determination" and by "a will to win."[46]

Financial worry took some of the bloom off all this recognition. His brother-in-law kept writing optimistically about his Vancouver investments, real estate and shares in some commercial concerns: they were sound, and in just a little while some return could be expected. One particular property in which Duff, Bird, and others had a substantial equity got caught up in government wartime regulations affecting real estate owned by enemy aliens. Duff and his associates had leased the property from its owner, a German national. Under wartime edict, it forfeited to the Crown, which jeopardized every penny Duff had put in. So serious was the situation that Bird asked Duff to intercede with the appropriate Ottawa official to have the property restored. It is not known whether Duff contacted the official personally, but either he or someone on behalf of his group did.[47] The ultimate outcome of all this is unclear; what is clear, however, is that Duff had to pay money out to help keep the investment afloat, and for that purpose took out a loan on the security of two life-insurance policies. In a manner that was typical of Bird's persuasive powers, he wrote to his sister:

> I will not consent for one moment to your suggestion of getting Lyman to loan me money on his insurance policies or from any other sources. At the same time you will know that such an offer is most gratefully received.[48]

That is precisely what happened. Duff borrowed approximately two thousand dollars, either sending the money to Bird or repaying debts already run up for the Vancouver property. On one policy he owed money for nearly fifteen years, and on the other for nearly twenty years. It seems probable that he lost both of them. His shortage of cash at this point nearly cost him his home for non-payment of taxes, and only the kindly intervention of the city solicitor kept his house off the tax-sale list.[49] This experience evidently brought home to him the gravity of his financial plight, for a year or so later he sold the beautiful house on Golbourne Avenue, filled with lovely English antique furniture, and lived in rented dwellings until 1946. His friend W.D. Herridge, R.B. Bennett's future brother-in-law and later ambassador in Washington, purchased the house for a handsome sum. And unhappy thoughts were far behind him when, on 20 June 1924, he and Lizzie sailed from Canada for several great English occasions that coincided to produce a halcyon period in his career.

English barristers belong to one of four Inns of Court: Lincoln's, Gray's, the Middle Temple, and the Inner Temple, all havens of tranquillity in busy London. Members lavish undying devotion on their Inns, rooted as they are in history and tradition. Even if a barrister becomes a judge he remains a member of his Inn, and in its privacy mingles freely with other judges and lawyers. A group called the Benchers is elected to administer each Inn's affairs, and one member, known as "Treasurer," is the senior Bencher. Each Inn, however, appoints as Honorary Benchers "those whose reputation and attainment in the legal profession was of the highest degree and whose personal character and charm made it a pleasure to associate with."[50] Lord Birkenhead, Treasurer of Gray's Inn, obviously impressed by Duff, asked him to become an Honorary Bencher. Duff, immensely flattered by the invitation which arrived just before he sailed for England, accepted wholeheartedly: "This is the crowning kindness I have received from the Bar in England, and a distinction which I prize more than I have ever received."[51]

In London, Duff attended various festivities connected with the combined meeting of the Bar associations of Canada and the United States. The event attracted over two thousand lawyers, judges, and their wives, who joined with many members of the English Bar in a week-long spate of speeches, lunches, dinners, garden parties, and trips to historic sites. Haldane, now Lord Chancellor and thus figurehead for the English bar and bench, did not relish his job:

> This is going to be a terrible week. We had dinner parties of Canadians last night, and the night before — and we have a bridge party (150) tomorrow night....Tomorrow morning I have to address (in wig and gold robes) 2,000 lawyers in Westminster Hall at 10:30 a.m. All the week banquets at the Guild Hall and Inns of Court — I loathe the prospect. It would have suited Birkenhead [his predecessor] to perfection."
>
> I wish this week were over. Still they are very nice boys, and me they hail as one of the fathers of the Canadian constitution...I wish these things could fall to someone who would enjoy them.[52]

Haldane gave no trace of these sentiments when with enormous pomp and ceremony, attended by tipstaffs and other functionaries, in the presence of the flower of the English legal world, he addressed a huge gathering in Westminster Hall, the great hall of William Rufus and cradle of the common law.

The four Inns of Court each held grand dinners two nights running attended by a suitable mix of English, Canadian, and American representatives. As a newly elected Honorary Bencher of Gray's Inn, Duff went to his first dinner there on 21 July, the first of the two evening events. The diners sat in the Tudor hall with its magnificent hammer-beam roof under the gaze of Queen Elizabeth, whose prized portrait, along with those of some of her courtiers including Walsingham and Burleigh, hung on the finely-panelled walls. Birkenhead presided and, as Haldane had rather sourly anticipated, enjoyed himself thoroughly. He gave a masterful performance. Urbane and witty, he had just the right touch for the occasion. Those present included the Duke of Connaught, H.W. Newlands, the Lieutenant-Governor of Saskatchewan, the American ambassador, Mr. Justice Riddell of Ontario, and Lord Justice Atkin of the English Court of Appeal. But Birkenhead was the star of the evening. His speechifying would have done justice to a clever stand-up comedian. On the second evening, though Duff did not attend, he was even funnier.[53]

Five minutes before the dinner ended, Birkenhead asked Duff if he would say something appropriate to round off the evening, "rather than leaving the thing at large to anybody."[54] Evidently the earl had overlooked one of the niceties of such an occasion, the formal thanks to the principal speakers of the evening. Duff managed to rise to the occasion, praising Birkenhead in a rare instance of his speaking to a distinguished gathering with any degree of spontaneity. Three days later, Lord and Lady Birkenhead, the Duke of Connaught, and Duff formed the receiving line at a garden party in Gray's Inn. They stood on the venerable lawn, shaded by ancient trees, to greet a large company of guests.

That evening he attended a gala dinner given by the Lord Mayor, not at the Mansion House as in 1903, but in the larger Guildhall. On this occasion, Duff knew beforehand that he had to make suitable remarks. Haldane led off the speeches, receiving applause but no laughter. Two Americans followed who spoke wittily and were roundly applauded. The Lord Chief Justice of England, Lord Hewart, after giving a humorous talk, introduced Duff and Sir James Aikins of Winnipeg, founder of the Canadian Bar Association. Duff delivered an earnest, laboriously prepared speech which drew polite applause. Aikins on the other hand spoke in a manner reminiscent of Birkenhead, carrying his audience with him on a wave of laughter.

The revels now were ended. After the meetings and parties, the exhausted delegates must have been relieved to sink into their berths in comfortable cabins for the sea voyage home. Duff remained to sit on a number of routine Privy Council appeals but also to help judge a far from routine case. In 1922 Eire and Great Britain had entered into a treaty called the Irish Free State Agreement Act. It provided that the boundary between the Free State and the six counties of Ulster remaining loyal to the United Kingdom should be determined by a commission formed of representatives of Eire, Great Britain, and Northern Ireland. With the intransigence which seems always to dog Irish affairs, the Ulster government refused to name a representative on the ground that since it had not been a signatory to the treaty it would not be bound by a decision which might conceivably award territory to the Free State. The stubbornness of Ulster cast in doubt whether the two other nominees could make a valid decision. Prime Minister Ramsay MacDonald pleaded with Sir James Craig, the prime minister of Northern Ireland, by appealing to his better instincts:

> Unless or until we can show that we ourselves know how to keep the law and to create friendship between ourselves in these islands, we can do little or nothing to bring back the verities of peace either to Europe, or the world at large.[55]

As the Northern Irish remained obdurate, MacDonald resolved to refer the question to the Privy Council for an opinion. He also decided that "in view of the constitutional importance of the question...it is proposed to include in the Tribunal eminent judges from the Dominions."[56] MacDonald asked Australia and India to send judges, and he asked the Canadian government to do the same. Haldane told the prime minister that since Duff would be attending the regular Privy Council sessions he would be the obvious choice. Duff agreed to serve and joined lords Dunedin and Blanesburgh of England, Sir Lawrence Jenkins of India, and Sir Adrian Knox, the chief justice of Australia, on the hearing of the case.

Lord (formerly Sir Edward) Carson, an Irishman who was Duff's colleague in the 1903 Alaska boundary hearing, had emerged as the leading advocate of Ulster home rule. He passed some extremely derogatory remarks about the overseas members of the tribunal, Duff included, accusing them of being unfit to settle any problem, let alone one as difficult as the Irish boundary. A Canadian journal commented that Carson's intemperate words had never been "equalled for insular parochialism." Carson, the paper said, was piqued because he had not been consulted about membership of the tribunal and his attitude made it regrettable that "so small a man should have risen to a mischievous eminence."[57] Six of the most eminent lawyers in England, including the attorney-general, Sir Patrick Hastings, appeared before the tribunal. The five judges decided that only a three-man commission could settle the boundary and if Northern Ireland persisted in its refusal, nothing could be done. In fact nothing more was done, and the boundary as originally fixed remained unchanged.

But Haldane wrote Duff: "You helped to render a great service in the P.C. on the Irish question, a new departure."[58] As he sailed home in August 1924, he must have reflected proudly on the events of the previous months. He had achieved distinction as an Honorary Bencher; he had been singled out for high praise in assemblies of famous judges and lawyers; and he had been asked to give advice on one aspect of the Irish question.

# 10

## The years of disappointment

IT HAD BEEN OBVIOUS for many months before his death in May 1924 that Sir Louis Davies could not continue much longer as chief justice. There was much speculation about his successor. It was agreed that Idington's age, even though he was the senior member of the court, put him out of contention. Duff, at age fifty-nine the next senior, hoped for the appointment with a nagging suspicion that there was a conspiracy afoot to bar him from it. The longer the prime minister delayed, the more worried Duff became.

Prime Minister Mackenzie King received much advice during the five months after Davies's death. Sir Allen Aylesworth reminded him of a conversation that they had two years earlier: "I said then that if it was to be one of the other judges of the Court I thought Anglin the best man. I still think so."[1] J.S. Ewart recommended Sir Robert Borden. Ernest Lapointe urged the appointment of his deputy E.L. Newcombe, but King objected, though he later repented by making him a puisne judge: "I oppose strongly because of his being a Tory thro' life. It wd. make our friends very much annoyed & there are plenty of good men in our ranks." Privately, he condemned the Canadian judiciary, most of whom had been appointed by governments of his own Liberal persuasion: "It is a difficult matter to decide: the Bench all over Canada is very weak."[2]

The attorney-general of Manitoba and the premier and attorney-general of Saskatchewan all urged that Duff be appointed. Sir James Aikins, recalling the eventful days in London, wrote King:

> May I now to you express my opinion which is that the appointment of the Right Honourable Mr. Justice Duff would be favourably viewed by the

profession. I know you are fully acquainted with his distinguished services as a member of the Supreme Court, but I may mention that this summer, while I was in London at the meeting of the Canadian Bar Association, several of Mr. Justice Duff's associates on the Judicial Committee of the Privy Council alluded in very high terms, to the eminent and valuable service which he has given during recent years as the active representative of Canada on that Committee. I am sure it is your desire, as it is the desire of the Canadian lawyers and the public, that the great office of the Chief Justice should be filled by a strong man whose judicial attainments and reputation will reflect credit upon the Court and the Dominion and that you will give your earnest consideration to the name of Mr. Justice Duff.[3]

In a spirit of compromise, King's defence minister suggested that Idington be made chief justice as a stop-gap to still the conflict.

King had his own ideas; he wanted Eugene Lafleur, and as early as 5 May, not a week after Davies had died, he summoned him to Ottawa for what turned out to be an emotional appeal to his sense of duty:

I...talked with him in my office, the tears came into his eyes as I spoke to him of the confidence of the govt. & the bar in his ability & of our desire to have him fill the position to strengthen the bench & uphold Br. [British] conception of justice.

When Lafleur averred that he was too old for the job and the Supreme Court needed younger men, King had a carrot ready for him: "I spoke of his going to Imp. Privy Council to take part with Law Lords there. He promised to re-consider, but did not give me any assurance. The Imp. P.C. may be the means of securing him."[4] King never slackened the pressure, writing yet again on 8 September:

You will permit me, I am sure, to make one more appeal to you to accept the position of Chief Justice of the Supreme Court of Canada....I need not tell you of the need which exists in Canada today to place at the head of our judiciary a man whose pre-eminence in his profession would gain for the Supreme Court the place it would hold in the respect of the bench and the bar not only of your own country but also of the British Isles....If you are in doubt about the wisdom of severing your Montreal associations, not being sure of how congenial the atmosphere of the Bench might be, let me suggest that you accept the position, with the understanding that it be held at your pleasure. You are the one man in Canada who can meet what today is our country's most imperative need.[5]

And Lafleur responded to these overtures with great honesty and feeling:

> Your letter of yesterday is so kind and so persuasive it requires all the
> courage I can muster to persist in my previous decision....I have long
> thought that what the Court needs most is to be rejuvenated, and it is not
> by appointing men who are nearing the 70 mark that you will really
> strengthen it.[6]

The prime minister delayed no longer. On 16 September he announced
Anglin's appointment. Anglin uttered suitable expressions of gratitude and
correctly predicted Duff's loyalty — loyalty, that is, so far as remaining a
member of the court was concerned.[7] In the legal profession, the choice
caused widespread dismay and much curiosity. But King spoke only to his
diary:

> I have tried very hard to secure Lafleur as Chief Justice, but in vain. It
> leaves the choice between Duff & Anglin. The former is prbably the abler
> but is dissipated, gets off on sprees for weeks at a time. Was intoxicated at
> last opening of prlt, & at Sir Louis Davies' funeral. I regard him too as a
> bit of a sychopant where the tories are concerned & more or less the
> favourite with the big interests. Anglin is narrow, has not a pleasant
> manner, is very vain, but industrious, steady and honest, a true liberal at
> heart. Both are personal friends. I imagine the bar as a whole prefer Duff,
> some do not know his habits...Lapointe [the minister of justice] wishes to
> appoint Newcombe, the dep. min. He will lose a good man & our friends
> will not like it, but it will please the Tories & will offset not appointing
> Duff....While I wish we could have secured Lafleur & I do not altogether
> like appointing Anglin because of the feeling of the bar against him, I
> nevertheless think in the interests of justice and the dignity of the bench,
> his appointment is preferable to any other all circumstances considered.[8]

King's description of him as a "sycophant" where tories were concerned
was questionable, but it is true that Duff, though an unwavering Liberal at
heart, maintained close connections with important Conservatives. He may
have thought it expedient to remain on good terms with both parties, hedging
his bets with an eye to judicial preferment. He and Borden were close friends;
they exchanged books and talked politics. Duff admired him immensely, more
than any other prime minister he had known.[9] W.D. Herridge, a prominent
Conservative, was an even closer friend. R.B. Bennett and Duff were not so
close, though Duff did admire him, grudgingly at first and then more warmly
over the years. In a letter to Duff not long before Anglin's appointment,
Bennett referred to himself as "ever your friend."[10] Duff had stayed in

Bennett's flat in London; he voiced satisfaction when Bennett took over the tory leadership in 1927.[11]

Relationships among the top people were studied assiduously in the hothouse society of Ottawa. And King, a past master at such studies, would look askance at Duff's association with the Conservative hierarchy. The "big interests" to which King referred would have included people like Sir Edward Beatty of the C.P.R., Sir Joseph Flavelle who had chaired the Imperial Munitions Board at the time of the hearings of the Shell Committee inquiry, and Sir James Dunn, head of the Algoma Steel Corporation, who shared Duff's interest in books and was also on excellent terms with Birkenhead.[12] Duff considered all these men his friends, and, as has ever been the case, friendship was the glue for continued power, political or otherwise.

The reference to Duff's intoxication raises something more serious. Others were making such charges. Lord Byng had told the prime minister that he hoped Duff would not be appointed because "of his being intoxicated [on the] day of State dinner and opening," in February. One wonders what reliance should be placed on Byng's appraisal; in the same conversation, he described Borden to King as "a man of very ordinary ability, and not very alert or bright."[13] Yet Peter Larkin, high commissioner in London, passed on to King a conversation he had had with Tilley, who urged him to use his influence with the prime minister for Duff's appointment. "I asked him," Larkin reported, "if the gentlemen named had not a weakness." Tilley replied that

> he thought he had no weakness as would disqualify him for the position and he was so eminently superior to anyone else in sight that his appointment was necessary if the Supreme Court was ever to attain such a standing as would justify the stopping of appeals to the Privy Council, for which he said there was no excuse other than the weakness of the Bench in the Supreme Court.[14]

This was a stout defence and a prescient remark on Tilley's part; six years after Duff had been made chief justice, the government introduced legislation to abolish Privy Council appeals.

The allegation that Duff had been drunk at Davies's funeral has persisted. Chief Justice Kerwin has said that he was'told of the occurrence,[15] and in 1946, when Duff made his last appearance as a member of the Judicial Committee in London, courtroom gossip there recalled the story.[16] And yet there is nothing that could be called evidence in contemporary accounts to support King's charge which, if true, would indicate that by 1924 Duff had been significantly affected by his drinking. There is certainly no evidence of illness to corroborate the "weakness" as there would be a few years later.

Towards the end of his life, Duff himself denied the funeral story, telling his confidential secretary that there

> were times when he made a fool of himself — when he was not appointed Chief Justice back in 1924 — when Anglin got the job, well naturally he was upset about this — he drank after that time...there was a period there where he was drinking.[17]

In fact, Duff's drinking was a superficial but not a real reason for King's decision. King came into office in 1921 with his Liberals winning every seat in Quebec, a backlash against the Conservative instigators of the Military Service Act. Even though in its later stages the Act had been administered by the Union government with Liberals in it, Quebec voters associated the hated measure with the Conservative Party. During that election campaign, Meighen vigorously though most unwisely attempted to defend conscription when he was in Quebec. Duff had become persona non grata there by refusing exemption to certain groups. One particularly unpopular ruling of his had been to deny exemption for seminarians. It caused consternation in the Borden cabinet, and Rowell was delegated to speak to him about it; but Duff would concede exemption only if the presence of a divinity student in a particular community was necessary to the continuance of religious observance there.

Even with every seat in Quebec, King did not have an overall majority in the House of Commons, and simply could not afford significant erosion of his support in that province. At a time when another election could not be far off, it would have been extremely dangerous to appoint as chief justice a man identified in the minds of Quebecers as one of the architects of conscription. Lapointe told Thibodeau Rinfret of the Supreme Court that he had given the prime minister this advice.[18] Arthur Meighen said that "Quebec's opposition" denied Duff the appointment, and this was also the opinion of J.W. deB. Farris, a prominent British Columbia Liberal lawyer and Duff's good friend.[19]

Even though Lafleur was a Protestant, King had badly wanted to appoint him, a prominent Quebecer, to cement his electoral hold on the province. When Lafleur let him down, however, the choice of Anglin, an Ontario Roman Catholic who had attended a Jesuit college in Quebec, would be almost as popular. Duff, anathema in Quebec and Protestant besides, could not be chosen. The reasons King intimated to his diary were personal; however shabby they were, they may have weighed, but the conclusion that political expediency was King's prime motive in the affair is reinforced by a similar occurrence of 1923. As a replacement for Brodeur, who had resigned the Supreme Court late that year, Fernand Roy of Quebec City had been mooted. Roy, a prominent and much respected lawyer, a member of the law faculty at Laval, had published a pamphlet shortly before the Military Service Act became effective urging his fellow citizens to abandon their opposition to the war — enlist or in any event accept conscription with good grace. Lucien Cannon, later solicitor-general but then a Quebec M.P., wrote to Sir Lomer Gouin, a former premier of the province who had joined King's cabinet, pointing out the political danger of appointing to the court a man who had condoned conscription. Roy was not appointed.[20] Duff well understood the political undercurrents; writing to Haldane a few months after Anglin's appointment, he told him:

> The turn of the political wheel brought Quebec into power in the last election, and the machine there is pressing the spoils doctrine to the extreme limit, and the present Prime Minister, who owes his office to his attitude of sympathy with Quebec during the war, is willing to acquiesce in that policy so long as Quebec's support is essential to him.
>
> Unfortunately, the whole thing is unprincipled. With the Quebec machine, office is the *summum bonum*. Its ascendancy in Quebec Province is maintained largely by keeping alive the anti-conscription bitterness and by avoiding offence to the clergy; subject to that, any policy is acceptable which assures political support elsewhere.[21]

King called an election in October 1925 and won every seat but four in Quebec.

King had twinges of conscience in later years. In a diary entry made two days before Duff's appointment as chief justice in 1933, he recorded,

> Just before waking I dreamt I was sitting at a table talking with dear Father. I was asking his assistance in revising something, each time he looked in the direction of Judge Duff who seemed to be the Chief Justice & who was the only other person I could see, & said to ask him. I seemed to be a little put out at Father always referring to the Chief Justice in this way as I felt he knew better himself.[22]

Two weeks later, he sat next to Duff at a luncheon party. He noted that

> I had not written to congratulate him as I thought he might naturally have felt I might have made the apptmt. years ago if I had wished to. I told him I was glad to see him where he was, that he had been spared to fill the post & hoped he might long be.[23]

In another dream fifteen years later, King's spirit returned to the days of 1924:

> I had a curious vision which seemed to me to relate more to the past than to the future. I seemed to be walking on the sidewalk opposite what in one way seemed my own residence and in another a building much like the house in which Sir Louis Davis lived. I passed some men who were talking opposite the house and seemed a bit perturbed about this. Walked across the road and up the stairs to the hallway through a double entrance. The house itself inside appeared like a public building more or less possibly a Court. I missed the presence of the dog in the hall, but there was evidence that the dog had been there.
>
> The vision seemed to me to clearly have reference to the appointment to the Supreme Court. Sir Louis Davis was a judge of the Supreme Court for a time Chief Justice. There was a sort of darkness over everything, but the thought mostly in my mind was that I had not been afraid of their faces. [24]

By any standard, this is an extraordinary entry, not least in his observing the evidence of a phantom dog. After the dinner at Government House in honour of Duff's retirement, King wrote in a more down-to-earth vein:

> I have become very fond of Duff and he equally I think warmly recipro- cates the feelings that we shared quite strongly when he and I first came to Ottawa. The appointment of Anglin as Chief Justice after we came into office inevitably made difficulties at the time but he has never alluded to it in any way and understood, I think, very fully the situation. [25]

For all that he may have understood, Duff suffered pangs of bitter disap- pointment that were not fully eased by many commiserations expressed to him by fellow judges and lawyers. In a letter to Mr. Justice Ferguson of Ontario, he expressed both disillusionment at past events and misgivings for the future:

> I must admit that on Thursday morning, when I saw the announcement, which was the first intimation I had of what had happened, I resolved to do what my wife and I had agreed should be done in the event of an appointment being made which was not satisfactory. Accidentally, I met Tilley before seeing the Minister of Justice, and it became very evident to me that my plan of action was seriously grieving him. Since then, I have had a good many talks with many members of the Bar with the result that I have determined not to resign...

I am afraid there will be no abatement of natural aggressiveness in a certain quarter as a result of the change. Present indications point to an enhancement rather.[26]

These last cryptic remarks probably refer to Anglin. Besides Tilley, D.L. McCarthy also urged Duff to stay on the Court; the influence of the two men undoubtedly persuaded Duff to remain at his post.

Duff had not liked Anglin to begin with, and he liked him even less after he became chief justice. Mackenzie King perceived the difference between the two. Acting as Administrator in the absence of a Governor-General in 1940, Duff swore King into office in the library of his own house. King recorded that "when I addressed him as 'Your Excellency'...he laughed as I rather expected he would. Duff has no side to him. Every difference from Anglin in those things. No pomposity."[27] A good example of what King had in mind occurred in 1932 during Bennett's term as prime minister. By separate commissions, the Governor-General, Lord Bessborough, appointed both Anglin and Duff to act as deputies in his absence — Anglin first if he was in Ottawa, otherwise Duff. At a time when Anglin was in the United Kingdom, Bessborough, about to leave on a lengthy trip to eastern Canada, asked Duff to act. Anglin returned to Canada earlier than expected and was miffed when Duff continued to act as deputy Governor-General after his return. Anglin's complaint reached the ears of the justice minister, who advised Bennett that the "return of the C.J. before the G.G. is taken legally '...to be a matter of little, if any, importance." '[28]

Anglin, in Duff's view, had a limited sense of the behaviour that was appropriate for a man in his position. A zealous layman, he gave an address to a Roman Catholic Education Association in Detroit in 1910. Writing of the occasion later, Duff described it as a "bitter speech to a congress of Irish-American Educationists, attacking the decision of the Privy Council in connection with the Manitoba School Controversy in 1905, ascribing the decision to political influence." He saw such a speech, especially given in a foreign country, as ill-advised and in bad taste.[29] Anglin was an extremely ambitious man, very conscious of his position and yet lacking the social graces and savoir-faire of someone on whom the mantle of distinction rested more deservedly. One time Duff was sitting at the Country Club among friends when Anglin, who had recently become chief justice, came over to speak about certain cases pending before the court. Duff reprimanded him openly: "Anglin, in case you don't know it, this is a gentlemen's club and not a business office."[30] That same year Anglin sent out pompous Christmas cards embossed with a gauntleted hand holding a dagger under which appeared the newly minted motto, "Vigueur Dessus." Duff would have noticed and disapproved of Anglin's solecism in having printed on the card, "Mr. Chief

Justice and Mrs. Anglin." "Chief Justice" is exactly that; only junior judges are "Mr. Justice so-and-so."[31]

At the opening of the court's winter term in October 1924, Duff gritted his teeth and, resolving to soldier on, sat with dignity beside the new chief justice. The first case on the list came from British Columbia, argued for the appellant by Duff's old friend E.P. Davis. The issue was whether the sale of standing timber by a company incorporated for the purpose of dealing in timber limits constituted capital or income. It remained important for many years, with Duff writing the judgement in favour of Davis's client.[32] In another income-tax case during that same session, Duff and his colleagues decided that profits from bootlegging could not be taxable income. The Privy Council very sensibly said that such a decision would throw an extra burden on honest taxpayers; profits, however illegal, were still profits and hence taxable.[33]

Anglin made an effort in his first years as chief justice to encourage the writing of a single judgement to embody the views of the majority, although dissents, by contrast to Privy Council practice, were disclosed. He could not make his views prevail, however, and gradually multiple judgements reappeared. Duff would attempt the same reform as chief justice with even less success. The Anglin period was also marked by the harmonious association of Duff and Newcombe; the two men thought alike. Newcombe had for thirty years served governments of both political parties as deputy justice minister; he served on the Supreme Court for only seven.

From 1924 on, the trivial cases began to disappear from the docket; amendments to the Supreme Court of Canada Act now restricted appeals to matters of some significance. Increases in the quantity and importance of the judges' work resulted in legislation in 1927 enlarging the court from six to seven members. The same statute introduced compulsory retirement at age seventy-five, legislation that was aimed at Idington, who retired unwillingly on the very day of its enactment.

The two most important cases heard by the court in Anglin's first session were, first, the decision upholding the validity of the Crow's Nest Pass rates for the railways,[34] and second, the decision dealing with the hours of work provisions contained in a convention of the League of Nations. There was no treaty involved as there had been in the earlier British Columbia case on the employment of Orientals; Duff and his colleagues ruled that the convention only required the federal government to refer it to the body having jurisdiction, whichever that might be, Ottawa or the provinces.[35]

A constitutional case decided by the Privy Council early in 1925 is one of the most important in Duff's career, even though he took no direct part in it; it established his pre-eminence as an interpreter of the Canadian constitution, and more importantly, it drew from him unique statements of extraordinary frankness contained in hitherto unpublished letters about the constitution and the process of government in Canada. In 1907, Parliament, guided by the then labour minister Rodolphe Lemieux, enacted the Industrial Disputes Investigation Act, an early attempt to provide mediation for labour disputes within provinces: it was actually the creation of Mackenzie King, by then deputy minister. The Act remained unchallenged until 1923 when, as the result of Ottawa's appointment of a board of inquiry into labour unrest in the Toronto Electric Commission, the commission brought court action to declare the legislation unconstitutional. After losing its case both at trial in Ontario and before the Court of Appeal, the commission went to the Privy Council which reversed the decision of the lower courts. The commission contended, successfully, that the legislation related to "property and civil rights," a provincial field of jurisdiction, and could not be supported on the principal argument advanced by the federal government that because it imposed penalties for non-compliance, it related to the federal criminal law.[36] Lord Haldane specifically quoted Duff's opinions in the *Reciprocal Insurers* case, saying that he had given "the true interpretation" of section 92, that under the guise of enacting criminal law Parliament could not oust the jurisdiction of the provinces in the specific fields assigned to them.

The decision, which overturned Dominion legislation of nearly twenty years' standing, drew bitter criticism from parliamentarians. Many felt the time had come to abolish the Privy Council's power to decide Canadian constitutional questions. The Toronto member W.F. Maclean, one of Duff's old friends, sent him a copy of a speech he had made in the House attacking the decision. "The Constitution of Canada," he said, "is being shot to pieces by the Judicial Committee in Great Britain."[37] Duff's reply is one of but a handful of surviving letters in which he utters his innermost thoughts and speaks critically of persons and institutions. He pointed out to Maclean that "there is a good deal of misapprehension abroad" about the interpretation of the British North America Act, and that

> you may take it from me that no court of competent lawyers in Canada would or could honestly have given any other decision as to the Lemieux Act. The truth of the matter is that Lord Haldane's judgment contains nothing which was not either expressed or implied in a judgment of February, 1924 which was written by myself here in Ottawa on behalf of the Judicial Committee and delivered there in my name, in the Reciprocal Insurers case....The truth is that the Dominion Parliament got into the habit of passing any legislation, however questionable constitutionally...and there is...a great deal of legislation which is utterly worthless....It records various illegal attempts on the part of the Dominion Parliament to exercise powers which it has no more authority to exercise than I have.

Duff described the Privy Council as a "court which is accustomed to giving effect to the law without regard to the feelings of politicians and the ambitions of the authors of acts of parliament," later describing these authors as "negligent and thoughtless legislators." He moved on to Newcombe, who as a deputy minister had attempted to get around the Privy Council's decision in the *Insurance Reference* case of 1916:

> This decision was much taken to heart by the then Deputy Minister of Justice — a gentleman for whom I have the greatest respect and regard, as well as friendship — who accordingly proceeded to attempt to escape the consequences of this decision by re-enacting this identical legislation in a slightly different form.

Newcombe had tinkered with the legislation and secured passage of an amendment to the Criminal Code, actions which led directly to the successful challenge in the *Reciprocal Insurers* case. Duff inveighed against deputy ministers whose legislative drafting had been invalidated by the courts and parliamentarians who "at the bidding of any deputy minister" pass "fraudulent" legislation for "the purpose of giving relief to his feeling of wounded vanity."

Speaking of the cases in which the Dominion Parliament had attempted to regulate the insurance business by making it a criminal offence not to comply with federal law, he decried the attitude of Parliament in "solemnly" passing laws which "competent constitutional lawyers knew [were] invalid but which businessmen could disregard only at their peril." He lamented that the "interests of the business community should be treated as zero compared with the feelings of the bureaucrat at Ottawa." Duff then trained his guns on the Ontario Court of Appeal and its aged Chief Justice Sir William Mulock, who with his colleagues had upheld the constitutionality of the Lemieux Act. After implying that Mulock was not one of the "limited number of Canadian judges [who] really understand the history of the judicial construction of the B.N.A. Act," he dismissed him contemptuously: "...one is not surprised when one finds that a Court sitting under the presidency of the Postmaster General of 1907 has made a mistake." Actually, Mulock had been postmaster-general in 1905.

Duff gave Maclean an admirable summary of his own attitude to the interpretation of the British North America Act as found in the history of its interpretation by the Privy Council over the previous forty years. His views are worth stating in full since they are apparently the only non-judicial expression of his constitutional rationale, and show that his decisions — up to 1939 at least, the year of the *Privy Council* reference — stem from inner belief rather than strict statutory interpretation.

I observe a disposition in some quarters to criticize the interpretation by the Judicial Committee of the BNA Act in this way: the tendency, it is said, has been in the direction of exalting the powers of the provinces at the expense of the Dominion and to that extent weakening the Dominion...

All this proceeds largely from a misapprehension. The BNA Act endows the Dominion with very great power indeed, and in the early days the Supreme Court of Canada was so impressed with the sweeping character of the language employed in defining the powers of the Dominion that it proceeded to give a series of decisions, the effect of which, if they had stood, would have been to take away from the provinces all but the slightest trace of political autonomy. What the Privy Council did was to protect the Constitution of Canada from this kind of judicial assault, and it has not gone beyond this. You and I, and everybody else who knows anything about the subject, know that according to the original design of the BNA Act, great communities like Ontario and Quebec were intended to possess individually a high degree of self-government — self government, that is to say, held under a tenure which did not leave it dependent in any way upon the policy of the Dominion or of the other provinces. The high degree of real self-government was what unquestionably was intended to be given; and it is just as unquestionable that if the Supreme Court of Canada of the 70's and 80's had had its way, the legislatures of the provinces would have been reduced to a status which would have made them little better than municipal councils. Now the Canadian courts, if left to themselves, it is not too much to say, had they stood, would have thrown our constitutional law into a state of chaos which would have required, before the exit of the 19th century, an entire revision of the whole position, but this was averted by the Privy Council.

Duff pointed out that whereas with the British North America Act the Privy Council by its decisions maintained the powers of the provinces, just the opposite had happened in the United States, where Chief Justice Marshall had made decisions which prevented the States from reducing the federal power to a nullity. But Duff did not regard the Supreme Court of the United States as "an ideal tribunal of law." Far from it:

American constitutional law is in large part arbitrary, illogical and, in many branches of it, chaotic in an incredible degree. In the beginnings of Australian constitutional interpretation, American decisions were looked to with almost a child-like sense of adoration, and for a time were slavishly followed. But Australians have come to see better and to find that an interpretation of their constitution in accordance with traditional British judicial methods that is, by really giving effect in a reasonable way to the intention of the constitutional instrument as manifested by the language of it, is the only safe course.

Responding to Maclean's argument for abolition of appeals to the Privy Council, Duff stated his beliefs in forthright fashion.

For my own part, I should much prefer, indeed, to see questions touching our constitution determined in Canada, but a Canadian court whose decisions should be subjected to such attacks as are now made upon the decisions of the Privy Council, merely because the results flowing from them happen to be inconvenient in a particular way, would be hopelessly discredited in five years...

He also vented his spleen at the quality of several recent judicial appointments which had implications for correct constitutional interpretation and the retention of the Privy Council.

Then the recent course of the present government with regard to judicial appointments is hardly calculated to create confidence. You know what has happened in Ontario, but you have possibly forgotten the appointment of Mr. Justice Malouin, who succeeded Mr. Justice Brodeur. Remembering that Sir Louis Davies was then the Chief Justice of our Court, and the age of Mr. Justice Idington, think of appointing a judge of the Superior Court of Quebec, 70 years of age, an invalid, to the highest court in Canada! Malouin is one of the nicest fellows in the world, but he was hopelessly at sea in any general question of law, especially on any constitutional question. Friends of mine in Quebec who, only three or four years ago were very strongly disposed to support a movement in favour of abolishing appeals to the Privy Council have, I believe, become quite convinced that until there is some evidence of a renewed sense of responsibility among public men as to judicial appointments, such a course would be altogether too hazardous.[38]

On 18 February 1925, prompted by the Privy Council decision overturning the Lemieux Act, Maclean introduced a motion in the House to "patriate" the constitution. It was implicit in the resolution and in subsequent debate that appeals to the Privy Council would be abolished. The two almost exactly foreshadowed the parliamentary proposals of 1981 which led to the passage of the Canada Act. Maclean called for unilateral action by the federal government to amend the B.N.A. Act without consulting the provinces so long as the rights of minorities, presumably Native, were preserved. He used the sovereignty argument: other nations could alter their constitutions, why should Canada not do likewise?

Since Maclean was a Conservative and in opposition, his motion was a private member's bill, but it still provoked a good deal of debate joined by M.P.s from all sides of the House and with contributions from Lapointe, the minister of justice, Arthur Meighen the opposition leader, and the prime minister himself. It is interesting to compare the positions taken then by the representatives of the three principal parties, the C.C.F. (now the N.D.P.), Liberals, and Conservatives with those taken in 1981 by representatives of these same parties. Lapointe, while supporting the motion in principle, doubted that the federal government could act unilaterally. He advanced the "pact" theory of Confederation according to which the B.N.A. Act was a contract which could only be altered by mutual agreement between the federal government and the provinces, and cited various scholarly opinions in his support. J.S. Woodsworth of the C.C.F., while deploring "legalities" which were "obstructive," agreed with Lapointe: let us pass the motion, he said, but only on first "obtaining the consent of all the provinces." These words can be compared with those uttered by Liberal ministers and their N.D.P. supporters in 1981: the wishes of the provinces were immaterial; the wish of Ottawa was paramount. By contrast, the Conservatives of 1981, unlike Maclean, would insist on the absolute need for consultation with the provinces. Lapointe passed eventually from doubt to conviction: "The Parliament of Canada has not the constitutional right to pass an address to the Imperial parliament to amend the Act of Confederation without first submitting the proposal to the provinces."

It was at this point that King joined the debate, delivering a carefully worded statement on the constitutional arrangements of the country, and drawing exactly the same distinction between the dictates of strict law and the strength of conventional usage which the Supreme Court of Canada drew in the constitutional reference of 1981.[39] King went on with characteristic obliqueness to say, however, that the "Canadian people, technically speaking," did not have the "right or power to amend the constitution" without permission from the United Kingdom Parliament; yet, he said, if both houses of Parliament at Ottawa, as the "agent" of the Canadian people, asked for amendment, Britain would undoubtedly "act in accordance with that request." Arthur Meighen, after pointing out that King and Lapointe obviously disagreed on the necessity of consultation with the provinces, urged strongly that appeals to the Privy Council be retained. The debate ended inconclusively; Maclean took his motion off the order paper.[40]

Duff, who devoured Hansard from cover to cover, would have read this debate with great interest. It would be instantly apparent to him that King had skirted the issue of whether the provinces' consent must be obtained before Parliament could ask the British houses, by convention or law, however it might be, to enact constitutional changes that could affect provincial powers. King was much less definite on this subject than his justice minister, and Duff sided with Lapointe on the issue, as he made clear in a frank and fascinating letter to Haldane, written immediately after the debate, in which he said the proposal was utterly lacking in merit.

> There was a good deal of discussion, and the upshot of it was that the proposals were laughed out of the House. Quebec and the Maritime Provinces, British Columbia and, generally speaking, Ontario, stood solidly by the Privy Council and by the principle that the B.N.A. Act could only be amended in any of its important provisions by consent of all the provinces.

This important affirmation flows logically from Duff's method of interpretation of the British North America Act, reinforced by decisions of the Privy Council.

He wrote scathingly of Mackenzie King and his views on constitutional amendment and the Privy Council's role. After pointing out that there was a feeling in Quebec "that the appeal to the Privy Council is a protection to them as a minority," and that "people are not at all in a mood to listen patiently to any suggestions for a change," he went on to say that people also were impatient with

> the present Prime Minister's theatricalities in relation to the conduct of Imperial affairs. People are tired of them, and the other day the Prime Minister was glad to escape the debate raised by Maclean's motion by declaring that, of course, amendments to the B.N.A. Act were entirely in the hands of the people in this country, and that nobody would presume to say nay to anything they might desire.

Duff exaggerated the effect of what King had said. The leader had delivered a reasoned dissertation on the constitutional arrangements of the country, but he certainly had no intention of supporting Maclean's motion.

Duff then gave Haldane a startling argument against establishing the Supreme Court of Canada as the final court.

> The Prime Minister himself is very jealous, I think, of the authority of the courts to deal with *ultra vires* legislation and I do not doubt that he would prefer to see the final authority in the Canadian Courts, with the idea that a court in Ottawa would be amenable to influence. You can have very little idea of the liberties some Canadian Ministers will allow themselves in

influencing judges where they think it is safe to bring pressure to bear.
Mulock, the C.J.O. who was responsible, with King, for the Lemieux
Act, brought every kind of pressure to bear on his colleagues to produce
the judgment delivered by Ferguson. Ferguson, no doubt, had honestly
convinced himself that he was right, but his view expressed to me about
two months before the delivery of the judgment was in the opposite
direction.

To substantiate his contention that the independence of the Canadian judiciary might be threatened if appeals to the Privy Council were abolished, he
gave an example of pressure from a Conservative government:

An instance of what I am referring to occurred a couple of years ago, in
Meighen's time when Doherty was Minister of Justice. A question was
before this court as to the validity of a proclamation to bring the Canada
Temperance Act into force in Alberta. The temperance people were
making a row about it, and the Minister of Justice, being anxious to
ascertain the probable result of the appeal then pending, sent for two
members of the Court, Anglin and Mignault, and obtained from them
information as to their own opinions of their colleagues and the probable
result of the appeal, and as a consequence legislation curing the defect was
introduced before our judgment was delivered. Doherty felt safe in that
case, because he and the two judges mentioned were educated at the same
Jesuit college in Montreal, with, you may imagine, very close reciprocal
affiliations.[41]

There speaks the authentic Duff. He rails at critics of the Privy Council. He
speaks scornfully of the wiles of politicians trying to influence the course of
justice. He describes a scheming deputy minister, a "mandarin" of his day,
securing passage of unconstitutional legislation by a compliant House. He
dismisses with contempt Sir William Mulock, the elderly chief justice of
Ontario, then eighty-one. He gives an excellent example of Mackenzie King's
political skill — avoid troublesome issues until forced to confront them.
    Above all, he affirms his view of Canada: a nation — two nations in a sense
— in which one segment cannot impose its will on the other. It sprang from a
compact among self-governing regions which, for the sake of nationhood,
chose to confer on a central government certain law-making powers for the
general good without detracting from their own regional powers. The nation
sprang also from two founding races whose diverse interests could only be
harmonized by a wise leader. Writing of Laurier's "lofty example," Duff said:
"One purpose he pursued steadily through good report and through evil
report...The development of a common Canadian spirit before which the

separatist tendencies arising from the divergence of race and religion should be minimized."[42] There can be no question what Duff's reaction would have been to the proposals advanced in 1981 by the federal government for changing the jurisdiction of the provinces by unilateral action: he would have condemned them out of hand as being totally inconsistent with the framework of Confederation and completely at odds with leading constitutional decisions of the courts, both in Canada and in England.

For similar reasons, he would have condemned entrenching a Charter of Rights on the American pattern in a constitution, which would essentially leave judges and not Parliament the power to determine the constitutional course of the country. In 1938, Loring Christie, then of the external affairs department, discussed with Duff a paper he was preparing for the prime minister on just such a subject; he sent Duff a copy of his lengthy memorandum. Christie, like Duff, believed that a comprehensive bill of rights enacted unilaterally by a federal government would quite properly founder on the rock of provincial jurisdiction.[43]

Soon after writing to Maclean, Duff sailed with Lizzie for England on a voyage that was fated to be her last. He had a busy time on the Privy Council, hearing appeals from various corners of the Empire. A Canadian case is worthy of note.[44] It was one of many testing the power of the provinces to regulate Sunday behaviour in the face of the federal Lord's Day Act. Duff and his colleagues had concluded, in a ruling affirmed by the Privy Council, that Manitoba could lawfully authorize the public transport of groups of citizens to resort areas within the province on the Sabbath. It may seem astonishing that such an innocuous matter could occupy the time of many highly paid lawyers and demand the attention of several courts, but Sunday observance in Canada has always been a contentious patchwork quilt, created with little apparent design. It is a curious fact that a significant portion of the constitutional law of Canada has resulted from people asserting the right to unrestricted Sabbath behaviour against the opposition of religious zealots who have viewed such horrors as the work of the Devil, and those asserting the right to consume liquor in the face of opposition by temperance societies.

While he was in London that summer, Duff called on the tailor from whom he had ordered, and received the previous year, the formal dress of a privy councillor, heavy blue cloth embroidered with gold trim. In the storied tradition of gentlemen of England, he had not paid the earlier bill but instead ordered still more garments to dispel any suggestion that he might take his custom elsewhere, unpaying though it was. The tailor waited until 1933 for payment in full. Duff did not take deliberate advantage; he simply had a chronic inability to match expense against income. From London, the Duffs went to Normandy for a holiday, staying at village *pensions*. Duff spoke French with the locals and read French novels avidly. On the return voyage, he absentmindedly took away a book he had borrowed from the *Montcalm*'s ship's library. A year later, the purser wrote tactfully to request its return.

He plunged into the work of the court when it reopened in mid-October. One case presented the same legal problem Duff had encountered on the Alaska boundary tribunal. In 1693 Count Frontenac, Governor of New France, had given a grant of "Lake Maatis" with adjoining lands. Ultimately the large Montreal paper firm of Price Brothers became the owner of this grant, but did "Lake Maatis" refer to only one body of water or did it, as Price Brothers contended, refer to several bodies of water connected by channels, an interpretation which would give the company much larger areas of contiguous woodland? A majority of the Supreme Court adopted the former view, but Duff dissented. In a most interesting judgement, he reviewed the history of the area, pointing out that the people living in it and officials had always considered "Lake Maatis" to be the larger body of water and governed themselves accordingly for many generations. Price Brothers appealed successfully to the Privy Council, which reversed the majority judgement, affirming Duff's opinion.[45]

Lizzie had been unwell before her summer trip to Europe. On her return in October her condition worsened, and she spent virtually all of the next five months in bed, forcing herself at the end of March 1926 to go with Duff to Atlantic City, where they hoped she would improve. Her spirits rebounded, if not her physical condition. Duff's friend Cromarty, also ill, wrote to Atlantic City: "I am delighted to hear Mrs. D. is feeling so well and strong. Just say to her that, although I am in bed, I will run her a race this summer and we will both be well again."[46]

But Lizzie could race no more. On her return to Ottawa she took to her bed, and death became only a matter of time. Duff continued to work, but Lizzie's state drove him to frenzied activity which caused a breakdown later in the year. Duff was quite unable to face serious illness in others. He might have been expected to stay close to home, but he did not. He employed a housekeeper to care for her in absences which became more and more frequent, with visits to the Country Club, the Rideau Club, the Golf Club, and to the houses of friends. He always went by taxi, a lifelong habit since he did not know how to drive and never owned a car. And on these visits he began to drink unwisely.

Early in July, Lizzie lapsed into unconsciousness. On the evening of the 8th she suffered a stroke and died peacefully in her home. Following a private funeral, she was buried in Beechwood Cemetery, not far from her first Ottawa house. The obituaries used such phrases as "Greatly Beloved Ottawa Hostess."[47] Condolences poured in from a wide circle of acquaintances and friends, among them Borden, Haldane, Aulay Morrison, Neville Chamberlain, and Sir Charles Fitzpatrick. Duncan Campbell Scott wrote Duff a graceful letter. Anglin left a calling card, but wrote nothing on it. Duff replied to them all.

It is obvious that many people were genuinely attracted to Lizzie and that she had not merely many acquaintances but numerous friends. It is also clear that whatever difficulties existed in earlier stages of the marriage had vanished; in spite of Duff's erratic absences, the two had, paradoxically, grown closer, and he was completely broken up by her death.[48] His good friend John Stevenson wrote Hume Wrong asking him to invite Duff for a weekend: "Poor old Judge Duff has just lost his wife and is very forlorn...[he said] he was sick of Ottawa and would like to go away somewhere even if only for a weekend but he had no one to go with and did not want to land in a strange place all alone." And then Stevenson gave Wrong a brief but affectionate portrait of Duff as seen by his friends: "A widower, and a very charming one, beloved by all who know him, fairly well off, the boon companion of august personages like Lords Haldane, Birkenhead and Dunedin and not a fanatical prohibitionist."[49]

Lizzie had died without a will; so often, lawyers fail to take care of their own or their families' business affairs. She did leave two letters, however, in one of which she said she wished all her estate to go to her unmarried sister Maggie, and in the other that she wanted her brother Edward and Maggie to share equally. Not a mention of Lyman, who, far from being offended and perhaps feeling the pangs of guilt, did his best to see that her wishes were carried out. Even though he was the sole heir, since the letters were legally ineffective, he wrote Edward Bird to tell him that he would not take one cent from Lizzie's estate. Bird replied that he would not accept any money and, very sensibly, told Duff not to be foolish; he "should rather be protected from his own generosity than be allowed to bleed himself white."[50] It seems that Duff followed his brother-in-law's advice, at least to the extent of taking some benefit from her estate, relatively small at less than twenty thousand dollars, rather than let it slip away.

Although he attracted women, Duff never remarried or formed a romantic attachment — never so much as took a woman friend to dinner or a play. Still, he enjoyed the company of women, and for years made a habit of sending flowers to his female friends, carefully selecting red roses for one, yellow for another, or gladioli of varying colours. He found safety in numbers, apparently, because he met his female acquaintances and friends at large social functions. To those who encountered him on such occasions, he might have seemed dull company unless there was the stimulus of intelligent conversation. But he had presence: when he walked into a room, he commanded the attention of all who did not know him. This was partly the effect of his carriage. He was not tall — perhaps five feet seven — but he had a head slightly disproportionate to the size of his body. He carried himself well. He had a strong face, exuding character and confidence heightened by the sharpness of his gaze. Partly it stemmed from his dress: always immaculate, perhaps even fastidious. He had a large wardrobe which he replenished by having at least two suits tailored for him in England every year.

Kathleen Black, who worked as his stenographer for about ten years until around 1935, had definite designs on Duff. She was a good friend to Duff's sisters, and often wrote to them on family matters at his request. The relationship between her and Duff went beyond mere stenography: they were obviously good friends, but her lack of social standing would have made it impossible for Duff to have carried the relationship any further.

In the only letter from her he seems to have kept, she was affectionate, sure in the knowledge that Duff would not be offended by the intimate tone. Writing to him when he was out of town, addressing him as "Dear Mr. J.," she typed a long, gossipy letter about books, people, works of art, and the doings of Duff's fellow judges. She urged him to prepare a "really clever speech" for a reunion he planned to attend at the University of Toronto, "entirely for your classmates' sakes, for they really do love and revere you." She finished her letter by hand, telling him, "This is the part you think should be written by hand. I am very proud of you, and pleased with Anna's report. I should have been much surprised if it had been otherwise." The reference to "Anna" and her "report" is mysterious, but that Duff had declared handwriting to be a more suitable medium than type for conveying personal feelings reveals some degree of warmth; perhaps he did reciprocate her feelings but, realizing his impotence, disciplined himself not to yield to them.[51]

The failure to secure the chief justiceship, followed within two years by the loss of his wife, led to increasingly heavier drinking which nearly robbed him of the chief justiceship when his chance came again in 1933. He was made ill by it a number of times in the six years following Lizzie's death, the first being in the fall of 1926, when he spent two weeks in hospital recovering from nervous exhaustion just before the court opened its October session. Those six were to be years of loneliness and misery.

# 11

# The bitter years

EARLY IN JUNE 1926, the federal cabinet made Duff chairman of a nine-man commission to apportion church properties between the newly created United Church of Canada and those Presbyterian congregations who had elected not to join the union. Methodists, Congregationalists, and some Presbyterians had banded together in 1923 to form the new body that was confirmed by act of Parliament in 1924,[1] but many Presbyterians, the "non-concurring congregations," chose to retain their identity along with significant Presbyterian church assets, including theology schools and endowment funds. Should these be part of the union? If not, how should they be divided? And what of funds for overseas missions? These and other questions had to be resolved in a reasonable, perhaps even in a Christian, fashion. To some it seemed that God and Mammon had joined forces, and one of the lawyers involved in the commission aptly summed up how incongruous it was for spiritual societies to be contending for temporal goods: "It is to me personally a pitiable thing that two bodies of those professedly following the [same] Christ should have required the services of a Commissioner to make a division of these assets."[2] Duff described the dilemma:

> Here you have two Churches, a United Church and a continuing Church proceeding. The United Church requires funds for a certain purpose; a continuing Church requires funds for precisely the same purpose. On what principle is the board to say that continuing Church may not require just as much, in proportion to its membership, as the United Church, or even more, possibly?"[3]

The statute creating the new church provided for the commission in case the two groups were unable to agree. As no agreement was reached, each side appointed three representatives and those six chose three neutral commissioners — Duff and two Toronto lawyers, Dyce Saunders and T.P. Galt.

Duff's choice was significant for two reasons. His father in 1892 and 1893 had been an early advocate of union among the three sects despite the fact that in his time, the strongest opposition came from his own Congregationalists.[4] It is also interesting that his sponsor for the chairmanship should have been Newton Rowell, a devoted Methodist layman who had played an important role in bringing about church union. It may have been because Duff had forsaken his Congregational upbringing by the 1920s to join Lizzie in the Church of England; obviously, to avoid conflict of interest, no Presbyterian or United Church member could have headed the tribunal, and a Roman Catholic would have been out of the question. The fact that Rowell wanted Duff is more evidence, if any were needed, that prior to his wife's death in July 1926 his faculties had not been affected to any degree by drink. No abstemious man such as Rowell would have recommended a known drunkard to preside over the parcelling of assets between two groups of strait-laced Protestants.[5]

The commission met briefly in Ottawa late in June to settle procedural details, but put off its actual sitting until September. The adjournment was convenient for the lawyers, but Duff must have been relieved too, as Lizzie clearly would not live much longer. The commission reassembled in Toronto, and starting on 14 September met intermittently until 22 January, the last of the fifteen full days of hearings. Tilley acted as counsel for the United Church and D.L. MacCarthy for the continuing Presbyterians.

The hearings were unusual in that no witnesses were called. Instead, the lawyers submitted long inventories of assets, property appraisals, balance sheets, and statistical lists of congregations throughout the country, and then presented cases based on these documents. Yet they still managed to be lively, and Duff himself took an active part with frequent questions and comments. The lawyers often agreed in mid-stream on the disposition of particular properties, and Duff gave his seal of approval, incorporating all these accords later into the formal orders of the commission.

Duff and Isaac Pitblado, a well-known Winnipeg lawyer and one of the United Church nominees, wrote most of the report. The total assets amounted to $10.5 million, and of these the commission awarded the non-concurring Presbyterians $3.26 million, or roughly 31 per cent. The United Church suffered its heaviest blow when the Presbyterians got Knox College in Toronto and Presbyterian College in Montreal, along with their endowment funds. Still, the commission's work received praise from all sides. Dr. W.L. Clay, a former moderator of the Presbyterian church and a non-concurring Presbyterian who had known Duff in Victoria, wrote him to recall a meeting the two of them had attended in that city at which Clay prophesied that "Canada might one day enjoy the benefit of your acute mind in some important judicial position."[6]

Not all the non-concurring felt that justice had triumphed, however. One of them, who chose to remain anonymous, wrote a parody of the well-known hymn, "The Church's One Foundation," which he suggested become "Hymn No. 1" in the new denomination's book. Two verses give the flavour:

Our church's one foundation
Is Mason's Union Bill,
She is his new creation
By legal craft and skill;
From Parliament he sought her
To force into his fold
and for law fees to slaughter
The Scottish kirk of old.

Mid toil and agitation
(And cold financial fear)
She waits the confiscation
of Presbyterian gear,
Till by that steal so glorious
Her longing eyes are blessed
And Union all victorious
Hath swallowed up the rest.[7]

G.W. Mason was a prominent Toronto lawyer who had played a role in getting the United Church Bill through Parliament. As with the Shell Committee inquiry, so with the church commission: Duff's colleagues accepted pay for their services, but he did not.

Duff heard an appeal afterwards that caused a sensation in United Church circles. A Presbyterian congregation in Nova Scotia had decided initially not to join the union, but changed its mind by a majority vote after the Act had come into force. Its non-concurring members went to court claiming that the pro-union resolution came too late because the Act contained no mechanism for delayed entry. A majority of the Supreme Court, though not Duff, agreed. Taking heart from Duff's support, the union faction appealed to the Privy Council; the London judges bowed in Duff's direction by referring to the "powerful assistance" the pro-union group had derived from his judgement, but they dismissed the appeal.[8] Two other church disputes reached the Supreme Court, both arising from difficulties in deciding how to dispose of Presbyterian trust funds held in private hands.[9]

His wife's illness kept Duff from going to London in 1926. Anglin, who as chief justice had been sworn automatically as an Imperial privy councillor, sat on a few appeals that year, but Haldane missed Duff: "The C.J. [Anglin] has done well, but we would like to have you too particularly."[10] Duff responded to this invitation by going over to sit with Haldane in 1927. Arriving, he learned of the death of his brother Rolph, who had been living in Michigan for over twenty years; following an active ministry in the Congregational church, he had been an executive assistant to two governors of that state, and when he died he was a member of the Michigan Public Utilities Commission. Lyman and he had virtually lost touch with each other, their only point of contact being their sister Emma, who sometimes passed news between them. Lyman was so little interested in his brother's activities, in fact, that for several years he had known nothing of his work, or even his address.

In an appeal from the court of the judicial commissioners of Oudh in India, Duff delivered the judgement of the board. The case concerned a death-bed will executed by "a taluqdar of Athgawan in the District of Partabgarh." Hoping to avoid a family quarrel over the division of his estate, the dying man summoned his children and asked all of them, plus two unrelated legal witnesses, to sign his will. One family member challenged the will's validity on the grounds that the signatories were barred from any inheritance, since under English law applicable in India, a beneficiary could not witness a will. Duff and his colleagues ruled that the children had signed only to allay their father's fear of a dispute — a vain hope, as it turned out — and not to validate the document.[11]

He did not see Haldane again; the statesman-philosopher-jurist died in 1928. Duff was saddened by the loss of his closest colleague at court. Later that year, he became ill. The details are sketchy, but his condition, caused by stress and overindulgence in liquor, was serious enough to worry his friends. One of them, his fellow-councillor Lord Hailsham, sent a discreet inquiry to R.B. Bennett in 1932:

> When I was in Canada in the autumn of 1929, I remembered that Mr. Justice Duff had been incapacitated by illness. I heard later that he had recovered and was quite himself again, but I really have no recent information as to whether he really has got rid of his weakness or as to whether it has left any traces on his great judicial power...

He wanted to know "what the position is," and if Duff was again the "outstanding figure" of former days.[12] Hailsham came to Canada a few months after this; Duff gave a dinner for him in Ottawa and no doubt laid his worries to rest.

Duff went to London in 1929 but did not go again until 1936. As far as 1931 and 1932 are concerned, the gap is explained by his commitments on the Transportation Commission, but in 1930 he was simply not well enough; heavy drinking had brought on a serious breakdown that kept him in hospital for over three months. Duff's alcoholism in this low period of his life was apparent in his behaviour at the New Year's Day levee given by the Governor-General in the Senate Chamber that year. A young subaltern attending with other officers of his regiment observed a man in formal clothes standing near the bar, obviously drunk, at eleven o'clock in the morning. Friends escorted him out of the chamber in a state of near-collapse. Struck by the episode and curious to know the man's identity, the subaltern learned that it was Duff.[13]

Three weeks before his breakdown, he heard a habeas corpus application on behalf of the rum-running distillery tycoon Harry Bronfman, described modestly as a "merchant," who had been jailed in Saskatchewan on a number of charges. Duff ordered that he be brought to Ottawa for the full hearing, at which he ruled that Bronfman had been validly imprisoned while awaiting trial and would have to return to Regina.[14] In his book on the Bronfmans, Peter Newman refers to this episode.

> Meticulously briefed on this complicated maneuver and assured that Harry was safely tucked in a Regina jail, McGillivray and his colleagues appeared before Duff on December 17th [1929]. They seemed to be convincing him, but for technical reasons the Supreme Court judge decided to put off his verdict until the following day. Instead, Duff went on one of his periodical benders and didn't return to the bench until two weeks later, leaving Bronfman pacing his cell in the interval. When he did return, Duff appeared to reverse himself and dismissed the application. Harry re-applied for bail, cursed his lawyers, and returned to his suite at the Hotel Saskatchewan to await the trial, which was eventually set for a courtroom in Estevan.[15]

Newman's account is grossly inaccurate. Bronfman had been charged in 1929 with offering a sum of money to a customs officer "with intent to interfere corruptly with the due administration of justice," an offence punishable under the Criminal Code. He made his first appearance on the charge at Regina on 20 December 1929; after a preliminary hearing on 18 January 1930, a normal procedure for this type of crime, a magistrate ordered him to stand trial. Bronfman also faced trial on two charges under the Customs Act. In an application before Duff on 22 January 1930, his lawyers secured a writ of habeas corpus ordering that Bronfman be physically produced in court on 1 February, at which time they could question the ruling that Bronfman must stand trial on all three charges. The merchant and his counsel duly appeared — among them Eugene Lafleur, on a case destined to be one of his last — to argue that the committals for trial were nullities because the prosecution had produced no legal evidence to establish guilt. Duff said that he would hand down his decision on the 3rd, which he did. He ruled that one of the three committal orders was invalid, but as the other two were not, Bronfman would have to remain in custody until trial.

There is no doubt that Duff drank heavily at this time in his life, but he did not go on a "bender" in the middle of Bronfman's case. In saying that Duff "appeared to reverse himself," Newman does not realize that his 22 January order was a routine one to ensure Bronfman's right to attend the formal hearing; he was not making a ruling on the merits of his case at that stage. And finally, Bronfman did not spend additional time in jail because of Duff.[16]

Lord Willingdon's term as Governor-General ended on 20 March 1931, but since his actual departure from Canada was planned for January, an

Administrator had to be appointed as acting head of state until his successor arrived. In a Governor-General's absence from the country, or disabling illness, or during a vacancy, the Administrator exercises all functions of the office and basks in all its privileges, including the aides and the pomp and the form of address, "Your Excellency"; this function differs from that of deputy Governor-General, a familiar one to Duff, who in the viceroy's temporary absence or indisposition gives the royal assent to bills and approves orders-in-council. As chief justice, Anglin would normally have acted, but he had fallen seriously ill and went off on three month's leave early in the new year. Duff, the next senior judge, was sworn to act in his stead.

An official in the secretary of state's office asked him to select an armorial device to be engraved on a privy seal. Duff gave this heraldry problem a good deal of thought, and on a number of occasions discussed it with the undersecretary, eventually selecting a crest of one of the many Duff families found in a book he had been poring over.[17] And he readied the privy councillor's uniform he had bought with just such an occasion in mind. Though Duff would have taken no pleasure in Anglin's illness, he must have reflected that, for once, fate had been kind to him, and that as a privy councillor senior to Anglin, he was actually the more logical choice. On 16 January 1931, moments after word arrived that the vessel carrying Willingdon back to England had left the shores of Canada, Duff presented himself before the clerk of the Privy Council to be sworn in. He felt great satisfaction and pride, natural emotions that were heightened by the expectation that he would open the coming parliamentary session. By mid-February, it was known that Parliament would reconvene on 12 March, some eight days before Lord Bessborough's expected arrival. Duff would indeed open Parliament, and read the speech from the throne.

As the days passed, however, he began to worry that the great moment might be denied him. A stomach disorder grew worse, and it became obvious to him and his doctors that something was seriously wrong. Fortunately, the condition did not disable him, and he was determined to carry on. On the morning of 12 March the new French ambassador presented his letters of credence. Early that afternoon, Duff dressed painstakingly in his gold-encrusted uniform, slipped the gilded sword into the scabbard that hung on a golden cord wrapped around his waist, donned a cocked hat, and set out from his home in a limousine for Parliament Hill. A cavalry troop from the Princess Louise Dragoon Guards escorted the car through the wintry Ottawa streets. As he stepped into bleak sunshine on the Hill, the regimental band of the Governor-General's Foot Guards played the national anthem. Duff inspected the guard of honour mounted by the same regiment while a nearby battery of artillery boomed a nineteen-gun salute. He walked with great dignity to the Hall of Fame in the Peace Tower where he was welcomed by two dozen senior officers of the navy, army, and air force, in full regalia. The ceremonial procession conducting him to the Senate Chamber included the prime minister and the leader of the Senate, military officers wearing full regimental dress, and senior government officials. When the Administrator and his party had reached the Chamber, Black Rod summoned the Commons, in obedience to ancient ritual, to hear the speech read by the Sovereign's representative in both English and French.

Leaving Parliament, Duff received a second artillery salute, the cavalry troop formed up, and the honour guard stood to attention as the band played the royal salute. As he settled into his limousine for the drive home, he reflected that he was the first person born in Canada to open the Canadian Parliament. His two sisters had come to Ottawa for the occasion and the dinner parties and receptions that followed, but Duff, unwell, could not do justice to these entertainments. Only four days later, his concerned doctor sent him to a specialist in Montreal, who diagnosed cancer of the colon. Duff underwent a successful operation for the removal of a large section of his bowel and made a complete recovery, although he could not return to work until July.[18]

The malignancy did not recur, but, not unnaturally, Duff worried for some years that it might. He took a deeper interest in cancer research, keeping up with the latest advances through the *Lancet*. On New Year's Day, 1935, Lord Bessborough announced the establishment of the King George V Silver Jubilee Cancer Fund that was his vicereine's inspiration. Lady Bessborough was also a driving force in the campaign which by June of that year raised over four hundred thousand dollars, a good round figure in the depression era. Duff willingly agreed to become one of the seven trustees, along with Bennett and King. His active role in the fund's affairs over several years brought him in touch with the surgeon who had operated on him, or, as Duff said, "saved his life," Dr. Edward Archibald of McGill. Archibald was one of the early advocates of an organization akin to the Canadian Cancer Society, and he talked about the quest of such a body to "find out the cause, and then the cure of cancer." In a striking metaphor he used to Duff, "You can't kill a dragon by keeping an eye open for him, especially if his hiding place is well concealed. We need St. George's spear which can kill him whether young or old, whether out in the open, or in his cave."[19]

A few months after his operation, Duff spent two months in an Ottawa hospital suffering from nervous exhaustion compounded by the effects of alcohol. His two sisters in Toronto, alarmed at their brother's behaviour so soon after surgery, began making plans to reform him. Quite literally, they were to rescue him from alcoholic oblivion and financial ruin.

During all these years of disappointment and illness, his financial troubles did nothing but increase; indeed he came closer to utter disaster in the five or six years prior to 1932, the year his sister Annie came to live with him, than at any other time in his life. His personal finances were in disarray, if not completely out of control. In what was probably a typical month during this period, September 1929, when his monthly salary did not exceed a thousand dollars, he spent more than $1,750. That sum included payments of five hundred dollars on his account with the Country Club and four hundred towards his taxi bill. He wrote cheques for over eight hundred dollars in cash at his bank, the Chateau Laurier, and the Rideau Club. Unquestionably, some of the cash and a large part of his Country Club account were going on liquor. In a two-day period in 1931, for example, he bought eight bottles of gin. Gin is not purchased to be laid down like wine, but to be drunk.[20] His banks in Ottawa and London wrote dunning letters demanding that he cover his large overdrafts, which, with difficulty, he managed to do. He had hired a manservant he could not pay; the man wrote on Duff's own note-paper pleading for his wages. Duff had a bit of money in shares which he lost in the stock-market crash of 1929. Yet in 1928, he sent two thousand dollars, a sixth of his annual salary, as a wedding present to one of Edward Bird's sons, telling Bird "I am rather hard up at present, but must do what I know Lizzie would have done if she had been alive."[21]

His acts of generosity, frequently impulsive, amounted to improvidence. Each year at Christmas, he gave a cheque for one hundred dollars to Archie Lacelle, the longtime doorman at the Rideau Club, and one for a hundred and fifty to Stella Malone, the Country Club stewardess. A group of nuns once called on him for a donation. One of them said in thanks, "Oh, dear Chief Justice. You are a very good man." Chuckling, Duff replied, "I am not. I am a very bad man."[22] He was a soft touch for hard-luck stories. One evening, Duff went into the Chateau Laurier to ask the cashier if he could have twenty-five dollars. Not knowing him, the cashier called the night auditor, who recognized Duff and cashed his cheque. Duff left, to return a few minutes later and request another twenty-five. The auditor, puzzled, asked him if he had lost his money. Duff's answer was, "I met a poor man at the front door on my way who told me a sad story and I gave him the twenty-five dollars."[23]

His financial troubles deepened with the depression. In 1932, he could not pay his medical bills; his coal merchant wrote a plaintive letter asking for payment, as he himself had heavy obligations to meet. And to top it all off, his name appeared on a list of members of the Royal Ottawa Golf Club "posted" for non-payment of dues.

The court was bound to feel the effects of Duff's absences during this time, but, surprisingly, the number of cases on which he sat in the period between Anglin's appointment and his operation in 1931 was not much less than for any similar period, nor was there the slightest sign that his intellectual capacity had been affected. He delivered a ruling that is still referred to by lawyers, defining in what circumstances close relatives may receive a larger share of an estate when they claim that a deceased has not bequeathed his assets fairly to his family.[24] He handed down a ruling — still valid — to settle in what circumstances an intoxicated person charged with murder may be convicted of the lesser crime of manslaughter.[25] This decision is one more example of an important case in which Duff ruled in favour of the accused. Also during this time, there were two notable constitutional cases; in each of them, his opinion was reversed by the Privy Council.

In the *Aeronautics* case of 1929, Duff and his colleagues ruled that the federal government did not have the sole power to regulate air transport in Canada, only certain parts of it such as the carrying of mail. The Supreme Court of Canada agreed in essence with the provinces' argument that air travel fell within their power to make laws relating to property and civil rights. The Privy Council disagreed, however, ruling that the whole subject of air carriage lay, in its every aspect, with the federal government of Canada. The decision is important, not only because of its result, but also because of the reasoning used in it. The board, headed by the Lord Chancellor, Viscount Sankey, evidently concluded that, from a practical point of view, federal regulation made a good deal more sense than the patchwork which would result if regulations were made by individual provinces. With that object in mind, it combed the British North America Act for language to support its proposition. The judges ruled, for example, that since air travel formed the subject of an international convention — not even a formal treaty — to which Canada was party, the treaty-making provision of the B.N.A. Act gave the federal government the power to implement it. Not only that, but the fact that Canada had signed a convention at all put the subject in the category of "national interest and importance," thus meeting the test formulated earlier by Duff and Haldane.[26] The decision came back to haunt constitutional lawyers, but a passage in Lord Sankey's judgement that describes the federal nature of the Canadian constitution is valuable in the light of contemporary political debate.

Inasmuch as the Act [British North America Act] embodies a compromise under which the original Provinces agreed to federate, it is important to keep in mind that the preservation of the rights of minorities was a condition on which such minorities entered into the federation, and the foundation upon which the whole structure was subsequently erected. The process of interpretation as the years go on ought not to be allowed to dim or to whittle down the provisions of the original contract upon which the federation was founded, nor is it legitimate that any judicial construction of the provisions of ss.91 and 92 should impose a new and different contract upon the federating bodies.[27]

The second overruling of a Duff decision occurred in a far more controversial case concerning the eligibility of women to be named to the Senate, famous as the *Persons* case. The question did not involve the distribution of powers between the various governments but whether the words "qualified persons," used in section 24 of the British North America Act authorizing senatorial appointments, included females. Five well-known feminists — Henrietta Muir Edwards, Nellie McClung, Louise McKinney, Emily Murphy, and Irene Parlby — had presented Mackenzie King's government with a petition demanding that a woman be appointed. True to his political style, King handed this hot potato to the courts. Every judge of the Supreme Court, Duff included, ruled that women were not eligible, but for different reasons.

Anglin and three other judges took the medieval approach to the question. In the Middle Ages, men went to the Crusades or to other theatres of male warfare leaving their womenfolk to tend the castle and manage the servants. Since only men fought in battle, so it was reasoned, only men were fit to govern. The historical fact became enshrined in a rule of common law which Anglin and some colleagues applied. Anglin said, for example, that clearer language would be required in the British North America Act in order to abrogate the common-law rule most succinctly stated by an English judge in the nineteenth century: "I take it that by neither the common law nor the Constitution of this country from the beginning of the common law until now can a woman be entitled to exercise any public function."[28]

Duff posed the problem for the court to solve at the very beginning of his judgement.

> Is the word "persons" in section 24 of the B.N.A. Act the equivalent of male persons? "Persons" in the ordinary sense of the word includes, of course, natural persons of both sexes. But the sense of words is often radically affected by the context in which they are found, as well as by the occasion on which they are used; and in construing a legislative enactment, considerations arising not only from the context, but from the nature of the subject matter and object of the legislation, may require us to ascribe to general words a scope more restricted than their usual import, in order loyally to effectuate the intention of the legislature. And for this purpose, it is sometimes the duty of a court of law to resort, not only to other provisions of the enactment itself, but to the state of the law at the time the enactment was passed, and to the history, especially the legislative history, of the subjects with which the enactment deals.

Having stated the question, he then analysed the "general character and purpose of the B.N.A. Act," concluding that the legislative authority of Parliament extends over all matters concerning the peace, order and good government of Canada; and it may with confidence be affirmed that, excepting such matters as are assigned to the provinces, and such as are definitely dealt with by the Act itself, and subject, moreover, to an exception of undefined scope having relation to the sovereign, legislative authority throughout its whole range is committed to Parliament.

This broad affirmation is striking, for when he was considering Parliament's authority to make laws for aeronautics, he seems to have reached the opposite conclusion. He went on to examine the language of section 24, rejecting the proposition that there was "a general presumption against the eligibility of women for public office." He then elaborated this view in carefully chosen language:

> It might be suggested, I cannot help thinking, with some plausibility, that there would be something incongruous in a parliamentary system professedly conceived and fashioned on this principle, if persons fully qualified to be members of the House of Commons were by an iron rule of the constitution, a rule beyond the reach of Parliament, excluded from the Cabinet or the Government; if a class of persons who might reach any position of political influence, power or leadership in the House of Commons, were permanently, by an organic rule, excluded from the Government.

He maintained, in laboured language, that

> the Constitution in its Executive Branch was intended to be capable of adaptation to whatever changes (permissible under the Act) in the law and practice relating to the Election Branch might be progressively required by changes in public opinion.

It might have been thought up to this point that he would hold in favour of the women, but he did not. Instead, he decided that "there is much to point to an intention that the constitution of the Senate should follow the lines of the Constitution of the old Legislative Council under the Acts of 1791 and 1840," from which women had always been excluded; according to the strict wording of section 24, only male persons were eligible.[29] Though he was more liberal in these matters than his colleagues, Duff could not bring himself to take that final leap. By this restraint, he failed to heed the advice he himself had given the Canadian Bar Association's 1915 meeting in Montreal:

Every lawyer knows that no system of law worthy of the name, whether it be cast in the form of a code or not, can be a mere collection of mechanical rules. By the law, a lawyer means the law in operation, the law in action; the law as it is commonly said is a living organism, possessing like every living organism, within limits, of course, the power to adapt itself to changing circumstances.[30]

Newspaper reaction to the decision was predictable, ranging from outrage to ridicule. An editorial in the Ottawa *Evening Journal*, typical of many other comments, put the court in a foolish light.

What? Women "Not Persons?"...the Supreme Court has made a terrible guess. How they came to make it, and they all married, only themselves and the Lord can know; and perhaps only the Lord. But in any case, the harm's done. Sitting there in their scarlet and ermine and with not a shadow of a smile on their legal faces, they said, emphatically and unanimously... "that women are not persons within s.24." Well, frankly, we don't believe it....The Fathers [of Confederation] may not have been sheiks or lounge lizards but there is no overwhelming proof that we've ever seen that any of them were asses...

Shame upon you gentlemen of the Supreme Court! Where is your gallantry, your chivalry?

...we're in the absurd position that a woman can sit in the House of Commons, where laws are really made and cannot sit in the Senate where they are merely reviewed. It looks as though Bumble ["the law is a Ass"] was right.[31]

Oddly, this editorial appeared barely a month after the same paper had pronounced, "We regret to say it, but it is true that women, as politicians, have been pretty much flat failures. The proof is complete, overwhelming."[32]

Undaunted by the decision — perhaps even heartened by it — the five women appealed to the Privy Council, supported, as they had been at the Ottawa hearing, by the province of Alberta. In constitutional cases, each province has the right to "intervene," or be heard, but as extraordinary as this may seem, only one other province, Quebec, thought the case important enough to take part in it, and then only in Ottawa. Newton Rowell had argued the women's case in Ottawa, and he also appeared in London. The federal government fought the London battle as well, hiring Eugene Lafleur to try to convince five English judges that women were not "persons."

Every lawyer knows that no matter how strong or weak his case, he may get one decision from one judge and an opposite decision on the same set of facts from another. Rowell was in luck. Sankey, the liberal-minded Lord Chancellor in a Labour government, presided over the four-day appeal. All Lafleur's charm and skill failed to sway him, and he wrote a judgement to rationalize what he believed to be a sensible result. He was embarrassed by the position taken by Duff, who knew far more about the Canadian constitution than he did. Acknowledging that Duff had correctly rejected the common-law rule excluding women from government, Sankey then demolished his contention that the senatorial provisions of the British North America Act were masculine:

> The word "person"…may include members of both sexes, and to those who ask why the word should include females, the obvious answer is why should it not? In these circumstances the burden is upon those who deny that the word includes women to make out their case.[33]

Sankey's decision and that of Duff in the *Persons* case represent diametrically opposite approaches. Commentators on the Canadian constitution and its interpretation by the Supreme Court of Canada and the Privy Council have tended to fall into two camps. One holds that courts should interpret the constitution in active response to social pressures, changing economic conditions, and shifts in public opinion. This group points with approval to the Supreme Court of the United States which, unlike the Canadian court, does not have general jurisdiction over lawsuits, but is limited to certain federal matters including the interpreting of the constitution. The judges of the U.S. Supreme Court have always made more broadly political decisions than the judges of the Supreme Court of Canada. It can be argued that every constitutional case has an element of politics, but the American court has generally been more conscious of this. Now, of course, Canada's Charter of Rights requires Canadian judges to assume a role akin to that of their American counterparts.

The second constitutional camp argues that to handle the B.N.A. Act differently from other statutes leads to uncertainty and confusion. It may be a constitution, but it is also an Act of Parliament to be interpreted by traditional and strict methods. As with any other statute — say, for example, the Goat Breeders Protection Act — the question is what precisely the words mean. If judges are allowed to interpret the constitution in any other way, they are asked to choose, according to their own notions, the social conditions that should determine the result of a particular case. It is better to leave Parliament the task of gauging the significance of social change, letting it respond by enacting laws that can then be interpreted in the traditional way by the courts.

Duff belonged to the second group, of course, and his decision in the *Persons* case, though his sympathies lay with the women, was a striking demonstration of his traditionalism. One must admire his ability to divorce himself from social considerations and confine his attention to legal detail. He was not a judicial activist, but a judicial traditionalist. Speaking of the American Supreme Court, he once told a friend, "I think that with a constitution that in so great a degree leaves the tone and drift of legislation to the courts for examination under such a system the statesmanship or lack of it of judges seems to be of legitimate public interest."[34] And yet, oddly, Duff appeared to favour the activist approach, at least when speaking off the bench. He made frequent reference to the great flexibility of the common law in adapting to new circumstances and conditions. Writing his friend Dafoe about a visit to Harvard, he commented:

> It is very comforting to see in operation such an admirable system for the training of lawyers for the practical business of the profession, which aims at the same time to liberalize their minds by appeals to the history of legal ideas and political institutions and by keeping constantly before them the function of the law as a social and political agent.[35]

Even Mr. Justice Rinfret, eulogizing Duff after his death, said that he had "treated the law as a social instrument for the preservation and development of new things that made modern life possible."[36] The truth is that Duff's view of the law as a "social instrument" had no application to the field of constitutional law, and limited application in other fields. His declarations from the bench somehow fell short of those uttered elsewhere.

Learning of the *Persons* ruling, the Ottawa *Evening Journal* exulted in an editorial headed, "The Privy Council Agrees With Us."

> We knew all along we were right. When our Supreme Court last year said that women weren't "persons" we got into a towering rage. We said that in our judgement a woman was not only a person but a personage....The Privy Council, of course, doesn't mention us...probably the reason he [Lord Sankey] didn't name us right out there in court was that he didn't want to create hard feelings, or sort of rub the thing in. Some people, and especially some judges, are terribly touchy.[37]

And so the five feminists had triumphed. Any of them would have been an ornament to the Senate, but Mackenzie King's mind ran in different channels. Perhaps as a rebuke to them for causing him so much trouble, King, not long before he went out of office in 1930, named Cairinne Wilson, a staunch Liberal, as the first female senator. She and Duff were close friends and saw a good deal of each other over the years; she would have a hand in his rehabilitation.

# 12

# Chief Justice at last

LATE IN 1931, the federal government appointed a "Royal Commission to Inquire into Railways and Transportation in Canada." The "Transportation Commission," as it became known, had seven members: Lord Ashfield, head of the London underground system; Sir Joseph Flavelle; L.F. Loree, president of the Delaware and Hudson Railway Company; Beaudry Leman of the Banque Canadienne Nationale, at the time of his appointment President of the Canadian Bankers' Association; Dr. Clarence Webster of Shediac, New Brunswick; Dr. Walter Murray, president of the University of Saskatchewan, who had also been a member of the United Church Commission; and, finally, Duff as chairman. The government intended that various regions of the nation should be represented; Duff, presumably, despite his long absence, could stand for British Columbia, but in fact, his former residence there had had nothing to do with the appointment; Sir Edward Beatty of the C.P.R. had urged the choice.[1]

The commission itself, however, had been suggested earlier in 1931 by Sir Henry Thornton, head of Canadian National Railways, as he told a select committee of the House of Commons about the financial difficulties of both major rail systems, conditions attributable in part to economic depression, in part to the advent of other means of transport, principally motor vehicles, and in part also to allegedly ruinous competition and wasteful duplication between the railways. The commissions's terms of reference went beyond the railways' plight to include "the whole problem of transportation in Canada...having regard to present conditions and the probable future developments of the country."[2] Despite a broad scope amounting to carte blanche, however, the spotlight was focussed on Canadian Pacific and Canadian National. Those sympathetic to the former feared nationalization and merger with C.N.R.;

those sympathetic to the latter feared the abandonment of the publicly owned system and its annexation by the C.P.R. Newspaper and political comment on the work of the commission concentrated on these fears.

Duff had accepted the job with reluctance, anticipating, correctly as it turned out, that it would place a heavy strain on his health. He told a correspondent that within two months he was "constantly assailed by regrets that I had not the obstinacy to decline the job."[3] At the time he was named on 20 November 1931 he was actually in hospital, but carried on preliminary correspondence from his bed, not leaving until 2 December. Two days after this, he and his colleagues greeted Lord Ashfield on his arrival at Ottawa Union Station; they all lunched at the Rideau Club, and dined the same evening with the Governor-General at Rideau Hall. The next day, Duff and his fellow members opened the commission sessions by listening to Dr. R.J. Manion, minister of railways and canals, and Sir George Perley, acting prime minister, emphasize the national importance of their work. Speaking for all seven commissioners, Duff replied that they would "spare no effort."[4]

The commissioners heard evidence that day and the next from Beatty and Thornton. As a matter of policy, they decided that testimony from these and other senior railway officials, as well as from representatives of the various governments, would be heard in camera. Not surprisingly, this move drew the censure of every newspaper in the country as well as many private citizens. Duff would not relax his ruling, though briefs to the commission as it travelled about the country were presented publicly. It is hard to see his rationale, but it may have had something to do with the rivalry, or antagonism, between Beatty and Thornton; they may well have been reluctant to give one another, or for that matter the general public, confidential information about railway finances and operations. When the commission delayed publication of its reports, the Ottawa *Evening Journal* observed: "We were aware that its sessions were to be held in secret, but we didn't know that secrecy was to be carried to the point where even the whereabouts of the commissioners would become a mystery."[5]

Duff and Flavelle worked closely together at the stage of organizing the commission's agenda. Their harmony may have been threatened by an incident which John Stevenson described to J.W. Dafoe:

> Sir J. Flavelle has his virtues but he is now aging sadly and is interminably prosy; he has tired out the rest of the Commission with long dissertations about his early experiences with the railways. Moreover, one day he got permanently on the wrong side of the Chairman by an unfortunate remark. Discussing the Grand Trunk decision, Sir J. said that he had always regretted its consequences in Britain and always felt that if his old friend, Sir Walter Cassels had not acquired unfortunate habits (Sir Walter

in his later days, I understand, drank heavily) and thereby impaired his mental faculties, a happier decision would have been rendered. The Chairman took this as a personal thrust at himself and was furious. Since then he has been down on everything that Flavelle proposed or argued and as Sir J. along with Leman are the leading paladins of the C.P.R., the consequences can be gauged....On such episodes turn the fate of governments, nations and railways.[6]

The commission thought it wise at the outset to travel back and forth across the country. However it had to tread delicately, not appearing to spend more time examining the roadbed and branch lines of one system than those of the other. Accordingly, the commissioners went to the Pacific by the C.N.R. and returned by C.P.R. They travelled in private cars with railroad officials, porters, stewards, and waiters dancing attendance. Duff was used to cross-Canada journeyings, but for some of the others the trip must have been an eye-opener. They went straight to the coast, crossing to Victoria by steamer to hear British Columbian submissions. On their way back they stopped in Calgary, making a side trip to Edmonton, and also visited Regina and Winnipeg. A writer for the Winnipeg *Free Press* caught them in an amusing vignette:

> The Commission on Railways looks reasonably imposing when its members group themselves at their table and confront the assembly which had turned out to meet them. Mr. Justice Duff is less massive than had been indicated by his portraits...the oil portraits of dead political worthies shone ripe and mellow in the thin yellow sunlight. There was a feeling of being in church; a solemnity; a pious interval. At eleven-thirty there were no more witnesses, and everybody went away.[7]

The commission granted J.W. Dafoe, the influential *Free Press* editor, the privilege of a private two-hour hearing, probably because of his long-time friendship with Duff. Before he appeared, he wrote Stevenson to express his suspicion that the commission intended to dismantle the C.N.R.:

> We may yet see a so-called National government appealing for a doctor's [Dr. Manion's] mandate to butcher the Canadian National Railway, and put the Canadian Pacific Railway in a position of monopoly under some pretentious camouflage of alleged protection of the public interest.[8]

After his private audience, he confided to a C.N.R. official that he was "not much impressed by the Commission; its members are too old...to have open minds on the issue which underlies the present situation." He thought that six of the commissioners would "feel that they have done a good turn if they find a way to stick a knife in the vitals of the Canadian National."[9]

Dafoe learned later, either from a member of the commission or from one of its staff, that although the majority of commissioners wanted the C.P.R. to operate all the railways, Duff might persuade them to accept a compromise. As he put it to a correspondent,

> It is therefore possible that Mr. Justice Duff and the one or two other members of the Commission who are in general agreement with him, may succeed in putting over a solution which they have roughly in their minds, and which I think would not be very far removed from the development which we in our conversations have come to think would be advisable. Nothing is, however, determined and my informant advised me that there was a doubt in his mind as to whether Duff would adhere to the cause for which he has expressed a preference if Mr. Bennett indicated a decided preference for a solution less favorable to the Canadian National Railway and, as we would think, to the country.[10]

He became so worked up at the possibility of C.N.R. being dismantled that he devised a subterfuge to draw what he saw as an alarming situation to the attention of the public. He asked an Ottawa confederate to mail the *Free Press* a letter he had written himself under a pseudonym to deplore the majority opinion. At the last moment, however, he changed his mind about sending it, evidently concluding that discovery would land him in trouble; certainly Duff would have had no more to do with him.[11]

On the way to Ottawa from Winnipeg, Duff made one more stop to inspect the grain terminals at Fort William, and trips to the Maritimes and Quebec in January wound up the travelling. Unquestionably the central issue before the commission was the relationship between the two railways, with Flavelle as Canadian Pacific's leading protagonist. At a February, 1932 Ottawa hearing, the issue emerged with great clarity during a submission in which A.R. Mosher of the Canadian Brotherhood of Railway Employees advocated nationalizing, not only the railways, but all other forms of transport as well. As reported by the Winnipeg *Free Press*,

> Flavelle emphasized that C.N. had not paid one cent to capital over five years and asked Mosher if this was what he was advocating for all Can. railways. He [Flavelle] said: "When Governments are in control politics play an important part, and when politics enter into business, it spells death."[12]

The American, Loree, expressed approval of these sentiments.

The commission wound up its public phase after fifty days of listening to a welter of advice. Trucking firms wanted more business; railways feared their competition; Saskatchewan farmers favoured, and Manitoba farmers opposed, the merger of the railways. Briefs were received from boards of trade, shipping companies, streetcar operators, automobile associations, bus companies, and a host of other transport groups. The enormous task of recording the material and reading it, let alone digesting it, fell principally on the shoulders of Duff and the commission secretaries, Arthur Moxon of Saskatchewan and G.W. Yates of Ottawa, to both of whom Duff expressed eternal gratitude for their skill. There was no report until 21 September 1932, owing in part to Duff's ill health. Dafoe had observed when appearing before him in mid-December 1931 that he seemed to be "in first-rate shape, with his mind crystal clear and probably devoid so far as man can be of bias,"[13] but the following months took a heavy toll. He did his loyal best to sit in court as often as possible, and the heavy commission work added to his judicial labours simply overwhelmed him. The day before the report came down, Grant Dexter wrote Dafoe, "Mr. Duff, I understand, is on a bit of a binge which has delayed things somewhat."[14] Dexter's comment is one of the few pieces of evidence of serious disruption in Duff's work because of his drinking. There can be no doubt of the truth of what he said: Duff had spent a month in hospital in May and June 1932 recovering from still another attack of drink-induced nervous exhaustion. Bennett became politically embarrassed by the delay and, bearing in mind the reason for it, made certain arrangements with Duff when appointing him chief justice in March of the following year.

When tabled in Parliament, the report proved voluminous. It contained a comprehensive history of public transportation in Canada, in itself a first-rate piece of historical writing which does not deserve the oblivion into which most of the commission's main recommendations sank. It examined the capital expenditures and profit-and-loss statements of the two major railways over many years, giving detailed descriptions of branch lines, hotels, and steamship operations. Qualifying the proliferation of unnecessary rail lines as a "tragedy," the report deplored the failure of C.P.R. and C.N.R. to prevent "irrational and wasteful competition." It pointed out that the competition had had more severe effects on Canadian National, whose crushing debt could not be serviced by revenue from operations which lacked the diversity of the private company's. Though the report commended C.N.R. for "welding together" the various railway systems acquired through the financial failure of others, it condemned "its red-thread of extravagance." This observation and others like it provoked Sir Henry Thornton, who took them personally, to violent protest.

The unanimous report's main recommendation had been anticipated by most observers. The two systems should continue their separate existences;

the commission rejected the idea of merger or, short of merger, a scheme by which the national road would lease its facilities to Canadian Pacific for either a short or long term to achieve economies of operation; the commission feared that merger would be the inevitable result. Duff and his colleagues wanted to correct the errors of the past by providing "machinery for co-operation between the two railways with a view to improving their financial position." They believed that preservation of the identities of the two roads, freedom of each from political interference, and economies of operation, were desirable objectives attainable only by "co-operation between the two systems." With these objectives in mind, they recommended the establishment of a board of trustees made up of three businessmen, not politicians, to replace the directors of Canadian National. They and the directors of the C.P.R. would have a "statutory duty" to

> adopt as soon as practicable such cooperative measures, plans and arrangements as shall, consistent with the proper handling of traffic, be best adapted to the removal of unnecessary or wasteful services or practices, to the avoidance of unwarranted duplication in services or facilities, and to the joint use and operation of all such properties as may conveniently and without due detriment to either party, be so used.

Failing agreement on practical measures to effect economy, an "arbitral tribunal" formed of the chief commissioner of the Board of Railway Commissioners as chairman with one representative from each railway should have "full jurisdiction as to measures, plans and arrangements for the joint use of tracks and facilities." Dafoe had been right about the strength of opposition to the thirteen-year-old Canadian National by some members of the commission, but Duff had mediated between the contending factions by persuading Loree, Flavelle, and Leman, all private entrepreneurs philosophically opposed to state ownership of industry, to join the unanimous report. He bowed in their direction with the statement that "some members would have preferred a plan which would have established a complete dissociation of the government of Canada from the responsibilities of competitive railway management or of any direct interest therein."[15]

The recommendations received widespread publicity across Canada, with coverage that concentrated on the railways and failed to note a significant lacuna in the report; there was not one word in it, let alone a recommendation, about the future of transport by land or air. The commission ignored its mandate in this respect; Duff, involved as he had been in the *Aeronautics* case, might at least have had something to say about the impact of air transport, if not road haulage. As its implications began to sink in, the report was damned by both Thornton and Beatty. Unlike Thornton, the C.P.R. president saw nothing in it which discredited him personally, but in two major speeches, in Toronto and Winnipeg, he claimed that its recommendations would significantly reduce his company's status as a public carrier. Not mincing words, he told the Canadian Club in the Manitoba capital that "the public interest and the interest of the company I represent, are identical. It is not the first time that the letters 'C.P.' stood both for the 'Canadian people' and the 'Canadian Pacific.' " Convinced that the C.P.R. knew what was best for the country, he declared:

> We are prepared to agree to all proper measures of co-operation, but we cannot consent to our property being administered for us, but at our expense, by others....This is not regulation; it is the assumption of complete powers of administration without financial responsibility.[16]

Duff was disturbed by his friend's attacks but he was prevented by the constraints of judicial office from engaging in public debate; he asked Yates to prepare a critique of Beatty's forthright criticisms, however, and no doubt made use of this in private. The Bennett government moved quickly to implement some of the commission's recommendations. Legislation authorized the creation of the three-man board of trustees but watered down Duff's statutory duty of co-operation to a mere direction that the railways "attempt forthwith to agree and continuously endeavour to agree" to co-operate in various ways. Finally, the bill proposed tribunals of the kind recommended by the commission, with authority to settle disputes between the railways and carry out any agreements between them on such matters as the joint use of terminals, tracks, or any other railway facilities.[17]

The Liberal opposition found itself in a quandary. One faction of the party approved the measure, but King believed that Bennett's government intended to destroy the C.N.R., and that Duff had abetted the millionaire prime minister's scheming.

> Personally, I believe the C.P.R. would really like the Arbitral Board to be established, despite all that Mr. Beatty is saying against it, and the kind of lobby being put up, and I told caucus so. I said that I was suspicious from the outset of the course taken — first an effort to prejudice the C.N.R. in every way, a tory trick — next the appointment of a commission by a tory gov't — its own chairman and men — Duff would do Bennett's bidding of that I am sure.[18]

Like so many of King's diary confidences, this encourages speculation. King wrote it on 1 March 1933; Duff was named chief justice on the 17th. In the close-knit Ottawa community, leading politicians, judges, and lawyers had been discussing a likely successor to Anglin since his death in February, and before that, during his time of incapacity. Was King hinting that Duff in his desire for the chief justiceship had become a "sycophant," as he had described him nine years earlier, toadying to Bennett? It seems incredible that King, even if Duff, understandably enough, thirsted for the post, had any basis for saying that he was part of a "tory trick" to carry out "Bennett's bidding." He would have no compunction in applying severe pressure on Duff, as a Liberal, to aid the party during the war.

The debate was long and acrimonious, with King aiming his fire at the board of trustees, whose powers, he claimed, usurped those of Parliament. The bill was enacted without amendment, however, and became law on 1 July 1933. It brought no real change to the operations of the two railways, and thus, in a practical sense, the Duff Commission accomplished virtually nothing. After King returned to office in October 1935, his government increased the number of trustees from three to seven, apparently on the principle that seven trustees were less likely than three to usurp the rights of Parliament, but there was no move to repeal,[19] and this innocuous law remained on the statute books unaltered for nearly twenty years. In 1955 the board of trustees disappeared, and eleven years later, with the passage of the National Transportation Act, the last vestiges of Duff's report vanished for ever.[20]

Although politicians believed at the time that the report had enormous significance, it can be seen in retrospect that such was not the case. Its main interest lies in the process rather than in its result: royal commissioners to settle a Canadian problem coming from the United Kingdom and the United States, lingering colonialism as the other commissioners trooped to Ottawa Union Station to greet Baron Ashfield from London, who played a modest role in the deliberations; and the commission's lordly progress in luxurious private cars across the broad expanse of the Canadian landscape. The decision to withhold important information from the public would not be tolerated today. Even as late as 1931, so the reasoning ran, ordinary citizens could not be trusted with knowledge of financial matters that could be revealed only in the proper setting of a Montreal or Toronto corporate boardroom. The one important aspect of the report was that it did not recommend either casting the wicked Canadian Pacific into the maw of government or allowing the innocent Canadian National to be devoured by its rapacious rival. It is a good example of that Canadian pattern, the inadvertent blend of state socialism and free enterprise which somehow seems to work.

Duff had hardly handed in the report before he went into hospital again with what R.B. Bennett described as a "complete nervous breakdown," so severe this time that the prime minister commented he would "not likely ever sit on the bench again."[21] This episode was clearly more dangerous than any of his previous attacks. After electric-shock therapy, he remained in hospital until the end of November and then went to Jamaica with his sister Annie to recuperate. Duff did not experience serious illness again until his death in 1955; from 1932 onward, he only occasionally, and then discreetly, lapsed into his former bad habits.

He owed his improved health and, in fact, his personal survival to his teetotalling spinster sisters Emma and Annie, both teachers. Eight years younger than her brother, Annie had taught continuously at Parkdale Public School in Toronto for more than thirty years until her retirement in 1930. A homely, shy person, she had the virtue of absolute devotion to her brother and his career. Annie also knew how to manage money; she had put aside a respectable amount in sound investments, the income from which, though reduced by the depression, carried Lyman through the difficult middle years of the 1930s, enabling him to pay all his bills and thereafter, under her watchful eye, stay on an even financial keel.

Even before the 1932 crisis, the sisters had resolved to take Lyman in hand. Annie moved to Ottawa in that year to persuade him to reform himself. Emma could not afford to stop teaching, and one suspects that she shared her brother's lack of financial acumen, but she sent five or six letters a week from Toronto where she taught for forty-five years at the same school, Queen Victoria, in the west-end Parkdale district. Two years younger than Lyman, she had made herself an international reputation as a kindergarten teacher and writer of stories for young children. This bright, attractive, and literate person was as devoted as Annie to her brother's career. Her letters to Lyman and her sister sparkle with lively news and comment. Duff, always a poor correspondent, partly because of his atrocious handwriting, seldom wrote back, but Annie kept her end up faithfully.

It was touch and go. When Annie arrived in Ottawa, she found Duff in very bad physical and financial condition. His finances were so appalling, in fact, that Annie felt compelled to write the prime minister for help a month after the transportation commission report was handed down.

> The illness of my darling brother is adding to our expenses daily and as his previous illness was a financial blow from which we had not yet quite recovered, I am becoming anxious if the special ten per cent income tax which he has cheerfully paid up till now were eliminated, things would run smoothly. I am now asking you if this can be done. I don't think he would approve of this request, but I am not asking his or anyone else's advice in this matter.[22]

Bennett replied to this remarkable request in a rather mysterious fashion:

> I find it is impossible to carry into effect the suggestion that you make, but

I am keeping before me an idea that I have with regard to your brother, which may enable me to be of some little help in meeting the difficulty.[23]

One wonders whether he had in mind a personal loan, an increase in salary, or the chief justiceship. Already regretting her boldness, Annie was relieved by his answer and responded to express pleasure that her scheme had not succeeded; her brother would have thoroughly disapproved of preferential treatment.[24]

Lyman improved fairly quickly with help from others besides his sisters. Senator Cairinne Wilson was one who probably spoke some home truths to him; whatever she did, it earned Annie's and Emma's gratitude. And simply by being there, Annie helped; Lyman's self-respect prevented him from abusing her sensibilities by irresponsible behaviour. From the instant of her arrival in Ottawa, she banned liquor from the house. Lyman used to smuggle some into his library or bedroom occasionally, but from the summer of 1932 onwards he never again offered an alcoholic drink at home. Annie hired a cook and housemaid and saw to it that Duff ate properly. She controlled the household expenses and held a tight rein on his personal expenditures, forcing him to live within his means. Whereas formerly he had been a spendthrift, he was now habitually short of ready cash; Annie insisted on paying all bills by cheque, and this new habit became a lifelong one for Duff.

Annie was heroic. Never in Toronto had she gone into "society," but she would in Ottawa, and she had steeled herself to the ordeal. Everywhere that Lyman went on social occasions Annie was not far behind. The endless invitations to dinner with ambassadors and important visitors from abroad, not to mention the ordinary run of Ottawa functions, now all came to the Right Honourable Lyman Poore Duff and Miss Duff. And they entertained — not in their own home except for tea, but in the Rideau Club or the Country Club, where Annie would tolerate a glass of sherry and one or two of wine during the meal. So determined was she to play the chatelaine that she took dancing lessons to spare Lyman the embarrassment of having to decline invitations to Rideau Hall or embassy balls. It is hard not to admire the spirit of a rather dowdy woman learning to dance at age sixty.

Emma followed the salvage campaign with continuous advice. Annie's letter about a proposed tea party drew a volume of it.

I really think, too, that the more of that sort of thing that you do, the better it is for L. He won't say much, but I'm quite sure he is very proud of the way you carry things off and of your appearance. It will all add to his social assurance (I mean his own assurance) to have people commenting on you — and the more of it you do, the easier it will be for you. — It always seemed to me when I was down there that Sunday was a bad time to get over (no occupation). Why not plan to have people drop in Sunday evening? — then he will be looking forward to it during the day, he will not want to go off...

Emma went onto praise the merits of serving food buffet style, telling Annie

that it was so much better to have refreshments where the men [poked] about and help serve — they love to do it — the "party" instinct from boyhood probably. I do feel that these things are going to be your weapons to fight that awful trouble — Lizzie would not do an original thing, it had to be like "Lady this" or "Mrs. that" and then in the end "but Lyman we could never hope to do it as well" — quite forgetting that people come to enjoy one another and most of all in *this* case to enjoy him — and everyone would understand if no "drinks" are served — just the best of coffee — I should be adamant on that — there is every reason for your not doing it and no good one why you should.

Three weeks later she wrote to remind Annie of the advice she had just given: "Don't forget what I said about going around with L. I know I am right. It may mean a great effort for you, but it is so good for him."[25] By January, 1933, if Duff had not slain the dragon, as Archibald might have said, he had wounded the beast grievously. His brief holiday in Jamaica had done him a world of good, and by February he was back on a regular working schedule.

By that month, Anglin had been ailing for more than a year, and it had been obvious to everybody that his absences would force a retirement. On 13 February 1933 he at last resigned. In open court the following day, Duff phrased a graceful but conventional tribute. The complimentary remarks came all the more easily since he had good reason to believe that he would be the successor. There was no disagreement that Duff as a jurist stood head and shoulders above his colleagues, but could he be relied on not to embarrass Bennett, who had responsibility for the appointment, or his colleagues, by repeating the excesses of the previous six years? Bennett had addressed himself to the question early in January, knowing full well that Anglin's retirement could not long be delayed. Duff had a strong ally in his friend Herridge, Bennett's brother-in-law, who knew just how excellent his sisters' influence made the prospects for Duff's recovery.

Bennett still had lingering doubts.[26] Laurier, when naming Duff's old friend and partner Gordon Hunter chief justice of British Columbia thirty years before, had extracted a pledge not to drink excessively that Hunter honoured more in the breach than the observance. Bennett took much the same approach with Duff. He talked to him about the composition of the court in view of Anglin's expected retirement and expressed his misgivings about

Duff's continued membership on it, the implication of course being that he might not succeed Anglin unless he reformed himself. Aware that his own shortcomings had made his future uncertain, Duff placed his fate squarely in the prime minister's hands.

> My Dear Bennett:
>
> I am taking advantage of the privilege of friendship to address you thus, because this letter is strictly personal, in the sense that it is not official.
>
> I have been trying to formulate my personal out in view of the present situation on the Supreme Court. That situation visibly demands from everybody having any responsibility in relation to it, not only the gravest consideration, but every reasonable effort to improve it; and it has seemed to me — I have been thinking of it for some time — that I ought to ask you, in explicit terms, to consider myself in your hands entirely, to dispose of as you think best with the view of securing the governing desideratum. If now or at a later time I can facilitate an improvement by resigning, I am anxious to take that course. If to remain as puisne judge would be better, I desire to do that.
>
> Without reserve, I should like you to know that, whatever your view may be, I shall not only be ready to act in accordance with it, I shall most gladly, most happily, cooperate in the fullest degree to attain the desired result.

Immediately, again writing in longhand, Duff wrote a separate letter:

> My Dear Bennett
>
> As complementary to my letter of this date I am enclosing a formal resignation which I put in your hands to act upon as you think best, now or hereafter.
>
> I am convinced that there is no impropriety in this, as the sole purpose of it is to enable you to act without further discussion upon any view you may form as to what will best serve the public interest. It differs toto caelo from the case of a device to serve the political convenience of a government or the personal convenience of one of its members.

The resignation itself was brief. Dated 10 January 1933 and addressed to "The Rt. Hon. The Prime Minister Ottawa," it ran: "I beg herewith to tender my resignation from the office of Justice of the Supreme Court of Canada. I have the honour to be, Sir, your most obedient servant L.P. Duff."[27]

Bennett, who had been expecting these letters, made no reply. When Anglin retired, he did not move on the appointment of a successor. Anglin died on 2 March; again Duff made appropriate utterances in court, and attended the funeral with his colleagues. Two more weeks of uncertainty passed. Finally, on 17 March Duff received a hand-written letter from the prime minister:

Dear Chief Justice,

It was my high privilege this day to recommend to his Excellency your appointment to the great office of Chief Justice of Canada.

I need hardly add that the exercise of the privilege gave to me the greatest pleasure both on public and private grounds. The public will rejoice that the most eminent Canadian jurist of our time has been called upon to discharge the duties of the highest judicial office in our country.

As an admiring friend of many years, I assure you that I have derived the greatest possible pleasure at seeing an old friend who has ever been most kind attain the position for which he is so singularly fitted.

I trust you may be long spared in health and strength to discharge with credit and distinction as well to the public and yourself the duties of your great position, reflecting added lustre upon our highest judicial office and adding a new fame and honour to the incumbent of the office.

With kindest regards I am ever yours sincerely, R.B. Bennett.[28]

This was great news, even if not entirely unforeseen. Duff replied immediately by hand.

My dear Prime Minister:

Please accept my thanks for your very kind letter. There are many things I should be tempted to write but perhaps you won't mind if I say just two things.

I know you will not suspect me of my trying to please you when I say that it has been a great source of happiness to me to realize especially during the last few months and from testimony which I do not think could be audible to you the comfort that people feel in the fact that in these extremely difficult times you are at the wheel. This confidence comes from gifts of mind & heart which even yr critics recognize, and most of them not unwillingly recognize. It is, of course, a great satisfaction to me to know that this great gift with which you have honoured me comes from a great Prime Minister.

Then I am sure you will understand me when I say — I am not forgetting the occasion, now some years ago, when you said to me speaking of the Chief Justiceship, "we want you" — that I value what you have done, in a degree I cannot begin to express as a gift of permanent friendship.

With the kindest regards, I am my dear Prime Minister, yours most sincerely, L.P. Duff.[29]

One could expatiate on these revealing letters. Duff's fulsome praise smacks of hypocrisy. It came from a grateful heart, but privately Duff did not think much of Bennett as either a lawyer or a politician.[30] To the extent that it existed at all, the friendship would wither ten years later in the wake of the Hong Kong inquiry.

Early on the morning of 20 March, the clerk of the Privy Council administered the oath of allegiance in the presence of the Governor-General, who for the occasion had inscribed the Bible Duff kissed. At a quarter to eleven that morning, wearing his ermine-trimmed scarlet robe, he and his colleagues, who were similarly attired, walked slowly into the Supreme Court, where he sat in the high-backed chief justice's chair. His brother judges paid him tribute, and his old friend D.L. McCarthy, who had been instrumental in persuading him not to resign in 1924, appropriately spoke on behalf of the Bar. Duff, visibly moved, had prepared a brief reply to the remarks he knew would be made, and this he read, not trusting himself to speak without notes.

Newspapers across the land applauded the appointment; congratulations poured in. Among the flood was an affectionate note from Borden, who told him, "Birkenhead once spoke to me of your eminence as a jurist in such glowing terms that I have never forgotten the pride I felt that a fellow Canadian had attained so distinguished a position in that tribunal."[31] Duff replied feelingly that he did not "think anything which could ever happen to me...could mean quite as much" as his appointment by Borden to the Privy Council.[32] For all his attacks on Duff's transportation commission, Beatty wrote a warm letter. Roscoe Pound told him that "the Common Law world is to be congratulated on having you in this place of influence upon the course of the law." Various law lords in England sent cables, and an old university classmate harked back to Duff's nickname: "I almost said 'L.P.' as I have been in the habit of doing for many years, in fact since we were together in the class of '87. At this distance you cannot commit me for contempt of court!"[33]

The glowing tributes in newspapers and letters rightly acclaimed him as a jurist of outstanding rank, but Emma and Annie knew where the real credit lay. A year after Duff's appointment, Emma wrote her sister: "We would both go down with teeth locked to have L's affairs carried through with honour —

and we have both fought a good fight in this regard — no one but our two selves knowing it." Several days later, she put it even more clearly:

> You know I've been thinking of what we were discussing — I don't believe Mr. B. would have appointed *L.* if he had not been sure of you. You see, they couldn't know what silly fool thing he might do — but now they are quite comfortable and assured that he is being looked after.[34]

By the end of 1934, the two sisters could congratulate themselves on a fight well and successfully fought:

> Isn't it fine that he has been in such good shape? I suppose you wouldn't tell me even if he were not — it seems to me that this has been a particularly good year in this respect and, as it is our most important objcct — we should congratulate ourselves. I say "ourselves" but should say "you" for I have been able to do less than nothing — just hope and pray that you are not being worried.[35]

And Duff himself was grateful to them for his restoration. At the end of 1935, he told a correspondent that "personally, I have during the past year, owing to family reasons, been living almost the life of a recluse. I do not find it irksome."[36] So it had all come right at last, but as Wellington said of Waterloo, it had been "a near-run thing." His sisters' intervention came just in the nick of time; had Anglin died or retired before they were on the scene, Duff could not have become chief justice.

# 13

# Sir Lyman Poore Duff

IN 1933, THE SUPREME COURT of Canada had seven judges on it. His twenty-seven years' service made Duff an awesome figure to more recently appointed colleagues, even though he was merely the first among equals; his vote had no more numerical weight than that of the most junior member of the court. Next senior to him stood Thibodeau Rinfret, appointed in 1924 and in 1944 his successor as chief justice; the two men respected each other's abilities. J.H. Lamont had come to the court from Saskatchewan in 1927; once, holidaying in Georgia, he received a Christmas message from Duff that with uncharacteristic blitheness announced, "May thy life be long in the land the Lord thy God hath given thee."[1] Lamont's judgements occasionally, along with those of Rinfret and, of course, Duff himself, are the only ones regarded as worthwhile sources of judicial wisdom from the court Duff then led.

Robert Smith from Ontario had also joined the bench in 1927; his unspectacular career there ended in retirement soon after Duff became chief justice. L.A. Cannon, Fitzpatrick's son-in-law, had come to the court in 1930, and his relations with Duff were particularly harmonious. O.S. Crocket had not been there a year; a Bennett choice, he had been an active Conservative in New Brunswick. Duff disdained him for his want of intellectual calibre and what he considered to be the too political cast of his appointment. The new chief justice thought that Ivan Rand, who was named eventually in 1943, should have received it. It will seem odd in the light of his own experience that Duff should have cavilled at patronage. Length of tenure may have altered his perception of it. He used to lecture Crocket, who once rushed out of Duff's chambers screaming, "Who the hell does he think I am — a student?"[2] The most junior member of the court, Frank Hughes, named a judge the same day

Duff became chief justice, served less than two years. Disenchanted with the cloistered judicial existence, he went back to private practice in Toronto. But Duff liked him as a jolly man who made him laugh. When Duff died, Annie made a point of asking Hughes to be an honorary pall-bearer.

In Duff's day there were three annual sittings of the court, the first of which — the January term — ran from the fourth Tuesday of that month through to Easter. The second started on the fourth Tuesday in April and ran to the end of June; the October term that began on the first Tuesday of that month continued until just before Christmas. If the judges took holidays, they did so between June and October, after they had prepared their judgements in reserved decisions. All seven judges, except in case of illness or other exceptional circumstances, sat on constitutional cases and murder appeals, as well as important cases involving new legislation. In all other matters that came before it, five judges formed the court. Duff almost invariably sat on Quebec cases involving the Civil Code.

By lawyers arguing cases before him after he became chief justice in 1933, Duff was generally regarded as a godlike personage whose pronouncements came down as if graven on stone; one such has recalled him as "a grim person who dominated the court."[3] Yet he could still unbend in private. A later Ontario chief justice, J.C. McRuer, appearing as counsel in a case before him, was summoned to his chambers. Because the opposing lawyers had not also been asked to attend, McRuer thought he must have committed some gaffe deserving a rebuke. In some trepidation, he was ushered into the presence. Duff, seated at his desk, said, "McRuer, where did you get your teeth?" Startled by the question, McRuer observed that Duff wore singularly ill-fitting dentures. What is more, Duff had observed that McRuer wore false teeth too, though his were a good fit. The two men discussed their teeth, and at Duff's request McRuer made an appointment for him with the well-known Toronto specialist who had done his set. For some reason, the appointment was not kept.[4]

Duff was of the old school; he believed the work of the Supreme Court to be so important that it could not be left to inexperienced lawyers, or, for that matter, to badly prepared experienced lawyers. He expected men in the top rank of the profession to appear on appeals; they would not waste their clients' money or the time of the court. If the lawyers happened to be old cronies, so much the better: he would fence with them in court, but avoid them socially until the conclusion of the argument. The mere fact that these friends appeared did not guarantee success. Tilley once argued a case until the luncheon adjournment. Duff was heard talking to himself as he went down the corridor to his chambers: "Tilley, what do you take me for, a damned fool? That's arrant nonsense. I don't believe any of it — there's nothing to it at all — arrant nonsense." And when the court reassembled after lunch, Duff was plain: "I think I should tell you quite frankly that I do not think there is any merit in your argument." Tilley knew his cause was lost.[5] It was quite beside the point that Duff considered him to be the finest all-round lawyer in the land; behind him, but not far behind, coming Eugene Lafleur and Aimé Geoffrion. Duff's conversation with himself was not at all unusual. Waiters at both the Country Club and the Rideau Club recall his arguing cases this way. One of them has said,

> The most vivid memory I have of him is how, in the quiet of an afternoon, he would pace back and forth in the upper lounge [of the Rideau Club] talking to himself. In fact, it was more than just talking...he paced vigorously up and down engaged in a most animated discussion with some unseen companion, gesticulating all the while and punctuating his strongest remarks with gestures, presumably appropriate to the point he was making at the time....In fact it seemed to me he was postulating arguments to both sides of a question — taking first the plaintiff's then the defendant's.[6]

Duff very much liked to control the flow of events in his courtroom, and tended to discourage his colleagues from putting too many questions to lawyers.[7] Yet he was not aloof, and his door was open to colleagues who might want advice. Though Duff took unmistakable charge of his court, there seems to have been little rapport among other members. Davis, for example, once expressed his surprise to Duff when he learned that two of his colleagues had been laid up with serious illnesses.[8]

Duff adhered to a fixed routine for the conduct and hearing of cases. He left home for court by taxi at nine o'clock in the morning, taking with him any books or papers he had carried home the evening before. On his arrival in chambers, Duff considered the case in progress or the one about to be heard, and fifteen minutes or so before the court opened, he met his colleagues in the conference room to go over the day's agenda and attempt a consensus on whether further argument on a certain point was necessary or not. At the end of each court day, he met the registrar to discuss administrative matters in general and make arrangements for the cases coming up.

He urged the importance of handing down a decision during the same term in which a case had been argued. It was not always possible, of course, but never in his time did a judgement appear later than the following term, or by June at the latest, when the court adjourned until the October sitting. Duff, however, could never persuade his colleagues to reassemble in the immediate aftermath of a case and reach agreement on a single judgement. Instead, judges dispersed to consider individual opinions that were eventually set down in draft decisions and circulated among themselves. Often, his colleagues did not know whether Duff himself would write a judgement. He would fix a day for formal judgements to be handed down, having regard to the importance or complexity of a particular case, and within two weeks of that assigned day, he and his fellows met to consider and discuss their drafts. A judge might agree with a draft subject to minor amendments, and concur in it without writing his own decision; he might also insist on writing a separate but concurring judgement, or he might dissent from the majority, in which case he would almost invariably write his own decision. Discussion was apt to be heated, particularly if judges were badly divided.

There were only a few cases of general importance during the first two years of his chief justiceship. One, yet another involving the admissibility of incriminating statements made to police by a person later accused of a crime, is still an important case cited by criminal lawyers. Duff, who gave the unanimous judgement, ruled that if the Crown wished to introduce into evidence a statement made by an accused in the presence of several police officers, the Crown's failure at trial to call all the officers, and thus dispel any suggestion of coercion, will render the statement inadmissible. He ruled in the same case that a reference by the accused in his statement to a previous conviction constituted an additional reason for exclusion, since the Crown cannot prove the commission of one crime by proving the commission of an earlier one. Today, however, Duff's latter ruling would not be strictly applied; the statement would be edited by withholding from the jury all reference to the earlier conviction.[9]

In a child custody case, one in which the natural parents of a child baptized as a Roman Catholic sought unsuccessfully to overturn a custody order granted to a Protestant couple, Duff ruled that a difference in religion between a child and its adoptive parents is not necessarily a bar to adoption, but forms only one element in the larger issue, the general welfare of the child.[10] And once again he agreed to head a royal commission. Bennett chose him to head one to inquire into allegations that Arthur Meighen had made corrupt profits from a hydro-electric development in Ontario. Meighen himself had urged the appointment to clear his name. Fortunately for Duff, the Ontario government set up its own commission to which the federal authorities deferred, and it absolved Meighen of any wrongdoing.

In January 1934, Duff reached another important milestone in his journey out of despair. Reversing the previous government's policy, Bennett no longer discouraged the conferring of titles on Canadian citizens resident in Canada: for a few years, Canadians were eligible for these distinctions again, and a number were knighted. In the King's New Year's Day honours list, Duff became a "member of the Knights Grand Cross of Our Most Distinguished Order of Saint Michael and Saint George." His investiture took place at Rideau Hall on 22 April.

Wearing the official morning suit, Duff arrived at precisely 4:30 in the afternoon and was met by the comptroller of the viceregal household, who conducted him to the ballroom where he stood under an arch to await the Governor-General's arrival. When Bessborough came in, Duff bowed, took nine steps forward, bowed again, advanced six steps, halted, and bowed once more. After the private secretary read the royal warrant, Duff approached Bessborough on the throne and knelt with his right knee on a footstool. His Excellency gave the accolade. Duff stood up. Bessborough ceremoniously placed the Riband and badge of the Order round his neck, attached the Star of the Order to the lapel of Duff's morning coat, and handed him an envelope containing the Grant of Dignity and the Statutes of the Order. Duff bowed again, and, wearing his insignia, took tea with the guests. The comptroller had admonished Duff to be sure to take the case for the insignia when he left. Sir Lyman Poore Duff, P.C., G.C.M.G., LL.D., picked the case up at the door of Rideau Hall and went home with Annie.

During that year he gave increasing attention to the coming hearings on the Canadian government's damages claim against the United States government for the U.S. coast guard's sinking in 1929 of a vessel registered in Canada, the *I'm Alone*. The affair was the most sensational example yet of the difficulties the Americans faced with the enforcement of their prohibition laws. Duff and Mr. Justice Willis Van Devanter of the U.S. Supreme Court had been named as joint commissioners to settle the claim.

This was not Duff's first experience with a case resulting from the illegal waterborne export of liquor from Canada to the United States, or rum-running, as the practice was commonly called. He gave judgement in the Supreme Court in 1926 in a famous British Columbia murder case involving two rum-runners, Baker and Sowash, who had been convicted of brutal murders in a pirate raid on a vessel carrying contraband liquor. A Canadian kept a large cache of liquor, purchased legally in Canada, in Barkley Sound on the west coast of Vancouver Island, from which he supplied a steady customer in the United States. Early in September 1924, the American purchased 350 cases of scotch whisky and gin, and, as he had done on other such occasions, hired a small vessel, the *Beryl G.*, to carry it to a rendezvous on Sidney Island, which lies in the Gulf of Georgia near the international boundary. Skippered by a man named William Gillis with his son as crewman, the *Beryl G.* made it safely to the anchorage, as it had done many times before, to meet an American boat which had slipped across the line into Canadian waters. After some of the cargo had been transferred, the American vessel returned to United States waters. The *Beryl G.* stayed at anchor to await its return for the balance.

Four other rum-runners who had learned of the shipment plotted to raid the *Beryl G.*, seize the spirits, kill the crew if necessary, and sell the booty themselves. Baker, the ringleader, laid the plans. Equipping themselves with revolvers, handcuffs, flashlights, and an ornate yachtsman's cap, which, Baker reasoned, would dispel the Gillis's suspicions of pending violence because of its resemblance to a customs officer's cap, the four men set out from Victoria by boat for Sidney Island. They crept into the cove under cover of darkness, drew alongside the *Beryl G.*, and, led by Baker with his cap on, boarded her. Baker shot the senior Gillis at once. The pirates then towed the *Beryl G.* away to transfer the liquor, 250 cases of it, to caches on other nearby islands. During these operations, Sowash shot the younger Gillis. Baker and his companions threw the two bodies into the sea, but first they took grisly precautions to prevent their discovery. They handcuffed the father's hands to the son's, tied the bodies to the *Beryl G.*'s bow anchor, and, after hacking the bodies apart with an axe. flung the anchor and the human remains overboard. They were never found. The *Beryl G.* was found drifting in the channel a few days later, her deck covered with blood. One of the four hijackers turned King's evidence, that is received immunity from prosecution by agreeing to testify for the Crown against the other conspirators. Another escaped to the United States, but Baker and Sowash were convicted at their trial, and the verdict was sustained by the British Columbia Court of Appeal, as well as by Duff and his colleagues. The two pirates were hanged.[11]

In 1931, another rum-running case came before the Supreme Court which had important implications for the *I'm Alone* affair. It began in 1929, when prohibition was still in force in Nova Scotia, although liquor could be landed legally at one port in the province, Halifax. Sylvester Dunphy, the owner of the Canadian-registered schooner *Dorothy M. Smart*, loaded her with liquor at the French island of St. Pierre in the Gulf of Saint Lawrence planning, as he said, to sell his cargo on the high seas. Intent on staying outside the twelve-mile limit, Dunphy headed his vessel to a point about fifteen miles from the north shore of Nova Scotia and, in the words of the trial judge, "from that time until the next afternoon about 4 o'clock it was jogging in various directions waiting for customers to come out in boats from shore." Possibly too busy serving his eager customers to pay close heed to his nautical position, Dunphy found himself eleven miles from shore in the clutches of a revenue ship under the command of a Canadian customs officer named Croft. In seizing the *Dorothy M. Smart*, Croft relied on the provision in the Canada Customs Act according to which, "If any vessel is hovering in territorial waters of Canada, any officer may go aboard such vessel and examine her cargo...and may...bring the vessel into port." The Act also defined " 'Territorial Waters of Canada' [to] mean the waters...within 12 marine miles [of the Dominion] in the case of any vessel registered in Canada," and stated that if "any dutiable goods or any goods the importation of which into Canada is prohibited are found on board, such vessels...shall be seized and forfeited."

Dunphy, nothing if not bold, and hoping to recover his liquor investment, sued Croft for damages for trespass and illegal arrest. His lawyers argued that the three-mile limit was the universally recognized zone within which nations could exercise police and customs jurisdiction. In the Customs Act, they contended, Canada had tried to acquire extra-territorial jurisdiction when nothing in the British North America Act gave the Dominion such legislative authority. That esoteric point formed the main argument ultimately put to Duff and his colleagues. He and two others, with Newcombe and Cannon dissenting, decided that in passing the British North America Act to provide for the confederation of former colonies, the British Parliament did not confer extra-territorial jurisdiction on them. The reason Duff gave was that "subordinate Legislatures" — the former colonial assemblies — "do not possess such extra-territorial jurisdiction unless it has been granted in express terms or by necessary implication."[12]

The government of Canada appealed the decision to the Privy Council, which disagreed with Duff. Lord MacMillan, giving the judgement, pointed out that for over two hundred years Great Britain had legislated against smuggling by so-called "hovering acts," and when Britain conferred sovereignty on Canada there was no reason to think that the power to pass similar laws was withheld.[13] Lord MacMillan made some gratuitous remarks which alarmed the Canadian government even though it had won its case; they also alarmed Foreign Office officials in Britain who, at Ottawa's instigation, took extraordinary steps to try to nullify their effect. What the law lord had said was:

> Whatever be the limits of territorial waters in the international sense, it has long been recognized that for certain purposes, notably those of police, revenue, public health and fisheries, a state may enact laws affecting the seas surrounding its coast to a distance which exceeds the ordinary limits of its territory.[14]

The pending *I'm Alone* case caused alarm precisely because its central issue was the right of the United States government to pursue a rum-runner beyond normal territorial limits. In that case, an American coast-guard vessel had chased a Canadian rum-runner and sunk it more than two hundred miles from U.S. territory. Lord MacMillan's remarks, the Canadians and British feared, played right into the hands of the Americans, strengthening their case immeasurably. W.N. Tilley, who acted for the Canadian government in the affair, commented after learning of the English decision that he would "go into the fight, to put it colloquially with one arm tied."[15]

Some background is needed in order to appreciate the dilemma the Canadian government faced as a result of its successful appeal. Winning litigants know chagrin if the fruits of victory are denied them, and this was precisely Ottawa's concern in 1932. Early in the 1920s, given the near-impossibility of enforcing its new prohibition law along thousands of miles of coastline, the U.S. had asked the British to enter into an accord that would give the Americans greater powers to deal with the liquor-smuggling trade than the ordinary rules of international law afforded them. Two years of discussions led to a 1924 convention between His Majesty the King-Emperor and the president of the United States. This document affirmed the three-mile limit as the norm for offshore sovereignty, but allowed American officers to inspect vessels "under the British flag," which included vessels registered in Canada, outside that limit. If these authorities found illicit liquor on board, they could seize the vessel and tow it to port. An important qualification stipulated that this extended right could be exercised only within a distance from shore equal to the distance which the confiscated vessel could sail or steam in an hour's time; a vessel capable of making seven knots an hour, then, could be stopped within seven nautical miles from shore.

As Canadian and British officials digested Lord MacMillan's words, it seemed to them that he had postulated yet a third "contiguous zone." And to further complicate the matter, the doctrine of "hot pursuit" overlaid all three zones: the right of a sovereign state whose legitimate territorial waters had been invaded by a marauder, piratical or commercial, to chase the intruder in immediate and continuous pursuit in the hope of capture.

Lord MacMillan's judgement appeared in the law reports section of the London *Times* on 29 July 1932. Foreign Office officials were concerned, first, that the three-mile limit should appear to be varied by something other than a treaty, and secondly, because the decision gave the United States more ammunition against the *I'm Alone* claim. Ottawa meanwhile contacted the Dominions Office in London to suggest that before the Privy Council judgement appeared in irrevocable form, the British government should attempt to have it "altered." In the following weeks, officials tried at high-level discussions in the Foreign Office, in the Privy Council office, and in joint meetings of various ministries, to find a tactful way of persuading Lord MacMillan to rephrase, if not discard, the inconvenient words. The main stumbling-block, however, lay in the fact that they had been published in *The Times*, almost the equivalent of Holy Writ. Any discrepancy between the version in *The Times* and a later one would not go undetected; every barrister and judge read its law reports. Lord MacMillan himself, though naturally disapproving, was willing to alter "a phrase or two," but when Lord Sankey, the Lord Chancellor, learned that mere civil servants had proposed the rewording of a Privy Council judgement, he wrote the registrar to express grave displeasure. The upshot was that the law lord's words went unaltered and were quoted by American lawyers to the discomfiture of the Canadians.[16]

The *I'm Alone*, well known to the American coast guard, had been smuggling tens of thousands of cases of contraband liquor on to the east coast of the
United States. On her last voyage she carried a crew of nine including her
skipper J.T. Randall of Nova Scotia, an experienced former captain in the
merchant marine who had seen service in the Great War. Perhaps to compensate them for the dangers of the trade, the owners provisioned the vessel in
handsome style, later claiming compensation for the loss of large quantities of
canned shrimp, lobster, salmon, hams, bacon, sausages, ox tongues, and
dozens of cases of every imaginable kind of canned fruit. Capt. Randall lived
in lordly state in his own quarters; he took his meals on fine china and silver.
The list of provisions lost in the incident included food but not drink — the
crew simply helped themselves to the cargo.[17]

The *I'm Alone* loaded its last cargo of liquor at Belize, British Honduras.
The customs clearance gave the value of the liquor as $39,000, but the owners
afterwards claimed that its illicit value was $125,000, a markup of over three
hundred per cent. Declaring to the Belize port authorities that he was bound
for Hamilton, Bermuda, Randall set the *I'm Alone* on course for the U.S. Gulf
coast on 12 March 1929.

On the morning of 20 March, the U.S. coast-guard vessel *Walcott* sighted
the *I'm Alone* moored off Louisiana and steamed towards her. Seeing smoke
that indicated she was about to get under way, the *Walcott* signalled her to
heave to for boarding and examination. The exact position of the *I'm Alone*
became important, because that moment marked the beginning of the search
procedures allowed by the 1924 convention and the pursuit, hot or otherwise.
It became common ground between the Americans and Canadians that the
*I'm Alone* had anchored by a shoal ten and a half miles from shore, and hence
the argument as to the legality of the *Walcott*'s action depended on whether
that distance fell within the treaty limit.

The *I'm Alone* made for the open sea with the *Walcott* sounding warning
blasts close behind. Recognizing his quarry, the master of the *Walcott* "spoke"
her by megaphone, ordering her to stop engines and head upwind. As the
vessel continued under way, he then fired blank shots across her bow to no
avail. The coast-guard captain appreciated the legal niceties of the situation
and the importance of correctly determining the *I'm Alone*'s position and his
own; he paused to verify his calculations with a passing tanker. The Canadians would argue that if there had been hot pursuit it ended with this
interruption, but the *Walcott* never lost sight of the *I'm Alone* and, resuming the
chase, caught up with her. The *Walcott*'s master, again by megaphone, asked
Randall to let him come aboard, and the Nova Scotian agreed. The two men
talked on deck for over an hour. The American testified later that Randall
refused to let him examine the cargo manifest but did admit he was carrying
contraband spirits. When he heard this, the coast-guard commander told

Randall that he must allow a full search. Randall's evidence was that he had convinced the American he lacked jurisdiction; the *I'm Alone* had been outside the treaty limit when first sighted, and in any event had anchored only because of engine trouble.

At the end of this curious discussion between the two skippers, the *I'm Alone* moved off pursued by the *Walcott* and later by another coast-guard vessel, the *Dexter*. About two hundred miles off United States territory the *Dexter*, after Randall's belligerent refusal to surrender, opened fire on the *I'm Alone* and sank her. One of the crew drowned in the rough seas; Randall and the others were arrested and taken in irons to New Orleans.

Because of the treaty limit — the distance equivalent to an hour's sailing — the speed of the *I'm Alone* seemed to be an important factor. There was conflicting evidence: Randall claimed that she could never make more than nine and a half knots; American skippers familiar with her from earlier expeditions said she could make over ten and a half. The question whether the *I'm Alone* had moored within the limit was a difficult one, but Duff and Van Devanter, in the view they formed of the case, did not need to resolve the problem.

The sinking led to an exchange of politely worded diplomatic notes between Vincent Massey, Canadian minister in Washington, and Henry L. Stimson, the secretary of state in the new government of Franklin Roosevelt. The Canadians argued that the sinking had been a deliberate act perpetrated on the high seas, for which compensation must be paid; the Americans made the courteous response that the rum-runner had been sighted within the treaty limit, that the doctrine of hot pursuit permitted the American vessel to act, and that her loss, while regrettable, was the inevitable outcome of her refusal to surrender. The Canadians contended that the doctrine of hot pursuit applied only if pursuit began within the three-mile limit; the Americans countered that the convention had created a new zone, the treaty limit, within which pursuit could equally begin, citing Lord MacMillan's words in support. The Canadians responded that even if the American contention was correct, the pursuit was not continuous: the *Walcott* had broken off the chase for a time and the sinking had been done by another vessel. And so the arguments went back and forth; it became obvious that no agreement could be reached by diplomats.

During her voyage to Louisiana, the agents in Belize had radioed instructions to the *I'm Alone* for the delivery of the cargo. These instructions came from one Dan Hogan in New York, whom the U.S. police arrested. The fact that he and another American named Bryan appeared to be the *I'm Alone*'s real or "beneficial" owners gave the United States what turned out to be their most powerful argument. American lawyers reasoned that since the treaty applied only to British vessels, it could not apply to the *I'm Alone* which, effectively owned by Americans, was therefore an American and not a British vessel. This contention seriously worried Canadian representatives, who prepared a lengthy aide-memoire for Duff outlining Canada's position. The Canadian government emphasized that the "registry of the ship is the determining factor," and that the Canadian shipping register, which showed the Eugene Creaser Shipping Co. of Nova Scotia as owner, was conclusive. The Canadians had a yet stronger argument, based on company law. The shares of the company may have been held by Canadians in trust for Americans as the United States government contended, but the company had a legal personality of its own separate from that of the shareholders; the Eugene Creaser Shipping Co., and not its shareholders, held legal title to the *I'm Alone*. The question really came down to whether Duff and his fellow commissioner would, as lawyers say, pierce the corporate veil by regarding the nationality of the true owners as the determining factor.

The Americans had a sound rebuttal to this Canadian argument, based on historic marine law, still valid today, by which ownership of a registered vessel is represented by a fictional sixty-four shares. Thus, the owner of a vessel does not own the hull per se, he owns sixty-four shares in a hull. Bills of sale of registered vessels, even now, transfer ownership of those sixty-four shares, and the sixty-four shares of the *I'm Alone*, the Americans maintained, were held by Canadians in trust for the Americans who had put up the money to buy them. The strongest argument of the Canadians was really the fact of the deliberate sinking of the *I'm Alone*. The treaty provided for the seizure of a rum-runner with incidental use of minimum force, but did not permit deliberate sinking by gunfire.

Arrangements for the hearings went forward at a leisurely pace. Duff and Van Devanter consulted privately from time to time, but not until 28 January 1932 did they hold a preliminary hearing attended by Canadian and American representatives, partly to discuss procedures for the formal hearing, partly to settle exactly what their own role should be — merely to make recommendations or to arbitrate in the usual sense of that term — and, finally, to consider the ramifications of the beneficial-ownership argument of the Americans. They had little difficulty in settling the mechanics; their role would be to make recommendations only, and no binding award.

Duff and Van Devanter told the hearing that they were uncertain of "the right of hot pursuit [where] the offending vessel is within an hour's sailing distance of the shore at the commencement of the pursuit and beyond that distance at its termination." Did Lord MacMillan's dictum create an extended zone from which a lawful pursuit could be launched? As matters turned out, the hot-pursuit argument became academic, for Duff and Van Devanter seized on the real weakness of the American case. The U.S. government could have used necessary and reasonable force to effect the boarding and searching of the vessel and bringing it into port; if sinking occurred incidentally to these activities, the Americans might be blameless. Then Van Devanter jolted his compatriots by telling them, "The Commission think that...the admittedly intentional sinking of the suspected vessel was not justified by anything in the Convention."[18]

Nearly three years went by before the hearings got under way on 28 December 1934 at Washington, D.C. W.N. Tilley and Aimé Geoffrion had worked up the Canadian submission, but John E. Read and Leon Mayrand, both of the external affairs department, appeared as counsel. George Wharton Pepper, member of a prominent Philadelphia family and a former United States senator, was leading counsel for the U.S. The American lawyers led by producing evidence of American ownership which showed that Dan Hogan and another man had bought the *I'm Alone* from a Canadian named Hearn of Montreal. Hearn, so the evidence went, had agreed to sell it for $15,000 and, by a complicated set of corporate manoeuvres designed to hide the true state of affairs, arranged for the apparent ownership of the vessel by the Eugene Creaser Shipping Co. He was shown as a shareholder when in truth he no longer had any financial interest in the company or the vessel.

Read brought Hearn to Washington to contradict that evidence. Hearn's testimony gives fascinating insights into the rum-running business, with its network of agents, importers, financiers, distillers, and sailors. Many of the people involved in the trade were decent, one might almost say honest, individuals like the skipper Randall, and even Hearn himself. He freely admitted to his rum-running activities, but denied being a front man for Hogan, stoutly maintaining that he was the true owner of the *I'm Alone*. He said that his many dealings with Hogan and Bryan had to do only with liquor. He hired Randall; he hired the crew; he, through his contacts in the U.S., supplied particular markets with particular brands. Hearn said that he stood to make no more than twelve dollars a case on the last voyage of the *I'm Alone*; anything over that figure would go to the Hogan and Bryan group. He clearly saw himself as a fair man, a reasonable man, interested only in a modest assured income from the sale of illegal liquor — not one greedy for gigantic profits. Pepper, who had prepared his case well, called in rebuttal to Hearn a lady who had worked for him; she testified, based on her knowledge of Hearn's personal business affairs, that he did not own the *I'm Alone* and the Hogan group did.

Randall gave evidence at length. His testimony was remarkable for its disinterestedness. He had been hired to do a job, navigate the *I'm Alone*, take it where directed, and get her there and back safely, for all of which he received handsome pay. He did not concern himself with the grubby, sordid details of the rum-running trade, nor did he soil his hands with money; other people looked after financial arrangements. He was a professional, a master mariner; the fact that he commanded a small vessel in an unlawful business did not concern him. He did his best for his employers; he would not allow the *I'm Alone* to fall into the hands of the American coast guard if he could prevent it; he knew his rights; he knew about hot pursuit and the treaty limit, but meekly to surrender was not his style.[19]

Read and Pepper finished their evidence on 2 January 1935. Van Devanter then asked the lawyers to meet privately with Duff and himself to see whether agreement could be reached on valuation of the various claims put forward by the Canadian government, both on its own behalf and on behalf of the owners of the *I'm Alone* and its crew. These totalled $386,000, including such obvious items as the value of the vessel and its cargo, but also the loss of the crew's personal belongings, the loss of the ship's provisions, and a claim by the widow of the drowned seaman for the loss of his life.[20]

By the time the hearings concluded, Duff and Van Devanter had made up their minds. They accepted the American argument that the *I'm Alone* was in reality an American vessel and thus ineligible for compensation under the treaty. As Duff said,

> The American case on the subject of the virtual ownership of the ship and cargo was as nearly complete as one could expect to get in a case of that kind. I had no manner of doubt about the conclusions of fact established by the evidence.[21]

Hogan and Bryan received nothing for the loss of the *I'm Alone* and its rich cargo of excellent liquors. Duff and Van Devanter held that the sinking of the vessel constituted an affront to Canada as the country of origin and recommended that compensation of $25,000 be paid by the United States. They also recommended compensation for Randall and his crew, and for the widow of the drowned crew member.[22]

For Duff, the hearings had been rewarding. Once again he had found himself in the international spotlight; the *I'm Alone* case had generated enormous interest and commentary in the United States and Canada. The New York *Times*, in an editorial headed, "A Voice from the Past," summed the episode up.

> Our Government was wrong. It can afford to say that it was, since the people have decided that Prohibition, which covered such a multitude of zeals, was wrong. But how far off this little marine incident looks! We who lived through the years of virtue have to rub our eyes and wonder "how the United States ever got that way."[23]

Duff enjoyed his stay in Washington, where Hume Wrong of the Canadian legation took him to various beauty spots. He and Pepper developed a mutual respect which led to the conferring of an honorary doctor of laws degree in 1940 by the University of Pennsylvania, an event Duff counted as a highlight of his life.

# 14

## At the pinnacle

ANNIE AND EMMA rejoiced in the acclaim Duff won for his role in the *I'm Alone* affair, seeing in it a complete vindication of their sisterly efforts to rehabilitate him; without them he could not have earned it. Emma died, three months after the hearings, of cancer, which she had endured for two years with magnificent courage, trying to conceal the true extent of her illness and its wracking pain from her brother all that time. Annie had urged her sister to move to Ottawa, but Emma would not hear of it:

> You simply couldn't stand it. There would be *three* down-&-outers instead of one. As it is, I can hang on but to know that I was upsetting L's work and worrying you to death would be the last straw, I would give in — take all the dope & be dead in three weeks.[1]

And a few months later, after a day of almost unendurable pain, she told Annie, "I am still suffering like hell — but I do not want L. to know this."[2]

Lyman could not, as Emma well knew, endure the sight of disabling illness. She not only attempted to hide her suffering from him, but actually discouraged him from visiting her. He did not see her once in those last two years, though Annie visited often. Nor did Lyman really know until shortly before she died how little money she had to live on; that was kept from him as well; Lyman used occasionally to make her a gift of money, though he could not afford much. On Boxing Day 1934, Emma opened up to her brother and sister in a heart-rending letter.

> Many thanks for the cheque — which I am to spend "on myself" — there is no doubt that I will do that. I am very hard up....For the first time in my

life I have not given a single Christmas present to anyone....Yesterday was a terrible day for me — not one moment free from pain — I hope I shall not see another such Christmas Day...

A day or two earlier, Emma had written a series of humorous verses poking fun at the staff of her old school for their annual Christmas party. Some of the pupils heard about this, and sent her a card to say that they hoped she would soon get well and come back to them. The indomitable teacher wrote her children,

> You must just think of me standing up very straight, a little bit crumpled because you have all hugged me a lot, but not a bit old, or sick, and singing in my best soprano (not a bit cracked, you understand). I thank you, I thank you, I thank you![3]

She died on 1 April 1935. Cairinne Wilson, whom Duff had called with the news, wrote Annie at once.

> We have passed through some very difficult times together and I am particularly sorry that I cannot be with you and your brother today. Please tell the Chief Justice that I appreciate his thoughtfulness in telephoning himself to let me know the very sad news.[4]

He and Annie went to Toronto for the private funeral. There he learned that the sale of Emma's pathetically few possessions might pay off a small bank loan with a few dollars to spare. He grieved for her.

That year also saw the death of perhaps his closest friend, J.A. "Dick" Ritchie, the Ottawa Crown attorney. A lover of literature like Duff, Ritchie could bring Duff out of his reserve with his personality and bright wit. News of his boon companion's death "completely upset" Duff, who interrupted an out-of-town visit to come home.[5]

Now seventy, Duff could look forward to only five more years' service on the court before mandatory retirement. Measured by the importance and number of cases that came before him in that time, they were fruitful years. Two decisions he considered his greatest judicial achievements: that defining the powers of provincially appointed judges to deal with such matters as the adoption and custody of young children, and the one later affirmed by the Privy Council upholding the federal government's right to abolish appeals to that body.

A few months after his return from Washington, he sat on still another rum-running case that involved the same sections of the Customs Act questioned in *Dunphy v. Croft*, though by 1935 no argument could challenge its validity. Within the twelve-mile limit a customs patrol boat had seized a vessel carrying 751 kegs of rum for illegal sale in Canada. While it was being pulled to shore, the owner grabbed the helm of the captured vessel, and, accelerating the engine, broke the tow-line and headed out to sea. Subsequently arrested and convicted of theft on grounds that at the time of his escape his vessel was lawfully in the custody of customs officials, he appealed to the Supreme Court of Canada. He got short shrift from Duff and his colleagues, who affirmed the three-year jail sentence. By an odd coincidence, the lawyer who appeared for him belonged to the same firm that had represented the American rum-runners Hogan and Bryan when buying the *I'm Alone*.[6]

In that year too, the Bennett government was defeated and the Liberals returned under Mackenzie King. Duff must have had mixed feelings; he had not yet completely forgiven King for his conduct in 1924, and he had reason to be grateful to Bennett. Since the Earl of Bessborough had resigned the month before the King government took office in October 1935, Duff acted as Administrator until the arrival of Lord Tweedsmuir. On the 23rd, formal in morning dress, he received King, who recorded in his diary,

> He shook hands very pleasantly, and said he was glad to see me again. After exchanging greetings in a formal way...I seated myself at the side of the desk at which Duff was seated. He said to me that he supposed the thing to ask was whether I was prepared to take over the Government. I replied that I was....He said: "I assume you have a Government that can take hold." I said that I had.

King and Duff discussed an unpleasantness concerning Fernand Rinfret, Thibodeau Rinfret's brother, whom King proposed to have in his cabinet. There were allegations that he had taken bribes in connection with illegal immigrants. Duff shared King's concern that no one be brought in who laboured under suspicion.

> I then told him what Bennett had said to me about having seen a photostat copy of cheques received by Rinfret....I mentioned what I had said to Bennett in reply, and that I had since gone into the whole matter very fully with Rinfret, as had also LaPointe [the justice minister] and we were both satisfied that the cheques were forgeries and that the whole matter was one of blackmail. I gave him the grounds on which we had reached this conclusion. I said I would not think of suggesting a name to him as representing the King, were I not quite sure that what had been reported to Mr. Bennett was without foundation, other than as I had indicated to him. His sole comment was: "Had LaPointe satisfied himself" and I said he had.[7]

A few hours later, Duff swore in a cabinet that included Fernand Rinfret as secretary of state. As the various ministers signed to acknowledge the oath of office, King buttonholed the chief justice.

> I talked with Duff about the significance of the fact that it was the first time a change of government had been made under the auspices of a Canadian. He reminded me that, as a Canadian, he had opened and closed Parliament. I said to him that, if a Canadian could perform the function of opening or closing Parliament, and received a new government into office, there was little need of bringing a Governor General to Canada from the Old Country. He concurred in the view that the office would be held, ere long, by a Canadian. As the men were taking the oaths, I said I hoped they would respect them, and commented on the shocking manner in which Ministers of the Crown had violated their Oaths of Office. I said that it was all part of the tendencies of the time to get away from moral standards and principles in public life. He agreed and said he had had the same difficulty at times with some of the judges in the Supreme Court — that they seemed to fail to recognize the scrupulous care with which they should regard their obligations.[8]

King's comment about the possibility of a Canadian Governor-General is puzzling. Five years later he did not think the time was ripe, though had Duff been in different circumstances he might have recommended his appointment:

> I told Judge Duff, at the High Commissioner's luncheon on Tuesday, that if he had been younger and were not needed for the Supreme Court (and, I might have added, if he had a wife still living) I would have been prepared to recommend him as G.G. This I gladly would have done. It would have been an admirable choice of a Canadian to fill the office. The obvious Canadian for that post has not yet come to the fore.[9]

Not until Vincent Massey's appointment in 1952 did a Canadian fill the viceregal post.

One wonders whom Duff had in mind in that remark about the shortcomings of some of his colleagues. He could not have meant his friend Hughes, who had resigned earlier in the year, but he might have been thinking of Smith or Crocket. Davis and Kerwin, appointed in January and July of 1935, both enjoyed his high respect, and Davis was a longtime intimate. It is just possible that the comment was simply judicial light-heartedness.

Before its defeat, the Bennett government had introduced a series of reforms to combat the worst effects of the depression. This so-called "new deal" drew on Roosevelt's programmes in the United States; W.D. Herridge, then Canadian ambassador in Washington, had urged his brother-in-law the prime minister to pass equivalent legislation. The various measures were hastily conceived, and fell short of a coherent policy; Bennett had neglected to consult his cabinet colleagues while drafting them. Even so, the newly elected King government faced a dilemma. Bennett's new deal had been an issue in the campaign, and since Bennett had been defeated, the electorate had presumably voted down the programme as well. At the same time, the Liberals had no legislative package for cushioning the depression's impact, and given King's background as a social reformer, inaction might be regarded as a confession of failure.

King decided to test the measures' constitutionality by referring them to the Supreme Court of Canada. Its opinions were delivered in six separate decisions, every one of which went to the Privy Council for the final word. Duff sat continuously from 15 January to 5 February 1936, and with his colleagues handed down the judgements on 17 June. On assembling for the first case, Duff gazed at an array of some of the most expensive lawyers in Canada: Gordon Sloan, then attorney-general of British Columbia, along with several other provincial attorneys-general, Rowell, J.W. deB. Farris, St. Laurent, and Geoffrion. The court first considered three amendments to the Criminal Code designed to combat restrictive trade practices. Duff held for the majority that the legislation was governed by his own earlier decision and that of the Privy Council in the *Proprietary Articles* case; the amendments were a perfectly valid exercise of the federal government's power to pass laws against crime. The Privy Council later agreed. The federal government had defined a new crime in a genuine, non-colourable fashion.[10] There followed the reference concerning the Dominion Trade and Industry Commission Act, which contained a number of questionable provisions including the establishment of a national trademark to be used in fixing commodity standards and the creation of a system of investigating complaints respecting unfair trade practices. The Supreme Court found the latter but not the former to be constitutional. The Privy Council agreed with all rulings of the Supreme Court except in holding that the federal government could create a national trademark, a finding which many constitutional scholars consider an aberration.[11]

Next came the Labour Conventions case, the longest with an argument of six days. Legislation had been passed pursuant to draft conventions of the 1919 and 1928 International Labour Conferences that called for a work week not longer than forty-eight hours, a weekly day off work, and the establishment of minimum wages in certain occupations. The case raised the vexed questions of the federal government's right to make laws implementing treaty obligations, and the extent to which such legislation could, if at all, intrude on provincial jurisdiction. It will be recalled that the Privy Council had upheld the validity of federal legislation concerning the Japanese treaty of 1913 by nullifying a British Columbia statute inconsistent with it.[12] In 1925, Duff and his fellow judges had also considered an hours of labour convention and decided that the federal government's treaty-making power did not empower it to implement the convention in law if to do so would affect specific provincial powers.[13] In 1929, Duff had rejected federal legislation in response to an international accord for the regulation of air transport only to be overruled by the Privy Council, partly on the basis of the same treaty-making power. And in a case concerning the regulation of radio communication, in which Duff took no part because of illness, the Privy Council had taken a somewhat similar view.[14]

It was small wonder, then, that in the 1936 Labour Conventions case, Duff concluded that despite his own previous opinion to the contrary, the Privy Council had endorsed Ottawa's treaty-making power to the hilt, even if it did whittle down specific provincial powers. Duff, as he was later to do in the case abolishing appeals to the Privy Council, asserted that nationhood was greater than those powers.

> As a result of the constitutional development of the last thirty years (and more particularly of the last twenty years) Canada has acquired the status of an international unit, that is to say, she has been recognized by His Majesty the King, by the other nations of the British Commonwealth of Nations, and by the nations of the world, as possessing a status enabling her to enter into, on her own behalf, international arrangements. These arrangements may take various forms. They may take the form of treaties, in the strict sense, between heads of states, to which His Majesty the King is formally a party. They may take, *inter alia*, the form of agreements between governments, in which His Majesty does not formally appear, Canada being represented by the Governor General in Council or by a delegate or delegates authorized directly by him. Whatever the form of the agreement, it is now settled that, as regards Canada, it is the Canadian Government acting on its own responsibility to the Parliament of Canada which deals with the matter. If the international contract is in the form of a treaty between heads of states, His Majesty acts, as regards Canada, on the advice of his Canadian Government.
>
> Necessarily, in virtue of the fundamental principles of our constitution, the Canadian Government in exercising these functions is under the control of Parliament. Parliament has full power by legislation to determine the conditions under which international agreements may be entered into and to provide for giving effect to them. That this authority is exclusive would seem to follow inevitably from the circumstance that the

Lieutenant-Governors of the provinces do not in any manner represent His Majesty in external affairs, and that the provincial governments are not concerned with such affairs; the effect of the two decisions [the *Radio* and *Aeronautics* cases]…is that in all these matters the authority of Parliament is not merely paramount, but exclusive.[15]

Such are the vagaries of the courts that Lord Atkin in the Privy Council — no Lord Sankey, he — reversed Duff. Atkin said that the *Aeronautics* and *Radio* cases dealt with subjects which were not enumerated in either section 91 or section 92 of the B.N.A. Act, whereas the legislation at hand had to do with matters that "were clearly reserved exclusively to the provinces as relating to property and civil rights." In discussing the distribution of legislative powers when considering the effect of a treaty, Lord Atkin uttered a striking metaphor that is now celebrated in the literature of constitutional law.

It must not be thought that the result of this decision is that Canada is incompetent to legislate in performance of treaty obligations. In totality of legislative powers, Dominion and Provincial together, she is fully equipped, but the legislative powers remain distributed, and if in the exercise of her new functions derived from her new international status Canada incurs obligations they must, so far as legislation be concerned, when they deal with Provincial classes of subjects, be dealt with by the totality of powers, in other words by co-operation between the Dominion and the Provinces. While the Ship of State now sails on larger ventures and into foreign waters she still retains the water-tight compartments which are an essential part of her original structure.[16]

The case in the Privy Council had another interesting aspect: apologetic for taking the unusual step of overruling Duff in a constitutional case, Lord Atkin went out of his way to praise him. Lawyers for the Dominion government had argued that the legislation could be supported by the general power of section 91 because the legislative scheme, being of such universal importance, had gone beyond being a merely local matter to become one of "national concern." Lord Atkin, pointing to attempts made by Ottawa over the years to use that sort of language to support encroachments on the provincial powers given under section 92, stated that the residuary clause must be very cautiously applied. He then paid homage to Duff:

The law of Canada on this branch of constitutional law has been stated with such force and clarity by the Chief Justice in his judgment concerning the Natural Products Marketing Act [the appeal from that case heard by Duff in January was heard by the the Privy Council before it heard the

*Hours of Work* case] dealing with the six Acts there referred to, that their Lordships abstain from stating it afresh....They consider that the law is finally settled by the current cases cited by the Chief Justice on the principles declared by him....The few pages of the Chief Justice's judgment will, it is to be hoped, form the *locus classicus* of the law on this point, and preclude further disputes.

In writing a tribute to Duff soon after the latter's death, Lord Wright, one of the judges who had sat on this appeal, expressed doubt about the correctness of the decision in an unusual if not unique example in that era of a judge of the Privy Council publicly expressing a view contrary to the majority, even after the fact. Although Lord Wright did not mention it, the decision was flawed because Lord Atkin assumed wrongly that Duff had rejected the federal treaty-making power as the foundation of the legislation. It cannot be known whether, if Lord Atkin had not erred, this would have made any difference to the result, but one can speculate in the light of what Lord Wright has written that there might have been greater reluctance to find the law unconstitutional.[17]

Duff still would not allow Ottawa to use its power to make laws concerning crime or trade for the invasion of specific fields of jurisdiction conferred on the provinces by section 92. He was prepared to allow such an invasion in the exercise of the treaty-making power. The distinction was between matters arising wholly within Canada and those flowing from international obligations, whether they were formal treaties or mere conventions. He would reiterate that view of national status three years later when he held that Ottawa could abolish appeals to the Privy Council, even those from provincial courts of appeal which bypassed the Supreme Court of Canada.

After the Labour Conventions case, the judges turned to the Employment and Social Insurance Act, the most important of all the Bennett new deal laws, which authorized the establishment of a manpower or employment service together with a contributory scheme of unemployment insurance. The majority of the court declared the legislation unconstitutional as trespassing on the provincial field of property and civil rights. Duff dissented, believing that it came under taxation or the public debt, both federal jurisdictions. His reasons are not convincing; after deciding that contributions to the unemployment insurance fund, whether from employees, employers, or the federal government, became in effect public money and hence "public property," he said,

It cannot, therefore, we think — and we do not think this was disputed on the argument, although we do not desire to put what we have to say upon any suggested admission — at all events, it cannot, we think, be disputed, even with plausibility, that, in point of strict law, Parliament has the authority to make grants out of the public monies to individual inhabitants of any of the provinces, for example, for relief of distress, for reward of merit, or for any other object which Parliament in its wisdom may deem to be a desirable one. The propriety of such grants, the wisdom of such grants, the convenience or inconvenience of the practice of making such grants, are considerations for Parliament alone, and have no relevancy in any discussion before any other Court concerning the competence of Parliament to authorize them.

Contending that the legislation could also be sustained as a form of taxation, he used language almost as laborious:

It would appear that, having regard to the nature of the legislative authority vested in Parliament, and to the wide discretion reposed in Parliament touching the matter in which moneys are to be raised...a court ought to observe a high degree of caution in pronouncing upon the invalidity of an enactment, by which moneys become by compulsion of law payable by individuals to the Dominion Treasury for a public purpose, on the ground that, in truth, it does not possess its prima facie character, that of a taxing statute, but is legislation intending to do what Parliament has otherwise no manner of authority to do.

He strains for the decision. One wonders if his innate liberalism guided his pen, or if his admiration for Roosevelt and sympathy with Bennett's efforts to cure the country's economic ills might have influenced him. According to the late R.K. Finlayson, the Conservative leader's executive secretary, Bennett used him during the court hearings as a messenger to take Duff explanations of the former government's legislative programme. Unwilling to intercede directly with the chief justice while the case was being argued, Bennett apparently had no compunction about using an intermediary to expound on his policies. Duff had once roundly condemned Mackenzie King for attempting to influence the court before the hearing of a far less important case. Bennett's intervention, and Duff's apparent willingness to listen, may be accounted for, if not excused, by the fact that the tory was out of office and merely trying to shore up his self-esteem.[18] At all events, the Privy Council disagreed with Duff here again, upholding the majority view. Mackenzie King later secured an amendment to the B.N.A. Act giving Ottawa specific jurisdiction over unemployment insurance, and reaped the political gains by claiming to be the architect of an important scheme of social welfare.[19]

The Supreme Court next heard the case referred to by Lord Atkin in his encomium on Duff, involving the validity of the federal Natural Products Marketing Act. This law regulated trade in such diverse commodities as meat, dairy products, fruit and vegetables, and honey. All the judges declared it invalid. Rowell argued unsuccessfully that the residuary power could justify it, and so could the federal trade and commerce provision. The latter argument prompted Duff to write a lengthy judgement reviewing the history of interpretation of the trade and commerce power by the courts, the exhaustive document that commanded Atkin's admiration. The Privy Council had no trouble dismissing the appeal brought by the Canadian government.[20] The final case was the least difficult to decide. To help insolvent farmers beleaguered by creditors, Parliament passed legislation creating a mechanism for the orderly payment of debts. The Supreme Court found this to be valid legislation relating to bankruptcy and insolvency, matters reserved to the Dominion government, a view with which the Privy Council agreed.[21]

It had been a heavy session; arguments from a battery of lawyers were tiring enough, but the judges had to find time to write their decisions while hearing other cases. Duff felt compelled to forgo the pleasure of a visit to Harvard. Roscoe Pound had invited him to speak at the university's tercentenary ceremonies, but, knowing the time and effort the pending appeals would require, Duff decided to tell him that

> we are now confronted with a series of [references] which will require us to pass upon the validity of a number of statutes dealing with such matters as the regulation of wages, hours of work, marketing, prices, etc., that, during the last session, were enacted by the Dominion Parliament. The question of the Federal authority in such matters is a highly controversial one and the consideration of these references, super added to the ordinary work of the court, will, in all probability tie me to Ottawa until the end of May.[22]

His labours on the Bennett legislation ended when the six decisions were delivered in mid-June. With great relief and pleasure, he and Annie sailed on the *Duchess of Bedford* for England and the Privy Council. He had written to his friend Farris not long before, "The Lord Chancellor has been pressing me to go over for the last two or three years and I have come to the conclusion for various reasons that I cannot properly delay my visit any longer."[23] The journey was a triumphal return; the Canadian high commissioner had contacted customs officials in the United Kingdom, and the Duff party was sped through customs at Southampton to find a limousine ready to whisk them up to London. Only three years after Lord Hailsham had expressed concern about his judicial powers, Duff, who had not attended a session of the board since 1929, now found himself its longest-serving member. Mere length of service did not ensure a place at the head of the table — that was reserved for the Lord Chancellor and other high-ranking English judges — but Duff's membership on the Judicial Committee since 1919 not only gratified him but impressed his fellows. Lords Atkin, Russell, MacMillan, and Sir Michael Myers, his colleagues on the first case he heard, could not claim with him that they had dispensed justice alongside all the colossi — Haldane, Birkenhead, Carson, and such lesser colonial giants as Ameer Ali and Sir John Edge.

At the end of his visit he received proof that he had indeed slain the dragon. As reported in the Court Circular of *The Times* for 29 July, "The Right Hon. Sir Lyman Poore Duff (Chief Justice of the Dominion of Canada) had an audience of the King [Edward VIII]."[24] Annie rejoiced with him, and Emma also, but from a distant shore. Duff and Annie returned home early in August to attend the annual meeting of the Canadian Bar Association in Halifax, where Duff was a special guest along with Lord Thankerton, a Privy Council colleague, and representatives of the legal professions of France and the United States. Dalhousie University awarded him an honorary degree, his sixth, in what was by now a routine ceremony. He slipped away from official functions to visit the scenes of his boyhood at Brooklyn. One can imagine the stir of emotion as he approached his old home after an absence of sixty years to re-visit his school, walk the streets where he had sold lobsters from a wheelbarrow, and tramp by the seashore to whiff the Atlantic spume. It is not given to many of us to return to our childhood after so long an absence.

When court reconvened in October 1936, Duff and his colleagues heard an unpleasant case involving John Brownlee, who had been hounded from office after serving as an effective premier of Alberta since 1925. Vivian MacMillan, a young secretary in the Edmonton legislature, alleged that on 13 October 1930 Brownlee had seduced her. She was then eighteen years old, and he a man of forty-five with a wife and family. She had testified that she engaged in sexual intercourse with him two or three times a week for the next two and a half years, not because she enjoyed the experience, but because Brownlee had wreaked his influence over her. Sometimes, she said, the sex took place in his car while they were out for a drive; on other occasions it took place in his home, or at his legislature office. Early in 1933, Vivian MacMillan met a young medical student who proposed marriage. Remorseful, she told him of her relations with Brownlee, though she still kept them up until July of that year. Since she showed no inclination to break off the affair, the student decided to do something about it himself, and hired a solicitor without her knowledge. The two set about to catch the couple *in flagrante delictu*. When Brownlee picked the girl up in his car one day, they followed it. Noting the trailing automobile, Brownlee drove on and eventually let her out. The game was up, however, when MacMillan and her father sued for damages for seduction. Brownlee, who through all the court proceedings strenuously denied having seduced her at any time, claimed later that he had been framed by political opponents.

The common law gave the parent or employer of a seduced girl a right of action for damages where pregnancy or illness resulted which prevented the girl, if living with her parents, from performing normal household tasks, or if employed, from performing her normal job at work. Vivian MacMillan had not become pregnant or ill as the result of her affair with Brownlee, but an Alberta statute, the Seduction Act, provided:

> Notwithstanding anything in this Act an action for seduction may be maintained by an unmarried female who has been seduced, in her own name, in the same manner as an action for any other tort and in any such action she shall be entitled to such damages as may be awarded.[25]

At trial a jury awarded the girl ten thousand dollars and her father five thousand, but the judge disallowed the verdicts on the ground that despite the broad language of the Act, she and her father must prove "loss of service" from illness or pregnancy in accordance with the common-law rule. The Alberta Court of Appeal agreed, and an appeal then went to Ottawa on behalf of the young woman only.

A majority of the Supreme Court of Canada, Duff and three colleagues, allowed the appeal and restored the ten-thousand-dollar award. True to his unwavering views on the interpretation of statutes, Duff held that the plain meaning of the words gave her a right of recovery, and that the common-law rule limiting that right should not be read into the section. Since she had not been affected physically, her father was not entitled to damages, but the jury had believed her evidence that she had been seduced; the jury had awarded her damages, and she was entitled to them. Brownlee appealed to the Privy Council, where an unusual situation developed. Vivian MacMillan, unable to afford the expense, took no part whatever in the appeal. The Privy Council still agreed with Duff and confirmed the award to the mortification of Brownlee's lawyer, who lost in the absence of opposition.[26]

The following year, Duff heard the most unusual case to come before him in his whole career. It had to do with the last will and testament of Charles Millar, the eccentric will of an eccentric lawyer that set off the famous "Stork Derby" to see which woman in Toronto would give birth to the largest number of children within ten years of his death. A number of entrants in the race came down to the wire in October 1936, the tenth anniversary.

Millar was the same man who had asked Duff to join his Toronto law firm in 1924, when rumour circulated after Anglin's appointment that he might retire: "I assume the Supreme Court is not as congenial to you as it might be. The counsel profession is more lucrative than the judicial one. If that is influential with you, this firm can make a proposal to you that might be worth your consideration."[27] Just two years after that letter, Millar, a bachelor, died suddenly in his office. Two months later, the extraordinary terms of his will became public. He had prefaced the document with these words:

> This will is necessarily uncommon and capricious because I have no dependents or near relations and no duty rests upon me to leave any property at my death, and what I do leave is proof of my folly in gathering and retaining more than I required in my lifetime.

The cynical Millar left shares in a race track to a former Ontario attorney-general, W.E. Raney, and a clergyman who had led a campaign to ban horse-racing, both of whom took the shares, sold them, and gave the proceeds to charity. He gave shares in a Jockey Club to clergymen "expounding the Scriptures to the sinners" in the Windsor-Walkerville area. To every Protestant clergyman and each Orange lodge in Toronto, he left shares in the O'Keefe brewery, a company controlled by Roman Catholics. Most beneficiaries claimed them, and, like Raney, sold them for charity.

Millar directed that the residue of his estate accumulate until a decade had passed, when it was

> to be given to the mother who, since my death has given birth in Toronto to the greatest number of children as shown by the registrations under the Vital Statistics Act. If one or more mothers have equal highest number of registrations under the said Act, to divide the said moneys and accumulations equally between them.

The pot of gold at the end of the rainbow lured various Toronto women and their husbands into the derby. Women without legal spouses or living with common-law husbands entered the race as well, but the resulting illegitimate children were eventually disqualified by the track stewards — the judges of the Ontario courts and the Supreme Court of Canada.

Millar's closest relatives were second cousins to whom he had left nothing. If the residuary clause could be broken, the legal position would be as if he had died intestate, and the cousins could then claim inheritance through blood relationship. The fact that they took no action until after the ten years had gone by, however, caused some of the judges to comment unfavourably on their bona fides.

By 31 October 1936 four married women were claiming the residue, each with nine children whose births had been registered in Toronto. However, they had to fight off two other claimants in the stretch, one who had had ten offspring in the stipulated period, though some had been stillborn, and another who had had nine, but only five of them by her lawful husband. When these two went to court to assert their claims, the four front-runners made an out-of-court settlement with them on the final division.

The case came first before Mr. Justice Middleton of the High Court of Ontario to whom lawyers for Millar's cousins put the argument that his bequest was of a nature to provoke uncontrolled reproduction, with attendant risks of physical harm to women who for ten years would be in near-continuous pregnancy. Middleton paid it scant attention since the damage, if any, had been done. The only point that took his and the higher judges' attention had to do with whether the bequest violated "public policy," an amorphous concept which in some instances allows courts to declare obligations unenforceable as being tainted by immorality or sin. For example, courts will not let anyone sue for an unpaid gambling debt or support a contract based on illegal grounds, as in Duff's early case involving fire insurance on a bordello. The cousins' representatives pressed that condoning the bizarre clause would be tantamount to encouraging "disgusting and revolting…competition among the mothers to obtain the benefits." Middleton disagreed:

> I would regard the clause in question as prompted rather by sympathy for the mothers of large families who are often extremely poor people, not unmingled with a grim sense of humour.
>
> The argument by the next-of-kin purports to be based on high motives of public policy and not upon mere greed, but the next-of-kin have waited until all the possible harm has been done, instead of prosecuting their claim immediately after Mr. Millar's death, when the evils, which it is said, result from the tendency detrimental to public policy set forth, might have been prevented.

In the Court of Appeal, only Mr. Justice Riddell echoed Middleton's irony:

> No objection was specifically taken to the inadvisability of the rapid increase of the population of our country, nor, indeed, in view of the tens of thousands of dollars we have spent and, doubtless, will spend on the encouragement of immigration by the steamboat, should there be any objection to the encouragement of immigration by the cradle.

In the Supreme Court of Canada only two judges, Duff and Crocket, wrote decisions. Each is utterly devoid of humour or any touch of irony. Duff declared the bequest valid and deplored the lengths to which the lawyers for the next of kin had gone in their attempts to undo it. In unwitting anticipation of the later fashion for surrogate parents, he added, "It is even suggested that in cases in which the husband ceased to be fecund in course of the race, the contestant might be tempted to resort to other males to do his office."[28] As the result of the decision, and after payment of all expenses, four Toronto families received approximately one hundred and sixty-five thousand dollars apiece.

Early in 1938 the court heard four Alberta appeals stemming from the Social Credit legislation of Premier William Aberhart, who had come into office in 1935 on a platform of Christian leadership and reform of the monetary system — an alliance of God and Mammon. Of more than twenty pieces of legislation ushering in the new economic order, three were disallowed by the Governor-General in August 1937, giving rise to the first case heard by the Supreme Court. The Alberta legislature had gone on after this to approve another three bills, the first to tax banks, the second to regulate credit, and the last to ensure newspaper publication of the government's viewpoint on any matter of public debate. Lieutenant-Governor John Bowen reserved assent and referred them to the Governor-General for possible disallowance, an action which moved Aberhart to close Government House in a fit of pique and force Bowen out of his mansion into a mere office. Rather than recommend disallowance, Mackenzie King referred them to the court at Aberhart's request.

In a highly charged political atmosphere, Duff correctly took a neutral approach.

> The three Bills referred to us are part of a general scheme of legislation and in order to ascertain the object and effect of them it is proper to look at the history of the legislation passed in furtherance of the general design.
>
> It is no part of our duty (it is, perhaps, needless to say) to consider the wisdom of these measures. We have only to ascertain whether or not they come within the ambit of the authority entrusted by the constitutional statutes (the British North America Act and the Alberta Act) to the Legislature of Alberta and our responsibility is rigorously confined to the determination of that issue. As judges, we do not and cannot intimate any opinion upon the merits of the legislative proposals embodied in them, as to their practicability or in any other respect.[29]

Though it was not one of the acts referred to the court, the Alberta Social Credit Act passed in April 1937 was at the heart of the constitutional question. It was asserted in the preamble of this key law that

> the people of Alberta, rich in natural wealth and resources both actual and potential, are yet heavily in debt and have been unable to acquire and maintain a standard of living such as is considered by them to be both desirable and possible; and…the existing means or system of distribution and exchange of wealth is considered to be inadequate, unjust and not suited to the welfare, prosperity and happiness of the people of Alberta.

Aberhart's government proposed to change that:

> In order to establish a system of circulating credit which shall at all times conform to the capacity of the industries and people of Alberta for the production of wanted goods and services, it is hereby declared to be the policy of the Legislative Assembly of Alberta to prevent the undue expansion of credit as well as to eliminate the contraction of credit in time of slackening trade. It is the true meaning and intent of this Act...that the controls over the supply of credit through open market operations and the discount rate shall be employed as heretofore to maintain a balanced credit structure.[30]

The statute elaborated a scheme for bettering the living standard of Albertans denied them, it was alleged, by an inequitable distribution of purchasing power, which was now to be tied to productive capacity. The various other pieces of legislation before the court, as Duff observed, arose from a

> fundamental postulate, viz., that the economic ills which they aim at curing arise primarily from financial causes and, particularly, from the circumstance that bank credit, which constitutes in the main, in point of volume, the circulating medium of payment and exchange in this country, is issued through private initiative for private profit.[31]

To overcome that evil, the Social Credit Act created a medium of exchange and payment called "Alberta credit." The provincial treasurer would circulate certificates with which citizens could obtain government services and discounts on retail goods, to mention only two of the wide range of uses to be made of them. As part of this scheme, every person over age twenty-one received a Consumers' Dividend or a monthly grant of Alberta credit. It was ridiculed as "funny money" by Aberhart's political opponents, and became a notorious object of derision in the press.

The scheme depended for its success on the willingness of Alberta merchants to accept provincial credit as a medium of exchange. To ensure the proper circulation of the medium, the Act set up what was in effect a banking system with certain limitations on the use of Canadian legal tender. A Social Credit M.L.A. of the time defined the solution and the predicament in which his government then found itself:

> We formulated certain Acts that would give us the power to use the credit of our people to give these same people the benefit of our production so that they could do away with any serious thought of this ridiculous

The Privy Councillor

Haldane as Lord Chancellor.
*Canadian Bar Association Proceedings,
vol. 9, 1924*

The Transportation Commission as seen by Arch Dale of the *Winnipeg Free Press* in December 1931: above, Beatty and Thornton peer up at a sphinx-like Duff. The *Winnipeg Free Press*

Duff and Annie aboard the *Duchess of Athlone* on their way to the Privy Council session of 1938

Duff at the Canadian Bar Association 1938 convention in Vancouver, as seen by local cartoonist Jack Boothe

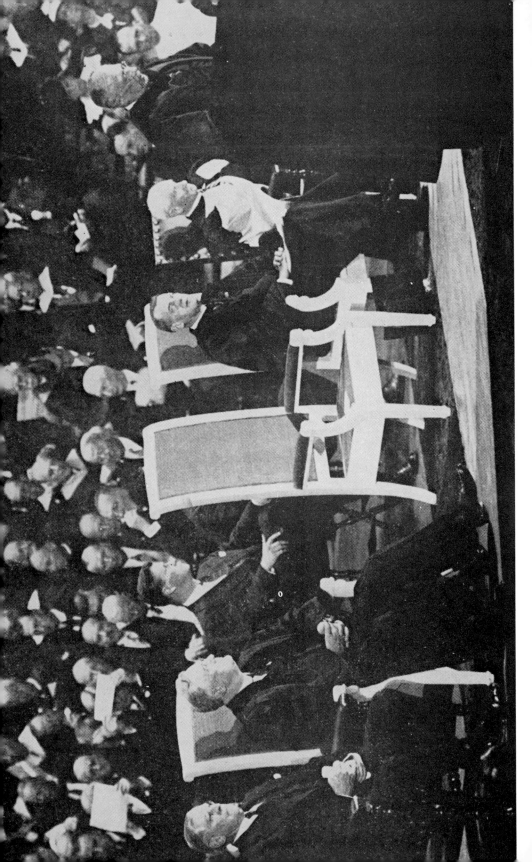

Duff the Administrator of Canada in wartime with his A.D.C., Col. Willis O'Connor, and F.S. Pereira. *Public Archives of Canada*

Duff — seated behind the speaker, President Gates — at the University of Pennsylvania convocation of 1940. Franklin Delano Roosevelt is sitting on the left. *University of Pennsylvania Archives*

The unveiling of Duff's bust in the new Supreme Court of Canada building, 1947. To the left of Duff, Justice Minister J.L. Ilsley and J.C. McRuer; on the right, Bar Association President J.T. Hackett, Mackenzie King, and Chief Justice Rinfret. *T.V. Little/Public Archives of Canada*

"Profession: Chief Justice of Canada." Duff's wartime passport

— 2 —

DESCRIPTION
SIGNALEMENT

Profession — Wife—Femme
Profession

*Chief Justice of Canada*

Place and date
of birth
Lieu et date
de naissance

*Meaford, Canada*
*January 7, 1865*

Residence
Résidence

Height — ft.   in.   pd.   po.
Taille — 5   7

— ft.   in.   pd.   po.

Colour of eyes
eur des yeux — *Blue*

ir yeux — *White*

NFANTS

Sex
Sexe

— 3 —

PHOTOGRAPH OF BEARER
PHOTOGRAPHIE DU TITULAIRE

WIFE
FEMME

Signature of wife—Signature de sa femme

The old man: Duff at the end of his life as he appeared in the Victoria *Colonist*, May 1955

The old friend, Douglas Alexander, with the baronet's dignities received for service in arms production during the Great War. *Vandyk photo/ Public Archives of Canada*

"depression" that was stultifying the lives of millions, and give them the benefit of the massive real wealth that they were producing, and which was piling up all around us...it soon appeared that the people didn't know what was good for them, and the Courts and the Federal Government decided in their supreme wisdom (mixed with a few other considerations that shall be nameless) that the province had no power to use their own credit to feed and clothe their own people.[32]

In its opening salvo before the Supreme Court, Alberta challenged the Governor-General's inherent right to the power of disallowance. The principal lawyer for the Alberta government on all four cases and Duff's old friend, O.M. Biggar, advanced a novel argument based on current practice in Alberta and some other provinces where the Lieutenant-Governor gave assent to bills passed by the legislature in the name of the Sovereign, rather than in the Governor-General's name as technically required by the British North America Act. Biggar argued ingeniously that the Governor-General's power of disallowance did not exist; it was the Sovereign's own, and not his Ottawa representative's.

Duff complimented Biggar on his "plausibility," but ruled against him.

The circumstance...that the assent of the Lieutenant Governor acting under the authority and on behalf of the Crown has been given in a form more august than that prescribed by the statute could not, of course, impair in any way the legal validity of his assent that is expressed as the assent of the Sovereign, which in truth, in point of law, it is and is intended to be.[33]

The court heard the argument in that case on 10 January 1938. A paper noted that "only a few spectators were in the courtroom";[34] constitutional cases are not crowd-pleasers. Over the next five days, submissions were heard on the validity of the three acts. Opposing Biggar were a dozen of the most eminent lawyers in the country, with Geoffrion, Tilley, J.L. Ralston, and S.W. Field among them. An argument arose immediately about what attention, if any, should be paid to the Alberta Social Credit Act, the validity of which, strangely, had not been referred to the court. Duff and his fellow judges resolved the dispute by holding that, since the Act had not been repealed or disallowed, it could be treated as the background against which the other acts should be scrutinized.

The Ottawa *Evening Journal* reported an exchange between the lawyers and Duff during that aspect of the appeal. Geoffrion in outlining the provisions of the Alberta Social Credit Act, referred to its implications as "staggering," whereupon "Mr. Biggar told the Court the measure Mr. Geoffrion called 'staggering' was not before the court and had nothing to do with measures before the Court." When Geoffrion retorted that "Light is needed," Duff picked up the metaphor by adding, "We need light more than heat." Observing that the temperature outside stood minus ten degrees Fahrenheit, Geoffrion quipped: "Well, it's a cold day...but I don't think there is much fuel in the word 'staggering.' " But Duff got in the last jab: "Well, it's a dry subject...and perhaps a little interlude like this doesn't do any harm."[35]

Courtroom humour is not always of high order. The Winnipeg *Free Press*, in its account of the argument between Biggar and Geoffrion, described Biggar as "suave, able, personable and persuasive," a man who was "struggling with every argument possible to prevent the thirsty Supreme Court Justices from imbibing at the fount of Social Credit wisdom."[36] Duff attempted further levity when Geoffrion referred to a decision involving the Esquimalt and Nanaimo Railway Company on Vancouver Island. He mangled the place names, and Duff corrected him. Geoffrion responded, "Your Lordship comes from that country. I would not argue with you on that, but I might on the pronunciation of some Quebec names," to which Duff, a true westerner still, retorted, "British Columbia is in Canada, you know."[37] Only old warrior-friends like Biggar and Geoffrion could get away with banter. On another occasion, Geoffrion concluded an argument just before the midday adjournment. When Duff returned, he told Geoffrion that before the break he had thought his argument had some merit, but he had changed his mind over lunch. Geoffrion told Duff that it was obvious he had suffered an attack of indigestion from which he hoped he would soon recover. Young lawyers would not have dared to take such liberties.

Having decided on the relevance of the Social Credit Act, the court looked at the other three acts one by one. The first, the Credit of Alberta Regulation Act, authorized the licensing of institutions to which the Social Credit Act related. The Bank Taxation Act imposed annual taxes on Canadian chartered banks of $1/2$ of 1 per cent on paid-up capital, 1 percent on reserves, and the same percentage on retained earnings. Duff commented that if other provinces were to impose similar levies, the Bank of Montreal, which he used as an example, would be subject to an annual impost of $6^1/4$ per cent on capital and $12^1/2$ per cent on each of the other two sources. In describing such a levy as "prohibitive," he took judicial notice — a phrase used by judges when drawing on their own knowledge and experience as distinct from facts proved in evidence — that banking in Canada could not survive a tax of such magnitude.

The third bill attracted by far the greatest publicity since it was aimed at newspapers. One of Aberhart's severest critics, the Edmonton *Journal*, had run numerous articles vilifying him and ridiculing his legislation as wild economic theory. In revenge Aberhart produced the Accurate News and

Information Act that required Alberta papers to print defences prepared by the government against critical articles and run these with equal prominence. More menacingly, it compelled publishers to identify their sources of critical comment to the government. A particularly obnoxious clause protected the government from libel suits, stipulating that a paper's refusal to print a story it believed to be libellous would be punishable by a fine of five hundred dollars and a possible shutdown.

Aberhart was clearly not a man to be trifled with, and now his anger turned to the federal meddlers. During the hearings, as if to egg on his lawyers in Ottawa, he made a speech to a general assembly of the Social Credit Party proclaiming, "I am calling you into economic war." He told party members that they needed "more and more of this thing called esprit de corps," for "the world is watching Alberta."[38]

The Supreme Court handed down its decision on 4 March along with its judgement on Biggar's disallowance argument. Duff began with an analysis of the Alberta Social Credit Act, which he ruled *ultra vires* as related to banking or trade, both exclusively federal topics. Duff drew a distinction between the Social Credit Act and various other acts which he had invalidated over the years, in the *Board of Commerce* case for example, and his more recent decision in the *Natural Products Marketing* case. He rejected the view that the legislation regulated a particular form of business and hence lay within provincial jurisdiction; the only particular business regulated was banking, and the province had no authority in that area.

Turning to the three acts in the case, he pronounced that the Credit Regulation Act, depending as it did on the Social Credit Act, must also fail — the tail goes with the hide. With regard to the tax on banks, he concluded that its object was punitive, making it economically impossible for banks to operate, and that therefore the pith and substance of the legislation related to banking. The prohibitiveness he had pointed out in the legislation came, of course, from his postulating what might happen if other provinces enacted similar measures. He appreciated the difficulty:

> As regards the excessive magnitude of the tax, the question may be asked: where are you to draw the line? The answer to that is, any attempt to draw an abstract line is difficult and, in dealing with questions of the kind before us, it is inadvisable to attempt it unless it be absolutely necessary. This case presents no such necessity. It is plain on the face of the Bill that the purpose of it is not to raise a revenue for provincial purposes, and equally plain that taxation of this character throughout Canada, if operative, would completely frustrate the purposes of the Bank Act.[39]

Duff declared the newspaper bill invalid for the principal reason that, like the Credit Regulation Act, it formed part of "the general scheme of Social

Credit legislation." He went on however, to make some gratuitous observations about the freedom of the press, taking his inspiration from Geoffrion's argument that the "free exchange of news [was] necessary to [the] Canadian political set-up."[40] Duff pointed out that the House of Commons was a representative body similar to Parliament in the United Kingdom, which worked "under the influence of public opinion and public discussion," and then ventured into relatively uncharted waters by attempting to define the legal basis of freedom of speech and public discussion in language civil libertarians in Canada have frequently turned to:

> There can be no controversy that [parliaments] derive their efficacy from the free public discussion of affairs, from criticism and answer and counter-criticism, from attack upon policy and administration and defence and counter-attack; from the freest and fullest analysis and examination from every point of view of political proposals...the right of public discussion is, of course, subject to legal restrictions; those based upon considerations of decency and public order, and others conceived for the protection of various private and public interests with which, for example, the laws of defamation and sedition are concerned. In a word, freedom of discussion means to quote the words of Lord Wright in *James v. Commonwealth* "freedom governed by law."
>
> Even within its legal limits, it is liable to abuse and grave abuse, and such abuse is constantly exemplified before our eyes; but it is axiomatic that the practice of this right of free public discussion of public affairs, notwithstanding its incidental mischiefs, is the breath of life for parliamentary institutions.

Having stated these broad principles, he turned to the immediate question of the bill's constitutionality.

> Some degree of regulation of newspapers everybody would concede to the provinces. Indeed, there is a very wide field in which the provinces are undoubtedly invested with legislative authority over newspapers; but the limit, in our opinion, is reached when the legislation effects such a curtailment of the exercise of the right of public discussion as substantially to interfere with the working of the parliamentary institutions of Canada as contemplated by the provisions of the British North America Act and the Statutes of the Dominion of Canada.[41]

That decision, as well as the others, drew shouts of praise and acclaim from every major newspaper in Canada. Duff overnight became a champion of press freedom, and the reaction from politicians outside the Alberta government was equally rapturous. Aberhart himself expressed surprise that the court had invalidated his legislation on the basis of a law that was not called specifically into question, and spoke of going to the Privy Council. Appeals were in fact launched, although by the time the Privy Council sat to hear them the Alberta scheme had collapsed with the repeal of the Social Credit Act and a return to conventional government, which left only the bank tax bill to be argued. All the same, the Privy Council went out of its way to declare that it had no doubt "as to the correctness of the decision of the Supreme Court" respecting the other two bills, nor was it troubled by Duff's postulate of the impact of such legislation if enacted elsewhere in Canada:

> It seems to their Lordships that the learned judges were justified in considering that the magnitude of the tax proposed for Alberta was such that, if it were applied by each of the other Provinces, it would have the effect of preventing banks from carrying on their businesses. It would be strange if each of the Provinces were successively to tax banks and the result of the question of *ultra vires* were to be that the Acts of those Provinces who were earliest in the field were valid, whilst the Acts of those who came a little later were to be held *ultra vires*.[42]

Only four days after Duff handed down his judgement in the Alberta references, he heard opening arguments in another important reference prompted this time by the province of Ontario. The case had to do with the authority of provincially appointed judges — justices of the peace, juvenile court judges, and magistrates — to decide matters under the Adoption Act, the Childrens' Protection Act, the Children of Unmarried Parents Act, and the Deserted Wives' and Childrens' Maintenance Act. Although only these Ontario statutes were directly involved, the provinces of Manitoba, British Columbia, Prince Edward Island, Saskatchewan, and Alberta had passed equivalent legislation and were thus vitally interested; all were represented at the hearing.

The issue turned on the effect of section 96 of the B.N.A. Act which requires Ottawa to appoint the judges of "Superior, District and County Courts." Plainly, magistrates and other provincial judicial officers do not fit those categories, but in interpreting section 96 the courts have ruled that judicial functions which would normally be discharged by federally appointed judges cannot be discharged by officials of the lower provincial courts, because such functions come within the "intendment" of the section. In this case, the Ontario Court of Appeal had decided that only judges appointed by Ottawa could adjudicate cases arising from the four acts in question. The Alberta Court of Appeal had made a similar ruling with regard to the equivalent Alberta legislation. The rulings alarmed provincial governments, partly because of the added cost of having the acts administered by judges of the higher courts, but mainly because of the inconvenience and delay that would be bound to occur if only a handful of high-court judges could hear such matters. The Supreme Court was asked to decide whether provincial judicial officers, forming courts of summary jurisdiction, were invested with the power of summary adjudication conferred by the provisions of the four acts which had been passed for the social welfare of children and their families.

As summarized by Duff, the attorney-general of Canada had argued

> that it is incompetent to the provincial legislature to legislate for the appointment of any officer of any provincial court exercising other than ministerial functions...and that, as regards all such courts exercising, at all events, civil jurisdiction, the appointment of judges and officers presiding over them is vested exclusively in the Dominion.

The argument sent Duff on a historical analysis of the role of summary jurisdiction courts in the provinces since Confederation and a review of cases in which the courts had considered aspects of that role. The attorney-general's argument, Duff pointed out, contained an "underlying assumption" that "the interest of the people of this country in the independent and impartial administration of justice" was best served by judges appointed by Ottawa and not by the provinces. Once again demonstrating his provincial orientation, Duff demolished the proposition:

> Throughout the whole of this country magistrates daily exercise, espe-cially in the towns and cities, judicial powers of the highest importance in relation more particularly to the criminal law, but in relation also to a vast body of law which is contained in provincial statutes and municipal by-laws. The jurisdiction exercised by these functionaries, speaking gener-ally, touches the great mass of the people more intimately and more extensively than do the judgments of the Superior Courts; and it would be an extraordinary supposition that a great community like the Province of Ontario is wanting, either in the will or in the capacity, to protect itself against this conduct by these officers whom it appoints for these duties; and any such suggestion would be baseless in fact and altogether falla-cious as the foundation of a theory controlling the construction of the B.N.A. Act.

The attorney-general then argued that the jurisdiction of provincial sum-mary courts as it had existed at Confederation remained fixed and immuta-ble. Duff pointed out in rebuttal that if that was a correct proposition of law, then the provinces would have had no right to increase the jurisdiction of the county courts, the judges of which were appointed by Ottawa; yet, as all lawyers knew, the jurisdiction of those courts had often been enlarged by provincial legislation which no one had questioned. He reached back to his own experience as a mining lawyer:

> Perhaps the most striking example of these enlargements of jurisdiction was that which occurred in British Columbia when the jurisdiction of the Mining Court...was transferred to the County Court, and the County Court in respect of mines, mining lands and so on was given a jurisdiction unrestricted as to amount or value with all the powers of a court of law or equity.
>
> It has never been suggested, so far as I know, that the effect even of that particular enlargement of the jurisdiction of the County Courts of British Columbia was to deprive the County Court and the County Court judges of their characters as such and transform them into Superior Courts and Superior Court judges [and thus come within the intendment of section 96].

Having lost that argument, the attorney-general submitted that giving provinces unlimited power to increase the jurisdiction of provincially constituted courts might lead ultimately to usurpation of the federal government's power to appoint judges. But Duff was not impressed with that proposition either:

> Even if I am satisfied that there is something in the nature of an abusive power, that in itself is no concern of mine. If, in its true character, the legislation is legislation concerning the administration of justice and the constitution of provincial courts and is not repugnant to the B.N.A. Act as a whole, that is the end of the matter.

He concluded that the four acts had to do with legislation for the administration of justice and the constitution of provincial courts, both powers given to provinces.[43] It was a common-sense decision and a great relief to the provinces whose side he had taken once again. Duff was rightly proud of his judgement and considered it one of his best; it is also a good deal more readable than many of his others.

The Canadian government did not appeal to the Privy Council, but in a 1948 case involving much the same issue, that body praised Duff's decision as "exhaustive and penetrating."[44] His judgement has been important in nourishing the growth of various provincial tribunals which adjudicate a wide range of issues; labour-relations boards are an example. The legal question still gives rise to litigation, however, for cases are constantly coming before the courts on whether the adjudication of certain issues must be discharged only by a judge appointed under section 96 of the B.N.A. Act.

At about the time the Alberta and Ontario references were being argued, Duff accepted an invitation from Senator Farris as president of the Canadian Bar Association to attend the 1938 annual meeting in Vancouver that August. In June, Duff had again become Administrator in Lord Tweedsmuir's absence from the country, and when the Governor-General had not returned by August, he cabled Farris asking whether, given the protocol his role required, the association still wished him to come. Farris repeated his invitation, and Duff made still another comfortable journey to the Pacific in a private railway car to be greeted on arrival by sundry dignitaries and, after the formalities, by Senator Farris and his son John. Asked by a reporter from the Vancouver *Province* to comment on changes in the law over his lifetime, Duff, conscious of his official status, said wryly, "I'm a poor man to interview; I can't very well comment on anything."[45]

He attended none of the business sessions of the association, but went to every one of the social events. The first was a banquet at the Hotel Vancouver at which he, R.B. Bennett, and the premier, T.D. Pattullo, were the honoured guests. At another banquet three days later Duff gave the address, affectionately recalling his days in British Columbia as a lawyer and judge, and paying tribute to such giants of the B.C. judiciary as Begbie and Hunter and to giants of the Bar like E.P. Davis. The meeting was also attended by Viscount Finlay, an English high-court judge and son of Sir Robert, later Viscount Finlay who had been leading counsel for Canada before the Alaska boundary tribunal. Duff remarked humorously that his own role in the arbitration would be recalled since mountains in the Yukon had been named for all the Canadian representatives.[46]

On 19 August Duff, Finlay, Farris, and the distinguished American legal scholar Arthur Vanderbilt, were made honorary doctors of law in a specially arranged convocation at the University of British Columbia. Finlay's attractive daughter Rosalind, afterwards the wife of Vice Admiral Sir John Hayes, accompanied her father. She met Duff for the first time at the luncheon at which the university entertained the doctoral candidates; the guests enjoyed a fine meal washed down with excellent wine. After this they trooped to the university auditorium where, in extreme heat, President L.S. Klinck conferred the degrees. Lady Rosalind recalled that the combination of the lunch, wine, heat, and a dull, lengthy speech by Dr. Klinck proved too much for Duff, who fell asleep in his chair on the platform. Her father nudged him awake to hear his presentation by Judge F.W. Howay, the well-known British Columbia historian, as a candidate for the degree. Following the ceremony the entire assembly took tea on the spacious lawns outside the pseudo-Gothic library. In all this, Duff the Administrator, "His Excellency," obviously warmed to Rosalind Finlay. She has remembered his animated conversation, his "great fun," and "approachable" manner. Instead of talking "at" her as elderly men are inclined to do with younger persons, Duff listened and spoke "with" her.[47]

The next day, she and her father, Duff, and other delegates boarded a steamer for the pleasant five-hour trip to Victoria, steaming past the lovely wooded islands dotting the Gulf of Georgia. Duff spent the next several days at Government House, only a few minutes from his old home; he walked past it sadly. The other delegates toured Victoria's beauty spots, but not Duff; he visited the Union Club of fond memories and called on old friends, among them the lawyer J.H. Lawson. The president of the Victoria Bar Association, H.W. Davey, later chief justice of British Columbia, presented him with the robe he had worn as a junior lawyer and had left in the barristers' room of the Victoria courthouse when he was made Queen's Counsel and required a new, special robe.

Apart from his 1932 tour as chairman of the Transportation Commission, he had not been in the city since 1908. The visit called up strong emotions in him: pride in his achievements, sadness at the loss of his wife and friends. Gone was Gordon Hunter, gone Senator Templeman; gone was Rattenbury, murdered in England ten years before; gone too were most of his old comrades at the Bar. The sense of loss made him drink unwisely, and one morning his friend Farris found him wandering about the Inner Harbour in a drunken stupor. The episode was not repeated. He returned to Ottawa late in August, and early in September, while he was still Administrator, he held an elegant dinner party at the Chateau Laurier for Finlay before his colleague's departure for England.

Hitler's invasion of Austria and his threat to Czechoslovakia filled Duff with uneasiness. In his Vancouver speeches Duff had doubted optimistically that "the light of France [would] fall into darkness," or that England would "become a mere outpost on the fringes of barbarism."[48] By the end of 1938, he could feel change all about him — the collapse of Europe, the winds of war, and, at a more personal level, the prospect of retirement after one more year of service.

# 15

## The old order changes

IN 1936 GEORGE V DIED. He had sworn Duff in as a privy councillor in 1919 and enrolled him in the order of St. Michael and St. George. The Prince of Wales succeeded his father as Edward VIII; he had received Duff in audience. On his abdication, his brother came to the throne as George VI and was crowned in May 1937. On 19 March of that year, Duff had a curiously worded note from Laurent Beaudry, the acting undersecretary of state for External Affairs:

> The High Commissioner for Canada in London has telegraphed stating that the Earl Marshal desires to know whether you and Miss Duff will be in London at the time of the coronation. If it is your intention to be in London at that time the Earl Marshal states that you would be eligible for an invitation to attend the Coronation in Westminster Abbey.[1]

Duff felt slighted. Many others had already been asked to the coronation; this invitation, if it really was an invitation and not a certificate of suitability, had come less than two months before the ceremony. His reply was testy.

> Since I am told that I would be eligible for an invitation to the Coronation if in London at the time, it must be that the office of Chief Justice of Canada is considered one of those offices which ought to be represented at the ceremony. It is, of course, the highest judicial office in Canada; relatively a higher judicial office than the Lord Chief Justice of England. In these circumstances, I really cannot understand what is meant by saying that if it were my intention to be in London at the time of the Coronation, I, as incumbent of the office of Chief Justice of Canada, and

my sister, would be eligible for invitations. I cannot help asking myself if that is the sort of intimation which has been received by the Lord Chief Justice of England — if he has been told that he is "eligible for an invitation if it is his intention to be in London at the time."

In Canada, judicial offices are justly held in the highest regard and esteem by the people generally; none other more so. The officials concerned with the ceremony of the Coronation ought to know something of the Constitution of the British Empire and ought to realize that this office is entitled to be treated with becoming respect.[2]

The unfortunate Beaudry referred the matter to Dr. O.D. Skelton, the undersecretary, who tried to mollify Duff by explaining that the note really did contain an invitation, ambiguously worded and regrettably delayed though it might have been. Skelton followed up with a printed invitation, but Duff decided he could not at that date rearrange the court's schedule for his own gratification. But he and Annie did go to London in June for the Privy Council. From 1936 onwards, these annual visits were vacations more than anything else; they were certainly not occasions for hard work. In 1937 he sat on only one case. The following year he sat on three and on one in 1939, in none of them rendering the judgement.

On the eve of sailing to Europe in June 1938, Duff heard still another important reference, on whether the Inuit of Quebec should be classified as "Indians" in the sense used in the federal Indian Act. At the time of Confederation, when Canada began to assume Britain's relations with the aboriginal societies, the Inuit population in the northern fief of the Hudson's Bay Company amounted to only four or five thousand souls as compared with an indigenous population in the whole of British North America estimated at over one hundred and fifty thousand. For Duff, trying to see if the few were part of the many, it was "important to consult the reliable sources of information as to the use of the term 'Indian' in relation to the Eskimo in those territories." He turned to the records of the great trading company, which had constituted for generations the government of the area, and found that such documents as census records invariably classed "Esquimaux" under the general "Indian" heading. When, in 1870, Rupert's Land and the Northwest Territories became part of the Dominion of Canada, the fact that virtually all the vast region's inhabitants were aboriginal imposed on Parliament the duty "to make adequate provisions for the protection of the Indian Tribes whose interest and well-being are involved in the transfer." Duff saw it as significant that the Hudson's Bay Company usage — Inuit equals "Indian" — had apparently been confirmed by Parliament. He also examined eighteenth-century documents relating to the coast of Labrador and found that, as in Rupert's Land, the Inuit had been included in the generic term "Indian" at least since 1774, when the boundaries of Quebec were extended to include portions of that territory. Proclamations of the time referring to "Esquimaux Indians," or "Esquimaux savages," turned up in missionary records as well. His research convinced him that the "Indian" designation legally applied. He obviously enjoyed this job; his judgement reflects pleasure in a well-conducted research expedition into the past.[3]

His decision coincided almost exactly with the passage through Parliament of a bill extending his term of office as chief justice of Canada for a further three years. His statutory time was to have expired at his seventy-fifth birthday, 7 January 1940, but in March 1939 King

> discussed with Lapointe position of Supreme Court, Duff's time being up in January. Four of the judges are anything but well. Court very weak. He could think of no one suitable being appointed Chief Justice — from B.C., or to take Duff's place on the Supreme Court Bench. I agreed to having Duff's term extended a year if he were agreeable.[4]

It is noteworthy that even in 1939, Duff was still regarded as a westerner on the court. A few days later, the prime minister spoke to him about the extension, a possibility he had never even contemplated. King recorded,

> I told him…that Lapointe was going to ask him to continue as Chief Justice, notwithstanding that his time was up in January, and that we would probably put through legislation to enable this to be done. He said that was extremely kind, the most flattering compliment ever paid him. I told him it was simply because the Court and the country needed him in the position of Chief Justice. He seemed very pleased at this.[5]

Duff himself said later that King had urged him to accept the extension as his "wartime duty."[6] On 2 May 1939, by a Special Act that did not mention Duff by name, Parliament authorized "the person holding the Office of Chief Justice of Canada" to retain the office for three years from 7 January 1940.[7] The bill was supported by all parties in the Commons. R.J. Manion, then in opposition, summed up the feeling of the House. Speaking of him as "a great Chief Justice, a great lawyer and a great scholar," Manion harked back to the days of the Transportation Commission to which he had appointed Duff:

> During the time he presided over the Commission both he and the Commission did splendid work, but he was the guiding force behind the decisions of the Commission and it was his skill that very largely helped to make those decisions clear-cut and well-balanced.[8]

In the Senate, however, there were murmurings. Sir Allen Aylesworth, one of the arbitrators on the Alaska boundary tribunal and a former justice minister who had favoured Anglin for the chief justiceship, carped at a measure which "to me means that members of the Bench who reach the age of seventy-five years will simply retain their positions at the will of the Government of the Day."[9] Duff's namesake Senator William Duff from the Maritimes, who as an M.P. during the shell scandal of 1916 had applauded his appointment as a Commissioner, now condemned the extension of his term, arguing that "there are hundreds of men of integrity and ability who could be appointed," or else "one of the present members of the Court could be elevated to the position of Chief Justice." When some senators remonstrated with him, Senator Duff joked solemnly that "all the Duffs have pride and a lot of conceit and they think nobody can do anything as well as they. That no doubt explains why the Chief Justice has agreed to have this Bill introduced."[10]

It was left to Arthur Meighen, at the opposite end of the political spectrum from the chief justice, to put the debate into perspective. In a tribute from one massive intellect to another, he doubted eloquently that anyone could equal Duff's abilities. From British Columbia, the same *Daily Colonist* that had patronized a man with perhaps some prospects of success forty-five years earlier, now spoke with awe: "Sir Lyman is more than a great Canadian judge: He is an Empire figure." Describing him as "the greatest jurist this country has produced," the newspaper praised the "human qualities" that "have endeared him to all his intimates, for though cultured, he is simple in his tastes, enjoys the society of both young and old, and seems invested with buoyancy of a perennial youth."[11] Duff had neither solicited nor expected the extension, but he was gratified by it.

Days afterwards came the laying of the cornerstone for a new courthouse, the culmination of four years of planning. In 1935, officials from the department of Pensions and National Health had made a room-by-room, brick-by-brick survey of the old Supreme Court structure, and reported:

> The building is antiquated, the rooms are small, the ceilings low, and the lighting and the ventilations very poor. This is particularly true of the rooms that are occupied by the Judges, which are considered the worst features of the building. These are comparable to old fashioned bedrooms in an old-time hotel, and there is no doubt that constant and prolonged occupancy of these rooms will have a deleterious effect upon the health of the occupants.[12]

Reviewing its shortcomings in detail, the officials concluded that "this building should be condemned."

There were other difficulties, caused mainly by the fact that the structure also housed the Exchequer Court of Canada presided over by A.K. Maclean. Two separate courts, each with its own judiciary and staff, were crowded into the same inadequate quarters. Not surprisingly, there were moments of friction. The Exchequer Court used the Supreme courtroom occasionally, and when Maclean found the door secured one day he wrote to Duff, even though they were good friends, to accuse him of deliberately locking the Exchequer Court judges out. Understandably offended, Duff sent back a stiff note saying that the door had been locked to keep out "riffraff" who were attending sessions of the Exchequer Court. He complained of being "jostled on the stair" by "groups of people who were wandering about," forcing him to lock his room "to protect myself against the intrusions of these people."[13] It is certain that Maclean never addressed such a letter to him again. But Duff probably wrote with tongue in cheek: even fewer showed up to watch proceedings in Maclean's court than came to Duff's, and those who did were litigants or civil servants.

As a result of the 1935 report, the justice department decided to replace the Supreme Court building rather than upgrade it, and a year later engaged the Montreal architect Ernest Cormier to design a new one. Cormier was not interested in a functional structure, built for those who worked in it; he planned a national monument to the supremacy of law. Duff too wanted to see a courthouse that would epitomize the dignity of the law, but he envisaged something on the lines of the Royal Courts of Justice on the Strand in London. Cormier did not agree, and the result is more grandiose than pleasing; it is also impractical, with much wasted space. Although Duff and Cormier had frequent consultations during construction, it was the architect and not the judge who won the day.

Early in 1939, Mackenzie King invited King George and Queen Elizabeth to come to Canada, and to his immense gratification they accepted. He asked the Queen to dedicate the cornerstone of the new Supreme Court building; she did so on 20 May 1939 in the presence of a large company that included the prime minister as well as Duff with his colleagues. Speaking in both French and English, the Queen remarked how it was "fitting that on these heights above the Ottawa — surely one of the noblest situations in the world — you should add to the imposing group of buildings which house your Parliament and the executive branch of government, a worthy home for your Supreme Court." In reply, Lapointe referred to the "massive architecture of this new temple of supreme judicial authority," and assured Her Majesty that "our judiciary and our Bar are greatly and justly honoured, and will remain protagonists of British ideals, of British traditions and of British justice."[14] Sadly, Duff never presided in the building: completed by the outbreak of hostilities in 1939, it housed wartime civil servants until 15 January 1946, when the Supreme Court sat in it for the first time two years after Duff's retirement.

Ten days before the cornerstone ceremony, Duff and his fellow judges heard an appeal by a Montreal black who had ordered a glass of beer in a tavern in that city and been refused service by a waitress who later testified that her employer had told her not to serve beer to black people. Only a year before, Duff had eloquently defended freedom of the press and speech, but he and the majority of the court now found that the complainant Christie had no civil right to be served. The case revolved around provisions of the Quebec Licence Act which made it an offence for restaurants to refuse to serve food to "travellers," defined as "persons paying money for food or lodging." Rinfret, who wrote the majority judgement in which Duff concurred, held that Christie could not be described as a "traveller" since he had asked only for a glass of beer. At all events, the majority decided, the tavern-keeper had an unqualified right to refuse anyone service: "Any merchant is free to deal as he may choose with any individual member of the public. It is not a question of motives or reasons for deciding to deal or not to deal; he is free to do either." Only Davis, who dissented, took an approach that would be commended today by civil libertarians, asserting that a merchant given special licensing status for serving alcohol to the general public could not "pick and choose those to whom he will sell."[15]

Change was being discussed more and more at this time for an institution of tremendous significance in Duff's life, the Privy Council as the final court of appeal for Canada. There was nothing new about this: the bill creating the Supreme Court in 1875 contained a provision to make its judgements "final and conclusive." Not until 1931 and the Statute of Westminster, however, could Canada pass laws affecting the prerogative right of appeal to the Privy Council.[16] In the wake of the Privy Council's 1937 decisions on new deal laws, politicians began seriously to debate the abolition of appeals. On 20 January 1939, C.H. Cahan, a former secretary of state in the Bennett government, introduced a private member's bill in the Commons to declare the Supreme Court of Canada the court of last resort for all Canadian cases. The bill would have repealed the Judicial Committee Act of 1833, an English law, in so far as it applied to Canada, a step made possible by the Statute of Westminster. The bill received little notice at this initial stage.[17]

On 14 April, after justice department officials had suggested certain amendments to improve his bill, Cahan moved its second reading. He defended it in the House as something that would strengthen rather than weaken the "imperial connection," since a fully independent Canada, no longer subservient to a British court, could the more willingly remain part of the British empire. Cahan paused to pay tribute to Duff in expectation of his retirement, expressing "profound regret that the present Chief Justice of

Canada, than whom no Canadian judge ever more fully enjoyed the respect, confidence and esteem of the Canadian people, is about to retire on account of the age limit prescribed by statute." He next touched on the main argument of those wanting to retain the right of Privy Council appeal, the rather doddering image that had become attached to the Ottawa court. Regretting that "physical frailties preclude two or more other justices from that active and onerous participation in judicial work which their official duties really demand," he stressed that the government must take "effective measures to change, increase and strengthen the present personnel of the supreme court...so that when it becomes the final Court of Appeal it will have the full confidence of the people." [18]

Another speaker rehearsed one of the more frequent arguments for abolition, the Privy Council's alleged heavy-handedness in constitutional matters.

> It narrowly interpreted the Canadian Constitution in the mistaken belief that by curtailing the powers of the central government to the advantage of the provincial governments it was strengthening, or at any rate preventing the loosening of, the ties that bind this Dominion to the mother country. [19]

Lapointe, the justice minister, wound up the debate. He thoroughly approved of the principle of the measure and believed that Parliament had the constitutional power to pass it, but, like many others, he was uncertain whether Parliament could abolish those appeals from provincial courts of appeal which bypassed the Supreme Court of Canada to go to the Privy Council directly. For that reason, he said, he would refer the question to the Supreme Court for an opinion. [20]

Duff at one time favoured the retention of appeals, though he never said so publicly. Speaking in 1925 to a large gathering of lawyers in Toronto, he extolled the virtues of the Privy Council, which embraced "the legal interests of one fifth of the human race," and addressed the abolition issue in these words:

> It will, I am convinced, be many a long year before we shall bring ourselves to abandon entirely the privilege of invoking the aid of the Judicial Committee in the determination of justiciable disputes — especially in the region of constitutional law. But the time may arrive when the people of this country will conclude that this responsibility, the burden of which has been so long and so generously borne by others, should, in great degree at all events, be assumed by ourselves....As I have said, I am not discussing the merits of the question, and of course I express no opinion upon it. But of this I am confident, and I am sure you will agree with me, that, if this change is to take place,...the tribunal upon whom the

responsibility shall fall can set before itself no loftier aim, can be actuated by no higher, no more exacting ambition, than to walk worthily in the spirit of the great judicial tradition of which it has received the keeping.

Just as the Privy Council ministered to different races and cultures, Duff continued, so the Supreme Court of Canada, if it were one day to be the court of last resort, would need to use a similar multicultural spirit to respect the French and English cultures.[21]

Duff's sympathy for retaining the Privy Council appeal, at least in constitutional cases, was just the logical outcome of his approval of the avenue of constitutional interpretation down which the council had travelled. Writing in 1926 to Senator Farris, then also a retentionist, he made the comment:

> There is no doubt that some curtailment of appeals in matters which, as between the parties, are comparatively unimportant, is desirable. Unfortunately, it is difficult to deal with the subject in a perfectly sane and dispassionate way. Extremists on both sides — people who regard any interference as a desecration of the Ark of the Covenant, and those, on the other, who would like to have a Declaration of Independence emanating from Ottawa — are only too glad to set up their bray at every opportunity.[22]

Many prominent lawyers and judges opposed abolition. Some believed that the Canadian judiciary was not strong enough, physically or mentally, to assume the responsibility for pronouncing the final word. Paradoxically, many in Quebec, far from wanting to rid themselves of an English and colonialist institution, saw the Privy Council as a bulwark against Ottawa's invasion of such critical areas of provincial jurisdiction as language and religion. Other retentionists felt that judges removed from the heat of Canadian politics could impart this detachment to their decisions.

The reference came to the court in June 1939 for three days of hearings. By that year, however, Duff had changed his mind, believing that his should be the court of last resort; there were enough well-trained Canadian lawyers to administer the law from its bench.[23] He had come to these views in spite of his long connection with the Privy Council and friendships with many of its luminaries. His relationship with it had been an affair of the heart, but his judicial mind convinced him that the Parliament of Canada had the constitutional power to end it.

Convinced that the case was the most important he had ever heard, he toiled over his judgement, not handing it down until the following January. The essence of his conclusion was that section 101 of the B.N.A. Act, which gave the federal government the power to constitute "a general court of appeal for Canada," implied the incidental power to make it the "ultimate" appeal court. He ruled also that by virtue of its general power to make laws for the peace, order, and good government of Canada, Ottawa could abolish appeals and that such legislation did not relate to a subject assigned specifically to the provinces by section 92.

In arriving at his decision, he renounced his strict legal approach to the interpretation of statutes, a most unusual thing for him to do.

> It would, indeed, be singular if the enactments of a legislature, charged with...responsibilities of the very highest political nature, should be interpreted and applied in a narrow and technical spirit or in a spirit of jealous apprehension as to the possible consequences of a large and liberal interpretation of them.

He reasoned that appeals from provincial courts to the Privy Council stemmed, not from rights inherent in the provinces, but from jurisdiction conferred by the Judicial Committee Acts of 1833 and 1844, statutes of the Parliament of Westminster, and thus there was no force in the argument that the abolition of such appeals would affect the right given to provinces by section 92(14) to make laws relating to provincial courts. It followed logically, therefore, that section 101 gave legislative authority to Parliament to make the Supreme Court's decisions binding on every other court in Canada:

> If there is authority in the Court as an appellate court to pronounce an effective decision, it is because such is the law that governs, not the appellate tribunal alone, but the inhabitants of Canada and the courts in Canada which carry out the decision. To say that the authority to adjudicate exists without the authority to make the adjudication effective in Canada would seem to be a self-contradictory statement...

As regards the general power to legislate which Duff had invoked in the *Persons* case but rejected in so many others in which he protected the specific rights of provinces, he ruled:

> The exercise of such jurisdiction for Canada by a tribunal exclusively subject to the legislation of another member of the Commonwealth is not a subject which can properly be described (as subject matter of legislative authority) as a matter merely local or private within a province. And again, the power to make laws for the peace, order and good government in Canada in relation to matters within section 101 being without restriction, the power of Parliament in such matter is, as I have said more than once, paramount....The primacy of Parliament under section 101 is just as absolute as under the enumerated clauses of section 91.

For Duff, finally, Canadian sovereignty was incomplete if courts outside the country could make final rulings on national issues. As an act of patriotism, he would bring home the court of last resort. He knew what the decision ought to be; he set out to achieve it.[24]

Several provincial governments were represented at the hearings in Ottawa, and, when the decision was announced, they began an appeal to the Privy Council. War delayed it, however, and not until seven years later did the appeal go forward. Ottawa meanwhile left its proposed legislation in abeyance.

On 24 August 1939 Duff entertained the Lord Chancellor, Lord Maugham, and his wife to dinner, along with Mackenzie King, who sat at a table flanked by Annie Duff and the wife of Judge Maclean. King recorded in his diary that "Mrs. Maclean talked incessantly against Hitler and the Italians in a babbling childish way, full of hatred, etc. With Miss Duff I had a very pleasant talk."[25] Less than two weeks later, the Canadian government declared war, doing so separately from Great Britain to demonstrate its independence. Duff moved over to his "wartime duty" of patriotic speech-making. Running the gamut from radio appeals on behalf of welfare services hard-pressed in time of conflict to exhortations at great universities, he took as his theme that the forces of evil must not be allowed to overpower enlightened civilization. His most forceful expression of it was delivered on 20 September 1940 at the University of Pennsylvania, where he was receiving an honorary doctorate of laws. The special convocation was part of the university's bicentennial celebration, and two other men, Justice Owen Roberts of the U.S. Supreme Court and President Franklin Delano Roosevelt, shared the platform with Duff.

George Wharton Pepper, an alumnus and former trustee of the university, had had much to do with planning the events to mark the anniversary, and it was undoubtedly he who recommended Duff as a man of eminence adequate to such a noteworthy occasion. The invitation had come in July from the president of the university, T.A. Gates, who told Duff, "We hope that you and your Government will feel as we do, that at this time it is important to strengthen the bonds between peoples who have common ideals of intellectual freedom and culture."[26] This statement gave Duff his topic, a summons to liberty in a country not yet at war but in sympathy with Canada.

He accepted the invitation on his own behalf and on behalf of the government for which he professed to speak. Several days later, he learned from the university that his and Roosevelt's words would be broadcast on a national radio hookup throughout the U.S. as well as beamed overseas by short wave. There followed elaborate arrangements for what proved to be less a trip than a progress. Samuel F. Houston, a pillar of the Philadelphia community and the university's senior trustee, agreed to be host to Duff and his party at "Druim Moir," his estate just outside the city.

Duff hired a taxi from the Ottawa firm he regularly patronized to drive him and his companion, F.L. Pereira, the viceroy's assistant secretary, to Philadelphia. Pereira made himself useful arranging funds from the Foreign Exchange Control Board. He also procured a passport for the chauffeur. He drew up an itinerary for the trip complete with dates and times. He made reservations for the stopping places on the way, which included Lake Placid and Atlantic City. He sent off publicity photographs of Duff. He made arrangements with the American legation and U.S. Customs for the shipment and return as diplomatic baggage of a trunk, too large for the car, that contained Duff's academic dress and regalia. For his part, Duff read books about the university and its history.

But it was the speech that preoccupied him. The university had first said that he should talk for eighteen minutes. In the face of Duff's evident consternation, however, a reduction to twelve minutes was negotiated. Duff then spent much of August and September going through at least five drafts. He sought advice from Pereira, but, realizing that he would be on radio vying with Roosevelt, he looked for more expert counsel from David Lewis, later leader of the New Democratic Party but then the secretary of its predecessor the C.C.F. As a young lawyer, Lewis had practised with O.M. Biggar and with him made appearances before Duff on patent cases. Impressed, Duff had asked him to come by his chambers for talks on politics, literature, and other non-legal subjects. Now, knowing Lewis's reputation as a public speaker, Duff asked for his help with both the content and delivery of his Philadelphia speech. Lewis has recalled the occasion:

> Democratic freedom was clearly the appropriate subject during a war against Nazi dictatorship. He asked me to prepare some notes, which I did, but the speech was very much his own. As I recall it, we met several times, once for lunch at the Rideau Club. He kept refining and rewriting. He looked for the same precision of meaning as he always demonstrated in his written judgements. I think he accepted many of the changes I suggested, which were delivered to him only a couple of days before he left for the University....Working with Duff was exciting. He had a restless mind and an intellectual impatience which challenged one. He was not easy to work with because of his impatience but it was, nonetheless, a very pleasant experience because of his unfailing old-world courtesy and kindness. After some discussion, he accepted the idea that social justice and universal human dignity were as essential to true democracy as liberty and cultural freedom. He not only accepted it but made it his own as part

of the Christian ethos and of the contribution of the English-speaking world.

I never had any doubt that Sir Lyman was not only a great jurist with an enviable capacity to unravel the most complicated web of fact and argument, but that he was also a learned and cultured man outside the law. His broadmindedness was evidenced by the fact that he was not deterred from approaching a well-known young socialist for help with a speech at a time when Socialism, or the C.C.F., was not overwhelmingly popular or even acceptable as an idea.[27]

Duff took Lewis's advice and made amendments, telling his young friend whimsically that he had thrown "one or two sops to Cerberus."[28] But Lewis did not think that the speech had been pruned enough. He wrote telling Duff that to hold the attention of the radio audience he should speak no more than a hundred and twenty-five words per minute and avoid long words and sentences. Duff did not receive these instructions before his departure; his secretary, however, sent them on to Atlantic City, just in time. Duff made further revisions to his draft, cutting it back to the twelve-minute mark by the elimination of some rather difficult language.

Duff and his party left Ottawa precisely at two o'clock in the afternoon of 13 September 1940. The progress was agreeable. The days at Atlantic City would have reminded him of the pleasant visits with Lizzie in former times. Exactly one week later and at the same hour Duff joined the academic procession which, minus Roosevelt but accompanied by band music, moved into Philadelphia's Convention Hall. At three o'clock, the U.S. president arrived to join his fellow candidates on the platform. Following Justice Roberts's speech, President Gates introduced Duff:

We are happy to greet you here as an eminent jurist and statesman, whose labors and opinions have had a profound effect upon the welfare of your countrymen. We welcome you no less as the representative of a great and friendly people to which we are bound in defense of common democratic ideals of justice and individual opportunity.

In recognition of distinguished service both in war and peace I confer on you the degree of Doctor of Laws, admitting you to all the rights and privileges which pertain to that degree, in token of which I hand you this diploma, signed and sealed with the Seal of the Corporation.[29]

Duff attacked his theme with a quote from Gladstone: "Liberty is a great and precious gift of God and human excellence cannot grow up in a nation without it." He paid tribute to the university, declaring that "it will be judged not only by the degree in which it has helped to advance the arts of life, but even more by the degree in which it has enriched the art of living." And Duff wound up with a war reference that became part of the extensive newspaper coverage the event received.

> With fire and sword, but also with a deep sense of service, the peoples of the British Commonwealth of Nations, with the help of those among their former allies who have retained their freedom, are today defending these ideals. They are defending, let me emphasize, not only the advance which they have already made along the road of progress, but the road itself for the further advance of humanity. As the people of London and Britain muster their every energy to withstand, successfully, the merciless enemy of freedom and of civilized living, they are moved by a fierce anger. But they are also animated by a spirit of grim determination not only to win this war, but, thereafter, with, they hope, the friends of civilization the world over, to apply themselves to the work of rooting out those conditions which prepare the ground for dictators who must make war because their power cannot endure peace.[30]

After Duff's speech the band played "God Save the King." President Roosevelt followed him. He spoke somewhat more guardedly, telling the students not to "withdraw into some ivory tower" or remain aloof "from the problems and agonies of society."[31] He too made reference to the dictators' onslaught on freedom and the need for "courage, humanism and faith in the future."[32] He had been upstaged by Duff, though neither man may have been aware of it:

> At the time, more personal attention seems to have been paid to Sir Lyman than to President Roosevelt; a large number of the Trustees, entrenched Republicans, objected violently to this honour to the President of the nation and pointedly looked away rather than at the speaker as he received his degree and addressed the Convocation. Evidently the espousal of Democratic principles in Philadelphia did not extend to all Trustees.[33]

A day or two later Duff returned to Ottawa, too quickly perhaps, for both his laundry and his trunk went astray. Both eventually turned up.

Duff took enormous personal satisfaction from the visit, but he also believed that he had made a genuine contribution to the war effort.

> I cannot conceal, either, my gratification at the expressions I met on every hand of sincere sympathy with our British battle and our aims. I found myself in Philadelphia, especially, among people who seemed to share our hopes and anxieties with as much depth of feeling as my people here.[34]

He paid all the expenses of the trip, including $132 for the taxi and a generous tip for the chauffeur. Pereira kept a record of every penny they spent; he typed up a statement and deposited the remaining U.S. funds in Duff's account.

Duff made a similar wartime expedition to Columbia University in June 1941. As in the case of Pennsylvania, the desire of one civilizing force to unite with others against the powers of darkness was behind the invitation. The institution's board of trustees, "in view of the world situation which now exists and the relation of the Government and people of the United States thereto," decided to ask three distinguished foreigners to receive honorary degrees at a special convocation: Lord Halifax, newly appointed as British ambassador to Washington, Duff, and the Brazilian foreign affairs minister. Three representatives of the American armed services were also invited.[35] Duff was informed in his invitation from Nicholas Murray Butler, president of the university, that

> at this critical time in the world's history we are anxious to associate ourselves with an outstanding representative of the people and the intellectual life of the Dominion of Canada and we wish to salute you as that representative.[36]

Duff asked Pereira to help him again, and once more the viceregal assistant handled the elaborate arrangements. To his great relief, this time Duff did not have to make a speech. One preparation, however, he believed he should make. Unlike the Pennsylvania ceremony, Columbia's would take place during the court's term. Even though his absence would be brief and cause no inconvenience, he wrote to Lapointe, still justice minister, "In the circumstances, I ought, I think to ask leave of absence from the Governor in Council. May I pray your good offices in that behalf? The leave should be for a week beginning the 31st of May."[37] Two days later, an order-in-council authorized his departure, noting that it would "not interfere with the due administration of justice by the court."

A large dinner given by Butler was the social highlight of the Columbia excursion. Besides Duff and Halifax as honoured guests, the company included Sir Wilfrid Greene, Master of the Rolls, and the well-known English legal scholar A.L. Goodhart.[38] This banquet was followed the next day by the commencement luncheon at which speeches were made by Butler, Halifax, and a retired rear admiral of the U.S. navy. In a voice "trembling with unusual emotion," the university president appealed to the four hundred and fifty guests "to carry the light of liberty and knowledge against the Nazi forces of darkness and reaction." The British ambassador spoke in the same vein, diplomatically urging the American nation to abandon isolationism and, in its own interests, enter the war. Agreeing with Halifax, the American admiral said bluntly that "should England fall we have got a war on our hands whether we want it or not — all the isolationists, pacifists and wishful thinkers to the contrary notwithstanding."[39] Duff applauded all of these sentiments.

The following afternoon Duff, in full regalia, joined the academic procession which filed into the South Court of the university to be greeted by a sea of over five thousand graduates and twenty thousand guests. Roosevelt, a Columbia graduate, did not attend, but sent a message deploring the "tragedy and chaos which today threaten all that we love." Presumably it received a more attentive hearing than that given his speech at Philadelphia. None of the degree recipients spoke, but Butler urged the American people to "take full responsibility for leadership in organizing the world of independent and liberal-minded nations."[40] When the six candidates were presented, he described Duff as

> receiving in the profession of his choice one important distinction after another and widely honored by the institutions of higher education in the Dominion of Canada; becoming Chief Justice of the Supreme Court of the Dominion of Canada in 1933 after long experience first at the Bar and then for more than a quarter century on the Canadian Supreme Court; distinguished for his contributions to the constitutional history of the Dominion; respected everywhere for what is recognized as his thoroughly well-stored mind and for his truly exceptional service to his country.[41]

The return to Ottawa was marred by a minor collision caused, not by Duff's chauffeur, but by a careless driver. At this point, Duff had what must have been his only experience of curbside justice. The investigating officer asked Duff if he wished to lay charges against the driver; Pereira advised against it. Negotiations followed: the driver offered sixty dollars cash for damage to the taxi, Pereira advised acceptance, the money changed hands on the spot, and the Duff party, feeling that justice had triumphed, resumed the homeward journey.[42] The Columbia visit proved to be the last public occasion of its kind for Duff. He thought he had "done his bit" and had been given an honourable discharge, but Mackenzie King soon recalled him to active service.

# 16

## Unhappy warrior

IN JULY 1941, Canadian-born General A.E. Grassett of the British army passed through Ottawa on his way back to England from Hong Kong, where for three years he had been commander-in-chief, and paid a social call on H.D.G. Crerar, an army friend who was then chief of the Canadian General Staff. When he reached London, Grassett reported to the War Office on conditions in the Far East. The experts believed there was "little danger of war with Japan,"[1] but Grassett told them that if the Japanese did invade Hong Kong "the garrison was too weak to withstand a serious attack," and suggested to the officials that to strengthen the colony's defence force, the course he recommended, reinforcements be requested from Canada. These discussions took place early in September. Churchill, who had earlier ruled out sending any more troops to the colony, changed his mind on the basis of Grassett's appraisal, for on the 19th the War Office sent the Canadian government a secret telegram asking for "one or two battalions."[2]

The Canadians complied and in great haste readied an expeditionary force. On 27 October the troop-ship *Awatea* left Vancouver by night with some nineteen hundred infantrymen. Her escort, the armed merchant cruiser *Prince Robert*, carried an additional hundred and twenty-five who could not be jammed on board the *Awatea*. Only when the two vessels reached Hawaii did the two battalions, the Royal Rifles of Canada and the Winnipeg Grenadiers, learn that they were bound for Hong Kong.

They arrived barely three weeks before the Japanese invasion. On 8 December the land and air assault began. The British, Indian, and Canadian defenders fought valiantly, but they were overwhelmed by a well-trained and numerically superior force moving in on them from the Chinese mainland. Newspapers reported heavy casualties, and the Ontario Conservative leader

George Drew chose the occasion to open a campaign for conscription with a letter that appeared in the Toronto *Globe and Mail* on Christmas Day.[3] It was the very day, by what turned out to be a tragic irony, that the British colony, its exhausted defenders overrun and its water supply cut off, capitulated to the Japanese. Churchill, who came to Ottawa at about this time, talked to Mackenzie King about the tragedy, with so many men dead and the survivors condemned to indefinite imprisonment. Still shaken by the loss of the battle-ships *Repulse* and *Prince of Wales* on 3 December, the British leader told King that "he regretted deeply he had ever asked us to send the troops."[4] Duff, who heard Churchill give his "some chicken, some neck" speech to Parliament on 30 December, learned the full dimensions of the disaster before long.

Drew soon afterwards unearthed some details about how the expedition had been mounted. He charged the government with incompetence in flinging raw troops into an area where it knew war might break out at any moment. First appearing in mid-January, his accusations were widely reported. As he reiterated them with growing stridency, King decided that there had to be a response. Accordingly, on 21 January Minister of National Defence J.L. Ralston made a House of Commons statement that became the official position from which, in public, the King government never deviated.

Ralston took the stage as a reasonable man buffeted by forces beyond his control. In calm, measured tones, he outlined the events leading up to the dispatch of the expedition. There had been no suggestion in the cable requesting reinforcements for Hong Kong that war with Japan was imminent; on the contrary, indications were that the prospect had receded. The request was considered by the cabinet's War Committee consisting of the prime minister, Ralston, air minister C.G. Power, naval minister Angus MacDonald, and several others. At its 2 October meeting, this committee had resolved to send the troops, and advised the British War Office accordingly.

It is of interest that King should have confided to his diary in 1948 that he remembered "opposing strenuously sending troops to cross the Pacific Ocean."[5] He made that entry when the Hong Kong controversy had flared up again; there is no hint of any opposition from his quarter in the War Committee minutes of 1941. His only concern about dispatching the troops recorded on that 2 October was the effect the expedition might have on the conscription issue: King

> observed that it should be clearly understood that the troops were available and that this further commitment would not contribute to the creation of conditions which would make conscription for overseas service necessary in order to meet all of our obligations.[6]

Ralston pointed out at the time that the prospect of conscription was not "the paramount consideration in these matters," and that the "situation ought to be considered in the light of the needs from time to time and the man-power available, having regard to the requirements of the service and of industry."[7]

Now, the defence minister conceded to the House that not all the men in the battalions had been adequately trained for combat, but then no one had expected their job to be anything more dangerous than garrison duty. No one in the government had any cause to expect an invasion by the Japanese. Ralston went on to disclose a piece of information not previously known outside the government: the mechanical and vehicle transport for the force, 212 vehicles in all had not gone with it. It might have been possible to load a few on board the *Awatea* — perhaps as many as twenty — but, unfortunately, these vehicles had not even reached Vancouver until after the ship had sailed. Ultimately, all this support equipment had been put on an American freighter that sailed for Hong Kong on 4 November but never reached her destination, being diverted to the Philippines because of the attack on Pearl Harbor. In all but two respects, Ralston told the House, the battalions were thoroughly and properly equipped and armed. Apart from their transport, they lacked only mortar ammunition, which would have been readily obtainable from the British garrison in the colony.[8]

The Conservative opposition leader R.B. Hanson did not at first grasp the significance of what he had just heard; he responded sympathetically, even approvingly, to Ralston's report. As a result of continuing political and public pressure, however, the government decided to hold an investigation. King had a series of discussions with colleagues and opposition members to decide whether to strike a parliamentary committee or set up a commission under the Public Inquiries Act. His motives in this were far from disinterested, as a diary entry reveals:

> It [the inquiry] really is a help to us as it will show where the onus really lies, how ready we were to meet a British request, and will put the blame where it ought to be on those responsible for taking some men overseas who should not have gone. Instead of helping the Tories in their determination to have conscription at all costs, it is going to react against them. The public will see that our whole war effort being what it is, that a mistake is being made in pressing matters so far. I hope the Defense Department will see the same. They have themselves to blame for getting this off right at the start.[9]

King saw the inquiry, however constituted, as a weapon with which to fight the tories on the dangerous conscription issue. A week later, while canvassing the commission issue with Hanson, King suggested that Duff head it, possibly with two other appointees. The two men agreed that a parliamentary inquiry would be undesirable because of the secret nature of much of the evidence.

Several days later, when Hanson said that he would be agreeable to Duff's sitting as sole commissioner, King took the unusual step of going to Duff's house surreptitiously after dark to ask if he would act. King recorded later that night that Duff "was very plucky and fine about the way in which he took the matter up." Any hesitation Duff had about the appointment was mainly because of his health, a matter on which he would have to consult his doctor before giving a definite answer. King, who badly wanted his respectability and credibility for the proceedings, began to apply pressure:

> I said to him that frankly I did not ask him to undertake the task except for two reasons: (1) he was the one man in whom all had confidence; (2) I really felt it might be a help rather than a burden to him if he would get an ad hoc Judge to act in the Courts and forget about the Courts for a time, and just interest himself in that question which was one of importance to the British Government as well as to our own. One which was an important war matter.

The two men went on to talk about the politics of the affair, their views being in complete harmony.

> [Duff] spoke of the present controversy being pretty much political and that it was shameful the way in which certain groups in Toronto were behaving. I know that he is not at all sympathetic to attempting conscription and feels that it is a great shame that the country should have become divided as it has, particularly when given a course on which all could unite.

They were both thinking of Drew's accusations and the prominence given them by the *Globe and Mail*. King left "with the feeling that he would accept. I can see that it is from a sense of duty and I think, too, of feelings that the government has considered him in every way, and that he should now consider it."[10]

In saying that the government had "considered" Duff "in every way," and that he should therefore "consider it," King would seem to have had a quid pro quo in mind. The government had extended Duff's term of office; he should take on the job. The later conduct of the hearings, as well as the evidence of Duff's partiality, also encourage the inference that King expected Duff to absolve the government and Duff knew King expected him to. That Duff understood the niceties of the situation is indicated by a remark to his colleague Davis: "I dislike intensely going on with the Government job, but it was put to me in such a way that I could not refuse."[11] Two days later, Duff telephoned the prime minister to say that he would accept. King noted how he was immensely relieved by the Chief Justice's ringing me up to tell me he would take on the Hong Kong inquiry out of a sense of duty in the present situation. I should not take it as a matter of his either seeking to oblige the Government or myself — that it was the only thing to be done at a time when others were all doing their utmost to help in the war effort.[12]

King knew from the start that the brass hats had made blunders in the dispatch of the troops. So did Ralston. The two men discussed which officials might be responsible.

[Ralston] is much afraid that Crerar may seek to slip out from under his responsibility by seeking to have it appear that the matter was one of political decision, though the records were clear that it was referred to the Chief of Staff for their approval before any action was taken.

...apparently the Department did not feel it necessary to go into the question of conditions at Hong Kong, but accepted the British request as covering that aspect, which involves complications with the Command — McNaughton being here at the present time.[13]

King had also known that war with Japan was not a remote possibility but an imminent probability. It was flagrant hypocrisy for him to maintain, throughout the controversy in 1942 and in 1948 when it erupted again, that the government had no reason to expect war. He had said himself in an Ottawa speech on the very day the *Awatea* sailed, "When we realize that any day we may see the Pacific as well as the Atlantic ocean the scene of conflict we realize this is vaster than anything that the human mind so far has conceived."[14] From the outset, he tried to head off public criticism of the actions of his colleagues and senior military figures. He was prepared to use any means to cover up the government's behaviour and its foreknowledge of war with Japan, even to the extent of editing an official British report and condoning blatant falsehoods in the House of Commons.

To head his investigation, he chose a fellow Liberal from whom he could confidently expect a report that would give every benefit of doubt to the government. Before Duff named a lawyer to act as commission counsel, he discussed the appointment with King and "suggested that he might have a word with Ralston just to make sure that he would not be picking anyone that would be objectionable."[15] In a real sense, it was the government and the army that were on trial, and for a judge to consult one of the accused before appointing counsel for the prosecution is nothing short of extraordinary. King had not misplaced his confidence. The explanation, of course, is that Duff was not impartial, as King realized full well.

> Chief Justice Duff spoke to me very strongly tonight [5 March 1942] about the Hong Kong inquiry. Said it would have been a crime if the inquiry had been held in public. He had reference to the behaviour of Drew who apparently has behaved very badly before the Commission. Duff said to me that he was really ashamed of the legal profession to see the way a certain gentleman had behaved. He said he would have much to tell me of the matter when the case is over. I could see that he was deeply incensed at the effort that was being made to play politics, and to misconstrue and pervert the whole business. It really was an act of Providence that we succeeded in getting this matter before him, and that Duff decided to have the hearings in camera.[16]

The prime minister had expressed "surprise" on learning that Hanson had gone to see Duff about the work of the commission and the appointment of a lawyer to act for the official opposition. King telephoned Duff and "agreed we might meet Hanson on the question of counsel, leaving it to him to appoint what counsel he wished."[17]

The hearings started on 2 March and continued until the 31st. Duff had named as commission counsel two Toronto lawyers, R.L. Kellock, later on the Supreme Court, and R.M. Fowler; George Campbell of Montreal represented the government, and George Drew appeared on behalf of the parliamentary opposition. Duff believed that the hearings should be held in camera, and, realizing that he had no legal authority in this, he asked King for an order-in-council giving him the power to enforce secrecy and compliance by proceedings for contempt of court.[18] The day hearings began, the cabinet approved an order-in-council[19] pursuant to the War Measures Act, which provided for "censorship and the control and suppression of publications, writings...communications and means of communication."[20] Duff awaited word that the order had been approved before compelling secrecy. Whatever might be thought of the wisdom of such an order in the circumstances of the Hong Kong inquiry, there could be no doubt of the validity of the order-in-council itself after Duff's own decision in the *Gray* case. He informed the lawyers that the hearings were to be held in camera or "in secret" — he used the terms interchangeably — and at their conclusion all documents, briefs, exhibits, and even notes made by the lawyers for their own use would have to be surrendered to the commission.

The order-in-council that appointed Duff required him to determine

> whether there occurred any dereliction of duty or error in judgment by those whose duty it was to arrange for the authorization, organization and despatch of the force that resulted in detriment or injury to the expedition or its members.[21]

If he did find any error or dereliction, he was not authorized to recommend measures to prevent their repetition. Throughout the hearings, Duff took the correct but narrow view that his function was to deal with the past and not draw lessons for the future. Drew, as might have been expected, took the opposite view. Convinced that there had been gross negligence and eager to fasten the blame on the Liberal government, he believed that the commission's work would be fruitless unless it generated improvements in military organization that would lead to greater efficiency in fighting the war. Drew's approach was sensible, certainly, but the wording of the order-in-council was against him: King and his advisors had phrased it deliberately to keep the commission within strict bounds. The differing approaches of Drew and Duff led to conflict in the course of the hearings and for years afterwards.

Drew quickly emerged as the dominant figure in the lawyer group. Though just as political in his motivation as King, or for that matter, Duff, he did a first-class job as counsel over the many days of hearings, combining a thorough grasp of detail with an excellent understanding of military organization and administration. During the twenty-two days, the commission heard a multitude of army personnel, from generals McNaughton and Stuart, the new chief of the General Staff, down to a private soldier who had deserted the ranks. Civilians testified as well, among them T.C. Douglas, then an M.P. from Saskatchewan. All the cabinet ministers for the armed forces gave evidence — Ralston, Power, and MacDonald. The commission also received written testimony from Crerar, by then in England.

These statements and the lawyers' arguments all focussed on four main questions. What intelligence reports had the government received concerning the likelihood of war with Japan after the request by Britain and before the departure of the troops? On what basis were the two battalions selected? What was the state of their training and, finally, why had the mechanical transport not gone with the troops? Their dreadful experiences hung like a pall over the proceedings.

Canada had no intelligence-gathering agency of its own in 1941, but it did have intelligence-receiving officers at the headquarters of each of the armed forces. For its appraisal of the situation in the Orient, the Canadian government relied on British intelligence, and in particular on a series of secret telegrams, none of which was published at the time, though some were disclosed to the commission late in its hearings. The first was the one of 19 September. Its contents were seen only by Duff and the lawyers. General Crerar had testified that when he received it he was

> already aware from his conversations with Gen. Grassett that the reinforcement of the garrison by two battalions would enable them to hold Hong Kong for an extended period against any force "...the Japanese could bring to bear against it."[22]

From his recollection of talks with Grassett, Crerar suggested, as did every other senior military officer as well as the cabinet members who appeared, that the government had no reason to fear imminent hostilities in the Pacific.

On 16 October, however, the Japanese government changed. Tojo, considered to be an extremist sympathetic to the Axis powers, became leader of the "War Party." The Americans took note of this ominous development and placed their Pacific forces on war alert; the Canadians ignored it. On that same day, the senior intelligence officer of the Canadian navy received a copy of a Japanese telegram sent by the Americans "in clear language," that is uncoded, and announcing a festival at the Yasuni shrine, on which every Japanese soldier wished to have his name emblazoned after dying for his country in glorious battle. Again, the significance of this message did not escape the Americans. The Canadian officer sent it off to the other intelligence branches in Ottawa, but did not see any significance in it himself or draw it to his seniors' attention. There was no evidence that anyone in authority paid the slightest attention to it.

On 24 October, three days before the troops were due to sail, Canadian intelligence received two messages, their tone disturbing to say the least. Sent from the Dominions' Office in London to the prime minister's attention, the first of these signals contained a lengthy review of the Far East military situation in the light of the change in Japanese government; though the cable did not use such words as "imminent," read as a whole it painted a bleak picture of the Allied position in the Pacific.[23] The same naval intelligence officer, who was brought to testify, received the second cable, a copy of one sent from the Admiralty in London to the British naval commander in China with the instruction: "In view of the altered circumstances request you will provide cruiser escort for *Awatea* from Manila to Hong Kong."[24] The Admiralty had requested specifically that copies be given to the quartermaster-general, the prime minister, Arnold Heeney, the clerk of the Privy Council, and Norman Robertson, undersecretary of state for External Affairs. Cross-examining this officer before the commission, Drew forced him to admit that the importance of the telegram was obvious because of the persons to whom it was directed.

The day before the troops left Vancouver, General Stuart in Ottawa received yet another cable from Canadian military headquarters in London. By that time, barring the actual outbreak of war, it was probably too late to delay the troop embarkation, but the *Awatea* could still have been recalled while at sea. Though this cable tended to discount the chances of war, it contained a darker intimation: "While no immediate action by Japan expected, however, will be probably more vigorous [when she considers] her rights." Canvassing the relative strengths of Japan, Russia, and China, the message left no doubt that Japan would indeed go to war, the only questions being when she would do so and whether she would attack Russia before moving "south against our forces."[25]

There was no indication that the Canadian government had given these messages any consideration whatsoever. Of the ministers who testified before Duff, only C.G. Power admitted frankly that the Far East situation was then so dangerous that war might have erupted at any moment: he had sensed, "perhaps, without any sound basis except having read these dispatches, that there was a very good chance of war breaking out with Japan, and in such a case our men would be in a very difficult position."[26] It was not clear just which dispatches Power meant.

Cabinet made the decision to send the troops. The choice of battalions was Crerar's. He decided not to select units from those already overseas or earmarked for European service. The remaining units based in Canada were at various stages of training but two of them, the Winnipeg Grenadiers and the Royal Rifles, had just returned from semi-overseas service. These were the ones Crerar chose, giving the cabinet precise reasons for so doing. Among them was geographical balance — one regiment from English-speaking Canada and the other from Quebec. No one connected with the hearings raised any question about the correctness of sending men to war who were selected at least in part for their ethnic and geographical backgrounds rather than their fighting qualities.

There was a reason for the choice of the Royal Rifles that was not revealed to the Duff inquiry. Major J.H. Price, second-in-command of the regiment, had written in September to his old friend C.G. Power to complain that his outfit was "fed up with being buggered about from pillar to post," and ask Power to help get it an assignment that would improve its fighting efficiency. Price said, "Our main problem is that of training."[27] The Royal Rifles got their assignment on 9 October. One places Price's remarks alongside Crerar's statement to the cabinet that the "primary consideration" was that the units be "efficient, well trained battalions."

Their state of readiness became one of the liveliest issues at the hearings. Evidence before Duff established beyond doubt that the two regiments, lacking actual combat experience, had not even trained under simulated battle conditions; moreover, many of the men were unfamiliar with the routine weaponry of the time — mortars, machine guns, and grenades. It was true that many other Canadian regiments shared these shortcomings, a point emphasized time and again by those who gave evidence to support the decision of the government, but these two had been allowed to swell their ranks with men who had almost no training at all. Testimony disclosed that when a fighting unit went into combat, provision was made to replace casualties with new men, the "first reinforcements." On an expedition going to an outpost like Hong Kong, thousands of miles away, casualties could not easily be replaced, and so the "first reinforcements" were sent with the force. This required enlistment over and above the regiments' establishment strength, but the recruiting officers had no difficulty locating volunteers. Duff listened to a great deal of evidence about the training these volunteers had received. Lists were submitted, man by man, of the rounds of ammunition they had fired on the rifle range; officers testified to the merits of each individual. Yet the truth was evident: though the men were high-spirited, they were ill-prepared for the task before them. There was nothing remarkable about this: Canada had mustered a raw army to be trained in the United Kingdom. It might have been reasonable to assume, as some officers testified, that the troops sent to Hong Kong would also have time to ready themselves for combat.

The arrangements for shipping the battalions' transport to Vancouver had been made by a group of relatively junior officers drawn from the various branches of army headquarters. Senior officers like General Schmidlin, the quartermaster-general, had not involved themselves in the planning of the expedition. Schmidlin had not even bothered to inquire about progress.

Although responsibility for the purchase of military vehicles rested with army headquarters, their actual shipment by rail or sea fell to the transport controller, a civilian with offices in Montreal. Division led to confusion. Anyone could have found out at a public library that the *Awatea*, a former passenger liner, could not possibly have carried the more than two hundred vehicles the army had blithely ordered. The transport controller authorized their shipment from the factory in Ontario, but when he learned that the vessel could not accommodate them, he halted shipment without consulting the army. He had done so, he testified, until a suitable carrier was available at Vancouver or an American Pacific port.

The junior officers of the army planning group then considered the possibility of putting at least a few of the vehicles on board the *Awatea*, and, after much discussion and consultation, they decided to ship twenty of them to Vancouver by rail. These "priority vehicles," as they became known, had finally left factories in Oshawa and Windsor on 20 and 21 October after some confusion over purchase orders and shipping manifests. Although the C.P.R. had given the rail cars expedited passage, bad weather on the Prairies and heavy eastbound traffic slowed the shipment down. The priority vehicles reached Vancouver on 28 October, the day after the *Awatea* had sailed, to the great surprise of local ordnance officers who had received no notice of their pending arrival.

After the last witness had been called on 31 March, Duff adjourned to wait for Crerar to respond from England to questions posed by Kellock, Campbell, and Drew. When the former chief of staff had answered, Duff adjourned again to give the lawyers time to prepare written submissions. In the interval, on 8

April, King and Duff attended a dinner for the external affairs minister of Australia. King recorded in his diary:

> I drove the Chief Justice home. We had a pleasant talk together. To me, he looked quite frail. Spoke several times of how well I looked and how strong I looked. He says he has his mind all made up on the Hong Kong matter, and material all together but has to wait for some further statement from Crerar and give opportunity to counsel for written argument. He gave me no hint of what his opinion would be, but I think the fact he mentioned it at all makes clear he is satisfied with the Government's position. He makes no bones about his feelings towards Drew.[28]

So Duff had his mind made up before all the evidence was in — worse, before the lawyers had made their final summations. King correctly surmised that the mere fact that Duff spoke in such a vein indicated the government would be absolved. These indiscreet remarks, combined with Duff's earlier comments to King about Drew, form the strongest possible evidence of his partiality.

In fact, when the written arguments were submitted on 22 May, Duff had his report drafted and ready. It came out in printed form only two weeks later. On 4 June he wrote King a personal note enclosing a copy. The government and the military were cleared of any wrongdoing. Only concerning the vehicles did Duff level any criticism, offering mildly that "more energy and initiative" might have been shown. In any event, he concluded, their failure to reach Hong Kong with the *Awatea* made no difference to the garrison defence, nor did any other official actions or inactions result in any detriment or injury to the troops, who would inevitably have been overwhelmed by the superior Japanese force.

King was delighted:

> I received a personal letter and a copy of the report on the Hong Kong expedition accompanied by a personal note from the Chief Justice saying that the report gave a clean bill of health...his wording really made me rejoice. It contains a first rate crack at Drew, the implication being that once there was possibility of fighting due to change of government in Japan the gov't should have reconsidered the force...
>
> Altogether the report is really a fine tribute to the Government and the efficiency of the Defence Department and its administration. There could not have been a finer vindication of the Government's whole attitude in undertaking the expedition and the manner in which it was handled.
>
> I phoned Ralston after reading the report and told him of its contents. I could feel the joy in his heart, and sense of relief which in his case I know is particularly great...how all things work together for good in the end.[29]

He replied to Duff at once, expressing his gratitude for the findings and the tribute paid to officials of the defence department. The next day he read a portion of the report to the House. When W.K. Campbell, Duff's private secretary who had also been secretary to the commission, recounted the favourable reaction in the Commons, Duff said, "Well, I think this occasion calls for a visit to the Country Club."[30] Off they went for a drink.

Duff had prepared his report in two sections. In the first and shorter section, he summarized his main findings; in the second, which he called an "appendix," he devoted over fifty closely printed pages to an analysis of the evidence relating to the four main issues, quoting extensively. He included the full text of a telegram sent by the War Office on 30 October:

> We are very grateful to you for despatching your contingent to Hong Kong on such short notice. We fully realize the difficulties of mobilization and of distance which have had to be overcome. The moral effect of their arrival in November will be much greater than it would have been two months later.[31]

He concluded his appendix by quoting a passage from the London cable of 26 October: "Consensus opinion that war in Far East unlikely at present."[32] The report passed in silence over the casual attitudes taken by Ralston, Stuart, and Schmidlin to the planning and organization of the force. Not one of them had known until well after 27 October that the vehicles had not accompanied the troops. Ralston, for example, was not aware of the problem until 15 December, when he read a month-old report brought back to Canada by the *Prince Robert*. In mid-December General Stuart had asked Schmidlin for a report on "what went wrong" with the vehicles;[33] the quartermaster-general disclaimed all responsibility, though he would eventually resign over the affair. For all this, Duff had not one word of surprise, let alone condemnation.

It was omissions of that sort that Drew had in mind when, the day after the report reached the House, he charged in an interview with the *Globe and Mail* that the "actual facts brought out in evidence were so blood-curdling that the public have a right to know what did take place," and that the evidence of "inexcusable blundering, confusion and incompetence had been hidden from the public."[34] Drew's accusations infuriated Duff. A few days later, when he was visiting the Senate Chamber to give royal assent to legislation, he discussed them with King:

> Duff, looks very frail....He spoke vigorously to Dr. King and myself about the behaviour of Drew during the Hong Kong Inquiry. Said he had all he could do to restrain himself from throwing Drew out of the court room altogether. He said his behaviour was intolerable. I spoke of it all being an

intimation of present-day politics to gain popularity by being subversive
of institutions. Duff remarked it was a terrible thing the way in which all
institutions were being undermined; how few sane men there were left to
manage affairs....I thanked him again and again for taking on the
task....I confess as I looked at him I felt he might pass away at any
moment.[35]

On 11 July Drew wrote King a highly critical letter in which he accused
Duff of whitewashing the government by failing to disclose critical evidence
and misinterpreting the evidence he did disclose; the chief justice had failed to
condemn proven incompetence. As he had done at the hearings, Drew
emphasized that the various cables, even if they did not point conclusively to
war, ought at the very least to have warned the government to reconsider its
decision to send the troops, or alternatively, find better-trained men. He
pointed out that Duff had included in his report two telegrams highly
favourable to the government's position, but omitted any reference to those
other telegrams and to portions of the ones he did quote which were less
favourable. Drew cited Duff's statement that the original "consideration" for
sending the troops, that is, the improvement in the general situation in the
Pacific, had not weakened but indeed "increased force" prior to 27 October;
in other words, by that date the prospect for peace had brightened. Drew
rightly condemned the finding: "This is not a case of mere misinterpretation
of evidence. The Report makes a positive mis-statement of fact."[36]

Drew went on to point out that the force commander, Brig. J.K. Lawson,
who died gallantly in the defence of his headquarters, had worried about the
state of the units' training, and yet Duff had somehow found that the men were
well trained. In reaching that conclusion he could not have failed to be moved
by the last message sent before surrender by Lt.-Col. Sutcliffe of the Winnipeg Grenadiers:

> Situation critical, Canadian troops...prisoners, residue engaged, casual-
> ties heavy. Lawson missing believed killed, Hennessy [second-in-com-
> mand] killed. Linden missing. Troops have done magnificent work. Spirit
> excellent.[37]

When the fighting ended on Christmas Day, just under three hundred
Canadians had been killed and some seventeen hundred taken prisoner. Their
resistance had been all the more remarkable after earlier "difficulties," as
Lawson put it, caused by the sudden addition of new recruits:

> some 30 or 40 men determined to break ship were, however, restrained,
> force being necessary at one period to do this. The men implicated were I

understand without exception those who had not been with the unit long enough to get to know, or be known by their officers.[38]

It was that incident, apparently triggered by overcrowding on the *Awatea*, that had resulted in the transfer of men to the *Prince Robert*.

But Drew was not questioning the men's spirit, or indeed the skill and dedication of their officers in welding them into a force with stomach for a fight; he was storming at decisions made on the home front, and, by Duff's report, defended on the home front. Duff had claimed naively, for example, that men trained to use a rifle and Bren gun could easily master an anti-tank rifle, and that experience with those weapons would ensure mastery in the use of mortars. Drew demolished him easily on this, and he condemned Duff's silence on the lack of co-ordination among the senior military. The Conservative was unanswerable on this point as well. Replying to Stuart's query about "what went wrong," for instance, Schmidlin conceded a "slight haziness" which would not have been the case "if we had talked things over before the Directors started to work — for example — I would have told you definitely that any considerable amount of M.T. [military transport] would require a second ship, and so on."[39] The fact was that the chief of the General Staff had received no co-ordinated information on progress in the planning for the expedition.

In drawing up his long letter to King, Drew had used a copy of the written argument he had submitted to Duff. This was in clear violation of the order to surrender all documents to the commission. Duff, incensed by what he regarded as a breach of confidence, believed that Drew had acted disgracefully, and was no gentleman but a "damned cad."[40] Worse, Drew's action was common knowledge: many people knew of the contents of the letter, copies of which had been sent to opposition leader R.B. Hanson and M.J. Coldwell, leader of the C.C.F. Coldwell asked King to table it in the House, but the prime minister refused until he had received legal advice from George Campbell.

King also asked Duff for advice. He prepared a statement to be made to the House on 15 July and discussed it with Duff, along with Drew's letter, the day before.

> He was, as I anticipated he would be, greatly annoyed at Drew's behaviour. Spoke of it as the worst he had ever known and of the whole proceeding as being a plot in Toronto to try and oust me. He spoke of the difficulty of doing anything in Toronto where influences were so terribly Tory, and where men who ought to know better would do the most outrageous thing to serve their own ends and to destroy others. He thought the letter should not be tabled on any account as it purported to

divulge information that was wholly secret. He spoke of Drew having violated his personal and professional honour.

After his visit, King "arranged to have Ralston and St. Laurent see the Chief Justice tonight."[41] These consultations involving the prime minister, his two senior ministers, and Duff did not become public knowledge. What is extraordinary about them is that Duff's role as commissioner had ended; he had reverted to his role as chief justice, and, as chief justice, gave political advice to the government in an attempt to conceal from the public the full weight of arguments which were embarrassing both to the government and to himself. Had Drew learned of these meetings, he would undoubtedly have called for Duff's resignation from the bench. Duff's behaviour as a submerged counsellor to the government of the day is impossible to justify on any grounds: hard to explain, let alone excuse. It can only be that his anger towards Drew and his admiration for King outweighed his better judgement, already compromised by the inquiry.

Campbell advised King that Duff's secrecy order bound all lawyers to disclose no evidence from the hearings and obliged them to turn "all writings" over to the commission. Campbell was not asked to, nor did he, discuss the extent to which Duff himself could reveal evidence heard in secret, but he did tell the prime minister that if he tabled Drew's letter, making it public knowledge, he would be as much in breach of the secrecy order as Drew was. Moreover, Campbell said, disclosure would violate the conditions under which the British government had permitted inspection of the secret telegrams. King told the House that he accepted Campbell's advice and would not therefore table Drew's letter.[42]

The government had deferred discussion in Parliament, but finally set aside two days, 27 and 28 July, for what proved to be an acrimonious debate on the Report, accompanied by personal attacks on Duff which the Speaker could not always deflect. The other unseen presence would, of course, be Drew. A group of Liberal backbenchers, all veterans of the Great War, mapped out some suggested debating lines for Ralston that reveal the intense dislike and indeed fear of Drew that existed in the government. Acknowledging that personal attacks "would make a martyr of him," the backbenchers still urged that he be painted as a "dishonourable man," who "broke his word" and "violated his undertaking." Ralston should tell the House that Drew's "word...when placed alongside that of the Chief Justice of Canada cannot be believed," and point out that "Drew is a 5th Columnist, pro-German, anti-Russian with Italian family connections" (a nasty reference to Drew's wife).[43]

The debate took place on an amendment to a motion for supply introduced by Howard Green, a Conservative member from Vancouver, asking the

House to condemn the "incapacity" of the military organizers of the expedition and calling for a complete reorganization of the department of National Defence. Green used all the arguments previously made by Drew. Ralston put the case for the government. To his credit, he did not use the intemperate suggestions of the backbenchers, taking essentially the same position he had in January, with some concessions. He admitted that with better staff work, the sailing of the troop-ship might have been delayed to await the arrival of the priority vehicles. He admitted that confusion had existed in the various branches of army headquarters, compounded by the actions of a civilian transport-control officer. He fastened the principal blame on Schmidlin, who had been "retired" along with another senior officer in the quartermaster-general's department. Not only had Schmidlin gone, but also, Ralston said, there had been "a very complete reorganization in the quartermaster-general's branch" as well as some twenty changes "in the senior staff appointments since the Hong Kong expedition." Although not all these changes had been dictated by the affair, "we shall have learned some lessons from Hong Kong." And then, picking up the very theme Drew had so long propounded, the defence minister remarked that the purpose of the debate was "not to find a scapegoat but to see that there is something in the experience which may be useful for the future." Ralston also defended Duff, praising his "courage" in performing a public service in an "impartial" fashion. He would have been well advised not to refer to Duff's impartiality, though none of the opposition M.P.s listening could have known just how partial he had been. The ensuing debate, which frayed the nerves of many members, ended in the overwhelming defeat of Green's amendment.[44]

On 29 July J.M. MacDonnell, a Conservative, wrote to J.W. Dafoe, a Liberal,

> I hope Hong Kong is over. I have loathed it and given low marks to everyone connected with it, though I think one must grudgingly admit that probably George Drew's outcry has led to a greater house-cleaning in the Department of National Defence than would otherwise have taken place.[45]

To this, Dafoe replied,

> I share your disgust about Hong Kong, though perhaps not precisely for the same reason. Among the problems of your party is what to do with George Drew. The Hong Kong episode might have been put to good public use by the opposition as we point out in an article which I enclose; but because George wanted to be in the limelight and play politics the opportunity was muffed.[46]

The article Dafoe sent was an editorial from his Winnipeg *Free Press* criticizing Drew for failing to concentrate on the government policy for training troops, an issue which

> might well have been a strong and cleansing breeze through the cob-web minds of our military experts, whose judgment and thinking about the war, as the Duff report clearly shows, is that of men without much independence of mind who go through life with blinders on.[47]

Drew's obvious thirst to score politically on Mackenzie King, whom he loathed, obscured the fact that much of what he had to say was sensible and cogent. It also let the King government extricate itself from its difficulties. As Grant Dexter, no friend of the Conservatives, told Dafoe after the Duff hearings,

> The truth is that the Army is in the hands of permanent force incompetents. On the one occasion when we had to organize an expeditionary (sic) force — Hong Kong — the General Staff, the Quarter master and the Adjutant General made a mess of it....If we are ever invaded, it will be a disaster. The only word for them is incompetent.[48]

Dexter used the corrective word "sic" sarcastically. Like Drew, he recognized that improvements should be made, and indeed some good did come of Duff's report.

At the time of the hearings, many wondered how such a relatively small episode, though one with obviously tragic overtones, could have engaged the time and attention of so many people. And the Hong Kong affair remains a matter of lively interest. The explanation may lie in the fact that Canadian troops had always been sent to Europe or Africa. The Hong Kong expedition was the first occasion on which Canada sent troops to the Orient, and it may be that the sense of strangeness and the unfamiliar ground keeps this concern alive. The political controversy might also help explain the continuing interest.

The inquiry was the last of four royal commissions on which Duff sat, three of them highly contentious politically, though none as highly charged as the Hong Kong affair. The 1942 inquiry shows in acute form the risks judges face when they accept such appointments. As Mr. Justice Brian Dickson of the present Supreme Court of Canada has observed "the danger of involving officers of the Courts in the politics of a particular dispute is that it may lead to the erosion of public confidence in the judiciary."[49] Duff was alive to the danger, but did not think it should deter him from performing a public duty.

After the Shell Commission of the previous war concluded, he had told Borden,

> I have met with a good deal of perfectly friendly criticism from members of the profession on the theory that the judges are wrong in exposing themselves to the risk of public partisan attack which such commissions may involve; but I confess that I have a perfectly clear conscience on that score. It is possible to carry the notion of judicial retirement from the world to the point of the ridiculous.[50]

Any citizen or newspaper is free to criticize the decision of a judge reached in court, but if the criticism becomes a personal attack it may be in contempt of court, or worse, criminal libel. A judge sitting as a commissioner, however, is not in court where the formalities apply. Duff believed that criticism of his report had gone beyond fair comment to attack him personally as a judge, a view that was shared by government supporters during the debate in and out of Parliament. Drew and many other opponents of the government passionately asserted their right to criticize Duff for what they saw as his failure to stigmatize incompetence; and they claimed that since he had stepped outside the courtroom, they were entitled to condemn him on personal grounds. In the House that 27 July, however, following an accusation that Duff had been "partial," the Speaker, relying on a passage from Beauchesne's Rules which categorized attacks on judges as unparliamentary, ruled that such an allegation could not be heard:

> The hon. member has made the statement that the Royal Commissioner Duff was partial. Certainly the statement implies that the Chief Justice, acting as royal commissioner was partial and therefore prejudiced in his report as submitted to the House, and I must rule that such a statement with regard to the Chief Justice of Canada is not admissible.[51]

That ruling stirred up a long debate in which opponents of the government maintained that they were criticizing, not the "Chief Justice of Canada," but the "Royal Commissioner." One opposition M.P. said in reference to Duff, "It is time that some of these fellows who are 78 years old or thereabouts be relieved of their obligations and replaced by men who are a little more active and probably better conversant with situations in war time."[52] Duff, who followed Hansard avidly, wrote private letters to members who spoke in his defence, even those not known to him, to express his gratitude.

He would have been so much more sensible to have pointed out in his report that the country was engaged in a war for which it was not prepared; an ally asked for help which could not in common decency be refused; military bureaucrats make mistakes and had done so in this case; tragically, men had been lost in a futile defence; those are the hazards of war; let us try to ensure that the same sort of thing does not happen again. Had the critics of 1942 known the facts surrounding the inquiry and its proceedings, the attacks on Duff would have been far stronger. As it was, Drew's charges and the persistent coverage they received made any reference to the Hong Kong affair painful to Duff for as long as he lived.

# 17

# Last judgement

THE HONG KONG inquiry exhausted Duff physically and mentally; from February until early June 1942, he had done nothing else. The
Supreme Court of Canada Act provided for judges from provincial high
courts to sit temporarily on the court, the "ad hoc" judges Mackenzie King
referred to, and these took Duff's place in those months.

Even before the inquiry, however, he had been doing less judicial work,
partly because the war had slowed down litigation and also because wartime
brought fewer big cases to Ottawa. There had been a couple of constitutional
questions in 1941[1] but they were far less important than the great constitutional cases of the prewar years. One personal injury case, inconsequential in
itself, was dealt with in a most unusual and in fact unique manner. After
consultation with the lawyers, Duff drew up a memorandum which he read in
court.

> The Judges...think it their duty to suggest to the parties that they should
> make an effort to agree upon a sum to be paid to the plaintiff in settlement
> of the action. If the parties are unable to agree, the Members of the Court
> would be willing, if the parties so desire, to award, as arbitrators, the
> amount that ought to be paid in settlement of the action and to give
> judgment accordingly.
>
> The Court wishes it to be distinctly understood that the parties must
> not feel themselves under any pressure by reason of this suggestion.[2]

The two lawyers were unwilling to accept informal arbitration by the judges
and they completed the appeal, the result of which was an order for a new trial.

The reason for the court's odd suggestion lay hidden; it is a good illustration of interconnections among members of the ingrown Ottawa community. For many years Landreville, the plaintiff, had operated a taxi business frequently patronized by judges of the court. As early as 1918, Duff had hired horse-drawn cabs from him. Typically, he was often late in paying his bills, for Landreville that year complained of an account "long past due" which caused him hardship because of the "very high price of grain and hay." Ten years later, by which time cabs were motorized, Duff quarrelled with him over the cost of repairing some damage he must have caused, perhaps while out on a drinking spree. Paying his account, Duff told Landreville testily,

> You are exceedingly lucky not to be dealing with a less indulgent person than myself; otherwise you would have to meet a claim for damages for careless driving. Your impertinent claim for broken glass is in the meantime ignored.[3]

Duff still continued to be his customer, though by the time of the appeal he had long since moved his business over to the Red Line firm. Nonetheless, Landreville was so confident of his long-standing relations with Duff and the other judges that on the eve of the hearing he wrote to them individually hoping for a good result. His embarrassed and angry lawyer wrote the court to dissociate himself from his client's gaffe and offer an apology.[4] Doubtless the judges made their unorthodox suggestion because of the Landreville letters.

Duff rested for a couple of weeks after bringing down his Hong Kong report and then turned his attention to whether the city of Ottawa and the municipality of Rockcliffe Park could levy municipal taxes on embassy buildings and residences of Commonwealth high commissioners. He took great pleasure in this type of case. He considered the historical relationship between an ambassador and the country to which he is accredited; he discussed the notion of diplomatic immunity, and quoted eminent English and American judges. With the majority he ruled that the structures were exempt from municipal taxation.[5] It became the last of a long line of important cases in which Duff applied what might be called the rule of history in interpreting the rule of law. True, in the *Deadman's Island* case and, later, at the Alaska tribunal, he had argued against the value of historical evidence of dealing in a particular way over long periods of time with a poorly defined land mass, but he had done so on his client's instructions. Lawyers are obliged to follow instructions, if not involving dishonesty, even though it may sometimes lead to anomalies.

It had taken him an uncharacteristically long time to prepare his decision — almost nine months. He was feeling his age, as he confided to his old friend Douglas Alexander:

> I am just getting through with one reference that concerns the position of the Legations here as regards taxation, raising points upon which you

could write a plausible judgment in several senses. I find that I do not welcome the opportunity of making decisions as I did up to about ten or fifteen years ago.

I do not believe you have ever experienced the sort of lethargy which seems to come over me in fits, when I feel as if I were utterly drained of energy and capacity for the simplest sort of action.[6]

He heard fewer cases for another reason, his pending retirement on 7 January 1943; it is unsatisfactory for a retiring judge to sit on cases in which decisions might have to be reserved. During the summer of 1942, there were rumours that Ralston might resign over the conscription issue to become chief justice, and Duff assured King privately that he would resign when asked.[7] By October, however, King had decided to ask Duff to stay on for another year:

I told him I regarded the extension as meaning we were glad to have him continue at this time of war, it would help all of us if he did, and I did not think the public would view the time limit as a factor, as long as he was capable of performing the duties of Chief Justice and able to do so.

After Duff expressed his willingness, the two men, as they always seemed to do when together, talked politics. Duff was warm about a recent speech by King, "and emphasis placed on consequences of a stalemate. He had not seen the argument presented so strongly and forcibly before. He was making use of it in something he is preparing."[8] The talk had been given in Toronto earlier that month at a meeting of the American Federation of Labor. King spoke of victory leading to a new world order created "by a spiritual interpretation of life" based on the "universal rule of law." In front of an organization of employees, he said that if the free nations could marshal their resources in wartime to conquer the enemy, they could do so in peacetime to conquer unemployment.[9] It was one of his more eloquent speeches, and had evidently struck a chord in Duff.

King raised the question of Duff with Ralston, who told him that, given the severe criticism of the Hong Kong report, failure to extend his term would be looked on as "giving in to our opponents."[10] That settled King's mind. He spoke to St. Laurent, then justice minister, and it was soon common knowledge that the government would bring in the necessary legislation. A problem arose, however: Duff's term would expire on 7 January, but Parliament did not convene until the 27th. What would Duff's status be during that interregnum? The justice department decided that his term could not be extended by order-in-council, but only by an Act of Parliament having retroactive effect, and accordingly St. Laurent introduced a bill in the House. There was strong opposition in and out of Parliament this time because of Duff's role in the

Hong Kong affair. The Vancouver *Daily Province*, for example, saw the government's action as a ploy to silence criticism of Duff's report as well as to gain support for its management of the expedition.[11] Two M.P.s, Conservative A.R. Adamson and T.C. Douglas of the C.C.F., were opposed on identical grounds, that Duff had ignored their evidence at the Hong Kong hearings. Douglas had testified to knowing some of the last-minute recruits for the Winnipeg Grenadiers, who had no more training than he had received himself as a reserve officer in Saskatchewan.

King never doubted that the measure would carry — he had an overwhelming majority — but he did worry that the criticism might deter Duff from carrying on:

> What I am now most afraid of is that Duff himself will not agree to continue on the Bench. I told St. Laurent we should see to it that he does not give in to the echoes of the Toronto gang, Meighen, Drew et al., and their attacks of the last year.[12]

St. Laurent ended the debate by saying that "this generation in Canada knows no greater jurist than the present chief justice...

> It was felt that in view of present conditions, when it is the duty of each of us to contribute to the service of his country in whatever capacity he may be best able to serve, it was indeed fitting to ask parliament further to amend the act so that the chief justice could continue for another year to perform services which are of such great value to the Canadian nation.[13]

In the resulting vote, Hanson and one other Conservative supported the bill, which passed by a wide margin. In the Senate it had a smoother passage and became law on 5 February.[14]

R.B. Bennett, by then Viscount Bennett and living in England, heard of the proposed legislation and sent Hanson an outraged cable on the evening of 4 February — two days after the end of debate in the House and the very day the bill went through the Senate. There were several reasons for Bennett's fury. In the first place, he was one of the many who felt that Duff had behaved badly in the Hong Kong inquiry.

> I really consider [the Bill] the most iniquitous legislation that was ever passed by any Parliament within the British Empire. The fact is that Duff has been made Chief Justice by a Statute after he had ceased to be a judge. It has caused a very great feeling of disgust amongst Judges and others in this country that we had a man who was willing to be legislated into a job which by law he had vacated because the Statute was not passed until he became an ex-Judge.

I am not interested, except that after reading a report that he made in the Hong Kong case, I realize that he is no longer fit for judicial duties, and in fact, if I had been in Parliament there would have been a very long struggle before he was permitted to avail himself of the benefits of the most iniquitous legislation that you will find in the Statute Book of any of the King's Dominions.[15]

In his wire to Hanson, Bennett also raised the issue of Duff's weakness for alcohol, sneering: "Suggest Prime Minister be asked if reason he gave for refusing appoint Senior Justice Chief Justice in 1929 have not since been greatly intensified."[16] Poor Hanson tried to put the best possible face on his support for the bill by reminding Bennett, "I did not feel I could pound the Chief Justice having regard to the fact that we helped build him up and you made him Chief Justice on Anglin's death. In another year, however, it will be different."[17] But Bennett had noticed something Hanson had missed: in the *Who's Who in Canada* for 1938 Duff had described himself as a Liberal. Bennett viewed the entry as "unusual and inconsistent with discharge judicial duties." The inept Hanson could only reply, weakly, "Had I known it was there, as I really ought to have known, I would have pounded it."[18]

Neither Bennett nor Hanson realized how many years Duff had been declaring himself a Liberal in *Who's Who*. He did so in every edition from 1913 until 1930-31, and from 1934 to 1940-41. In the edition of 1930-31 he also listed himself as "ex-president, Victoria Liberal Club."[19] The gaps from 1931 until 1934 and after 1941, may or may not be significant. The former coincided with Anglin's decline in health, a period when Duff, under a Conservative government, hoped to succeed him. In 1942, his conduct as commissioner had been harshly criticized as being partial to the King government. Although it would be unthinkable today for a sitting judge, much less a chief justice, to publicize his politics, attitudes in Duff's time were different. Everyone knew that virtually all judges of the higher courts were appointed from the ranks of the governing party. Prominent lawyers of a party in opposition reconciled themselves to waiting for the party's return to power. Citizens did not often become exercised by this, since most judges really were impartial or made an honest effort to be so. A reading of Duff's decisions in the Supreme Court of Canada over thirty-seven years would not reveal where his political sympathies lay. Only in the Hong Kong inquiry did his politics directly influence his decision.

Bennett was wrong about Duff's appointment being illegal; the supremacy of Parliament as expressed in a Special Act overrode the provisions of the Supreme Court of Canada Act. Yet Duff was sufficiently conscious of the delicate position he occupied for the month between 7 January and 5 February that he sat on no appeal; he busied himself deciding those he had already heard and gave judgement only after the latter date. As he told Alexander, "There was an interregnum of about a month during which I had no judicial character and was engaged in working feverishly on some difficult issues of law." He also gave his friend his reasons for agreeing to stay on: "Looking at the thing from a selfish point of view, I fancy I will be happier during the next year with something definite to do. As to the public side of the matter, I feel that I was left no choice."[20]

Three days after the bill extending his term became law, the Supreme Court of Canada heard an appeal in a constitutional case. Duff did not sit on it, the first time since 1906, barring illness or the pressure of extra-judicial commission work, that he had been absent for one. He had probably been uncertain whether his status would be confirmed in time and assigned other judges to hear the case. No other constitutional matter came to the court before his retirement.

A month later, he again displayed his old tendency to sympathy for abandoned women. The case was the last and perhaps the most remarkable of its kind. A woman had brought an action for breach of promise of marriage. The common-law relationship between her and the male defendant dated back to 1908. She testified that they had both agreed to defer marriage until his prospects in life had brightened. Finally, in 1941, she felt that her fiance's means had satisfied the condition. When he refused to marry her, she sued him. After a jury trial, the lower court dismissed her case on the ground that the passage of time had eroded the legal basis of her claim, and the decision was affirmed by the Ontario Court of Appeal. On appeal to the Supreme Court of Canada, Duff decided that, contrary to rulings of the lower courts, there was sufficient legally admissible evidence which, if believed by a jury, could sustain an award for damages. He ordered a new trial.[21]

In this case, as in the *Brownlee* case Duff demonstrated his belief in the integrity of a verdict by a jury, a belief consistently affirmed from his earliest days on the Supreme Court of Canada. Quoting a British judge in 1907, he said that where the issue in a case was one of fact, as distinct from a legal question, "'the verdict of the jury, once found, ought to stand; the setting aside of such a verdict should be a rare and exceptional occurrence.'"[22] In criminal cases, verdicts of juries are frequently overturned because their validity depends on the legal correctness of instructions given by a trial judge and also because the liberty of an accused person is at stake. In civil cases, although verdicts also depend on judges' instructions, Duff was equally inclined to take the side of the jury.

On 6 October he heard argument in the appeal of a man convicted of murder. The accused, Beatty, had been arrested on suspicion of stealing a revolver. He admitted the theft, and, while he was being interrogated by the police, blurted out the words, "I killed Phil Davis." Davis, a taxi driver, had been found shot dead, but the police had had no inkling that Beatty might be the culprit. At his trial, his statements to the police, including the confession that he had stolen the revolver, were admitted into evidence. After conviction, he appealed on the sole ground that the reference in his confession to another crime, theft, invalidated his conviction for murder. Despite his generally lenient view of those accused of serious crimes, Duff dismissed the appeal in a judgement delivered on 6 January 1944, one day before the effective date of his retirement.[23] It was his last judgement.

He scheduled the routine handing down of judgements in reserved cases for 15 December. When it became known that that day would be the last on which he would grace the Supreme Court bench, the justice minister and lawyers wanted to mark the occasion. Duff opposed the idea, desiring no "imposition on the Bar to come from all over the place to attend such a ceremony."[24] To avoid any ceremony, he decided not to sit on the 15th after all, but St. Laurent told him that the legal profession genuinely wished to do him honour and his failure to sit that day would be read as discourteous. The argument succeeded. Duff, still reluctant, said he wanted to avoid any appearance of a "public function," and would accept only "a fairly general spontaneous expression of the wish of the Bar" with no speeches by anyone except lawyers and colleagues, and certainly not by members of the government. He would limit his own remarks to "one or two paragraphs only."[25]

At noon on 15 December 1943, a large crowd filled the courtroom. Duff presided for the last time, his colleagues flanking him. Thibodeau Rinfret was the senior judge. After him came H.H. Davis, Duff's closest friend among his fellow judges. Patrick Kerwin, later to succeed Rinfret as chief justice, had joined the court in 1935. A.B. Hudson from Manitoba had been a judge since 1936. Robert Taschereau, who was to succeed Kerwin as chief justice, had come to Ottawa in 1940. The junior judge, Ivan Rand, next to Duff perhaps the brightest of them all, had been a colleague for only a few months. Duff had regretted Crocket's appointment in 1932, believing Rand to be the better man; Rand had filled the vacancy caused by Crocket's resignation in 1943. Duff could take justifiable pride in his colleagues. As a group, they formed a far stronger court than any other in his experience.

After the conclusion of formal business, E. Philippe Brais, vice-president of the Canadian Bar Association, representing its president, R.L. Maitland, who was ill, made remarks suited to the occasion, as did C.F.H. Carson of Toronto, representing D.L. McCarthy, treasurer of the Law Society of Upper Canada, who was also ill. But only Aimé Geoffrion wrenched Duff's heart. Speaking with feeling, he recalled the great days in London when they had both worked on the Alaska case.

> There were five juniors on that Commission. One was Mr. F.C. Wade, who has just died. Another was S.A.T. Rowlatt, who has since been made a member of the Privy Council. The third was Mr. Simon, later Sir John

Simon, who is now Lord Chancellor. The fourth was Mr. Duff, who later became the Chief Justice of Canada, and the fifth myself — I am the only plain one left.

...the result of that association for me was a friendship that has lasted forty years, and of which I have always been very proud. I have been able to know the Chief Justice, not only as a public man but as a private individual. I admire him in the one capacity, I like him in the other. I can only say this in the sense that I am probably losing more than others by his departure. I wish him the long days of rest which he has so richly earned.[26]

Far from the "one or two paragraphs" Duff had spoken of, he read a carefully prepared speech about fifteen minutes long, recalling his "forty years (less ten weeks)" on the bench and his pride in that long service. He mentioned a favourite theme: the unique ability of the Supreme Court, administering as it does two systems of law, to deal with "new problems that arise from time to time as the law adapts itself to novel conditions." He spoke, as he had often done before, of the values of an independent Bar and the hallmarks of a great lawyer — honesty, habits of detachment, loyalty. As at Philadelphia, he praised the British people and the nations of the Commonwealth for taking "their stand across the path of the power of evil" and summoning "the world to defend the rights of mankind." He uttered his final words from the bench: "I thank you all for this manifestation of kindness, one of the most memorable of my life, the recollection of which I shall always cherish."[27]

It was a good speech, but one wishes he had thrown it away and spoken directly from the heart with the easy grace of Geoffrion. He wrote Alexander a week later to tell him, "The other day I made my last appearance on the bench and I think it is right that I should give place to a younger man; although I think that fate has dealt with me quite as well as I have deserved."[28] No complaint from Duff — a sturdy acceptance of the loss of position.

On 6 January the Governor-General, the Earl of Athlone, invited Duff and Annie as guests of honour to a gala dinner at Rideau Hall. Most of the guests were judges, but the prime minister attended as well. Athlone "made a nice little speech," according to King, who recorded that the

chief justice merely rose and speaking with great sincerity and naturalness, said he would not be expected to say anything, but how deeply grateful he was to His Ex. for his kindnesses at all times towards himself and for his kind words of the evening.[29]

Duff badly disappointed those present who, with affection, wished him to speak longer.[30]

Next day, the actual day of retirement, King wrote Duff a long letter by hand to thank him "for the help you have given to the Administrations in office while in your position as a member of the Supreme Court, and the Chief Justice; and, particularly, in helping to meet the demands of war-time emergencies."[31] And among the flood of messages and letters came one from George VI, happy in its phrasing.

> I have learned with sincere regret that the time has come when you will be retiring from your position as Chief Justice of Canada, after having served as a member of the Supreme Court for no less than 37 years. During that time you have helped to build up the reputation and authority of your great Tribunal and to secure for the administration of the law in Canada the respect and admiration of all. Your services to your fellow-countrymen in that Dominion as Administrator of the Government, as Deputy to successive Governors General and as Chairman of important Commissions both in war and in peace are gratefully remembered, and I would wish especially to thank you for your most valuable aid from time to time on the Judicial Committee of my Privy Council.
>
> The Queen and I send you our best wishes, with the hope that you may long enjoy your well-earned retirement.[32]

This letter touched Duff above all others. Although he believed appeals to the Privy Council should be abolished, he never lost his emotional ties with the United Kingdom or the monarchy, identifying strongly with the great British traditions of law and parliamentary democracy.

And so it was all over. He gathered up his few possessions from his chambers and took them home. Thereafter his study was his office. In that study a few months later, he met J. W. Estey, newly-appointed to the Supreme Court, and made an agreement for the sale of his judicial robes. To seal the bargain, Duff invited Estey to the Country Club for a drink, telling him that he would take him there because he kept no liquor in the house. Duff was nonplussed to learn that Estey did not touch liquor.[33]

Retired as a judge, he could have practised law again had he chosen to do so, but he never considered the possibility. He did become an Honorary Bencher of the Law Society of Upper Canada at the instance of his friend D. L. McCarthy, but he attended none of the meetings, which were always held in Toronto.

Seldom did he leave Ottawa after his retirement, but he cherished the hope that he might be able to make one more journey to sit on the Judicial Committee. He knew, of course, that the appeal from his decision to abolish recourse to it would be heard some time after the end of the war. It would be appropriate for his final appearance to be made before the hearing of that appeal, if it could be managed. He did manage it. Learning that the abolition appeal had been scheduled for the autumn of 1946, he resolved to travel to London in June. His former private secretary, W.K. Campbell, by then an intimate friend, accompanied him. They had booked passage on the *Queen Mary* from New York but Duff caught a bad cold on his arrival in that city; a doctor confined him to bed, and they had to wait for the next sailing in two weeks' time. Duff, who received his travelling expenses and an allowance from the Canadian government, later refunded a sum proportionate to the time spent in illness in New York; profligate in his own spending habits, he never took advantage of the public purse.[34]

By happy coincidence, Lord Wright, the eminent English jurist and an old acquaintance, was also sailing on the *Queen Mary*, and the two men saw much of one another on the Atlantic crossing. Among the other passengers were Alan Bronfman, Lazarus Phillips, who had been one of the lawyers for Harry Bronfman, and Phillips's son. A waiter came to Duff and Campbell at dinner one evening to say that the Bronfman party wished to send wine to their table. Duff sent his thanks but declined the offer, telling Campbell he would never accept anything from the Bronfmans. The Canadian high commissioner arranged for a vehicle at Southampton which carried them swiftly up to London and the Dorchester Hotel.

Dr. C.J. MacKenzie, head of the National Research Council, had also been a passenger on the ship, travelling to London for a scientific conference. Duff wished to entertain MacKenzie and some of his fellow scientists at a cocktail party but he had no liquor. Without his knowledge, Campbell phoned the younger Phillips at the Savoy, telling him that he, Campbell, wished to entertain friends, and asking if Phillips could help him out with some liquor. Phillips readily obliged with a supply of gin and Scotch whisky which Campbell turned over to Duff. Duff held his party but never asked, nor did he ever learn, the source of the liquor.[35]

For Duff, the return to London at age eighty-one must have been exhilarating, if tinged with regret. He had been a member of the Judicial Committee for nearly twenty-seven years, far longer than any other Canadian judge. He had sat on over eighty appeals, far more than any other Canadian and far more than many English or Commonwealth judges had heard. He enjoyed an international reputation as a jurist; he and Haldane had run in the same harness. This would be his last appearance and perhaps the last occasion on which any Canadian judge would sit as a member of the Judicial Committee. Duff foresaw the end of the Judicial Committee as a Canadian institution, and though he was convinced intellectually that this was as it should be, the prospect saddened him.

Nevertheless he enjoyed himself. He visited his Inn, and he had lunch at the Inner Temple with Lord Greene whom he had last seen at Columbia

University in 1941. He and MacKenzie were invited to the garden party at Buckingham Palace. The Canadian high commissioner arranged a limousine for them and, dressed in morning clothes, they joined thousands of other guests in the Palace grounds. The High Commissioner had done more than arrange transport: through his good offices, Duff and MacKenzie were among the four Canadians presented to the King and Queen.

As if to make up for his rather perfunctory appearance in the late thirties, on this last shift Duff worked hard, sitting on five cases, all from Canada. Sir Brian McKenna, a retired high court judge who appeared before Duff as a lawyer on one of these cases, has remembered him as being alert and keen. Sir Brian commented that Duff's reputation had preceded him, and the lawyers who appeared before the Judicial Committee all recognized his ability.[36] On one appeal, Lord Simon and Duff sat as colleagues. A.B. Robertson, one of the lawyers on a British Columbia case and later a judge of the court of appeal of that province, has recalled that at the end of the first day of argument he and Senator Farris, also appearing, had apparently convinced Simon of the soundness of their case, and felt confident that they would succeed. Duff and Simon went off to Simon's house in the country for a long weekend, Thursday until Sunday evening. While there, Duff, not convinced by Robertson's argument, persuaded Simon to change his mind. That appeal was ultimately dismissed.[37]

It is fitting that the last case which Duff heard in London, the last case on which he would ever sit, came from the Supreme Court of Canada. While he was a member of that court he would not hear appeals from it, but that impediment was now removed. Late in 1945, several months after the war with Japan had ended, the federal government passed three orders-in-council authorizing the deportation of Japanese nationals and, in some circumstances, British subjects of Japanese origin. A civil liberties group called the Cooperative Committee on Japanese Canadians challenged the validity of the orders-in-council, which had been passed under the War Measures Act. There had been a difference of opinion among the judges of the Canadian supreme court on some aspects of the case, but they generally upheld the validity of the orders-in-council.[38] At the Privy Council, Lord Simon presided over the board, which included, besides Duff, lords Wright, Porter and Uthwatt. Though the subsequent judgement appeared under Wright's name, he collaborated with Duff in the decision, supporting the orders-in-council in their entirety.[39] Both the Supreme Court of Canada and the Judicial Committee were guided by Duff's decisions in the noteworthy *Gray* case from the time of the First War, and the *Chemicals Reference* case from the recent war.[40] The effect of both decisions was that an order-in-council passed in relation to a specific subject set out in the War Measures Act — deportation in the Japanese case — had the force of an Act of Parliament and could not be questioned. Just as in 1918 the conscript Gray lost his exemption under the Military Service Act because of such an order-in-council, Japanese nationals and their families were now liable to deportation by order-in-council passed under emergency conditions.[41]

Duff did not record his emotions when, a day or two after the argument in that case had ended, he embarked for Canada. He was tired, certainly, because the work had been difficult, but worse, he was heavy-hearted. He would not visit London again, or sit as a member of the board. He may have hoped secretly for a moment that the Privy Council would reverse his own decision on the abolition appeal.

That appeal was argued in London between 23 October and 1 November 1946 before an exceptionally able court, perhaps the strongest ever assembled to hear a Canadian appeal: the Lord Chancellor, Jowitt, lords Simon, MacMillan, Wright, Greene, and Simonds, and the redoubtable Lord Goddard. The case is an excellent example of a judge with a certain cast of mind being presented with the opportunity of solving a problem which only he can solve. Jowitt, Lord Chancellor in a socialist government, delivered the judgement. It cannot be told from the official records whether his views represented unanimity or a majority. In 1946, however, the times called for the dismantling of empire, and the Privy Council, led by Jowitt, responded by agreeing with Duff that appeals could be abolished.[42]

The decision, handed down on 13 January 1947, opened the way for Parliament to legislate, but the government moved very slowly, mainly because Quebec members of the Liberal caucus feared a loss of provincial rights if the Supreme Court of Canada was given the last word.[43] Not until eighteen months after the ruling did the government now led by St. Laurent introduce legislation to follow the decision up. George Drew, by then in the federal House, attempted unsuccessfully to delay its passage to allow consultation with the provinces, whose constitutional position, he argued, would be affected. M.J. Coldwell of the C.C.F. put forward the centralist argument of those in favour of abolition: "our federal system as visualized by the fathers of confederation has been seriously impaired and the powers of this parliament greatly reduced by the decisions of the privy council from time to time."[44]

The new law abolished appeals to the Privy Council in all lawsuits started after 1 January 1950.[45] Those already under way could continue. Not until 1959 did the Privy Council hear the last case from Canada. Involving the ownership of a lease for petroleum and natural gas, it began in Alberta just before the passage of the law, and took more than ten years to reach its conclusion in London. A group of Alberta lawyers enjoyed the distinction of arguing the last Canadian case in that forum.[46]

Those who voted in 1949 to make the Supreme Court of Canada the final court of appeal thinking that this would mean significant change in the interpretation of the British North America Act were to be disappointed, for the constitutional direction of the country has not been much affected. The reason lies in the well-established rule of precedent; the significant rulings on the Canadian constitution by the Privy Council, and by Duff, remain essentially unchanged.

# 18

# The Hong Kong cover-up

IN JULY 1946 Maj.-Gen. C.M. Maltby, who had been the British commander at Hong Kong, completed his official report of the battle, and the War Office sent a routine copy to the Canadian high commission in London. The contents were so inflammatory that officials there recommended to Ottawa that the report be toned down for Canadian sensibilities. Maltby had scathing things to say about the Canadians. With their lack of training, they should never have been sent to Hong Kong, where, as everyone knew, war was about to break out. Everything he wrote contradicted what Duff had concluded. There were quiet consultations involving King and Lt.-Gen. Foulkes, chief of the Canadian General Staff, Field-Marshal Montgomery, and other British and Canadian officials, as a result of which the Maltby draft was watered down considerably. Even in its amended form, however, the report, not published until 29 January 1948, stirred up another political storm.

In early February of that year Brooke Claxton, then defence minister, asked Foulkes for his advice. The general took Duff's main findings and compared them with what Drew had said in his July 1942 letter to Mackenzie King and what Maltby had written. Foulkes did not deal with the question of whether the Canadian government should or should not have been aware of the intentions of the Japanese, but he did say in a revealing aside that there was "no evidence of the receipt of the telegram of October 24th," the "altered circumstances" telegram, even though he had asked defence department officials to search for it. In spite of its being marked for the prime minister and other important figures, the message had never reached the minister of defence. Concerning the expedition itself, Foulkes agreed with virtually everything Drew had said in 1942. Troops were not "adequately trained" as Crerar had asserted and Duff had accepted; Foulkes could not reconcile the woeful deficiencies in the training of the men with Crerar's "proven efficiency" of the two battalions. He told Claxton that the shipment of transport vehicles had been so badly mishandled that if officers under his command displayed such incompetence he would have them court-martialled. Duff had merely said that the officers had shown a "lack of energy." Nonetheless, Foulkes believed that the affair should be stifled. He saw no value in renewed debate or revelation.[1]

As he had in 1942 on publication of Duff's report, the prime minister felt compelled to make some response to the clamour. Among the people he talked to was Power, who told him that "our men were not too well trained," but the British troops had been no better prepared.[2] On 18 February John Bracken, leader of the Conservative opposition, moved the tabling of all the evidence from the Duff Commission. King replied that since this evidence made reference to confidential British telegrams, the British would have to give consent to their release, which he had asked for but not yet received. The motion was stood over.[3] Two days later, King told the House that he had received a reply to his request and would make a further statement after he had digested it.[4]

The government had before it opposition requests for the tabling of Drew's 1942 letter to the prime minister as well as the Duff material. British approval would be needed for both. King decided to make a statement to the House on 24 February, a draft of which he discussed with cabinet on the 23rd. Cabinet was so badly divided on the question that King left the decision until the following day. After the meeting, he redrafted his statement and then "phoned Chief Justice Duff and said I would like to let him look at it and get an opinion from him later as to whether he approved." King noted, "The worst feature is the reopening of wounds but I believe that once we bring down the material, if the papers start that kind of thing, the public's feelings will be roused against them."[5] Duff went over the statement carefully. The prime minister telephoned him to discuss it later that evening. Duff strongly advised King to table the evidence lest the public think the government had something to hide. He used harsh words of Drew, calling him a "blackguard and a fool" and totally unpredictable. King emphasized that he did not wish to take any step that would embarrass Duff, who replied rather sententiously that in spite of "pot shots" from the Toronto *Globe*, "no man could do anything in life that was worthwhile without someone misrepresenting things." The sometime apostle of free speech in the Alberta newspaper act case went on to complain that a C.B.C. newscaster, commenting on the Maltby Report, had said that "Drew had been right." Really, Duff went on, the "C.B.C. should be spoken to about matters of that kind." After their conversation, King recorded, "I feel now quite at ease in my mind about giving the statement as it stands."[6]

Comforted by Duff's advice, King rose in the House the next afternoon.

After reviewing the secret nature of the telegrams from the British and emphasizing that any reproduction of them must be by paraphrase so as not to compromise the cypher code used, the prime minister agreed to table the evidence, which, he said, would refer only to such of the telegrams as the British agreed to disclose. King refused to table Drew's letter, which contained extracts from those secret telegrams meant only for the eyes of the commissioner and counsel. He left it to Drew to "decide for himself whether he wishes to break the confidence reposed in him and to disclose information which the government of the United Kingdom wishes to have kept secret."[7] Power, independent of mind as always, followed with the remark that he would be "unhappy if every dispatch, every report and every item of evidence is not laid before the people of Canada."

Although the government tabled the evidence, it did not include the lawyers' written arguments. There was a certain irony in this, since Duff had paid no attention whatever to them.[8] On 10 March Claxton laid a single copy before the House. Bracken asked: "The Minister, then, does not intend to provide us with more than one copy of the evidence. That is all we are to have. Is that correct?"[9] The government later relented, and printed more.[10]

Mulling over the 24 February debate, King had reread Maltby's report and commented in his diary, "I have never been able to understand why the people of the Defence Department were so anxious to send the men they did in such a hurry except to make a name for themselves and the Dept."[11] His old newspaper foe the *Globe and Mail* ran an editorial on the 26th suggesting that the reason he refused to table Drew's letter was that it would show he had known on 24 October 1941, the day the "altered circumstances" telegram reached Ottawa, that the troops would face "the virtual certainty of brutal war."[12] Leading off the debate for the Conservatives in Parliament that day, Gordon Graydon attacked the government along the same lines. In King's absence, Claxton took on the defence of the government, stating that it had received no warning of impending hostilities. He blamed the furore on the release of Maltby's report, which "was made in accordance with well-established practice under which general officers make their reports," and went on, "In his report, General Maltby has this to say, and this only, on the subject of training,"[13] quoting the first sentence of the report's summary as amended: "These two battalions proved to be inadequately trained for modern war under the conditions existing in Hong Kong."[14] Claxton knowingly concealed from the House the fact that Maltby had originally made far harsher statements about the Canadians' training. He announced that he did not intend to "go into the facts" of the affair because "I for one, until I have some other evidence, accept completely the report of the royal commission."

J.G. Diefenbaker, then Conservative member for Saskatchewan Lake Centre, asked, "Was he [Claxton] or any other member of the Cabinet made aware of the contents of the report of General Maltby prior to its release by the British War Office on January 29th?" Claxton replied blandly,

> I cannot speak for my colleagues, because I have not asked them, but I feel reasonably certain that none of them was; and I certainly had not been. That would not be usual....In this war the allies were fighting combined operations under unified commands, with the representatives of various nations associated under different commands. As far as I know the practice was not followed of consulting with the representatives of all the countries concerned when it came to the preparation of a report by the General Officer Commanding, although no doubt there would be exchanges at the official level to verify details.[15]

Honourable members were not aware that the government had tailored the original report to its liking, and they were never told.

King spent much time the next day "reading over yesterday's debate in the House between Graydon and Claxton on Hong Kong," as well as various documents: the Drew letter, Duff's report, and "later the dispatches to and from Britain at the time to Hong Kong." He was

> immensely relieved to find that there was nothing in all of the correspondence that could in any way reflect on either myself or run counter to the judgment of Chief Justice Duff. There is, of course, much that would indicate that our men were sent far too quickly, insufficiently trained, etc. but there is enough in the telegrams from the U.K. to make clear there was no reason to expect they would be involved in any engagements as soon as they were.[16]

So the government had known all along that the expedition was mishandled. It also appears that King had just read all the October 1941 telegrams for the first time. Cabinet does not even seem to have been briefed during the five weeks from 19 September, the date of the British request, to the day the expedition left.

Drew accepted King's challenge, releasing his letter to the press; it appeared in the Ottawa *Citizen* on 1 March. King saw its publication as a tory plot

> to make a battle between Drew and the ex-Chief Justice though I can see the Tory plan is to seek to make me the scape goat by Drew's assertion that I knew there was a certainty of war against Hong Kong 3 days before our troops left.
>
> I have taken part of the afternoon to go over correspondence again. I

think the Chief Justice is absolutely right in his decision. I am glad tomorrow to have the opportunity of raising the question of privilege and saying that Drew is wrong in his assertion. Of course, we shall be embarrassed at not being able to produce telegrams which support the truth of our position.[17]

Next day King engaged in some deception himself. As the first order of business in the House he rose to deny the allegations that

> after the government of Japan changed on October 16th, 1941 and before the expedition sailed on October 27, I received messages from the United Kingdom government in the nature of the most complete warning of the probability of early hostilities....In my opinion, such information as the Canadian government received, at the time, from the British authorities is in complete accord with the finding of the Commissioner, Chief Justice Duff, in his report, namely, that "the best informed opinion available to the Canadian authorities was that hostilities would not arise in the near future.[18]

King was less than candid in referring to "such information as I received" as if to suggest that the information was innocuous. The two telegrams of 24 October were anything but innocuous, and he himself had predicted on 27 October that the war would spread to the Pacific "any day." His statement stirred up a hornet's nest; members on both sides of the House jumped to their feet, shouting and interrupting; the Speaker, unable to control the debate, called "Order" fruitlessly until at last not even he could be heard.[19]

A week or so later, Bracken unsuccessfully requested the government to table

> all correspondence, written communications or memoranda respecting...communications between (a) the British Government and the Canadian High Commissioner's Office in London;...(c) The British and Canadian governments, either through Ministers of the Crown or public office, relative to the Maltby report on Hong Kong made public by the British War Office on January 29 last.

It is not clear whether Bracken had heard rumours that the original report had been revised. On receiving notice of his motion, King had asked Arthur Beauchesne, clerk of the House and an eminent authority on parliamentary procedure, for an opinion. Beauchesne said it would be "unusual" to produce such papers; if it were otherwise, letters "written by senior officers...to the governments of other countries" would become public knowledge. It would, he said, be "unsafe and unwise" to do so as tending "to destroy the harmony which should exist between the different powers in the state," and would, in effect, put power in the hands of those not "sworn in to administer the Country's affairs." King relied on a tenuous argument to justify non-disclosure.[20]

The debate also raged outside the House, led by the *Globe and Mail*, which ran an editorial on 12 March that cut Duff to the quick.

> Directly contrary to the findings of Commissioner Sir Lyman Duff, the evidence makes it clear that the two battalions sent from Canada on October 27, 1941, were untrained for war, inadequately equipped, and without the military transport considered necessary by its commanding officer.

Pointing to Power's evidence that there was "a real chance of war breaking out," and making reference to the "altered circumstances" telegram, the *Globe and Mail* said,

> All these facts were disregarded by the Commissioner in his report, and his findings were false on the four points at issue. The troops were untrained, inadequately equipped, without essential transport, and the government was well aware that there was a real danger of war with Japan. Every one of these facts is documented in the evidence, and all have been confirmed by the Maltby report to the British Government.[21]

The editorial also stung King, who said that it was "really criminal libel saying the Chief Justice was guilty of falsehood....A perfectly shoking communication."[22]

The next day King's aide J.W. Pickersgill wrote by hand to Norman Robertson, then high commissioner in London, about a plan he and Brooke Claxton had devised to ease the pressure on the government. To avoid further "grave" injury "to Duff and the P.M.," he asked whether Robertson might be able to find a well-disposed M.P. to ask a planted question in the British House of Commons, the answer to which would absolve the government from the charge of foreknowledge that there would be war with Japan. Pickersgill sent Robertson a copy of the *Globe and Mail* editorial with the comment that the contents clearly amounted to criminal libel, but the Ontario attorney-general, a Conservative, would never initiate proceedings. Still, Pickersgill thought, "there must surely be some M.P.s who have encountered Drew" and would like to turn the tables on him. Nothing came of this Machiavellian suggestion.[23]

On 17 March Senator Farris made a heated speech in the Senate, hitting out at Drew and the *Globe and Mail*, singing Duff's praises, lauding King, and castigating the tories who, he said, were dragging down the reputation of the country's most renowned judge.[24] Duff was grateful to his old friend, and King said it was the "kind of thing that every Member of Parliament should be doing for all he is worth."[25] The prime minister was still gnawing away at the point that preoccupied the *Globe and Mail* and most other critics: whether the government had any warning after 16 October 1941 of impending hostilities with Japan. In mid-April King sent a long wire to Clement Attlee, the British prime minister, asking him to confirm that no messages had been sent to Canada containing "a complete warning of the probability of early hostilities." King told the House later that month that he had asked for this assurance because "the veracity of Sir Lyman Poore Duff, the former Chief Justice of Canada, and myself as Prime Minister of Canada...[had been] called into question." He read out a reply from Attlee declining to give the full texts of the telegrams but confirming that "any such suggestion as has been mentioned is entirely contrary to the facts, and...none of the telegrams contained any warning that action by Japan of the kind was expected."[26] According to Pickersgill, he had drafted the telegram confident of the reply. Because of groundwork laid in London by Norman Robertson, who often played bridge with Attlee, King knew in advance what the British prime minister's response would be. Sympathetic to King, Attlee helped him in his difficulty.[27]

What Attlee said was, strictly speaking, true, and King was also right in a sense in saying that he had received no message stating explicitly that war would soon break out. Drew undoubtedly exaggerated the effect of the October telegrams, but it is undeniable that the cabinet did not see all of them at the time and that the intelligence officers who did see them saw no particular significance in them.

Drew was also a key figure in the second episode. In suppressing information and editing Maltby's report, the prime minister had an eye on the past — Ralston's statement of innocence made to the House in January 1942. But King also had an eye on the future. By 1948, Premier Drew of Ontario was moving into federal politics and thinking of becoming Prime Minister Drew. King would not give him the slightest satisfaction by conceding that he had been right, and concealed the truth accordingly.

Was Duff implicated in the deception? In giving advice to King on the February 1948 statement, Duff, a retired judge, did no wrong. King sent him a copy of the edited Maltby report and Duff followed the debates avidly in Hansard. When one considers his close relations with King, and his own partisan role in 1942, it is hard to believe that he knew nothing of the efforts by King and his advisors to stifle criticism of his own report, but no evidence to support such a belief has yet come to light.

# 19

# Nightfall

FOR TWENTY YEARS after his wife's death, Duff had lived in a succession of rented apartments and houses. In 1946, after a disagreement with a landlord over the cost of some repairs, he decided to buy a last home, and asked Campbell to find one for him. Campbell chose a house on Clemow Street, an upper-middle-class area in the Glebe district of Ottawa. Campbell told Duff he thought he had found a suitable place but that he should look at it before completing the purchase. Duff didn't bother.

He was very happy in it. A dignified but thoroughly comfortable three-storey house, it had a wooden bow front and peaked porch, long mullioned windows, and high chimney. Entering through a small vestibule, one came into the central hall with Duff's study on the left and on the right, the spacious sitting room with a handsome dining room next to it. Duff's and Annie's large bedrooms, each with a fireplace and comfortable furniture, were on the second floor, where Duff also kept his library. The third was taken up by their two servants' quarters and rooms for storing books. Duff was surrounded by books. He did not know how many volumes he owned, but there were thousands of them, in French as well as English. Not long after retirement, he decided to sell his holdings of legal titles to the Supreme Court library. An appraiser set their value at twenty-five hundred dollars; he said he would not take a penny more than fifteen hundred. Officials from the justice department insisted on paying the appraised value; Duff, adamant, refused to sell at all. The department capitulated and paid him the fifteen hundred.[1]

He had always bought quantities of books, though he was often unable to pay for them. Not only did he buy them, he read them. It is hard to imagine a field unrepresented in his library: he had cookbooks, novels by Disraeli, medical journals and texts, detective stories, Herodotus, Boswell, scientific works like Maxwell's *Matter and Motion*, tomes on economics — the range was astonishing. But he borrowed great numbers of books as well, mainly from the Parliamentary Library. Often he failed to return them. Sorting out his effects after he died, Campbell discovered two dozen library books which were duly returned.

Yet none of his vast reading appeared directly in his judgements. There are no quotations from Caesar or Shakespeare or literary allusions of any kind; his reading undoubtedly honed his intellect, but there is no evidence of it in his judicial writings. He wrote judgements dispassionately, and displayed the knowledge gained by wide reading in places other than the courtroom — his speeches, for example.

A year after his retirement he resigned from the board of governors of the University of Toronto of which, as a representative of the alumni association though formally appointed by the Ontario government, he had been a member for twenty years. His attendance at meetings had been sporadic at best, but on one occasion in 1926 when he offered to resign both Sir Robert Falconer, the president, and Howard Ferguson, the premier of Ontario, persuaded him to stay on.[2] Duff's first meeting on 24 September 1925 had turned out to be an interesting one. The board was considering the investment of $310,000 which had been raised by public subscription for the Banting Foundation to carry on its research into the cause and treatment of diabetes. Its decision was deferred because a Mrs. Jessie Ramsay had written claiming that she had discovered insulin long before Banting. The board was concerned enough about her assertion to appoint a special committee headed by the dean of medicine, Alexander Primrose, to investigate it. The committee reported that her claim was a sham.[3] Banting and Duff had received their knighthoods at the same investiture in 1934.

Duff's board colleagues over the years included a number of distinguished Canadians — Flavelle, Rowell, Mulock, and Reuben Wells Leonard among them. Though Duff attended few meetings he kept abreast of the board's activities, carefully reading all the material sent to him and frequently offering advice on various aspects of university affairs. Two controversies erupted towards the end of his term. In 1940, Professor Frank Underhill made pacifist remarks which were widely condemned, leading to accusations that he was a communist. In December of that year the board decided that he should be fired, but deferred its formal action to the following June. In the interval a deputation of faculty members appeared at a board meeting to protest the disciplinary action. Duff's friend John Stevenson, by then in Toronto with the *Globe and Mail*, wrote him to say that one member of the delegation, Prof. Charles Cochran, had told President Cody (who favoured firing Underhill, and Duff would have supported him), "Why, Mr. President, I've known Frank Underhill all my life. All this talk about his being a communist is just nonsense: I'll tell you what he is, a North York Grit, like old Mulock."[4]

Duff resigned from the board as a result of some unpleasantness involved in the election for chancellor in 1944. Sir William Mulock, by then nearly a century old and wishing to "die in harness," decided to run again, but someone nominated Vincent Massey, then high commissioner in London. A strong faction of the board protested that Massey's decision to run was in poor taste, and the registrar sent the high commissioner a brusque telegram suggesting that he withdraw; if he persisted in running, an inquiry would have to be held to determine his eligibility, which hinged on his being a resident of Ontario. The wording of the telegram led to bitter board disputes that lasted for months. Massey bowed out, and Mulock was re-elected in September 1944 only to die a few days later. Cody was made chancellor to fill out Mulock's term. Duff did not want to serve under Sidney Smith, who succeeded Cody as president; he had also thoroughly disapproved of Massey's behaviour, and no longer wished to be associated with people who had condoned it.[5]

He did preserve long after retirement his connection with another body far closer to his heart, one he had founded himself, the Dinner Club. Early in the 1920s — the exact year is uncertain — Duff conceived the idea of assembling a small group of kindred souls once monthly on an informal basis to enjoy a good meal and good conversation. The group would never be larger than twelve or fourteen and would have no by-laws or constitution: members were by invitation only. One of the group, the host for the evening to be known as the "symposiarch," would be responsible for arranging the dinner, and he was allowed to invite one guest. All meetings were held at a round table in a private dining room at the Ottawa Country Club. The group gathered at seven o'clock for drinks, with dinner at eight. Members drank moderately but talked a great deal in the ambiance of fine port, liqueurs, and cigar smoke. Among the early members of the group were Duff's old friend Biggar and his law partner Russell Smart, the poet Duncan Campbell Scott, and Dr. R.H. Coats, the Dominion statistician. Later came Grattan O'Leary the journalist, M.J. Coldwell, Arnold Heeney, Norman Robertson, Mr. Justice Rand, and Dr. C.J. Mackenzie. No speeches were made at these gatherings, but a distinguished guest such as the British scientist Sir John Cockcroft might be asked to say something informally.

Duff took more pleasure in the club than he did in any other organization. Like all its members, he would move heaven and earth to be present at a meeting. He particularly enjoyed the company of O'Leary. Irish, witty, an excellent conversationalist, he made Duff roar with laughter. The two of them tried to outdo each other with quotations from literature. Duff would say, "Oh, O'Leary, that damned little Irishman, I love him."[6] Norman Robertson described Duff as "the true Symposiarch who, wherever he sat, was at the head of the table. We all knew that Sir Lyman was a very great man indeed, and felt privileged at his company."[7] Mackenzie has agreed that Duff's powerful intellect made him the "ruling person in the group," in fact "the ablest man in Canada — a man of great intellectual power."[8] Duff kept up with the club almost until his last illness. Though it continued after his death, the mainspring had gone and it eventually wound down. Mackenzie has explained that the club ended because "the next meeting did not take place."[9]

Duff's long association with Mackenzie King continued until King's death in 1950. The two men developed a genuine affection for each other and, as they grew older, their letters were increasingly warm. In earlier times when King held office and Duff occupied the bench, their relationship had been more that of two politicians cut of the same cloth than that between elderly men recalling with fondness the long days of their friendship. When Duff as Administrator had read the speech from the throne in May 1940, the two men chatted and King recorded, "Duff spoke highly of it to me."[10] After a church service which they had attended in their official capacities a few months before, when the two of them looked "at the Justice Building immediately opposite, he [Duff] said 'your name is visibly written in that building.' I said to him: 'I am glad that ours will be associated together there.'"[11] In 1944 King went to London, and his speech to the two houses of Parliament on Canada's role in the war prompted a cable from Duff extending "warm and proud congratulations." King replied, "Deeply grateful your kind cable."[12]

In 1946 King became, like Duff, an honorary member of Gray's Inn. Duff wrote at once to congratulate him, telling him that Laurier had also been elected an Honorary Bencher in 1897, a fact unknown to King. Duff's letter pleased King immensely.

> How exceedingly kind of you to write me as you have of my election...the fact that I am privileged to share that distinction with yourself has added more to this honour and pleasure of receiving it than I can begin to tell you...the association of the honour with the names of Sir Wilfrid and yourself have lent it a new lustre in my eyes, as it will in the eyes of all Canadians.

Then King gave credit where credit was due:

> What touches me most deeply of all is what the knowledge of this association would have meant to my dear Father. I like to think as indeed I do believe, that what I have received of honour in this and in other directions is due more to what I owe to him and to my Mother than to all the other influences and circumstances of my life.[13]

At the end of 1947, King told Duff of his plan to give up office.

I am indeed grateful that my health is what it is at 73, but I must confess that I feel I should not seek to continue in office much longer, and, if spared to complete 21 years, should have a word with his Excellency concerning my successor — that assumes of course that I may continue to hold the confidence of the House of Commons until June.[14]

The two men invariably exchanged birthday greetings and Duff and Annie occasionally took tea with King; they often met at social functions, and rejoiced to see each other. They met at the Governor-General's annual levée on New Year's Day 1949, and later that same day King wrote Duff, "Nothing has given me quite the same pleasure at the beginning of this new year as to have had the good fortune to see you at this morning's levee and to shake you by the hand."[15] As he said he would, King stepped down in August 1948. Duff's letter to him on the occasion prompted King to write:

As I look back upon this old year [1948] I can think of no communications received in the course of its days that I shall treasure more than the two letters I received from you — the one you wrote on the eve of my retirement from the office of Prime Minister, and the other on the eve of my 74th birthday anniversary. That you should have found it possible to write as you have of my years in parliament, and at the government of our Country touches me deeply. I could ask for no greater reward of such public service as I have sought to render. That you could hold for me the wishes you do, and cherish the hopes expressed in your letter of greeting on my birthday is also something for which I shall be forever grateful, with your example behind your words, they come as a veritable inspiration.

I have been long in writing largely because writing by hand has become for me almost a lost art, and, since I was laid up, a bit of strain for my eyes. You will have known, however, what my feelings have been, I can only describe them as of the profoundest gratitude to, and deepest affection for you.[16]

Duff and St. Laurent, who succeeded King as prime minister, also had a warm relationship; the Liberal leader referred to Duff as "my dear and highly esteemed lifelong friend."[17] St. Laurent had been a successful lawyer before succeeding Lapointe as justice minister in 1941. On his appointment, he asked if he could pay a courtesy call on Duff and his colleagues at the Supreme Court, as he would no longer be appearing before them; his tact pleased Duff very much. He had often come to argue cases before Duff, who had a high opinion of his talents as an advocate. When he became prime minister in 1948, Duff wrote to congratulate him.

I recall with pleasure a conversation I had with Aimé Geoffrion, not many years after my arrival in Ottawa, in which your name and that of another of the then junior members of the Bar came up. Your professional distinction which was even then quite well recognized is not the topic that most sharply stimulates my recollection now; it was the tribute to character and personality that left the most lasting impression on my mind. It is very gratifying that the expectations of my dear friend have been so completely fulfilled, although he probably did not at that time anticipate the final stage.

Of all the prime ministers who have been lawyers, Duff put St. Laurent at the head of the list: "We have had Prime Ministers who have been called to the Bar, but no Prime Minister of Canada whose career as an advocate had approached in distinction that of yours."[18]

The federal election of June 1953 returned St. Laurent to power, but with a slightly reduced majority. Senator Cairinne Wilson viewed the results as a triumph, telling Duff, "I have no doubt that we are able both to rejoice over the results of Monday's voting....I even feel sorry for George Drew...[then leader of the opposition]"[19] However St. Laurent felt downhearted about the loss of even a few seats, so much so that he came to ask Duff's advice about whether he should carry on. Rather surprisingly, Duff told him that he should go back to law. His reason was not that St. Laurent had failed as a politician, but that he would leave office sooner or later, and if he waited too long he would find it very difficult to pick up the threads of his practice.[20]

Following his retirement, Duff went only twice to the new Supreme Court Building which the war had prevented him from occupying. In 1943, the Canadian Bar Association commissioned a bust of Duff for the building from the Montreal sculptor and architect Orson Wheeler. Duff completed his sittings for Wheeler in March 1943, but the wartime shortage of metals delayed the casting. Duff had enjoyed the sittings and he liked Wheeler, who found him a patient subject. The Bar association had asked prominent lawyers to contribute to the cost, including R.B. Bennett who, before the debate on the bill to extend Duff's second term, promised fifty dollars. Afterwards regretting he had done so, he delayed sending his money until he was reminded of a pledge made as a man of honour; reluctantly, he forwarded the funds.[21] Duff may have been unaware of Bennett's anger, for he sent him a cordial birthday message later that year.

The Bar association decided to unveil the bust in conjunction with its 1947 annual meeting at Ottawa. On 5 September the ceremony took place in the great hall of the Supreme Court attended by Mackenzie King, Chief Justice Rinfret, Lord Jowitt, Sir Norman Birkett, and a multitude of judges and lawyers. Minister of Justice J.L. Ilsley was the main speaker. Duff uttered only a few words of thanks. The unveiling revealed a figure of forbidding countenance quite unlike what might have been expected after the cordiality of the sittings. Duff liked the bust, however, and those who knew him best have said that it is a good likeness of him wrestling with some difficult problem.[22] Set on a plinth on the landing between the main and second floors of the courthouse, the bust gazes into the vast space of the bare hall.

The other occasion on which Duff went to his old court occurred in 1954; it proved to be his last appearance in public. On 21 June a ceremony like the one tendered Duff was held to honour the departure of Rinfret, who with great thoughtfulness asked his former chief to join him on the bench. Duff gladly did so, not robed like his fellows on the dais, but in an impeccably tailored suit. Rinfret, who had served the court for thirty years, nearly as long as Duff, commanded everyone's affection. Duff carefully prepared a brief speech, not once referring to himself but talking warmly of his colleague of old.

Rinfret's retirement posed a problem for St. Laurent. The logical successor was Kerwin, but he, like Rinfret, was a Roman Catholic, though from Ontario. It is hard today to understand how troublesome were the questions of religion and ethnic background when governments considered high judicial appointments. St. Laurent called on Duff for advice, and to his credit, Duff told him to ignore the question of religion; Kerwin, who had come to the Supreme Court of Canada after trial court experience in Ontario and earned his spurs in Ottawa, merited the appointment. St. Laurent followed his counsel.

Duff had been eighty-nine the previous January but looked well, indeed quite spry for his age. He had on the whole enjoyed excellent health for twenty years; apart from the occasional attack of lumbago, he suffered from no disabling ailment. He never entirely cured his drinking habit, but, out of necessity, had learned to control it. According to a waiter at the Country Club, Duff, at least until 1939, had come to the club at lunch several times a week for his "usual," which consisted of three or four of his customary drinks — double Gordon's gin and grapefruit juice. The grapefruit juice was preferred freshly squeezed into the drink pips and pulp and all for "maximum nutritive value," as Duff said. Failing that, he endured canned juice. When he went to England in 1946 he took many cans with him, fearing that they might be unobtainable there.[23] Duff never drank any liquor but gin, although on appropriate occasions he would take wine, champagne, and liqueurs. Occasionally, according to the same waiter, he would arrive at the club in the early evening for a drink, asking him, "If my sister calls, tell her I just left and bring me another gin and grapefruit juice." In such an event, Duff would take home his unfinished drink in a bottle for a nightcap.[24] Three or four double gins at lunchtime would sink a person much younger than Duff; he must have retained a considerable tolerance for alcohol.

Campbell started to work for Duff in 1940; only once after that date did he see Duff in his cups, and that was years after retirement. Annie phoned Campbell one afternoon to ask him to come to the house because "Lyman had been drinking." Campbell went at once to be greeted by a surprised Duff, who soon guessed why he had come. Duff said to him, "We are going out to the Country Club and I want you as a friend and as a gentleman to come with me; we will go and have one drink and then we will return." They took a taxi, had one drink each, Duff ordered his nightcap, and they returned home. Evidently Duff had become upset at the death of a friend, for on the way back to the house he told his companion, "You know, Campbell, it's hell to grow old. You lose your friends; they are dying away; you're alone; there's nobody to talk to and you haven't any good friends."[25]

On 7 January 1955 Duff celebrated his ninetieth birthday. A photo taken of him at the time shows a rather bird-like man with grey hair and Van Dyke beard. The eyes are piercing and unwavering. He had a happy day. The Queen telegraphed; the Prime Minister congratulated him; there was a deluge of calls and cables from former colleagues, and neighbours whom he hardly knew called to wish him well. Even George Drew, mellowing, sent a warm message. No sooner did the day end, however, than he began to fail. It was as if he had striven to reach his ninety-first year without yielding, but having scaled the height he let down his guard, and age conquered the citadel. His appetite diminished; he spent more time in bed. Still, he read as voraciously as ever. His doctor diagnosed incurable kidney failure. He could remain home while practicable, but he would eventually have to go to hospital to die.

One day Campbell phoned Annie to say that he was bringing Sir Lyman "oysters and some refreshment," knowing Duff's liking for the mollusc. He did not tell Annie until his arrival that the "refreshment" was champagne. Learning of the feast prepared for him, Duff got out of bed and the two friends went into the library where they devoured the succulent oysters and drank the excellent champagne. Not since Annie came to Ottawa had spirits been served openly in the house. On this occasion she knew and understood.

Not long afterwards Duff went into the Ottawa Civic Hospital. Once there, he began to lose interest in reading, an ominous symptom to those who knew him. One day Campbell asked him if he would like a drink. Duff said he would, but worried about what his physician — Dr. S.F. Service, a brother of the Yukon poet — would say. Campbell smuggled in a gin and grapefruit juice which Duff drank with gusto, telling him, "That's pretty good, Campbell."[26]

Very few people visited Duff during his last days. His closest friends — Ritchie, Biggar, Tilley, Geoffrion — were all gone. One close friend still living, W.D. Herridge, did come. Many knew he was dying, but it is often awkward for the living to visit those soon to die. Annie could not endure the ordeal of calling on him; she had the family trait of abhorring the sight of illness. Campbell went daily. And he was called on by Archdeacon Hepburn of All Saints' Anglican Church in the Sandy Hills district of Ottawa, which Duff had supported financially for many years, though he attended infrequently. At the conclusion of one visit, Hepburn, after a prayer, said, "God bless you, Sir Lyman." To which Duff replied, "And God bless you too, padre."[27]

Ten days before Duff died, Mr. Justice Rand told Campbell that he would like to see him. A bit awkward at the prospect of visiting a dying judicial deity, Rand asked Campbell what he did when he was with Duff. Campbell said that he smoothed his hair, sat down, held his hand, and talked to him. Rand did the same. Duff, who had enormous respect for Rand's abilities, clutched his hand, telling him, "Rand, you are my friend." Greatly moved, Rand could say nothing.[28]

As he knowingly approached death, Duff worried about Annie; he had only his house and a few dollars besides. Campbell promised him that he would look after Annie by buying the Clemow Street house at its proper value, turning the money over to her, and ensuring that she could live in it rent-free for the rest of her life. Those arrangements were completed before Duff's death.

In the last few days of his life, Duff stopped reading, a sure sign of the approaching end. He suffered the discomfort of a catheter, but no real pain. At eight o'clock in the evening of 25 April 1955, he lapsed into unconsciousness. About one o'clock the next morning, Chief Justice Sir Lyman Poore Duff died, peacefully.

News of his death brought widespread expressions of tribute and regret from the monarch on down to her humblest subjects. Duff might have valued three tributes above all others. In the Privy Council on 27 April, Lord Radcliffe, together with Lord Somervell and Mr. L.M.D. de Silva, were hearing an appeal from west Africa. Phineas Quass and Dingle Foot were opposing counsel. Before the proceedings started, Radcliffe, who had just that morning read Duff's obituary in *The Times*, had this to say:

> Mr. Quass and Mr. Dingle Foot, before this case is called on you would have noted in the morning paper news of the death of Sir Lyman Duff, formerly a Chief Justice of Canada, and for many years a distinguished member of this Board.…It is in the nature of things and the passage of time that there can be few, if any, members of this present Board who can claim to have sat as his colleagues, but the nature of his character and of his attainments is familiar to all of us who took any part in the work of the Board during the years when he sat, to all who are interested in the administration of the work of the Judicial Committee.

He brought to his work a singular richness of gifts, his great knowledge of the law of Canada and its various Provinces, and of the Constitutional Law of Canada of which, both in form and in spirit, he was an acknowledged master, and the hearing of the diverse appeals in which he assisted, from all the various territories and systems of law which come under our notice here, he contributed by common consent a grasp of legal principle a true learning of the law and mature experience that was, we all know of great assistance to the work of this Board.

On this day, when we get the news of his death, we would like to place on record, as I know you would, on behalf of the Bar, our sense of the loss that has been sustained by the legal systems of the Commonwealth in the death of a great lawyer.[29]

Word of Duff's death reached the Supreme Court of Canada in the midst of an appeal in which all involved, lawyers and judges, conscious of the solemnity of speaking in tribute to Canada's greatest jurist, expressed their sadness. But the third tribute might have touched Duff most of all. For more than twenty years he had patronized the Red Line taxi firm; he had been its best customer during all that time, spending, even during the depression years, perhaps a hundred and fifty dollars a month, and taking at least four journeys a day. The proprietor, Omer Lahulle, "and the Red Line Boys" sent Annie their "heartfelt understanding." Duff would not, however, have been pleased with the obituary in the *Globe and Mail* which reminded its readers of his role in the Hong Kong inquiry: "This inquiry, like others he was called upon to conduct, involved him in political controversy which he no doubt regretted; and which to some extent shadowed an otherwise illustrious life."[30]

Annie Duff wished her brother's funeral to be held in his house. She and Campbell collaborated on the arrangements. There were to be no active pallbearers, but many honorary ones: the prime minister, Chief Justice Kerwin and the other judges of the court, Frank Hughes, W.D. Herridge, Grattan O'Leary, Francis Hardy, the parliamentary librarian, Dr. Service to whom Duff had become devoted, and W.K. Campbell. The day before the funeral, the members of the Dinner Club came to the house as a group to pay tribute to their deceased "symposiarch."

Duff's embalmed body lay at Annie's request in an open casket in his library. The house was far too small to accommodate all the people who attended the service, and many of them stood outside on the lawn in the sunshine, listening through the open windows. Padre Hepburn read the Anglican Service for the Burial of the Dead. There were no hymns; there was no eulogy. After the service Duff's body was carried to Beechwood Cemetery to be laid beside Lizzie. Annie could not bring herself to attend the interment, staying at home to grieve. She lived for another ten years, to be buried beside her brother and his wife.

# Epilogue

Duff practised law and served as a judge during the period in which Canada completed its transition from colonial status to full nationhood. In 1903, he had acted as one of its lawyers at the Alaska boundary tribunal before which Canada was merely a pawn in a power play between Great Britain and the United States; the Canadian government had virtually no influence on the course of events and what little it might have had was undermined by Laurier. In 1939, Duff as chief justice of Canada had upheld the authority of the Canadian government to abolish appeals to the Privy Council from any court in Canada. The Duff who in 1903 had been a colonial counsel lived to become a national judge who conferred on Canada a wholly indigenous court system, surely a distinctive badge of nationhood.

Simultaneously with its odyssey from colony to nation, Canada changed from an essentially rural society to a modern industrial state, a trend reflected in decisions of the Supreme Court of Canada during Duff's tenure. Increased commercial activity produced the multitude of cases between 1908 and 1916 in which the court sought to define the scope of business activities of companies incorporated in the provinces and those incorporated under Dominion legislation. Decisions of the courts developed an approach which allowed companies incorporated in both jurisdictions to carry on business. The increase in commercial activity was also reflected in cases involving patents and trademarks between competing business enterprises, and cases in commercial law generally increased throughout the period.

The flight from the countryside — the growth of the cities — is reflected in the increase of lawsuits involving the automobile rather than the railway and, in the field of criminal law, cases of violent crime and fraud. Greater industrial activity fostered the establishment of workmen's compensation boards to supplant courts in the adjudication of industrial mishaps. And perhaps most striking of all, the increase in the nation's wealth was manifested in the succession-duty and income-tax cases which, after the Great War, came to the Supreme Court with increasing frequency.

Duff had a hand in all these developments. So, of course did his fellow judges, but the fact is that lawyers today looking for guidance from cases decided in the Duff era pay far more attention to his pronouncements than they do to those of his colleagues. The reason lies in his strength and, conversely, in their weakness.

There is no question that in the early and middle stages of Duff's service, the Supreme Court was mainly a collection of mediocrities. Duff himself thought so. He had no respect for Fitzpatrick, Davies, Brodeur, Smith, Malouin, Maclennan, Crocket, Mignault — all of them judicial and jurisprudential nonentities. Except for constitutional ones, however, the types of cases that came to the court until about the nineteen-thirties did not call for much intellectual ability. Surveying cases before World War I and, indeed, until the late twenties, one is struck by the utter triviality of a great many of them. Gradually, as legislation changed, limiting the right of appeal to cases involving more significant issues, demands on the judges increased, and by the time Duff retired in 1944, the calibre of the court was far higher than any with which he had previously been associated.

Throughout Duff's entire career on it, the Supreme Court was not the court of last resort; appeals in certain instances, depending on the nature of the litigation and the amount of money involved, could be taken to the Judicial Committee of the Privy Council in London. Virtually every important case involving the Canadian constitution went to London for a ruling. As an active member of the Judicial Committee for twenty-seven years, Duff sat on several of these appeals and, in one of them, delivered the judgement in what has become a leading case. The Supreme Court in Duff's time lay in the shadow of the Privy Council, but Duff's membership of both bodies, and the commanding reputation he won in England, undoubtedly lightened that shadow. Only in a handful of appeals did the Privy Council overrule him on a constitutional issue, and seldom in other types of cases.

The subservient position of the Supreme Court had implications for the quality of men appointed to its ranks. Politicans could appoint loyal friends and repay political debts without risking too much damage to the legal fabric of the country. Those who wished appeals to continue — the retentionists — always cited the weakness of the Canadian courts to justify the continued role of the Privy Council. Abolitionists argued that the Canadian courts could not be strengthened until appeals were abolished. But which was to happen first? Abolish appeals when the judiciary was weak, or wait until the courts in Canada grew stronger, an unlikely event so long as the Privy Council retained its ascendancy? Altering his views of the twenties, Duff cut the Gordian knot in 1940 by holding that appeals could be abolished, partly because he sensed that developing nationhood demanded he do so and partly because the increasing sophistication of the country was producing judges of higher intellectual calibre. When King was considering the replacement for Davies in 1924, he remarked on the weakness of all the courts in Canada. W.N.

Tilley, alive to the same weakness, saw that Duff's appointment as chief justice would markedly strengthen the judiciary and pave the way for the eventual abolition of appeals to London.

Because Duff was surrounded by mediocrity for most of his time on the court, it may be thought that he himself was not the dominating figure he is commonly believed to be, and that although he stood above his fellows, his own stature must be measured by the small scale of theirs. To put it another way, it may be argued that he was a small hill on a level plain. His judgements, however, belie this notion. More cogently, perhaps, his international reputation belies it: Lord Haldane, Lord Hailsham, Lord Simon, Lord Atkin, Roscoe Pound, and Felix Frankfurter all spoke of Duff as one whose learning was equal, if not superior, to theirs. The collective opinion of these judicial giants is unarguable: Duff did stand apart from his contemporaries, a colossus by comparison.

Because the amount of money and the nature of the dispute governed the court docket, appeals to it in Duff's time originated in an episodic and haphazard fashion. Judges were obliged to hear appeals as they were presented. They could decide in what order cases would be argued, but they could not pick and choose the appeals they would hear. (Today the court, with a few exceptions, can and does determine its own docket, limiting appeals to those which have national significance.) It should not be surprising to learn, therefore, that no pattern emerges from the decisions of the court during Duff's time on it except in constitutional and, perhaps, criminal cases. The judges did not assemble to discuss the legal condition of the country, the social climate, the state of the economy, or the relations between English- and French-speaking citizens, with a view to shaping future events by developing trends in particular fields of law, or to remedy perceived needs, or reverse undesirable trends. They did not consciously render decisions to respond to social conditions or further their philosophical beliefs. Nor did they do so unconsciously, because there is no evidence that any of Duff's colleagues was innovative or, to use the current term, activist. Not even Duff was an original thinker, and although perhaps in the Social Credit cases from Alberta and in the *Adoption* case he shows some sign of originality, he remains essentially a talented student and exponent of the law, not a creator of it.

The truth of these assertions can be found in the myriad decisions of the Supreme Court, but those cases relating to what we now refer to as civil rights cases afford good examples. His decision in the *Saskatchewan* case upholding provincial legislation forbidding the employment of white women by Chinese, his decision upholding the validity of orders-in-council forbidding the employment of Japanese on Crown lands in British Columbia, his decision in the *Bedard* case, the forerunner of the Padlock Law in Quebec, his decision supporting the right of restauranteurs to refuse service to blacks, his decision in the Japanese deportation case — none of these can endear him to civil liberties groups today. Yet it would be wrong to think on their basis that Duff was unconcerned about the rights of citizens and, more particularly, the rights of Oriental citizens. In 1919, in the case of a Chinese set free on a habeas corpus order, the Crown tried to appeal but was met by Duff's objection that the Supreme Court Act then in force did not clearly sanction an appeal. To permit one in the absence of specific language authorizing it would, he said, "amount to a sudden reversal of the policy of centuries in regard to the summary determination of the right of personal freedom and...such a reversal of policy ought not to be inferred from general language which, having regard to the context, was reasonably open to another view as to its effect."[1] Duff could not pen a simple ringing declaration that the liberty of citizens was not to be taken away by vague language, but in spite of his laboured words, he can be seen as a bulwark against assaults on their liberties.

To him and his fellow judges, the phrase "civil rights" meant the words used in section 92 (13) of the British North America Act which gave the provinces the power to legislate for "property and civil rights"; it did not mean freedom from oppression or discrimination. Duff and his colleagues were no different in that respect from most of their fellow citizens. They lived before the era of human rights commissions, and must not be judged by the changed values of a later generation.

It is not a question, then, of whether Duff was a good or bad man, or judge. In cases involving non-whites he was not racially discriminatory as that term would now be understood. In those cases, as indeed in all types of cases presented to him, he simply expounded the law impartially as he believed it to be; if Orientals or blacks were affected or householders barred from their homes, these were not his direct concerns.

A more innovative or activist judge might have been able, however, to reach opposite decisions in the same firm belief that he was expounding existing law and not creating it. Such a judge was I.C. Rand, from the Maritimes, appointed to the court in 1943, whose career as a lawyer had been concerned mainly with Government-regulated enterprises such as railways, grain elevators, and shipping. He had argued many cases in Duff's court, and Duff wrote to congratulate him on his appointment. Rand thanked him for his "generous message," telling Duff it was "like the sign of approval from the great teacher to the humble disciple," and that "my highest aspiration has been to sit on a court presided over by you." There is a certain conventionality in these utterances, true, yet Rand was no sycophant but a man of strong intellect like Duff: their mutual respect did credit to both of them. Unfortunately, they served only eight months together on the court. Legal scholars frequently speculate on the influence they might have worked on one another had the overlap been longer.

One might have expected from a man with Rand's background a dry, technocratic approach to the solution of legal problems, yet he brought soul to the court. He was not radical, but feeling. His decisions in the landmark cases from Quebec in the Duplessis era affirmed the ascendancy of law over arbitrary actions of government. Duff, by then retired, hailed them from afar. Did Duff, perhaps wistfully, applaud Rand's decisions as the kind he himself might have rendered, given more judicial boldness?

Although Duff often spoke of the importance of the rule of law and its beneficent influence on society, he was really a judicial technocrat, not a judge of broad sweep and vision. A judgement he delivered three years after joining the Supreme Court of Canada gives an excellent illustration of the conservatism of his judicial approach, a trait which remained with him all his days:

> Hardship is not necessarily attended by injustice; the truth is, that a failure to comply with the statutory conditions of statutory rights often results as do other kinds of improvidence in individual loss; but when such lapses give rise to litigation (and they are a considerable source of the litigation arising out of the administration of the laws governing the acquisition of rights of various kinds of the public lands) judicial efforts to mitigate the seeming hardship of particular cases by departing from settled paths rarely fails to lead to general confusion and in the end I think not seldom to injustice.[2]

Duff was not prepared to yield to the temptation of curing an apparent injustice at the expense of strict interpretation of the law. One gets a close, concentrated analysis of the legal problem at hand and the application to it of all relevant principles deduced from earlier decided cases, but no eloquent expression of judicial fervour.

He had a remarkable capacity to identify and grasp an issue quickly, a skill that came variously from acuteness of mind, wide knowledge in virtually every field of law, and wide reading in fields outside the law. When confronted with new legal problems, lawyers and judges frequently become instant experts on obscure subjects only to lose their expertise after the case ends. Duff's eclectic reading enabled him to remain expert long after the conclusion of a particular case. His influence sprang from two main sources: first, his immense knowledge of the law and leading cases in different jurisdictions and countries and, secondly, the sheer length of his service on the Supreme Court — nearly thirty-eight years. If one adds to that period the two years spent on the Supreme Court of British Columbia, Duff worked as a judge for nearly forty; few judges in the common-law countries could match that record.

His numerous judgements give no hint of the inner man. None of his knowledge of history and literature seeped into them. It is as if he had set up a barrier between the literary-humanist side of his nature and the legalistic. Knowing no more of him than what could be deduced from reading those judgements, technically flawless though they may be, one would not want to meet him at a social gathering. Yet he was a most convivial companion; he was not pompous; he could talk vivaciously and intelligently for hours on all sorts of subjects unrelated to the law. On these occasions he spoke animatedly, but was always well poised, forcefully yet gracefully giving utterance to his thoughts. A resonant voice added lustre to the orderly and grammatical language.

The contrast between appearance and reality in so many of Duff's actions makes it difficult to find his mainspring. He professed to have drunk from the river Lethe, but could be importuned by a prime minister seeking a return for favours conferred. He professed to be impartial, but he could not always submerge his political loyalties. On the public platform he described the law as a living social instrument,yet in the courtroom he was a judicial conservative. The public image of sobriety is belied, until 1933, by the reality of alcoholism. The awesome person in the courtroom cannot be the warm, charming man chatting with counsel and visitors in his chambers. The man who unless among intimates or friends of like spirit finds it difficult to converse easily can talk comfortably to taxi drivers, doormen at hotels, and waiters in restaurants and clubs. With all his forensic experience, he found it difficult to speak freely to large gatherings; he was sexually impotent, yet remained faithfully married in a loveless match which ripened towards its end; he was hopelessly improvident, yet constantly called on in court to settle the financial problems of others.

To chronicle the contradictions is to wonder whether in his case the appearance was reality. Perhaps all that needs to be said is that he was a human being wracked by inner torments, without displaying them, who left a mark on the judicial history of Canada that has yet to be matched.

# Sources

PUBLIC DOCUMENTS AND RECORDS

*Alberta Statutes*, 1922 et seq.

British Columbia, *Journals of the Legislative Assembly of the Province of British Columbia*, session 1903–04, vol. XXXIII.

Canada, *Claim of the British Ship I'm Alone — Brief Submitted on Behalf of His Majesty's Government in Canada in Respect of the British Ship I'm Alone Under the Provisions of Article IV of the Convention concluded the 23rd of January 1924 between His Majesty and the United States of America*. Ottawa: King's Printer, 1933.

*Claim of the British Ship I'm Alone — Statement with Regard to the Claims for Compensation submitted by the Canadian Agent pursuant to Directions given by the Commissioners dated the 30th of June, 1933*. Ottawa: King's Printer, 1933.

Department of External Affairs file #152–AS, RG 33 16 (PAC).

Department of External Affairs file AR414/5/3, RG 25 A–12, vol. 2115 (PAC).

Department of Justice file #142360 (PAC).

Department of Justice Registers for the War years, RG 13 (PAC).

Great Britain, *Further Correspondence Relating to Article 12 of the Articles of Agreement for a Treaty Between Great Britain and Ireland, C.M.D. 1560*. London: His Majesty's Stationery Office, 1924.

*Hansard*, House of Commons, 1914 et seq.

*Hansard*, Senate, 1909 et seq.

"Machin Report," *Report of the Director of the Military Services Branch to the Hon. the Minister of Justice on the Operation of the Military Service Act, 1917*. Ottawa: King's Printer, 1919.

*Manual for the Information and Guidance of Tribunals in Consideration and Review of Claims for Exemption*. Ottawa: King's Printer, 1918.

Minutes of the Cabinet War Committee, July 1941 — June 1942, RG 2-7(c), reels C 4654 and C 4874 (PAC).

Miscellaneous Inspectors Reports and Correspondence, 1870–1908, RG 2, Ontario Archives, Toronto.

Ontario, County Board of Education Records, 1850–1910, RG 2, Ontario Archives, Toronto.

Proceedings (transcripts, exhibits, memoranda, notes and arguments of counsel) of Royal Commission on Canadian Expeditionary Force to Hong Kong RG 33/120 (PAC).

*Report of the Military Service Council on the Administration of the Military Service Act, 1917.* Ottawa: King's Printer, 1918.

*Report of the Royal Commission to Inquire into and Investigate into and Report upon Certain Contracts made by the Committee known as the Shell Committee and upon such other matters relating to the acts or proceedings of the said Shell Committee as may be referred to the said Commission by Order-in-Council from time to time.* Borden Papers, MG 26H (PAC).

*Report on the Canadian Expeditionary Force to the Crown Colony of Hong Kong.* Ottawa: King's Printer, 1942.

*Report of the Royal Commission to Inquire into Railways and Transportation in Canada,* 1931–32. Ottawa: King's Printer, 1932.

*Report to Dr. Woodhouse, Department of Pensions and National Health,* December 9, 1935. Duff Papers (PAC).

*Revised Instructions for Dealing with Deserters and Absentees without Leave.* Ottawa: King's Printer, 1918.

*Sessional papers,* House of Commons, 1918–20.

*Statutes of Canada,* 1906 et seq. Ottawa: Queen's (King's) Printer.

*Statutes of British Columbia* (S.B.C.), 1890 et seq. Victoria: Queen's (King's) Printer.

United States, *Hearing on the Claim of the British Ship I'm Alone,* George W. Reik Shorthand Reporter, Washington, D.C., December 28, 1934. Duff Papers (PAC).

*Claim in respect of the Ship I'm Alone — Documentary Evidence and Affidavits Submitted by the Agent for the United States.* Washington: U.S. Government Printing Office, 1935.

Upper Canada, Law Society of, *Journal of Proceedings of the Convocation of Benchers of the Law Society of Upper Canada, Hilary Term 1879 to Michaelmas Term 1891,* vol. 1; *Journal of Proceedings of the Convocation of Benchers of the Law Society of Upper Canada, Michaelmas Term 1891 to Michaelmas Term 1896,* vol. II.

Victoria Land Titles Office, Deed AFB 20-259/7010-C and CB 14-761/4340-D. Victoria, British Columbia.

UNPUBLISHED SOURCES

Minutes of the Board of Governors and Senate of the University of Toronto 1901–02 to 1940–49. University of Toronto Archives, Toronto.

Privy Council Judgment Registers. Privy Council Office, Downing Street, London.

Proceedings of the Supreme Court of Canada, No. 5477, Jan.–Feb., 1930, Ottawa.

Rolls of the Law Society of Upper Canada, Osgoode Hall, Toronto.

Proceedings, Church Union Commission, Church Union Collection, vol. 2, Notes, Papers and Transcripts. United Church of Canada Archives, Toronto.

University of Toronto Class and Prize Lists, 1852, 1861, 1862, 1887. University of Toronto Archives, Toronto.

Bennett, R.B., Papers. University of New Brunswick, Fredericton.

Bennett, R.B., Papers. MG 26K, microfilm reels seriatim, PAC.

Biggar, O.M. Papers MG 30 E 85, PAC.

Bird, Henry, family Bible, in possession of the family.

Borden, Robert, Diaries, 1916, 1917, 1919; MG 26 H, PAC.

Dafoe, J.W., Papers. MG 30 D 45, PAC.

Dexter, Grant, Papers. Queen's University Archives, Kingston, Ontario.

Drew, George, Papers. MG 32 C 3, PAC.

Duff, Sir Lyman Poore, Papers. MG 30 E 141, PAC.

Farris, J.W. deB., Papers. University of British Columbia Special Collections, Vancouver.

Fitzpatrick, Charles, Papers. MG 27 II C 1, PAC.

Flavelle, Joseph, Papers. MG 30 A 16, PAC; Papers, Queen's University Archives, Kingston, Ontario.

Frankfurter, Felix, Papers. Container 92, Library of Congress, Washington.

Gouin, Sir Lomer, Papers. MG 27 III B-4, PAC.

Grant, Fred, Scrapbooks. Barrie Public Library, Barrie, Ontario.

Haldane, Lord, Papers. MS 6001–6006, National Library of Scotland, Edinburgh.

King, William Lyon Mackenzie, Diaries and Papers. MG 26 "J" Series, PAC.

Lang, Robert J., "Annals of Liverpool and Queen's County, 1760–1867." Perkins House, Liverpool, Nova Scotia.

Lapointe, Ernest, Papers. MG 27 III B 10, PAC.

Laurier, Wilfrid, Papers. MG 26 G, H, J, PAC.

Meighen, Arthur, Papers. MG 26 I, PAC.

Pope, Joseph, Papers. MG 30 E 86, PAC.

Power, C.G., Papers. Queen's University Archives, Collection 2150, Kingston, Ontario.

Sifton, Clifford, Papers. MG 27 II D 15, PAC.

St. Laurent, Louis, Papers. MG 26 L, PAC.

Walkington, Douglas, "The Congregational Churches of Canada: A statistical and Historical Summary," 1979. United Church Archives, Toronto.

PUBLISHED SOURCES

*The Calender of the University of Toronto and University College, 1887–1888.* Toronto: Henry Rowsell, 1887.

"Ceremony at Supreme Court Building — Unveiling of a Portrait Bust of the Rt. Hon. Sir Lyman Poore Duff, P.C., G.C.M.G., LL.D.," in *Proceedings of Canadian Bar Association*, vol. 30 (1947), 69.

"Farewell Ceremony for Sir Lyman Poore Duff, G.C.M.G." in *Canadian Bar Review*, vol. 22. Toronto: The Carswell Company Limited, 1944.

*The Canadian Congregational Year Book, 1903–04*. Toronto: Congregational Publishing Co., 1904.

*The Canadian Independent*. United Church Archives, Toronto.

*The History of Speedside Church, 1845–1945*, Fergus, Ontario: *The News Record*, 1945.

*University of Toronto Class and Prize Lists, 1888*. Toronto: Rowsell and Hutchison, 1888.

*Who's Who in Canada*. Toronto: International Press Ltd., 1913 et seq.

*Who's Who and Why*. Toronto: International Press Ltd., 1913 et seq.


Armstrong, Elizabeth, *The Crisis of Quebec, 1914–18*. Toronto: McClelland and Stewart, 1974.

Bliss, Michael, *A Canadian Millionaire: The Life and Business Times of Sir Joseph Flavelle, Bart., 1858–1939*. Toronto: Macmillan, 1978.

Borden, Henry, ed., *Robert Laird Borden: His Memoirs*. Toronto: Macmillan, 1938, 2 vols.

Brown, G.P., *The Judicial Committee and the British North America Act*. Toronto: University of Toronto Press, 1967.

Byerly, A.E., *Fergus*. Elora, Ontario: Elora Express, 1932–34.

Cairns, Alan C., "The Judicial Committee and its Critics," in *Canadian Journal of Political Science* (1971) vol. IV, 3.

Campbell, A.E., *Great Britain and the United States, 1895–1903*. London: Longmans, 1960.

Campbell, Charles S., Jr., *Anglo-American Understanding, 1898–1903*. Baltimore: The Johns Hopkins Press, 1957.

Campbell, W. Kenneth, "The Right Honourable Sir Lyman Poore Duff, P.C., G.C.M.G.: The Man As I Knew Him," in *Osgoode Hall Law Journal* (1974) vol. 12, No. 2.

Cook, Ramsay, *The Dafoe-Sifton Correspondence, 1919–1927*. Altona, Man.: D.W. Friesen and Sons, Ltd., 1966.

Dafoe, John Wesley, *Clifford Sifton in Relation to His Times*. Toronto: Macmillan, 1931.

Dawson, R. MacGregor, *William Lyon Mackenzie King: A Political Biography*. Toronto: University of Toronto Press, 1958.

Dennett, Tyler, *John Hay — From Poetry to Politics*. New York: Dodd, Mead, 1934.

Dickson, Hon. Brian, "The Role and Function of Judges," in *The Law Society of Upper Canada Gazette*, July, 1980.

Duff, Lyman Poore, "British Columbia: A Retrospective," in *Canadian Bar Review* (1938) vol. 16.

———. "The Common-law Judge and Lawyer," in *Canadian Bar Review* (1933) vol. 11.

———. "Privy Council," in *Canadian Bar Review* (1925) vol. 3.

English, John, *The Decline of Politics: The Conservatives and the Party System, 1901–20*. Toronto: University of Toronto Press, 1977.

Friedmann, W., "Judges, Politics and the Law," in *Canadian Bar Review*, October, 1951.

Gardner, Melbourne M., *History of Pilgrim United Church*, Brooklyn, Queen's County, Nova Scotia. Dayspring, N.S., 1961.

Garraty, John A., *Henry Cabot Lodge: A Biography*. New York: Knopf, 1953.

Gosse, Richard, "The Four Courts of Sir Lyman Duff," in *Canadian Bar Review* (1975) vol. 53.

Graham, Roger, *Arthur Meighen*. Ottawa: Canadian Historical Association, 1965, No. 16.

Granatstein, J.L., *Mackenzie King: His Life and World*. Toronto: McGraw-Hill Ryerson, 1977.

———. and Hitsman, J.M., *Broken Promises: A History of Conscription in Canada*. Toronto: Oxford University Press, 1977.

Henderson, L.G., *Henderson's British Columbia Directory and Street Index*. Victoria and Vancouver: Henderson Publishing Co., 1895, 1899 and 1900.

Hodgins, J. George, *Documentary History of Education in Upper Canada from the passing of the Constitutional Act of 1791 to the Close of Rev. Dr. Ryerson's Administration of the Education Department, 1876*. Toronto: Warwick Bros. & Rutter Printers, 1894–1910, 28 vols.

Hogg, Peter W., *Constitutional Law of Canada*. Toronto: The Carswell Company Limited, 1977.

Honsberger, John D., Q.C., ed., *Law Society of Upper Canada, 1797–1972*. Toronto: Law Society of Upper Canada, 1972.

James, Norman B., *The Autobiography of a Nobody*. Toronto: Dent, 1947.

Jennings, Ivor W., "Constitutional Interpretation, the Experience of Canada," in *Harvard Law Review*, vol. 51, 1937.

Jessup, Philip C., *Elihu Root*. New York: Dodd, Mead, 1938.

Johnson, L.P.V., and MacNutt, Ola J., *Aberhart of Alberta*. Edmonton: Institute of Applied Art, 1970.

Langton, H.H., ed., *The University of Toronto and Its Colleges, 1827–1906*. The University Library: published by the Librarian, 1906.

Laskin, Bora, "The Supreme Court of Canada: The Final Court of and for Canadians," in *Canadian Bar Review* (1951) vol. 29

Le Dain, Gerald., Q.C., "Sir Lyman Duff and the Constitution," in *Osgoode Hall Law Journal* (1974) vol. 12, No. 2.

LeSueur, William Dawson, *William Lyon Mackenzie: A Reinterpretation*. Toronto: Macmillan, The Carleton Library, 1979.

Lowe, A.V. and Young, J.R., "An Executive Attempt to Re-Write A Judgement," in *Law Quarterly Review* (1978) vol. 94.

McConnell, W.H., "The Judicial Review of Prime Minister Bennett's 'New Deal,'" in *Osgoode Hall Law Journal* (1968) vol. 6.

McDonald, Vincent C., "The Privy Council and the Canadian Constitution," in *Canadian Bar Review* (1951) vol. 29.

MacKinnon, Frank, "The Establishment of the Supreme Court of Canada," in *The Canadian Historical Review* (1946) vol. 27.

MacMillan, Lord, "The Writing of Judgments," in *Canadian Bar Review* (1948) vol. 26.

Mallory, J.R., "Federal Overthrow of Social Credit Legislation," in *Social Credit and the Federal Power in Canada*. Toronto: University of Toronto Press, 1954.

"Maltby Report": Supplement to the London *Gazette*, 29 January 1948.

Marsh, D'Arcy, *The Tragedy of Henry Thornton*. Toronto: Macmillan, 1935.

Medland, Harvey, *Minerva's Diary, A History of Jarvis Collegiate Institute*. Belleville, Ontario: Mika Publishing, 1979.

Neatby, H. Blair, *William Lyon Mackenzie King*. Toronto: University of Toronto Press, 1976.

Newman, Peter C., *Bronfman Dynasty: The Rothschilds of the New World*. Toronto: McClelland and Stewart, 1978.

O'Leary, Grattan, *Recollections of People, Press and Politics*. Toronto: Macmillan, 1977.

———. "Rt. Hon. Sir Lyman Poore Duff, G.C.M.G.," in *Canadian Bar Review* (1955) vol. 33.

Parsell, H. & Co., *Historical Atlas of Waterloo and Wellington Counties, Ontario*. Toronto: Walker and Miles, 1881–1887.

Penlington, Norman, *The Alaska Boundary Dispute: A Critical Reappraisal*. Toronto: McGraw-Hill Ryerson, 1972.

Pickersgill, J.W., *The Mackenzie King Record, vol. I, 1939–1944*. The University of Chicago Press and The University of Toronto Press, 1960.

———. and Forster, D.F., *The Mackenzie King Record, vol. 4, 1947–1948*. Toronto: University of Toronto Press, 1970.

Pierce, Lorne, ed., *The Chronicle of a Century, 1829–1929, the record of one hundred years of progress in the publishing concerns of the Methodist, Presbyterian and Congregational Churches in Canada*. Toronto: Ryerson Press, 1929.

Pope, Maurice, ed., *Public Servant: The Memoirs of Sir Joseph Pope*. Toronto: Oxford University Press, 1960.

Pound, Roscoe, "The Theory of Judicial Decision," reprinted in *Canadian Bar Review* (1924) vol. 2.

Rand, I.C., Hon., "Rt. Hon. Sir Lyman Poore Duff, G.C.M.G.," in *Canadian Bar Review* (1955) vol. 33.

Reksten, Terry, *Rattenbury*. Victoria: Sono Nis, 1978.

Rinfret, Rt. Hon. Thibodeau, "Sir Lyman Duff," in *University of British Columbia Legal Notes* (1955) vol. II, No. 4.

Robertson, J. Ross, *Robertson's Landmarks of Toronto — A Collection of Historical Sketches of the Old Town of York from 1792 until 1937, and of Toronto from 1834 to 1904*. Toronto: J. Ross Robertson, 1904.

Schultz, Harold J., "Portrait of a Premier: William Aberhart," in *Politics of Discontent*. Toronto: University of Toronto Press, 1967.

Stacey, Charles P., *Six Years of War, volume I of the Official History of the Canadian Army in the Second World War*. Ottawa: Queen's Printer, 1955.

Tansill, Charles Callan, *Canadian-American Relations, 1875–1911*. Toronto: Ryerson Press, 1943.

Thomson, Dale C., *Louis St. Laurent: Canadian*. Toronto: Macmillan, 1963.

Wallace, W. Stewart, *A History of the University of Toronto 1827–1927*. Toronto: The University of Toronto Press, 1927.

———. *The Macmillan Dictionary of Canadian Biography*. London: Macmillan, 1963.

Walsh, H.H., *The Christian Church in Canada*. Toronto: Ryerson Press, 1956.

Weir, E. Austin, *The Struggle for National Broadcasting in Canada*. Toronto: McClelland and Stewart, 1965.

Wright, Lord of Durley, "Rt. Hon. Sir Lyman Poore Duff, G.C.M.G.," in *Canadian Bar Review* (1955) vol. 33.

LEGAL REPORTS AND PUBLICATIONS

*Appeal Cases* (A.C.) The Incorporated Council of Law Reporting, London, 1875 et. seq.

*British Columbia Reports* (B.C.R.) Burroughs and Co., a division of Carswell Company Limited et al., 1897 et. seq.

*Canadian Bar Review*, The Carswell Company Limited, vol. I et. seq.

*Supreme Court Reports* (S.C.R.) Ottawa, Queen's Printer, 1907 et. seq.

*The Supreme Court Rules 1890*. Queen's Printer, Victoria.

# Notes

CHAPTER ONE

1. H.H. Walsh, *The Christian Church of Canada*, 221
2. Toronto *Globe*, 7 January 1905
3. Sarah Duff to Ann Duff, in possession of C. Kent Duff
4. *Canadian Independent*, f-58
5. Ibid., f-68
6. Ibid., f-71
7. Ibid., 1868, vol. XIV
8. Ibid.
9. In 1940, Duff was acting as Administrator of Canada following the death of Lord Tweedsmuir, the Governor-General, an event which got extensive newspaper coverage. A Mrs. Carrie McLeod wrote him from Winthrop, Massachusetts.

   To the Governor-General of Canada

   Congratulations on the appointment of your new position!
   Do you remember the red-haired boy Harvey McLeod, who sat on the same old wooden bench in the village school at Brooklyn?
   He often desired to have you know his kindly interest in your advancement since leaving school...
   I, after due consideration, became the wife of that red-haired boy.

   She told Duff that she had cut his picture from a newspaper, going on to comment, "This noble man I remember & his dear father I loved and admired."

   If Duff replied to this charming letter, which was written by the daughter-in-law of the man who allegedly cured his illness with a cup of rum, he did not keep a copy. (Duff Papers, vol. III)
10. Duff Papers, I, Duff to Douglas Alexander, 25 March 1878
11. J. George Hodgins, *Documentary History of Education in Upper Canada...*, XXV, 96.
12. Ibid., XXIII, 83
13. Ibid.
14. In one of the numerous letters that Duff, when famous, received from people soliciting his help in an endless variety of ways, a former classmate at Speedside reminded him of their school days, and how the two boys used to hoe turnips on a nearby farm. Duff had been employed on the farm for two weeks in the summer of 1878. The writer concluded by asking Duff to intercede with the department of Immigration in some matter; Duff did write to the department.
15. *Canadian Independent*, 1875, XXIII, 246
16. Miscellaneous Inspectors' Reports...1870–1908. Fergus, 1878
17. Duff Papers, I, Duff to Alexander, 9 February 1877
18. Ibid., 19 March 1877
19. Ibid., December (n.d.) 1878
20. Ibid., 15 July 1879
21. Ibid., 28 June 1880
22. St. Catharines *Daily News*, 26 February 1881
23. Ibid., 30 April 1881
24. Duff Papers, I, Duff to Alexander, 3 April 1881

CHAPTER TWO

1. There is no doubt that he attended the institute: an engaging history of the school attests to the fact. On 29 September 1922 Duff was a guest at what was described as "the largest school reunion in Canadian history," a gala event which attracted seven hundred persons to celebrate the laying of the cornerstone for a new school building. As a "graduate" of Jarvis Collegiate Institute, Duff was invited to give the toast to "Our School." It was not the type of ceremony Duff would normally have enjoyed, but he accepted nonetheless. Except for one or two relatively small reunions of university classes, he never attended another one like it. He may have been induced to attend by his close friendship with two other graduates, Angus MacMurchy, a well-known lawyer in Toronto, and Sir Henry Drayton, politician and railway commissioner, who was one of those asked to respond to Duff's toast.
2. Toronto *Globe*, 7 January 1905
3. Liverpool, N.S. *Transcript*, 5 April 1867
4. Toronto *Globe*, 22 November 1881
5. *Varsity*, 25 November 1881
6. Ibid., 2 December 1881
7. Duff Papers, III, Thomas Marshall to Duff, 10 January 1944
8. Ibid., I, Duff to Alexander, 27 December 1881
9. Ibid.
10. Ibid.
11. G.G. Langton, ed., *The University of Toronto and its Colleges 1827-1906*, 84
12. Annie Duff to Richard Gosse, 17 March 1964, in the latter's possession
13. A. Bruce Robertson to Richard Gosse, 2 August 1963, in the latter's possession
14. Fred Grant Scrapbooks. Barrie Public Library, Barrie, Ontario
15. Barrie *Northern Advance*, 30 April 1885
16. Ibid., 5 November 1885
17. University of Toronto Class and Prize List, 1887
18. *Varsity*, 11 February 1888
19. John D. Honsberger, *Law Society of Upper Canada 1797-1972*, 44
20. Fergus *News Record*, 23 November 1893
21. Annie Duff in conversation with Richard Gosse

CHAPTER THREE

1. He was well remembered by his colleagues of the club: "What a good speaker you were and how keen you were in the debates! I can still see your eager face. There has never been another political Club in Toronto equal to that one. There was no subject that we were afraid to tackle. It is remarkable how many Chief Justices it has produced — Gordon Hunter, Horace Harvey, Macdonald (the present Chief Justice of British Columbia) and now yourself." (Duff papers, XI, W.D. Gregory to Duff, March 1933)
2. Quoted in A.E. Byerly, *Fergus*
3. Duff Papers, I, Duff to Ernest Burns, 28 December 1938
4. *Canadian Bar Review*, XVI, 527
5. Duff Papers, XVII, Belle Armstrong to Duff, 19 December 1894
6. Ibid., 3 January 1895
7. Ibid.
8. Ibid., 8 July 1895
9. In 1896 Belle married Alexander Fasken, who later became prominent in legal and business circles in Toronto where he founded a law firm which still bears his name. He died in 1944, she in 1957. Those who remember Belle describe her as a handsome, gracious woman, utterly devoted to her husband. There is no indication that she and Lyman ever met again.
10. Duff Papers, VI, Annie Duff to Duff, circa 1895
11. Senator J.W. deB. Farris in conversation with Richard Gosse
12. Donald Lawson in conversation with Richard Gosse
13. Madden v The Nelson and Fort Shepherd Railway Co. (1897) 5 B.C.R. 585
14. Section 92(1), B.N.A. Act
15. Laurier Papers, 14841-2, Lyman Duff to Laurier, 17 May 1897
16. Victoria *Daily Colonist*, 3 November 1897
17. Ibid., 16 February 1898
18. Henry Bird Family Bible
19. Barrie *Examiner*, 7 July 1898

20. H.I. Bird in conversation with Richard Gosse
21. Stevenson in conversation with Richard Gosse
22. Marjorie Carnsew in conversation with Richard Gosse
23. Ibid.
24. H.I. Bird in conversation with Richard Gosse

25. Marjorie Carnsew in conversation with Richard Gosse
26. Senator J.W. deB. Farris in conversation with Richard Gosse
27. Henry Angus in conversation with Richard Gosse

CHAPTER FOUR

1. S.B.C. 1897 c.56
2. Victoria *Daily Colonist*, 13 December 1898
3. Stoddart v. Prentice (1897–99) 6 B.C.R. 309
4. Victoria *Daily Colonist*, 16 December 1898
5. Ibid., 22 December 1898
6. S.B.C. 1899 c.20
7. Victoria *Daily Colonist*, 12 November 1898
8. Ibid., 11 October 1898
9. Victoria *Daily Times*, 11 October 1898
10. Wensky v. Canadian Development Co. (1901) 8 B.C.R. 190
11. Gill v. Ellis (1898) 6 B.C.R. 197; Green v. Stussi (1898) 6 B.C.R. 193
12. Victoria *Daily Colonist*, 8 June 1899
13. Ibid., 17 May 1899
14. Ibid., 3 May 1899
15. Ibid., 21 December 1900

16. Vancouver *World*, 10 June 1899
17. Victoria *Daily Colonist*, 5 May 1900
18. Ibid., 23 August 1900
19. Ibid., 24 October 1900
20. Ibid., 28 October 1900
21. Ibid., 26 October 1900
22. Rossland *Record*, 24 July 1900; 23–24 October 1900; Victoria *Daily Colonist*, 4 August 1900
23. Henderson's *British Columbia Directory and Street Index*, 1900
24. See, e.g., Reksten, *Rattenbury*
25. Land Titles Office, Victoria, Deed AFB 20-259/7010-C
26. Ibid., CB 15-761/4340-D
27. Henderson's *British Columbia Directory and Street Index*, 1899
28. Ibid., 1895

CHAPTER FIVE

1. Victoria *Daily Colonist*, 8 February 1902
2. Ibid., 8 May 1902
3. Ibid., 2 June 1903
4. Quoted in Tansill, *Canadian-American Relations 1875–1911*, 127
5. Dennett, *John Hay — From Poetry to Politics*, 224
6. It was precisely evidence of that nature — uncontested maps drawn by public officials — that determined the decision in the Deadman's Island case.
7. Charles Campbell, *Anglo-American Understanding 1898–1903*, 326
8. Norman Penlington, *The Alaska Boundary Dispute: A Critical Reappraisal*, 88
9. Clifford Sifton Papers, 151, 120946
10. Laurier Papers, 791G, 225798
11. Sifton Papers, 275, 120993-4
12. Ibid., 140, 111861-3
13. Tansill, 159

14. A photograph recorded the event. Years later, Duff, on running across a copy of it, wrote Geoffrion: "Poor Wade, like yourself and myself, he does not give evidence of a particularly amiable mood. Perhaps we were all impatient for the bar to open." (Duff Papers, II, Duff to Geoffrion, circa 1935)
15. London *Times*, 9 October 1903
16. Roosevelt correspondence quoted in Philip C. Jessup, *Elihu Root*, 397
17. Quoted in Penlington, 95
18. *Canadian Bar Review* (1938) XVI, 526
19. Jessup, 397
20. Campbell, 336
21. London *Times*, 14 October 1903
22. Ibid.
23. Maurice Pope, *Public Servant: The Memoirs of Sir Joseph Pope*, 298
24. Duff Papers, II, Geoffrion to Duff, 5 March 1929

25. Victoria *Daily Colonist*, 14 November 1903
26. Ibid., 5 February 1904
27. *Journals of the Legislative Assembly of the Province of British Columbia*, Session 1903–1904, XXXIII

## CHAPTER SIX

1. Duff Papers, XI, Sen. G.H. Barnard to Duff, 18 March 1933
2. Victoria *Daily Colonist*, 16 October 1903
3. Laurier Papers, 294, 79 and 907-8
4. Laurier Papers, 303, 81904-6
5. Ibid., 81907
6. Ibid., 304, 82249-50
7. Vancouver *Daily Province*, 26 February 1904
8. Ibid., 29 September 1904
9. Sifton Papers, 174, 141404-09
10. *Canadian Bar Review*, 16, 526
11. Downie v. Vancouver Engineering Works Ltd. (1904) 10 B.C.R. p. 367
12. Re Gray (1918) 57 S.C.R. 150

13. Re Sea (1905) 11 B.C.R. 324
14. Scott v. Fernie (1904) B.C.R. 91
15. Wexler v. The King (1939) S.C.R. 350
16. Rex v. Kay (1904) 11 B.C.R. 157
17. Gach v. The King (1943) S.C.R. 250; Boudreau v. The King (1949) S.C.R. 262
18. Vancouver *Daily Province*, 22 May 1937
19. Duff Papers, IX, Duff to A.M. Johnson, 29 December 1918. On another occasion, early in 1904, Duff received a money order which he apparently mislaid. His former partner found it in Victoria in 1908 and sent it to Duff, who never cashed it. It may still be seen among his papers (vol. xv)

## CHAPTER SEVEN

1. Laurier Papers, 264, 73052, Bodwell to Laurier, 19 May 1903
2. Ibid., 75053
3. Ibid., 242, 113203
4. Duff Papers, II, Duff to Ghent Davis, 6 April 1940
5. Victoria *Daily Colonist*, 11 October 1906
6. These pews figured in a remarkable episode. A well-known Montreal criminal lawyer appeared before Duff and his colleagues to argue what proved to be a losing case. By the time of adjournment for lunch, the lawyer realized which way the wind was blowing, but instead of bowing to it, he went to his hotel and drank too much liquor. On his return to the courtroom in an alcoholic haze, he became uncontrollably voluble and abusive. When Duff threatened to call the constable to have him taken into custody for contempt of court, the lawyer flung down his papers, jumped from his seat, and ran from the courtroom by hurdling the pews, hardly touching them in his headlong flight. Duff, a few days later, generously wrote the man inviting him to appear before the court to apologize, on which the episode would be utterly forgotten. The lawyer did not reply, nor did he ever appear in the court again.

(In re M.B. Singer, 5 October 1943; W.K. Campbell in conversation with the author)
7. Mr. Justice W.Z. Estey in conversation with the author
8. (1906) 37 S.C.R. 676
9. (1907) 38 S.C.R. 198
10. Duff Papers, I, W.B. Common to Duff, 16, 20 December 1938
11. LaLiberté v. LaRue (1931) S.C.R. 13
12. *Proceedings*, Supreme Court of Canada, 8 February 1928
13. *Canadian Bar Review* (1934) 12, 417
14. St. Catherine's Milling and Lumber Co. v. R. (1888) 14 A.C. p.46
15. Province of Ontario v. Dominion of Canada (1909) 42 S.C.R. 1
16. Burrard Power Co. v. The King (1909) 43 S.C.R. 27
17. Marks v. Marks (1908) 40 S.C.R. 210; The King v. Proud (1924) S.C.R. 599
18. Montreal West v. Hough (1931) S.C.R. 113
19. Quon-Wing v. The King (1914) 49 S.C.R. 440; Union Colliery v. Bryden (1899) A.C. 580
20. Sydney Post Publishing Co. v. Kendall (1909) 43 S.C.R. 461
21. Woolmington v. D.P.P. (1935) A.C. 462
22. Girvin v. The King (1912) 45 S.C.R. 167

23. Gilbert v. The King (1907) 38 S.C.R. 284

24. Eberts v. The King (1912) 47 S.C.R. 1

25. Morang & Co. v. Le Sueur (1912) 45 S.C.R. 95

26. Undated letter, Duff to Lord Haldane, 1925, prob. February; copy in author's possession

27. In 1945, King again played the role of literary censor. In that year, an author, Elizabeth Smart wrote a novel about a love affair between a young woman and an older married man. Her father, a prominent Ottawa lawyer, learning of its publication outside Canada and believing the novel to be more autobiographical than fictional, asked King to intervene with the customs officials to prevent the book from coming into Canada. King obliged him; the book stayed out. It was recently distributed in Canada.

28. King Diaries, 11 February 1940

29. King Papers, 13, 12706-8

30. Borden Diaries, 24, 8529-31

31. In re: Marriage Laws (1912) 46 S.C.R. 132

32. (1907) 39 S.C.R. 405

33. *Statutes of Canada*, 50–51 Vict. c.50, s.1

34. British Coal Corporation v. The King (1935) A.C. 500

35. Naden v. R. (1926) A.C. 482

36. Colonial Building and Investment Association v. Attorney General of Quebec (1883) 9 A.C. 157

37. (1913) 48 S.C.R. 208

38. Attorney General of Canada v. Attorney General (Alberta) (1916) 1 A.C. 588

39. In Re: Companies (1913) 48 S.C.R. 331

40. John Deere Plow Co. v. Wharton (1915) A.C. 330

41. Bonanza Creek Gold Mining v. The King (1916) 1 A.C. 566

42. In Re: Companies (1916) A.C. 598

43. Victoria *Daily Times*, 15 January 1907

44. Laurier Papers, undated letter to Laurier, 1-3 January 1908, 134486

45. Senate, 11 March 1909

46. Laurier Papers, 6 April 1909, 154955. The "mutual friend" could have been either Duff or Templeman.

47. Duff papers, I

## CHAPTER EIGHT

1. Borden Diaries, 28 March 1916

2. Ibid., 29 March 1916; Borden Papers, 337, 1267-8

3. Borden Diaries, 29 March 1916

4. Ibid., 30 March 1916

5. Borden Papers, 337, notes 1916, sec. 2, 232-3

6. Ottawa *Evening Journal*, 31 May 1916

7. Borden Papers, 62, 31507, Hugh Clark to Borden

8. Borden Diaries, 1 January 1917

9. R.S.C. 1906, c.139, s.7, and c.138, s.33

10. *Revised Statutes of Ontario*, 1914, c.57

11. Borden Papers, 363, 40497-501, Reid to Borden

12. Borden Diaries, 16 June 1917

13. J.W. Dafoe, *Clifford Sifton in Relation to His Times*, 425; Borden Diaries, 5 July 1917

14. Borden Diaries, 10 August 1917

15. Ibid., 11 August 1917

16. See, e.g., John English, *The Decline of Politics: The Conservatives and the Party System 1901-20*

17. Borden Papers, 78, Part I, File 0C362, p.40375, undated letter Duff to Borden, prob. 29 August

18. Ibid., 40376

19. Borden Diaries, 31 August 1917

20. Ibid., 1 September 1917

21. Ibid., 3 September 1917

22. Ibid., 6 September 1917

23. Grant Dexter Papers, Folder T-28, 1943-44

24. Machin Report, 10

25. Military Service Act Manual, 1917, 5

26. Machin Report, 5

27. Duff Papers, undated letter Duff to Lord Haldane, 1925, prob. February; copy in author's possession

28. House of Commons, 5 April 1918

29. Ibid.

30. Machin Report, 26

31. Laurier Papers, Reel C917, Item 200.399-401, Item 200. 756

32. Re Gray (1918) 57 S.C.R. 150

33. The Charter of Rights enacted in 1981 would not prevent a future government from invoking the same provision, unless first the War Measures Act itself is changed or repealed, or a future Supreme Court of Canada overrules the *Gray* case

34. Duff Papers, II, Duff to Viscount Greenwood, 6 April 1940

35. Grant Dexter Papers, Correspondence July–December 1941; 22 December 1941 memorandum

CHAPTER NINE

1. Dominion Fire Insurance v. Nakata (1916) 52 S.C.R. 294
2. Local Union No. 562 U.M.W. v. Williams (1919) 59 S.C.R. 240
3. Vandry et al. v. Quebec Railway (1916) 53 S.C.R. 72
4. Johnson v. LaFlamme (1916) 54 S.C.R. 495
5. Borden Diaries, 30 October 1918
6. Duff Papers, XI
7. Lord Strathcona Steamship Company Limited v. The Dominion Coal Company Limited (1925) A.C. 603, Privy Council Judgment Register 1925
8. Fort Frances Pulp & Power Company Limited v. Manitoba Free Press (1923) A.C. 695; Haldane Papers, ms 6006, letter to mother, 27 June 1923
9. A.G.B.C. v. C.P.R. (1927) S.C.R. 184, (1927) A.C. 934; the Hon. J.L. Farris in conversation with the author
10. J.W. DeB. Farris in conversation with Richard Gosse
11. Haldane Papers, ms 6002; letters to mother, 14 July, 1 August, 2 August 1919
12. Ibid., ms 6005, 6 July 1922
13. Ibid., 26 and 30 June 1922
14. United States of America v. Motor Trucks (1924) A.C. 196; Haldane papers, ms 6006, letter to mother, 11 July 1923
15. Duff Papers, XI, W.P.M. Kennedy to Duff, 18 March 1933
16. Haldane papers, ms 6004, letters to mother, 9 July and 2 August 1921; ms 6006, 11 July 1923
17. In re Insurance Reference (1913) 48 S.C.R. 260
18. Attorney General of Canada v. Attorney General of Alberta (1916) 1 A.C. 588, 597
19. (1913) 48 S.C.R. 311
20. In re Board of Commerce (1920) 60 S.C.R. 456
21. In re Board of Commerce (1922) 1 A.C. 191
22. (1923) A.C. 695
23. Bora Laskin to I.C. Rand, 3 April 1962, letter in the author's possession
24. In re Board of Commerce (1920) 60 S.C.R. 456
25. (1924) A.C. 328
26. Duff Papers, X, Duff to Neish, 24 November 1923
27. Ibid., Duff to Haldane, 20 December 1923
28. Ibid.
29. Clark v. The King (1920) 61 S.C.R. 608; Smythe v. The King (1941) S.C.R. 717
30. Ross v. Dunstall (1921) 62 S.C.R. 393
31. In re The Chief Justice of Alberta (1922) 64 S.C.R. 135
32. Canada Law Book Company v. Boston Book Company (1922) 64 S.C.R. 183; Duff Papers, I, Cromarty-Duff correspondence 1923, 1924, 1925
33. C.P.R. v. Ouellette, (1924) S.C.R. 426. This case, incidentally, offers a good example of Idington's style of writing judgements which stands in sharp contrast to Duff's. In short, staccato paragraphs, he fired verbal bullets as if from an automatic weapon. After pointing out that common knowledge as well as the legislation itself "tells us they [the tender and engine] are separate," he went on:

   "When parties are driven to such arguments and no better, it makes it rather hard, I must respectfully submit, to understand why leave to appeal was granted.

   "That evidently was given because of it being urged that the judgment would impose serious loss upon all railways in Canada.

   "Just imagine a serious loss arising from being forced to carry the tender in its proper place instead of putting it in the reverse order of things!

   "I prefer the interpretation of any statute which will tend to avoid the sacrifice of human life, even if some careless employee is put to a little trouble.

   "I am of the opinion that this appeal should be dismissed with costs."
34. Union Colliery v. Bryden (1899) A.C. 580
35. Attorney General of British Columbia v. Brooks-Bidlake & Whittal Limited (1922) 63 S.C.R. 466; (1923) A.C. 450
36. Re Employment of Aliens (1922) 63 S.C.R. 293, (1924) A.C. 203
37. (1936) S.C.R. 461
38. Bedard v. Dawson (1923) S.C.R. 681
39. Saumur v. City of Quebec (1953) 2 S.C.R. 299; Switzman v. Ebling (1957) S.C.R. 285
40. Duff Papers, IV, Roscoe Pound to Duff, 16 October 1923
41. Ibid., Duff to Pound, 25 January 1924
42. Ibid., Duff to Beale, 25 January 1924
43. Ibid., Duff to Pound, 25 January 1924

44. Frankfurter to Richard Gosse, 10 January 1964, letter in Gosse's possession; Frankfurter to I.C. Rand, 31 January 1956, Container 92, Frankfurter Papers, Library of Congress
45. Duff Papers, III, Duff to Frankfurter, 27 March 1936
46. London *Times*, 29 July 1921
47. Duff Papers, XIV, J.E. Bird to Lizzie Duff, 8 August 1920
48. Ibid., 14 October 1920
49. Ibid., IV, Duff to Proctor, 15 September 1920
50. B.M. Cocks to Richard Gosse, 28 August 1963, letter in author's possession
51. Duff Papers, II, Duff to D.W. Douthwaite, 4 June 1924
52. Haldane Papers, ms 6007, letter to his mother, 20 July 1924
53. One should perhaps not pay too much attention to remarks made by lawyers and judges at gatherings of this nature where laudatory speeches are frequently made. But what Lord Atkin said of Duff is worthy of remark because he need not have said it. Although Atkin overruled Duff in the Labour Conventions case, he respected his judicial talents. At the dinner, Atkin commented that in compiling a catalogue of distinguished jurists, one should include Chief Justice Marshall of the United States, Coke, Oliver Wendell Holmes, and "the name of Duff" (*Journal of the Canadian Bar Association* (1924) 34) Fulsome praise perhaps, but, considering the source, noteworthy.
54. Duff Papers, I, Duff to E.H. Coleman, 20 September 1924
55. MacDonald to Liam Maccosgair, 26 June 1924, reprinted in *Further Correspondence Relating to Article 12 of the Articles of Agreement for A Treaty Between Great Britain and Ireland*, C.M.D. 1560
56. Ibid., 2 June 1924
57. *Saturday Night*, 8 June 1924
58. Duff Papers, X, Haldane to Duff, 28 September 1924

## CHAPTER TEN

1. King Papers, 96, 81835-6, Aylesworth to King, 1 May 1924
2. King Diaries, 1 May 1924
3. King Papers, 96, 81595-6, Aikins to King
4. King Diaries, 5 May 1924
5. King Papers, 102, 86521, King to Lafleur, 8 September 1924
6. Ibid., 86522a, Lafleur to King
7. King Diaries, 15 September 1924
8. Ibid., 12 September 1924
9. W.K. Campbell in conversation with the author, July 1979
10. Duff Papers, I, Bennett to Duff, 8 February 1924
11. Ibid., VII, Emma Duff to Duff, 15 October 1927
12. Ibid., II, Dunn to Duff, 21 December 1922
13. King Diaries, 4 May 1924
14. King Papers, 103, 87345, Larkin to King, 29 August 1924
15. In conversation with Richard Gosse, 1962
16. Sir Brian McKenna in conversation with the author, November 1980
17. W.K. Campbell in conversation with the author, July 1979
18. Ibid.
19. Duff Papers, IV, Travers Sweatman to Duff, 26 September 1924; J.W. deB. Farris in conversation with Richard Gosse
20. Gouin Papers, 27, Cannon to Gouin, 14 December 1923
21. Duff to Haldane, 1925 (prob. February), copy in the author's possesion
22. King Diaries, 15 March 1933
23. Ibid., 30 March 1933
24. Ibid., 10 February 1940
25. Ibid., 6 January 1944
26. Duff Papers, II, Duff to Ferguson, 20 September 1924
27. King Diaries, 11 February 1940
28. Bennett Papers, reel M1048, 208142-5, memorandum minister of justice, 7 October 1932. King was not altogether accurate in referring to Duff's lack of "side," for Duff could be a stickler for protocol on occasion. As Administrator, he arranged a reception in Quebec City for Lord Tweedsmuir on his arrival as the newly appointed Governor-General. Chief Justice Greenshields of Quebec wrote Duff to wangle an invitation to the party. Duff replied rather punctiliously that the only people living outside Quebec City to be invited (Greenshields lived in Montreal) were those directly connected with the welcoming ceremony. Since Greenshields did not qualify, he could not go to the reception. (Duff Papers, II, Duff to Greenshields, October 1935)

29. Duff to Haldane, 1925 (prob. February), copy in the author's possession
30. W.K. Campbell in conversation with the author, July 1979
31. Duff Papers, XV
32. Anderson v. The King (1925) S.C.R. 45. Davis, incidentally, told Duff some years later he had been so incensed at King's treatment of him that he changed his politics from Liberal to Conservative
33. Smith v. The Minister of Finance (1925) S.C.R. 405, (1927) A.C. p.193
34. The Attorney General of Alberta et al. v. C.P.R. (1925) S.C.R. 155
35. Re Hours of Labour (1925) S.C.R. 505
36. Toronto Electric Commissioners v. Snider (1925) A.C. 396
37. House of Commons, 12 February 1925
38. Duff to Maclean, February 1925, in the author's possession
39. (1981) 1 S.C.R. 753
40. House of Commons, 12, 18 and 19 February 1925
41. Duff to Haldane, 1925 (prob. February), copy in the author's possession. The reference to "Ferguson" is to Mr. Justice Ferguson, who sat as a member of the Court of Appeal and formed part of the majority in declaring the Industrial Disputes Investigation Act valid. The case to which Duff refers is Gold Seal Limited v. Alberta (1921) 62 S.C.R. 424
42. Duff Papers, I, Duff to T.A. Crerar, 19 November 1941
43. Ibid., memo Christie to Duff, 31 December 1937; letter 18 March 1938
44. Lord's Day Alliance v. Attorney General of Manitoba (1925) A.C. 384
45. The King v. Price Brothers (1926) S.C.R. 29
46. Duff Papers, I, Cromarty to Duff, 24 March 1926
47. Ottawa *Journal*, 9 July 1926
48. Duff Papers, VII, Rolph Duff to Emma Duff, 13 July 1926
49. Hume Wrong Papers, Stevenson to Wrong, 1 August 1926
50. Duff Papers, XIV, J.E. Bird to Duff, 26 July 1926
51. Ibid., VI, Kathleen Black to Duff, 3 September 1927

## CHAPTER ELEVEN

1. *Statutes of Canada*, 1924, c.100
2. Duff Papers, X, R.S. Cassels to Duff, 26 May 1927
3. *Proceedings*, Church Union Commission, 2, Box 10
4. Lorne Pierce ed., *The Chronicle of a Century 1829-1929*
5. N.W. Rowell to W.N. Tilley, 1926, undated (prob. 30 June). United Church Archives, Church Union Coll., 2, Box 13
6. Duff Papers, X, Clay to Duff, 27 June 1927
7. Ibid., undated memorandum
8. Trustees of Saint Luke's Presbyterian Congregation v. Cameron (1930) A.C. 673
9. (1930) S.C.R. 344, 630
10. Duff Papers, X, Haldane to Duff, 28 July 1926
11. Privy Council Judgement Register, 1926
12. Bennett Papers, reel M3175, 599270, Hailsham to Bennett, 21 April 1932
13. Gray Campbell in conversation with the author, 1980
14. Ottawa *Evening Journal*, 28 January, 1 February, and 3 February 1930
15. Newman, *The Bronfman Dynasty*, 119-20
16. In Re Bronfman, Supreme Court of Canada proceedings No. 5477, January–February 1930
17. Duff Papers, III, Duff to Thomas Mulvey, 8 January 1931
18. Bennett Papers, reel M1048, 208126, Dr. Edward Archibald to R.B. Bennett
19. Duff Papers, I, Archibald to Duff, 4 April 1937
20. Ibid., II, XV
21. Ibid., XIV, Duff to Bird, 28 April 1928
22. W.K. Campbell in conversation with the author, 1979
23. Phil Dugas to the author, 30 November 1979
24. Walker v. McDermott (1931) S.C.R. 94
25. MacAskill v. The King (1931) S.C.R. 330
26. In re Board of Commerce (1922) 1 A.C. 191
27. Re Regulation and Control of Aeronautics in Canada (1932) A.C. 54
28. Lord Esher in Beresford-Hope v. Sandhurst 23 Q.B.D. 79, 95
29. Reference Re Meaning of Word "Persons" in s.24 of the B.N.A. Act (1928) S.C.R. 276
30. Canadian Bar Association *Report* 1915, 56
31. Ottawa *Evening Journal*, 25 April 1928

32. Ibid., 30 March 1928
33. Edwards v. Attorney General of Canada (1930) A.C. 124
34. O.M. Biggar Papers, I, Duff to Biggar, 23 April 1945

35. Duff Papers, III, Duff to Dafoe, 26 January 1924
36. Toronto *Daily Star*, 26 April 1955
37. 19 October 1929

## CHAPTER TWELVE

1. Duff Papers, XI, Beatty to Duff, 20 March 1933
2. Order-in-council 2910, 20 November 1931
3. Duff Papers, IX, Duff to Mulock, 9 January 1932
4. Winnipeg *Free Press*, 5 December 1931
5. Ottawa *Evening Journal*, 1 April 1932
6. Dafoe Papers, 6, Stevenson to Dafoe, 25 April 1932
7. Winnipeg *Free Press*, 19 December 1931
8. Dafoe Papers, 5, Dafoe to John Stevenson, 9 December 1931
9. Ibid., Dafoe to H.J. Symington, 23 December 1931
10. Ibid., 6, Dafoe to Harry Sifton, 24 February 1932
11. Ibid., Dafoe to Dexter, 25 February 1932
12. Winnipeg *Free Press*, 15 February 1932
13. Dafoe Papers, 5, Dafoe to H.J. Symington, 23 December 1931
14. Ibid., 6, Dexter to Dafoe, 13 September 1932
15. Transportation Commission *Report*, 1932
16. Duff Papers, IX, "The Way Out," a second address on the Canadian Railway situation by E.W. Beatty, K.C., LL.D. delivered before the Canadian Club, Winnipeg, 8 February 1933
17. Canadian National-Canadian Pacific Act, *Statutes of Canada*, 1933, c.33
18. King Diaries, 1 March 1933
19. Canadian National-Canadian Pacific Act, *Statutes of Canada*, 1936, c.25
20. *Statutes of Canada*, 1955, c.29, and 1966–67, c.69

21. Dafoe Papers, 6, Dexter to Dafoe, 16 October 1932
22. Bennett Papers, reel M1079, 251855-6, Annie Duff to Bennett, October 1932
23. Ibid., 251857, Bennett to Annie Duff, 17 October 1932
24. Ibid., reel M3175, 598299-300, Annie Duff to Bennett, 19 October 1932
25. Duff Papers, VII, Emma to Annie Duff, 25 October, 16 November 1934
26. W.K. Campbell in conversation with the author, July 1979
27. R.B. Bennett Papers, University of New Brunswick; notable persons file, Drury to Finlayson (all letters dated 10 January 1933)
28. Duff Papers, II, Bennett to Duff, 17 March 1933
29. Bennett Papers, reel M3175, 598307-09, Duff to Bennett, 17 March 1933
30. W.K. Campbell in conversation with the author, July 1979
31. Duff Papers, XI, Borden to Duff, 1933 (prob. March)
32. Borden Papers, 269, 150933, Duff to Borden, 1933 (prob. March)
33. Duff Papers, XI, A.H. O'Brien to Duff, 20 March 1933
34. Ibid., VII, Emma to Annie, 11 and 14 September 1934
35. Ibid., 14 December 1934
36. Ibid., VIII, Duff to Martin, 31 December 1935

## CHAPTER THIRTEEN

1. Duff Papers, II, Duff to Lamont, 22 December 1934
2. W.K. Campbell in conversation with the author, July 1979
3. W.R. Jackett to the author, 10 January 1981
4. Hon. J.C. McRuer in conversation with the author, October 1981

5. Canada Permanent Mortgage v. Cheese (1942) S.C.R. 291; W.K. Campbell in conversation with the author, July 1979
6. R.A. Rich to the author, October 1979
7. J.J. Robinette to the author, January 1981
8. Duff Papers, II, Davis to Duff, 9 December 1935

9. Thiffault v. The King (1933) S.C.R. 509
10. DeLaurier v. Jackson (1934) S.C.R. 149
11. Baker and Sowash v. The King, 37 B.C.R. 1 (1926) S.C.R. 92
12. Dunphy v. Croft (1931) S.C.R. 531
13. One should observe that the precise problem in the case would no longer arise since the passage of the Statute of Westminster in 1931, two years after Mr. Dunphy's liquor-vending voyage. The British and Canadian diplomats responsible for its enactment had him and others like him clearly in mind, for section 3 expressly gave to Canada "full power to make laws having extra-territorial operation."
14. Croft v. Dunphy (1933) A.C. 156
15. A.V. Lowe and J.R. Young, "An Executive Attempt..." in *Law Quarterly Review* (1978) 94, 255
16. Ibid.
17. Randall, when in the merchant service, had visited the principal Caribbean ports many times, and being the skipper of a rum-runner did not discourage him from keeping up his social contacts. Thus, he kept on board the vessel an array of clothing: six mess jackets, eleven white uniforms, dinner jacket, opera hat and cape, and a dozen pair of shoes. His personal accoutrements would have done justice to a captain of a Cunard liner. When asked at the hearings why he kept so many personal effects, he said that he had been accustomed to entertaining and being entertained at various colonies in the Caribbean: "I knew the highest people in these colonial places, and had been a guest, and also of the Governor, and knowing that all of these people had been at one time or another my guests, and that I would not be classed as the captain of a rum-runner, but would hold the same social status in the colonies as before." (Duff Papers, VIII.) He convinced Duff and Van Devanter that a

man of his standing required an extensive wardrobe, because they recommended $7,900 compensation for its loss.
18. Duff Papers, VIII
19. Randall impressed Pepper as a completely honest man. Pepper's cross-examination of Randall reveals as much of the lawyer as it does of the captain. The former was also an honest and decent man who never once, in his cross-examination of Randall, questioned his personal integrity or professional competence. The two men, the rum-runner skipper and the eminent lawyer, chatted with each other as one professional to another. In its written submissions the U.S. Government had quarrelled with Randall's calculation of his position when first sighted and with his evidence of the speed of the *I'm Alone*, but not Pepper. In his concluding question put to Randall, Pepper said, "You have done exactly, sir, as an honest man should do, and I am very obliged to you." Randall, impressed (perhaps relieved) by Pepper's unfailing courtesy, replied, "Thank you sir. I appreciate that."
20. One claim might have caught Duff's attention. The Canadian government claimed, on behalf of Randall and the shipping company, an account of over twenty-seven thousand dollars in legal fees paid to Lazarus Phillips, a well-known Montreal lawyer who had acted both for Randall and the company following the sinking. Phillips, Duff would have recalled, had also been involved in the Bronfman case in 1930. However, in their recommendations neither Duff nor Van Devanter thought that the United States Government should pay his legal bill.
21. Duff papers, VIII, Duff to Martin, 31 December 1935
22. *New York Times*, 10 January 1935
23. Ibid.

CHAPTER FOURTEEN

1. Duff Papers, VII, Emma to Annie, 12 July 1934
2. Ibid., 13 November 1934
3. Ibid., XV, Toronto *Mail and Empire*, 2 April 1935
4. Ibid., VII, C. Wilson to Annie Duff, 2 April 1935
5. Ibid., II, Duff to Davis, 6 December 1935
6. Mason v. The King (1935) S.C.R. 513
7. King Diaries, 23 October 1935
8. Ibid.
9. Ibid., 4 April 1940
10. (1936) S.C.R. 363 (1937) A.C. 368
11. (1936) S.C.R. 379 (1937) A.C. 405
12. Re Employment of Japanese (1924) A.C. 203

13. (1925), S.C.R. 505
14. (1932) A.C. 304
15. (1936) S.C.R. 461
16. (1932) A.C. 326, 353
17. Lord Wright of Durley, "Rt. Hon. Sir Lyman Poore Duff, G.C.M.G.," in *Canadian Bar Review* (1955) 33, 1123
18. McConnell, *Osgoode Hall Law Journal* (1968), 39
19. (1936) S.C.R. 426 (1937) A.C. 355
20. (1936) S.C.R. 398 (1937) A.C. 377
21. (1937) S.C.R. 384 (1937) A.C. 391
22. Duff Papers, IV, Duff to Pound, 16 November 1935
23. Ibid., II, Duff to J.W. deB Farris, 23 May 1936
24. London *Times* 30 July 1936
25. The Seduction Act, *Revised Statutes of Alberta*, 1922, c.102, s.5
26. (1935) 1 W.W.R. 199 (1937) S.C.R. 318 (1940) A.C. 802
27. Duff Papers, III, Charles Millar to Duff, 3 October 1924
28. (1936) O.R. 554 (1937) O.R. 382 (1938) S.C.R. 1
29. Reference Re Alberta Statutes (1938) S.C.R. 106-7

30. The Alberta Social Credit Act, *Statutes of Alberta*, (1937) 1st sess. c.10, s.33
31. (1938) S.C.R. 110
32. N.B. James, *The Autobiography of a Nobody*, 222
33. Reference Re the Power of Disallowance (1938) S.C.R. 77
34. Ottawa *Evening Journal*, 10 January 1938
35. Ibid., 12 January 1938
36. Winnipeg *Free Press*, 14 January 1938
37. *Vancouver Sun*, 10 January 1938
38. Ottawa *Evening Journal*, 15 January 1938
39. (1938) S.C.R. 130
40. Ottawa *Evening Journal*, 13 January 1938
41. (1938) S.C.R. 133-5
42. (1939) A.C. 132
43. "The Adoption" Reference (1938) S.C.R. 398
44. Labour Relations Board of Saskatchewan v. John East Iron Works Ltd. (1948) A.C. 134
45. Vancouver *Daily Province*, 16 August 1938
46. Sir Lyman Duff, "British Columbia: A Retrospect," in *Canadian Bar Review* (1938) 16, 524
47. Lady Rosalind Hayes in conversation with the author, 1980
48. *Vancouver Sun*, 19 August 1938

CHAPTER FIFTEEN

1. Duff Papers, I, Beaudry to Duff, 18 March 1937
2. Ibid., Duff to Beaudry, 30 March 1937
3. (1939) S.C.R. 104
4. King Diaries, 9 March 1939
5. Ibid., 14 March 1939
6. W.K. Campbell in conversation with the author, 1980
7. An Act Respecting the Chief Justice of Canada, *Statutes of Canada*, 1939, c.14
8. House of Commons, 24 April 1939
9. Senate, 26 April 1939
10. Ibid.
11. Victoria *Daily Colonist*, 22 April 1939
12. Duff Papers, report to Dr. Woodhouse, department of Pensions and National Health, 9 December 1935
13. Duff Papers, III, Maclean to Duff, 22 April 1937, and Duff to MacLean, 23 April 1937
14. Memorandum, 1939 S.C.R. iii
15. Christie v. York (1940) S.C.R. 139
16. Frank MacKinnon, "The Establishment of the Supreme Court of Canada," in *The Canadian Historical Review*, (1946) 258

17. House of Commons, 20 January 1939
18. Ibid., 14 April 1939
19. L.P.A. Robichaud, House of Commons, 14 April 1939
20. House of Commons, 26 April and 8 May 1939
21. *Canadian Bar Review* (1925) 3, 273
22. Farris Papers, Duff to Farris, 4 June 1926. Special Collections, University of B.C.
23. W.K. Campbell in conversation with the author, July 1979
24. Reference Re Supreme Court Act (1940) S.C.R. 49
25. King Diaries, 24 August 1939
26. T.A. Gates to Duff, 29 July 1940, letter in the author's possession
27. David Lewis to the author, 29 July 1980
28. Duff to Lewis, 12 September 1940, copy in the author's possession
29. University of Pennsylvania Bureau of Publicity, Philadelphia, 20 September 1940
30. Drafts of speech, University of Pennsylvania, 20 September 1940, in the author's possession

31. Montreal *Gazette*, 21 September 1940
32. The *Pennsylvania Gazette*, 39, 1, October 1940
33. F.J. Dallett to the author, 30 June 1980
34. Duff to Gates, 5 October 1940, copy in the author's possession
35. Columbia University to the author, 25 July 1980
36. Butler to Duff, 3 February 1941, in the author's possession
37. Duff to Lapointe, 19 May 1941, Department of Justice file #142360
38. New York *Herald Tribune*, 3 June 1941
39. *New York Times*, 4 June 1941
40. Ibid.
41. Citation, Columbia University, 3 June 1941, in the author's possession
42. F.L. Pereira to C.H.B. Garland, 6 June 1941, copy in the author's possession

## CHAPTER SIXTEEN

1. Grassett to Richard Gosse, 15 May 1967, in the latter's possession
2. *Proceedings*, Hong Kong Royal Commission, ex. 1
3. Toronto *Globe and Mail*, 25 December 1941
4. King Diaries, 25 February 1948
5. Ibid.
6. Minutes of the Cabinet War Committee, 2 October 1941
7. Ibid.
8. House of Commons, 21 January 1942
9. King Diaries, 22 January 1942
10. Ibid., 4 February 1942
11. Duff Papers, II, Duff to Davis, 7 February 1942
12. King Diaries, 6 February 1942
13. Ibid., 9 February 1942
14. Toronto *Daily Star*, 27 October 1941
15. King Diaries, 6 February 1942
16. Ibid., 5 March 1942
17. Ibid., 12 February 1942
18. House of Commons, 27 July 1942
19. Order-in-council P.C. 1639, 2 March 1942, quoted in House of Commons, 15 July 1942
20. War Measures Act, *R.S.C.* 1927, c.206, s.3(a)
21. Order-in-council P.C. 1160, 1942, quoted in *Report* of Hong Kong Royal Commission
22. *Report*, Hong Kong Royal Commission, 14
23. Dept. of External Affairs, file AR 414/5/3 RG 25 A-12, 2115
24. *Proceedings*, Hong Kong Royal Commission, ex. 293
25. Ibid., ex. 45
26. Ibid., transcript of evidence, 1875
27. J.H. Price to C.G. Power, 13 September 1941. Directorate of History, III. 1009 (V-2 Papers re "C Force") received from Hon. C.G. Power in 1953; also 1 October 1941. Public Archives of Canada
28. King Diaries, 8 April 1942
29. Ibid., 4 June 1942
30. W.K. Campbell in conversation with the author, July 1979
31. *Proceedings*, Hong Kong Royal Commission, ex. 44
32. Ibid., ex. 45
33. Ibid., ex. 291
34. Toronto *Globe and Mail*, 6 June 1942
35. King Diaries, 12 June 1942
36. *Proceedings*, Hong Kong Royal Commission, (memoranda); Drew to King, 11 July 1942, copy in the author's possession
37. Ibid., ex. 138
38. Ibid., Lawson Report, 15 November 1941, ex. 51
39. *Proceedings*, Hong Kong Royal Commission, ex. 291
40. W.K. Campbell in conversation with the author, July 1979
41. King Diaries, 14 July 1942
42. House of Commons, 15 July 1942
43. Directorate of History III.13 (D66) Misc. Memo's, Hong Kong 1941–48
44. House of Commons, 27, 28 July 1942
45. Dafoe Papers, 13, MacDonnell to Dafoe, 29 July 1942
46. Ibid., Dafoe to MacDonnell, 31 July 1942
47. Winnipeg *Free Press*, 29 July 1942
48. Dafoe Papers, 13, Grant Dexter to Dafoe, 14 April 1942
49. David B. Goodman Memorial Lectures, reprinted in *The Gazette*, Law Society of Upper Canada, July 1980
50. Borden Papers, 75, 395402, Duff to Borden, 1 January 1917
51. House of Commons, 27 July 1942
52. Ibid.

## CHAPTER SEVENTEEN

1. Atlantic Smoke Shops v. Conlon (1941) S.C.R. 670; Re Debt Adjustment Act (1942) S.C.R. 31
2. Duff Papers, X
3. Duff Papers, XII, Landreville to Duff, 1 February 1918; Duff to Landreville, 9 March 1927
4. Duff Papers, II, Auguste Lemieux to Paul Leduc, 17 June 1941
5. Reference Re Ottawa, etc. (1943) S.C.R. 208
6. Duff Papers, I, Duff to Alexander, 14 February 1943
7. King Diaries, 9 July 1942
8. Ibid., 23 October 1942
9. Toronto *Daily Star*, 10 October 1942
10. King Diaries, 9 November 1942
11. Vancouver *Daily Province*, 4 January, 4 February 1943
12. King Diaries, 2 February 1943
13. House of Commons, 2 February 1943
14. Statutes of Canada, 1943, c.1
15. Bennett Papers, reel M3175, 598331, Bennett to Haig, 23 March 1943
16. Ibid., reel M3175, 498321-2, Bennett to Hanson, 4 February 1943
17. Ibid., reel M3175 598321, R.B. Hanson to Bennett, 5 February 1943
18. Ibid.
19. *Who's Who and Why* and *Who's Who in Canada*, seriatim
20. Duff Papers, I, Duff to Alexander, 14 February 1943
21. Mott v. Thrott (1943) S.C.R. 256
22. The Windsor Hotel Company v. Odell (1908) S.C.R. 336
23. Beatty v. the King (1944) S.C.R. 73
24. Department of Justice file 142360
25. Ibid.
26. Quoted in *Canadian Bar Review* (January 1944), 22, 4
27. Ibid., 6 et seq.
28. Duff Papers, Duff to Alexander, 22 December 1943
29. King Diaries, 6 January 1944
30. W.K. Campbell in conversation with the author, July 1979
31. King Papers, 359, King to Duff, 7 January 1944
32. Duff Papers, XI, H.M. George VI to Duff, 15 December 1943
33. W.K. Campbell in conversation with the author, July 1979
34. Ibid. He would, for example, occasionally be asked by fellow judges to campaign for higher salaries, but consistently refused to do so
35. W.K. Campbell in conversation with the author, May 1981
36. Sir Brian McKenna in conversation with the author, November 1980
37. A.B. Robertson to the author, January 1981; British Columbia Electric Railway Co. Ltd. v. The King (1946) A.C. 527
38. (1946) S.C.R. 248
39. W.K. Campbell in conversation with the author, July 1979
40. (1943) S.C.R. 1
41. (1947) A.C. 87
42. (1947) A.C. 127
43. King Diaries, 3 February 1948
44. House of Commons, 23 September 1949
45. An Act to Amend the Supreme Court Act, *Statutes of Canada*, 1949, c.37
46. Ponoka-Colmar Oils Ltd. v. Earl F. Wakefield Co. et al. (1960) A.C. 18

## CHAPTER EIGHTEEN

1. Directorate of History III. 13(D66) Misc. Memo's re Hong Kong 1941–8. Public Archives of Canada
2. King Diaries, 18 February 1948
3. House of Commons, 18 February 1948
4. Ibid., 20 February 1948
5. King Diaries, 23 February 1948
6. Ibid.
7. House of Commons, 24 February 1948
8. King Diaries, 9 March 1948
9. House of Commons, 10 March 1948
10. Ibid., 29 April 1948
11. King Diaries, 25 February 1948
12. Toronto *Globe and Mail*, 26 February 1948
13. House of Commons, 26 February 1948
14. Supplement to the *London Gazette*, 29 January 1948
15. House of Commons, 26 February 1948
16. King Diaries, 27 February 1948
17. Ibid., 1 March 1948
18. House of Commons, 2 March 1948
19. Ibid.

20. Ibid., 19 March 1948
21. Toronto *Globe and Mail*, 12 March 1948
22. King Diaries, 13 March 1948
23. Department of External Affairs File No. 152-As, Pickersgill to Robertson, 14 March 1948

24. Senate, 17 March 1948
25. King Diaries, 19 March 1948
26. House of Commons, 29 April 1948
27. J.W. Pickersgill in conversation with the author, October 1981

CHAPTER NINETEEN

1. Department of Justice, file 146766. Public Archives of Canada
2. Duff Papers, X
3. Minutes of the Board of Governors, 1925–26: University of Toronto Archives
4. Duff Papers, IV, John Stevenson to Duff, 20 March 1941
5. W.K. Campbell in conversation with the author, July 1979
6. Ibid.
7. Duff Papers, VI, Robertson to Annie Duff, April 1955. Perhaps the most famous "symposiarch" was Dr. Johnson to whom one of his biographers, Sir John Hawkins, applied the term, meaning "a person to preside in all conversations."
8. Dr. C.J. Mackenzie in conversation with the author, May 1979
9. Ibid.
10. King Diaries, 16 May 1940
11. Ibid., 14 February 1940
12. King Papers, 359, 311121-2
13. Duff Papers, III, King to Duff, 16 December 1946
14. Ibid., 16 December 1947
15. Ibid., 1 January 1949

16. Ibid.
17. Duff Papers, VI, St. Laurent to Annie Duff, April 1955
18. Duff Papers, VI, Duff to St. Laurent
19. Duff Papers, VII, Senator Wilson to Duff, 12 August 1953
20. W.K. Campbell in conversation with the author, July 1979, and also Grattan O'Leary, *Recollections of People, Press and Politics*
21. Bennett Papers, reel M3175, 598332, Aylen to Bennett, 24 March 1943
22. W.K. Campbell in conversation with the author, July 1979
23. Ibid.
24. Cedric Callahan to the author, October 1979
25. W.K. Campbell in conversation with the author, July 1979
26. Ibid.
27. Ibid.
28. Ibid.
29. Minutes of the Judicial Committee, 27 April 1955: Privy Council office, London
30. Toronto *Globe and Mail*, 27 April 1955

EPILOGUE

1. The King v. Jeu Jang How (1919) 59 S.C.R. 175
2. Vaughan v. Eastern Townships Bank (1909) 41 S.C.R. 286

# Index